# Creating Political Presence

# Creating Political Presence

*The New Politics of Democratic Representation*

EDITED BY DARIO CASTIGLIONE
AND JOHANNES POLLAK

THE UNIVERSITY OF CHICAGO PRESS     CHICAGO AND LONDON

The University of Chicago Press, Chicago 60637
The University of Chicago Press, Ltd., London
© 2019 by The University of Chicago
Published 2019
Printed in the United States of America

28 27 26 25 24 23 22 21 20 19     1 2 3 4 5

ISBN-13: 978-0-226-58836-0 (cloth)
ISBN-13: 978-0-226-58853-7 (paper)
ISBN-13: 978-0-226-58867-4 (e-book)
DOI: https://doi.org/10.7208/chicago/9780226588674.001.0001

Chapter 6, "Varieties of Inclusive Representation," first published in French as "La représentation inclusive," in *Raisons politiques* 2, no. 50 (2013): 115–35. © Presses de Sciences Po

Library of Congress Cataloging-in-Publication Data

Names: Castiglione, Dario, editor. | Pollak, Johannes, 1969– editor.
Title: Creating political presence : the new politics of democratic representation / edited by Dario Castiglione and Johannes Pollak.
Description: Chicago ; London : The University of Chicago Press, 2019. | Includes bibliographical references and index.
Identifiers: LCCN 2018029040 | ISBN 9780226588360 (cloth : alk. paper) | ISBN 9780226588537 (pbk. : alk. paper) | ISBN 9780226588674 (e-book)
Subjects: LCSH: Representative government and representation. | Democracy. | Political parties.
Classification: LCC JF1051 .C743 2019 | DDC 321.8—dc23
LC record available at https://lccn.loc.gov/2018029040

♾ This paper meets the requirements of ANSI/NISO Z39.48-1992 (Permanence of Paper).

# Contents

Acknowledgments   vii

Introduction   1
*Dario Castiglione and Johannes Pollak*

CHAPTER 1.   The Logics of Democratic Presence in
Representation   16
*Dario Castiglione and Johannes Pollak*

PART I.   **Representation as Democratic Empowerment**

CHAPTER 2.   How Representation Enables Democratic Citizenship   39
*Mark E. Warren*

CHAPTER 3.   Judgment Alone: Cloven Citizenship in the Era of
the Internet   61
*Nadia Urbinati*

CHAPTER 4.   Political Parties and Conflict Handling   86
*John Erik Fossum*

CHAPTER 5.   Populist Twist: The Relationship between the Leader
and the People in Populism   110
*Paula Diehl*

PART II.   **Representation as Democratic Inclusion**

CHAPTER 6.   Varieties of Inclusive Representation   141
*Samuel Hayat*

CHAPTER 7.   Radical Democracy: The Silent Partner in Political
             Representation's Constructivist Turn   162
             *Lisa Disch*

CHAPTER 8.   Who Counts as a Democratic Representative? On Claims
             of Self-Appointed Representation   186
             *Laura Montanaro*

CHAPTER 9.   Future Generations and the Limits of Representation   204
             *Kerry H. Whiteside*

PART III.    **Changing Contexts**

CHAPTER 10.  Synecdochical and Metaphorical Political Representation:
             Then and Now   231
             *Frank Ankersmit*

CHAPTER 11.  Externalities and Representation beyond the State:
             Lessons from the European Union   254
             *Christopher Lord*

CHAPTER 12.  Liminal Representation   276
             *Michael Saward*

CHAPTER 13.  Recursive Representation   298
             *Jane Mansbridge*

List of Contributors   339

Index   343

# Acknowledgments

The research and many discussions leading to this volume have been generously supported by the Institute for Advanced Studies, Vienna, Austria; and ARENA, Centre for European Studies, University of Oslo, Norway; with a contribution from the University of Exeter in the United Kingdom. One highlight in these many years of cooperation was the workshop kindly hosted by the Ash Center for Democratic Governance and Innovation at Harvard University in November 2015. We thank the participants in those discussions, who endured our enthusiasm for the topic of political representation at countless conferences and whose insights and comments were highly appreciated. We also thank the contributors to this volume, in particular Jenny Mansbridge, not only for their individual contributions but also for their support throughout the making of the book and for their advice in shaping it and putting it together.

Our editors, Charles T. Myers and Holly Smith from the University of Chicago Press, have shown greater patience than one can habitually expect with our struggle in bringing this project to completion. Their subtly applied pressure contributed to its successful conclusion as much as the comments from the two anonymous reviewers did. Those comments were invaluable toward the revision of the manuscript and improved the focus of both the individual contributions and the volume as a whole. In times when crude forms of direct democracy are sold as the panacea to the ills of our current systems of representative democracy, their support for this volume is greatly welcome.

Finally, we would like to thank the other people who have helped make this a better and more accessible book: At the University of Chicago Press, Melinda Kennedy managed the marketing and Christine Schwab and Tamara Ghattas supervised the copyediting and proofreading process. On behalf of the press, Carol McGillivray also managed the copyediting with skill and sensitivity. Their professional help has been invaluable. We hope that the errors and ambiguities the careful reader might still find in the text and the presentation of the arguments are few and far between—but they are there, no doubt, and they are exclusively our responsibility as editors. Perhaps such errors will be the trigger to support renewed discussions on a topic that remains of worthwhile interest: the future of representative politics and democratic representation.

# Introduction

Dario Castiglione and Johannes Pollak

The crisis of representative democracy is a commonplace in contemporary political debates. Considered as the dominant political form of the modern constitutional state in advanced industrial societies, representative democracy is increasingly seen as incapable of satisfying the demands of participation, recognition, and governance that come from society at large. Moreover, its institutional machinery is often regarded as inadequate to deal with the greatly intensified speed and complexities of decision-making in the politics of the global age. In different ways, populism and antipolitics, the dominance and personalization of executive power, societal self-regulation, and technocratic power all seem to challenge the traditional institutions, practices, and principles of representative democracy. As suggested by the late Peter Mair (2013; see also Crouch 2004 and Mastropaolo 2012), we are witnessing the hollowing out of representative democracy, insofar as the citizens are feeling disempowered and apathetic, while the political class has become increasingly insulated—all of which has led to ever greater and more desperate attempts by the political class to portray itself as similar to so-called ordinary people. This crisis of representation is not new. Some of its phenomenology may look worryingly similar to the crisis of the parliamentary regimes in the first two decades of the twentieth century. Discussions about the crises of parties and representative institutions have proliferated since the 1970s. In political theory, representative democracy, though generally regarded as the only viable form of democracy in large-scale societies, has been the direct and indirect object of criticism from many quarters, with the elaboration of alternative democratic models emphasizing in turn participation,

deliberation, and agonism, while questioning the democratic nature of representation itself.

And yet, during the last couple of decades, there has also been a resur-
gence of interest in the theory of political representation from a distinctly
democratic perspective. A new literature has developed proposing a rethinking of representation itself—of both the basis of its legitimacy and
the ways in which it can be combined with other democratic forms. In
reflecting on this revival of interest amid the crisis of representation, two
broadly though naturally overlapping perspectives can be seen to emerge.
Both are captured by the idea of *political representation*, but one looks at
the issue from the perspective of democratic theory and of *representative
democracy* as a form of government, while the other looks at the way in
which *representation* operates in politics as an element of the governing
process, irrespective of its democratic form. In the past, these two perspectives have often been confused in discussions of democratic representation
for the simple reason that *modern* democracy and representation were
collapsed into a single entity. No less than Hanna Pitkin bears testimony
to this, when in a 2004 article she admitted that, at the time she wrote her
famous book *The Concept of Representation* (1967), she had taken the
relationship between representation and democracy to be "unproblem-
atic": "Like most people even today, I more or less equated democracy
with representation, or at least with representative government. It seemed
axiomatic that under modern conditions only representation can make
democracy possible" (2004, 336).

On the contrary, disentangling democracy from representation may allow us to ask a number of questions regarding how political representation
can (or, perhaps, following Rousseau, cannot) be an important moment
of democratic government in modern societies, and how mechanisms and
processes of representation work in political governance contexts (here
meant in a broader sense than the political system). Such a distinction
allows for a better view of both the macro- and microprocesses of representation, of their efficacy and legitimacy. With respect to its democratic nature, the distinction allows us to investigate whether different
democratic theories, emphasizing different principles and moments of the
democratic process (constitutive, participatory, deliberative, and representative) can perhaps be reconciled. It also allows to reassess what are the
main models of democratic government that operate in modern societies,
whether the mix of institutions and constitutional principles that characterized the consolidation of democratic forms of government in the twentieth

century are still in place or are dramatically changing in front of our eyes—and in what directions. In this respect, new theories of representation are part of the debate about forms of democracy, providing what has been called a "representative turn" in democratic theory (Näsström 2011). Even though not entirely new, one intuition that may be worth pursuing is that representation, as part of democratic government, needs to be understood as a complex "system" rather than viewed through individual moments, processes, or institutions. Thinking of representation in systemic terms implies looking at it in its multiple functions: as the central instrument for the transference of popular sovereignty and legitimacy; as a means of opinion formation through public and legislative deliberation; and as a more widespread mechanism of democratic empowerment throughout society. Such a way of looking at representation has the potential of bringing into dialogue different theories of democracy; it can help us rethink our theoretical and conceptual vocabulary, while forcing us to being more attentive to the institutional transformations that take place as a consequence of other social and political changes, like the revolution in communication and the spread of global interconnectedness.

The second perspective, which looks at representation independently from democracy, is more attentive to the actual operations of representation itself: the kind of meanings that the acts and performances of representation imply, particularly in a political context; the role that representation plays in constructing political identity; and the different ways in which the very process of political representation takes place. What has been described as the "constructivist turn" (Disch 2015) and, more generally, performative and identity-shaping understandings of representation capture important aspects of how political representation operates. They emphasize the artificiality of "constituencies"; the entrepreneurial function of representatives in making what Michael Saward has influentially described as "representative claims" (2006 and 2010); the way in which such claims necessitate a more complex structure of validation and intelligibility, going beyond the dualistic structure of principal-agent and thus involving tertiary figures such as "audiences" and "publics." A fresh look at the meanings (including symbolic ones) and the mechanisms of representation has therefore pushed the discussion beyond some of the more traditional categorizations that consolidated throughout the last century, offering a more nuanced view of the dynamic relationships and political processes that constitute political representation, while expanding its scope from formal to more informal settings. These new lines of investigation have also posed the specific question of the political nature and democratic legitimacy of nonelectoral, nonauthorized forms of representation and hence of whether representation can be democratic in character even when considered independently of the institutional role it plays within representative democracy.

The two perspectives on the study of political representation thus outlined may be regarded as its two faces. One face considers political representation as part of democratic theory and practice, examining the role that it plays, as both a theoretical and institutional construct, in democratic forms of government. The other face looks at representation itself, exploring the ways in which it functions in politics at large and inquiring whether it has a logic and legitimacy of its own, independently of its specific role within representative forms of democracy. The intention of this book is to engage with both sides of the problem. While being analytically attentive to the ways in which different types and processes of representation operate in our everyday politics, giving form to societal demands and connecting them to the decision-making powers, the various chapters explore the conditions under which the latter processes may be considered democratic, in the hope also of finding ways of reactivating the link between the disaffected citizens and insulated elites described by Peter Mair and others. In other words, is there a way in which political representation can facilitate democratic empowerment and inclusion by providing legitimate and effective channels through which the citizenry is given some form of *presence* (through voice and influence, or by recognition and a sympathetic hearing) in decision-making and in the administration of power?

The scope of the volume is therefore to highlight the way in which rethinking representation contributes both to revisiting our conception of democracy and to redefining the ways in which the practices of representation may be made to work *for* democracy and not against it. The volume collectively shows that there are different approaches to this problem and that the recent revival of interest in the theoretical study of representation offers divergent characterizations of the relationship between representation and democracy amid the conditions of contemporary politics. But there is a common preoccupation in the contributions to this volume, which is to investigate whether the new theoretical interest in the field advances new paradigms of democratic representation, subverting the long-established models developed through the constitutional debates of the eighteenth-century revolutions and the successive metamorphoses of representative government, centered first on the legislative role of parliaments and eventually on the ascendancy of mass parties and executive government (see Manin 1997). Both theoretically and institutionally, political representation is a moving target, and so is its relation to collective forms of self-government. As already suggested, in this volume we are trying to come to terms with both sets of transformations. While assessing the democratic potential of new forms, practices, and conceptions of political representation, many of the contributors give attention to the quality of representation and the criteria that make it either legitimate or effective. Above all, most of the authors in this volume investigate how represen-tation contributes, when it does, to the formation of those capacities and self-identities that make political agency possible, thus also creating the conditions for the political *presence* of citizens in the public arena. The opening essay of this collection aims to tackle the very issue of the con-ceptual implications of thinking representation in relation to presence, and the practical ways in which political representation may contribute to the creation of democratic presence.

In attempting to give coherence to the plurality of perspectives offered in this volume, we have divided it into three parts, highlighting different aspects of the relationship between representation and democracy. The first part more directly speaks to the way in which representation con-tributes to democratic empowerment. This is done by examining different ways through which political representation may either facilitate or im-pinge upon the capacity of citizens to develop the autonomy of judgment required for collective decision-making. The chapters composing part I look at the issue from the perspective of the citizens (Warren), of the role of some of the agents of representation (Fossum), or from that of the forms and characters of political action in modern times, such as populism (Diehl) and the tendency toward "audience" democracy in the internet age (Urbinati). The second part looks at democratic representation from the point of view of inclusion. The focus of this part is on different ways in which representative relationships and representative claims may ar-ticulate the demands of those who are or feel excluded or without voice. Particular attention is given to the interplay between the social and the political in the articulation of representative claims: how, for instance, artic-ulating such claims may require a more active role from the represented in order for representation to be inclusionary (Hayat); or how the hegemonic projects played out in representation constitute the political subjectivity of the citizens from their own standpoint (Disch). The other two chapters in this part investigate how social figures who have no direct presence in the politics of representation may perhaps find a more visible space through self-appointed representatives (Montanaro); and how other subjects, like future generations, may have to rely on deliberative innovations for their needs to be properly considered (Whiteside). The third and final part of the book looks at political and democratic representation from a more general and contextual perspective. This part therefore explores the relationship between political representation and democratic sovereignty across different historical phases (Ankersmit) and in the face of growing forms of transnational and international governance (Lord). But it also redesigns the context of representation by going beyond its traditional political boundaries and distinctions, suggesting, for instance, that there is a more general practice of democratic representation of which representative democracy, as a form of government, is only a part (Saward); or outlining a complex system of interdependence between political, administrative, and societal representation all amenable to the legitimating principle of recursive communication (Mansbridge).

Although we have divided the chapters in relation to issues of empowerment, inclusion, and the changing contexts of representation, many of them speak across all three areas. As already noted, not all authors speak from the same perspective. Occasionally, they also may disagree on the normative fit between democracy and representation. The scope of the book is therefore not only to illustrate the new ways in which the dynamic between political representation and democratic legitimacy works but also to air the analytical and normative disagreements that animate the new literature by making our contributors enter into dialogue and speak with each other, often between the lines but at times more critically and directly. Our understanding of political phenomena can only benefit from such a plurality of voices.

## A Brief Synopsis

The book opens with a substantive introductory chapter by Dario Castiglione and Johannes Pollak, exploring the vexed problem of the meaning of representation as the paradox or dialectic of presence and absence. The focus, however, is neither linguistic nor conceptual. It does not aim to solve the puzzle but to show what lies behind it, in more concrete political terms. The essay attempts to identify distinct logics of presence—meant as the creation of a political subjectivity—which tend to give different accounts of the principles and institutions involved in representation as part of the political and democratic process. This is a problem for political theory, institutional design, and political practice rather than one of philosophical and conceptual clarification, even though such clarifications may greatly help the articulation of political discourse and practice. Outlining different ways in which political representation offers a space for citizens to have a voice and some *presence* in the process of governance—that is, some approximation to the ideal of self-governance—moves us forward a step toward a theory of democratic representation. In this sense, political representation needs to be more than a process of reflection but also one of creation of democratic subjectivity. Creating political *presence* remains therefore a normative aspiration for representative democracy as a political regime; though the problem for most of the other contributors remains whether and how this is still possible in the contemporary conditions of politics, and whether the institutional instruments and political practices of democratic representation need a radical overhaul, going beyond the traditional terrain of representative democracy.

## Part 1

The central idea of the first part is looking at representation as an interactive relationship that allows for the empowerment of the represented. The view adopted by the contributors is not one that takes the interests/preferences of the represented as preformed, conceiving representation as a transmission belt but one in which citizens need to have an ongoing (deliberative and participatory) engagement with the representatives, as well as the possibility/opportunity to develop their competences as citizens. Accordingly, Mark Warren's contribution focuses on the political activities of the represented, analyzing what the citizens are doing when they assess representative claims, authorize representatives to act and speak on their behalf, and, finally, hold them to account. From a more normative perspective, Warren asks how representative relationships construct and enable the capacities of democratic citizenship. While the constructivist turn in representation theory is not disputed, it has little to say about the substantial democratic objectives of representation per se. Warren shows how the representative relationship induces capacities for autonomous judgment, frames individuals as members of a collective, enables moral judgment, and makes discursive accountability possible.

In her contribution, Nadia Urbinati takes up Warren's point on autonomous judgment. She considers this as part of the diarchy of will and judgment in modern democracy, of which political representation is, in her view, a constitutive part. Declining voter participation and increasing opinion formation via online media has the power to undermine the standard model based on electoral representation. These two trends provide a challenge to the traditional mechanisms of opinion formation and political expression represented by the parties and traditional media, suggesting instead that citizens tend to multiply the moment of judgment formation, through a more diffuse array of media, but as a surrogate to participation and political autonomy. Citizens' political judgment manifests itself more in continuous discussion than in the political autonomy that comes from active citizenship, and in her view this discussion must translate into acts of democratic will through decision-making. Urbinati sees such developments with some normative concern and therefore considers those theories of representation that emphasize the phenomenology of claim-making as concentrating on only part of the practice and institution of democratic representation. The danger, in her view, is that of a cloven type of citizenship, rich in deliberation but with no real influence.

The role of intermediary institutions such as political parties and media is also central to John Erik Fossum's contribution, which discusses the way in which political parties perform a representative role through conflict handling that is fundamental to the construction of the democratic political space. Under which conditions are parties still able, if at all, to mediate societal conflicts? How can they do so and at what price? It may well be that political parties uphold their role in civilizing conflicts at the cost of fully expressing their voters' democratic voice. But this civilizing function remains essential in order to provide a framework for democratic politics. Fossum sketches such an analytical framework, which in his view allows us to understand the various ways in which parties relate to their voters as well as handle conflict. A proper understanding of this important function is, according to Fossum, an essential element for a normative reassessment of the representative role political parties play in modern democracy.

In her contribution to the volume, Paula Diehl approaches the question of how representation may contribute to the creation of political subjectivity, and hence potentially the empowerment of citizens, by an analysis of the topical issue of how populist parties and populist movements claim to represent the people or popular demands. Populism, which is often associated with charismatic leadership, embodying some of the aspects or the alleged aspirations and feelings of the people, seems to present, in modern politics, a countertendency to individualist fragmentation and political disenfranchisement. Understanding the kind of link that populist rhetoric tries to establish between the leader and the people is the key element for understanding the way in which populist discourse changes and challenges democratic representation. According to Diehl, populist rhetoric emphasizes both horizontal equality among the people, whose presence populists constantly evoke in their politics, and the more vertical and hierarchical relationship between the leader and the masses, whose characteristics and passions are often embodied and symbolically represented in the former. Diehl sees in such tension and in the identitarian link between the leader and his or her followers a worrying antidemocratic feature of populism insofar as it threatens democracy's central features of transparency and control, which in her view are central to empowering citizens as autonomous political subjects.

## Part 2

The contributions to the second part of the volume—on inclusion—tend to look at representation from a more constructivist perspective, posing the question of how it is possible for those who are de facto excluded from political decisions still to be given some form of presence. It suggests that the political subjectivity of the represented is often shaped by the representatives and by the claims the latter make to speak and act in their place. But this process is anything but a one-way system. The essays in the second part, therefore, tend to focus on less formal and traditional forms of political representation or on its main institutional mechanisms, such as voting, parliaments, parties, career politicians, and the political establishment at large. The rejection of traditional political representation has been given particular attention of late and characterized under various labels from antipolitics to celebrity politics and from informal representation to civil society advocacy. In all these instances, informal representatives often claim to be much closer to the real needs, demands, and wishes of the people or of particular groups of citizens, such as the dispossessed, insofar as they are untainted by particular political allegiances or because they stand outside the traditional apparatus of politics. Besides, they often tend to combine their claim to represent either particular groups or more general interests by combining these together with more participatory and deliberative processes.

Samuel Hayat's essay offers a historically grounded but also general defense of inclusive representation by critically engaging with a traditional view of representative democracy, which he contrasts with citizen participation. According to Hayat, who in this regard follows other recent contributions to the debate such as Plotke's (1997), representation and participation are not in direct opposition. This is because representation presents two different aspects and can be institutionalized accordingly. One aspect consists in the exclusion of citizens from decision-making, allocating their function instead to variously chosen elites. The other, however, consists in the role that representation can play in the inclusion of citizens, by making them participants in politics through different forms. Hayat singles out two: "inclusion through politicization," which concerns individuals and can happen through either partisan or autonomous channels, and the inclusion of social groups, which allows certain social identities to be formed and hence represented in the political arena.

Lisa Disch offers a general reflection on the constitutive power of political representation, and of its inclusive aspects, by providing a strong defense of a constructivist conception of representation. Her analysis speaks also to the concerns of theorists that the constructivist approach may not have the necessary resources to address the demands of legitimacy. She characterizes the "constructivist turn" as implying a performative, rather than a merely reflective and vicarious understanding of the act of representing in politics. She is insistent that the "rediscovery" of representation as contributing to the formation of the political subjectivity of the represented should not be seen simply as a way of integrating representative government within consent-driven processes of opinion formation and democratic deliberation but as part of the more agonistic battle for political hegemony. In her opinion, this constructivist reading of representation is indebted, although not always with acknowledgment, to more radical views of democracy and particularly to Laclau and Mouffe's (1985) conception of hegemony (not in the sense of domination but in the more specific sense of constructing commonalities through conflictual practices). From a democratic perspective, representation therefore involves the continuous reconstruction and challenge of hegemonic discourses and practices.

The remaining two essays of the second part of the volume deal with forms of surrogate representation, where the represented are truly absent, and their interests and voices therefore literally require the representative to speak or act in their stead. Laura Montanaro's chapter on self-appointed representatives analyzes the increasing prevalence of such radically independent representatives, since the constituency on whose behalf they claim to speak is neither consulted nor participates in their selection. While the critique that such self-appointed representatives are not democratic is not disputed by Montanaro, she holds that they still have the potential to fulfill an important democratic function: to speak for those who are affected by decisions but who for various reasons are excluded from the political process and lack any opportunity for their voice to be heard. From such a perspective, self-appointed representatives have an important role in democratic governance—particularly in a complex and globalizing world—where electoral constituencies may fail to coincide with those interests affected by collective decisions. But in such a capacity, self-appointed representatives should also be subjected to some form of democratic accountability.

What if the represented do not form a community at all—however loose and dispersed—but are merely a potentiality, such as future generations? How can they ever be subjects of representation if they cannot exert their inherent right to hold to account those who make decisions in their name? In the final essay of part two, Kerry Whiteside addresses this conundrum by admitting that the language of political representation may ultimately fail such an occasion and instead makes a case for using randomly selected minipublics to deliberate over decisions that may impact on future generations. Such deliberative processes, however, should not be merely consultative but carry real power within the legislative process. Whiteside thinks of these deliberative bodies as groups that, though not making law or policy directly, would pass judgments to decision makers and monitor the execution of their directives. They would be more than advisory councils. He proposes a more empowering form of deliberative minipublics, which would give them a unique and consequential role to play where the legitimating credentials of representative democracy are at their weakest, as in the case of future generations. This ensemble would not replace representative processes, but it could help create a distinct pillar of effective future-regarding concern in the overall architecture of contemporary democracy.

## Part 3

The final section of the volume addresses the context (or overall system) that gives meaning to both the process of democratic representation and to the political conditions that make it possible for the politics of representation to provide the institutional instruments for the democratic voice to be organized into a form of collective rule. The question is whether, in the

new conditions of political governance, it is possible or indeed desirable
for representative institutions to provide some form of unity and collective
self-government or whether we should look for a more diffuse system of
representation, encompassing social and administrative as well as political
moments and operating at a national and supranational level.

Contemplating this new context requires us to think in more comparative terms, including searching for historical examples of radical shifts,
returning patterns, and changing meanings. Frank Ankersmit does so by
concentrating on what he regards as the fundamental relation character-
izing modern democratic government, that between representation and
sovereignty. The way in which sovereignty and representation come together in modern democracy is the fundamental context within which to
understand how the latter operates. In a very stylized form, if democracy
means sovereignty of the people, then the political representation of the
people is how that sovereignty is exercised in decision-making. Ankersmit
suggests that this combination has been achieved historically, but that the
"synecdochical" (pars pro toto) conception of representation seen in the
Middle Ages has given way to the "metaphorical" conception of representation that predominates today. Ankersmit's archaeology of the concept of representation from the Middle Ages to modernity—and how
this affects the formation of modern democratic government—has more
than historical value; synecdochical representation, he claims, is making a
return in modern political discourse, changing the very core of democratic
government and the way in which sovereignty and representation (in its
more metaphorical sense) find their reconciliation within it. In his view, the
return of more synecdochical conceptions of representation are worrying
insofar as they put into question the centrality of sovereignty, jeopardizing
modern democratic government as we know it.

The place of sovereignty in the scheme of representative government is
of course an important element in discussions concerning the transnational
context of politics. This is the object of Christopher Lord's contribution
to the volume, though, significantly, rather than framing the question in
terms of sovereignty, he prefers to draw some of his concepts from the
more economic language of externalities. His focus is on representative
politics within the context of European integration, which he regards as an
almost ideal laboratory for exploring representation beyond the nation-
state. Contrasting the "all-affected principle" with the "all-subjected principle" he holds that both principles lack a conception of externalities. Defining under which conditions and at what point everyone affected by a

decision shall have a right to be represented may prove impossible. On the other hand, the all-subjected principle is based on the preservation of one's polity, which in itself may well require the management of externalities to guarantee the ideal of self-government. To dissolve this impasse Lord suggests analyzing the formal properties of externalities with the help of economic theory to understand how such an approach might impact core democratic values. By combining this with the literature on the possibilities and problems of deliberating and deciding laws through representatives, he arrives at a new and original formulation of the problem: Under what conditions should people permit the representation of outsiders' interests in their own decision-making process? And how far should they go in seeking representation in the decisions of others?

For Michael Saward appraising representation nowadays involves rethinking both its contexts and its phenomenology. In his words, "whatness matters," and it is only by attending to representation's performative phenomenology, rather than trying to find an essence or some referent, that we can move to the more normative terrain of what is right and what is wrong in (democratic) representation. On the phenomenological side, he argues that representation has a "dynamic liminality," which makes many of the traditional distinctions that we use to analyze democratic representation less than solid. Representation instead traverses familiar empirical and conceptual distinctions and boundaries and defies neat categorization. By accepting the liminal character of representation, we can track its conditionality—its changeable character in different circumstances, times, and situations. Saward suggests that by embracing the liminality of representation, and the fuzzy borders between elective and nonelective, formal and informal, institutional and noninstitutional, normative and descriptive, we are also in the position to appreciate the important distinction between "representative democracy," as the generally recognized form of democratic and legitimate representation, and a wider field of "democratic representation" itself, where acts of representation take place. The latter comprises a variety of practices that traverse the three somewhat artificially separated domains of political representation in a generic sense, societal democratic representation, and state-based representative democracy. It is by attending to the way in which representation may take place across all of these levels, rather than concentrating on the functioning of the latter, that we may better appreciate what representation does and how it does it.

In the final chapter of the third part, Jane Mansbridge takes up Saward's distinction between representative democracy and democratic representation and his map of the three concentric domains across which representation operates. Although she considers democratic representation as something that operates at multiple levels, she focuses on the electoral and administrative processes of representation in the state-based domain and on the support they receive from nonelectoral representation across the three domains. Her approach is more normative than Seward's. Building on some of the arguments earlier in the volume, she suggests that we should replace the standard linear model that establishes a chain of representation from voters to representatives, and from these to administration and finally back to citizens (as subjects of the law), with a more dialogic communicative model, where feedback loops operate throughout the system and throughout time. She maintains that, in this revised model, two-way communication is critical for maintaining not only an appropriate mutual constitution of represented and representatives but also warranted trust between them. The main part of the essay outlines different ways in which the various chains of electoral, administrative, and nonelectoral representation can be restructured, supported, and recalibrated to offer renewed normative standards of democratic representation across the system.

In conclusion, we hope that by approaching political representation through both of its faces—its own autonomous working and its relation to democratic self-government—the chapters of this volume will contribute both to the reassessment of representation and to a more considered theory of democracy in our time.

## References

Crouch, Colin. 2004. *Post-democracy*. Cambridge: Polity.

Disch, Lisa. 2015. "The 'Constructivist Turn' in Democratic Representation: A Normative Dead-End?" *Constellations* 22 (4): 487–99.

Laclau, Ernesto, and Chantal Mouffe. 1985. *Hegemony and Socialist Strategy*. London. Verso.

Mair, Peter. 2013. *Ruling the Void: The Hollowing of Western Democracy*. London: Verso

Manin, Bernad. 1997. *The Principles of Representative Government*. Cambridge: Cambridge University Press.

Mastropaolo, Alfio. 2012. *Is Democracy a Lost Cause?* Colchester: ECPR Press.

Näsström, Sofia. 2011. "Where Is the Representative Turn Going?" In *European Journal of Political Theory* 10 (4): 501–10.

Pitkin, Hanna. 2004. "Representation and Democracy: Uneasy Alliance." *Scandinavian Political Studies* 27 (3): 335–42.

Pitkin, Hanna F. 1967. *The Concept of Representation*. Berkeley: University of California Press.

Plotke, David. 1997. "Representation Is Democracy." *Constellations* 4 (1): 19–34.

Saward, Michael. 2006. "The Representative Claim." *Contemporary Political Theory* 5:297–318.

———. 2010. *The Representative Claim*. New York: Oxford University Press.

CHAPTER ONE

# The Logics of Democratic Presence in Representation

Dario Castiglione and Johannes Pollak

If we conceive democracy as some form of citizen *self*-government—however attenuated and qualified—we inescapably invoke a *self* in some guise. Hence, citizens' presence would seem to be congruous with the very idea of democracy. It is partly for this reason that modern representative government has historically been construed (and fought over) as either aristocratic, in that it keeps citizens away from the levers of power, or democratic, in that it provides them the political instruments to deliberate, direct, or check the exercise of power. The idea of political *presence* is therefore integral to disputes over *democratic* representation.

As the title of this volume suggests, citizens' political presence is not something that comes naturally. However it is created—and the contributors to this volume offer different views of the process—such presence needs to be identified, explained, and justified; or simply ruled out as either impossible or unnecessary. If one important element of the crisis afflicting a representative conception of politics in general—and the institutions of representative democracy in particular—is that people feel unrepresented, their interests and aspirations unheard, then an important way out of the impasse is to see how their presence as political agents can be reconstructed in the modern conditions of politics. While other contributions in this volume offer more substantive arguments about a "new politics of democratic representation," we wish to reflect on what it means to provide democratic presence (i.e., a conceptual and practical space for self-government) within a system of representation. In the past, some of the disputes about presence *in* representation have been fought over the meaning(s) of *representation*. We return to these debates, not to offer conceptual clarification but with the intent to show the political purport, or logic, that lies behind conceptual definitions. Our intent is to show that disputes over the meaning(s) of representation do not settle questions of political theory. Overall, they are rhetorical and persuasive means for political arguments; it is on the latter that we should concentrate. If we are right, as we try to argue throughout this chapter, neither a conceptual nor an essentialist solution exists to the problem of how to create democratic presence in political representation, only more or less convincing arguments for how to approach the problem in a coherent and efficacious way.

## Presence *in* Representation?

The idea of presence is central to much theoretical speculation on the meaning of representation in general and of democratic representation in particular. As Mark Warren reminds us in his contribution to this volume, a powerful rendering of the way in which representation works—as the reduction of the costs and difficulties of democratic (direct and autonomous) decision-making in large and complex societies—is through the representatives *making present* the represented by standing for, speaking for, and acting for them, while, at the same time, the represented remain de facto *absent*. Authorization and accountability mechanisms operate as effective (or at least formal) means for securing the democratic legitimacy of the representatives' vicarious performances. In the Anglo-American literature, the most powerful and sophisticated account of this paradoxical rendering of representation as "making present what is absent" is Hanna Pitkin's *The Concept of Representation* (1967). Pitkin stresses, in both the book and a subsequent article (1968), that what is absent must be made present "in *some* sense," but not "literally," otherwise "it would simply be 'present' rather than 'represented'" (1968, 41). This account has a natural appeal, capturing in linguistic terms some important tensions in the more substantive meaning of political representation—tensions well illustrated by the historical and constitutional disputes between "free" and "imperative" conceptions of the representative mandate, or by the related arguments over trustee- and delegate-based conceptions of the duties and functions of political representatives, particularly within parliamentary settings. The conceptual paradox highlighted by this assumed linguistic meaning of representation is at the very core of Pitkin's classic book (as also evinced in Pitkin 1968) and has been taken up by others to illustrate both the relational, reflexive, and contested aspects of political representation (see Castiglione and Warren 2006, among many). More recently, David Runciman (2007) has further elaborated the paradox by suggesting a somewhat more negative, possibly more realistic form of *presence* of the represented in the political process. Runciman suggests that what he calls the "non-objection criterion" can already be found in Pitkin when she argues that "the substance of the activity of representing seems to consist in promoting the interests of the represented, in a context where the latter is conceived as capable of action and judgement, but in such a way that he *does not object* to what is done in his name" (Pitkin 1967, 155; Runciman 2007, 95; emphasis added). Runciman also qualifies this criterion through an important categorical distinction in the asymmetrical ways that individuals and corporate groups exercise their power to object—that is, the differences in status that arise between individuals' and groups' capacities for "non-objection" when their objections are related to the legitimacy of representation. (We shall return to such a difference in the next section.)

Despite the persuasiveness of the argument that the paradox of *re-presentation* has important consequences for substantive understandings of what is going on in political representation, such a conception is not without its opponents. One criticism is the well-rehearsed argument that the *substance* of real, effective political representation is often misconstrued as existing only in the politics of action and ideas. According to the standard view,[1] the key test of the presence of the represented in the actions of representatives lies in the way in which the latter promote the former's interests, as well respond to their judgment. This view assumes, or stipulates, a kind of virtuous and reinforcing circle between the representatives' judgment and that of the represented. Criticisms of this view emphasize instead that vicarious presence can carry little weight if based only on the force of judgment. The argument developed by Anne Phillips (1995) and other supporters of a more balanced representation of gender, race, and ethnicity in legislative and other political bodies takes aim at one of the central distinctions that Pitkin draws between two forms of substantive representation: one focused on what the representative *does* ("acts for," captured by the German *vertreten*) and the other on what the representative *is* ("stands for," captured by the German *darstellen*) (Pitkin 1967, 59). In her own work, Pitkin accepts that the stands-for group of conceptions complement and enlarge formal understandings of representation primarily based on authorization and accountability. When "stands for" is meant in a more descriptive sense, it points to the importance of likeness and resemblance between the representatives and their constituencies. When it is meant in a more symbolic sense, it emphasizes more imaginative, albeit often irrational, ways in which representatives take on the role of signifiers[2] and how this can emotionally affect or persuade constituents (111). But neither of these forms of substantive representation is decisive, for neither captures what Pitkin regards as the fundamental aspect of political representation: *action* based on *judgment*, which, particularly in democratic representation, is open to the contestation of the represented (who are themselves seen as "capable of action and judgment" [155]). Supporters of the *politics of presence* maintain that vicarious action in general is either insufficient in promoting the interests of the represented or structurally unresponsive to their demands, unless it is backed by a more concrete form of representativeness. In any case, a system of representation mainly or exclusively based on "acting for" tends to favor what Bernard Manin calls the more aristocratic "principle of distinction" (1997, 94), whose selection processes may yield representative bodies so different from the constituencies they are meant to represent that the system lacks representativeness or seems unfair, failing the crucial test of democratic inclusion (Phillips 1995, 5). It follows that, instead of being marginal to substantive political representation, descriptive representation can be construed, as indeed it has been, as a way of promoting not just the representativeness of the representatives (who they *are*) but also their capacity for democratic action (what they *do*—i.e., the kind of decisions they make). Given that the quality and efficacy of substantive representation is thus predicated on representativeness, it becomes necessary to provide a stronger and more descriptive presence in representation than that offered by vicarious action. In this sense, democratic representation must stand for something closer to *depiction*, as implied in the German *Darstellung*.

Another criticism of the paradox of representation argues that, in the standard theory usually identified with Pitkin, presence is not just *thin* but *unreconstructed*. From a more constructivist perspective, such as that proposed by Michael Saward (2006, 2010, 39–43; Disch 2015), the central issue of political representation lies in the process of representation itself, in the *how* of representation rather than in the *what* may be present or absent. Saward (2010) suggests that there are several failings in the "presence approach" and that these must be corrected by a radical shift to what he names an "event approach" focused mainly on the "*rendering* of such a claim of presence" (39). In brief, the main failings of the presence approach identified by Saward consist in it being too centered on linguistic meanings and stipulative definitions; too inclined to slide from these to the simple, uncontested social facticity of fixed roles and institutions; too prone to reductive binary thinking,[3] and too conducive to a kind of abstract, unsituated normativism that legislates for the legitimacy of representation rather than interpreting its phenomenology and assessing the democratic force of conviction as seen from the citizens' standpoint (Saward 2010, chap. 6; see also Disch 2015). Saward does not deny some utility to the presence approach, but he regards it as restrictive, since it takes the presence of the represented and the role of the representatives as being both fixed and given, and reduces them to a few traditional roles (legislators), institutional mechanisms (elections), and places (parliaments). By contrast, in the event approach, discursive processes spread across state and society; representatives' claims gain a more tentative purchase on the represented, and representatives are capable of invoking, rather than reflecting, the political subjectivity of the people they represent through their own claim-making (43). The event approach is more interested in the performativity of political representation (a point further developed in Saward 2014 and 2017), both as a performance (in the sense of its theatricality) and as a construction of interpretative categories of political action. To put it in a different way, if one considers that *representation* is one of those verbal nouns that shows process/product ambiguity, referring to both the *act* and the *thing*, one may suggest that, whereas the presence approach looks mainly at the product of representation, the event approach emphasizes the process itself. Both can be valid in their own way. In terms of political analysis, however, the constructivist reading of representation, such as that suggested by Saward, makes a considerable change to the way in which we conceptualize modern political representation, highlighting a number of features also embraced by the literature more generally referred to as the "representative turn."[4] We can summarize those features in three broad ways that, if they do not entirely subvert the standard theory, amend it decisively.[5] First and as already indicated, the new literature draws particular attention to the processual aspects in representation, hence opening up the institutional black box of political representation and emphasizing its more discursive, interpretative, and conflictual aspects, which are never exhausted by the more formal and institutional acts (or mechanisms) of authorization and accountability. Secondly, by stressing performativity, this literature puts a premium on the creativity inherent in the act of representing, which contributes to the construction of political subjectivity and the self-understanding of the represented. Finally, the literature conceives representation as a relationship that is intrinsically dynamic and recursive[6] but that may not be exhausted in the simple dual structure of principal-agent. For insofar as representation is a semiotic act involving production and conferment of meaning, it must engage and maintain an audience's conviction, which gives the audience itself a third-party analytic role that on many occasions can be empirically separated from both the represented and the representatives.

Where does the constructivist criticism leave the paradox of representation? Saward (2010), for one, does not deny that "representation may well have a core meaning" and that this may consist in the presence/absence paradox (39); but Saward criticizes the stress put on "presence" as the sign of a narrow and mistaken attempt to retrieve some ultimate referent, an operation that in his view inevitably misses the more constitutive, discursive, and dynamic aspects of the practices of representation. Nonetheless, as we shall see in the next section, that very agreement on a core meaning can be challenged. Note that Pitkin's approach to the concept of representation is far from an attempt to get to an essentialist meaning. Pitkin (1967) suggests that there are different theories (or concepts) of representation and that these offer different pictures of a "rather complicated, convoluted, three-dimensional structure in the middle of a dark enclosure" (10). Each theory gives a snapshot of the structure from a different angle, and Pitkin's own conceptual exploration aims to contextualize these visions, "making explicit . . . how the word is used," which, as she adds, "is a vital element in knowing what the thing *is*" (11; emphasis added). Yet, in a footnote that reads like an afterthought to the whole book, she tries to correct the impression that theories are partial "images" of a more essential concept; she now believes, Pitkin writes, "on the basis of reading Wittgenstein, that the *metaphor is in some respects profoundly misleading about concepts and language*. But on the concept of representation it happens to work fairly well. Since it is central to the structure of this book I have let it stand" (255n20; emphasis added). As is clearly evidenced by this as well as another footnote (254n14; see also Pitkin [1972]1993, xxi), Pitkin's conceptual approach was greatly indebted to Austin's philosophy of ordinary language, but her subsequent reading of Wittgenstein put a different perspective on how she understood conceptual reconstruction and the study of political language and action. She now saw her conceptual exploration of representation not so much as a collection of partial images of a transcendent reality but as a first-order philosophical and political reconstruction of the ways in which people *do* things with language ([1972] 1993, chap. 2). Although she never rewrote her book from a more Wittgensteinian position, which would have avoided what she believed to be an unsatisfactory background vision of language as a "picture" of reality, she was convinced that her analysis of representation could still stand, if only one read it not as an exercise in linguistic and conceptual typology but as an analytical and critical reconstruction of conceptual controversies behind which emerged the "problems" of political representation.[7] Such a problem-based approach to the study of the languages of politics is more clearly outlined in her subsequent book on political theory and Wittgenstein (Pitkin 1993, 287–315 and particularly 313–15). In her 1968 article on the "paradox of representation," she is even more explicit, suggesting that philosophical clarification of the concept of representation, if even possible, would still leave plenty of work for political theorists to do. And, yet, in that very piece she still maintains that there is something important in the "core" meaning of representation as the making present of something absent.

## Representation, Personification, and Identity

As we have seen, there is no simple answer to the question of whether—and if so in what precise sense—the presence/absence model helps us solve the issue of political representation. The question, however, may be worth a second look, for in its complexity we may find, if not representation's *real* meaning, its *uses* in relation to democracy. First, it is not that clear that "making present something absent" can be taken as the core meaning of representation, even when this statement is shorn of any essentialist implication. In his monumental book on the "word" and "concept" of representation from medieval antiquity to the nineteenth century, Hasso Hofmann ([1974] 2003) denies that this is the case. As he states in his introduction, his intention in the book is to clear up a number of historico-terminological confusions that emerged during the twentieth-century German constitutional debate over representation.[8] The main target is the conviction, shared by authors such as Leibholz and Schmitt but also others (Pitkin is cited in this context), that from a supposedly original and persistent understanding of representation as "making present something absent" one can derive a more substantive theory of political representation. Instead, Hofmann believes that meaning must be found in the way in which "words"—that is, specific linguistic markers—are used in contextualized discursive practices and intellectual traditions. He insists on the importance of retracing the uses and sedimentations of the meanings of *representation* (*Repräsentation*) by painstakingly reconstructing its lineages from the classical and medieval usages of the Latin word *rapraesentare* and through its *derivata* into other languages. He identifies three broad linguistic usages, defining distinct semantic fields. The first set of meanings aligns the use of *rapraesentare* with the relation between *original* (*Urbild*) and *image-copy* (*Abbild*), an issue central to medieval theological disputes over the sacramental character of the Eucharist and to later, more general philosophical inquiries into perception and knowledge. The second set of meanings emerges from liturgical and ecclesiological contexts that used *rapraesentare* in the sense of "standing for," a usage also increasingly employed in legal language and practices. Both sets of meanings deal with the presence/absence dialectic but in different ways. As for the third set of meanings, this emerges in relation to the problem of corporative action and personality, which Hofmann calls "identity representation" and which carries a sense more of embodiment and personification. Whether or not one agrees with Hofmann's historical and terminological reconstruction, his analysis suggests that, in view of the polysemic nature of the idea of representation, there is no original or universal meaning on which one can establish a theory of political representation (Sintomer 2013; Mulieri 2016).[9] At best, the three sets of meanings overlap each other and interact in the uses people make of them in constitutional and political debates. Moreover, Hofmann observes that in the context of civil law classic and medieval usages of *rapraesentare* referred to immediate performance, often through ready payment; while, in the context of a legal trial, it meant the production and exhibition of witnesses. In neither case did the term convey the sense of vicarious performance, nor did it point to something absent but rather to something immediately present and manifest.

Interestingly, Hanna Pitkin admits that in Latin "*repraesentare* does seem to have meant to make literally present," though she also qualifies this by saying that "*repraesentare* is not exactly 'to represent'" (1968, 41). Nonetheless, this is not entirely true either. As Roger Chartier (2013) shows in the case of the French language, at least two apparently contradictory meanings of *repraesentare* have been documented since the seventeenth century.[10] One has the sense of substitution, as in the case of the image or the memory of an absent object; the other, as one of the entries in Furetière's dictionary testifies, means the "exhibition de quelque chose ... monstration d'une presence, présentation publique d'une chose ou d'une personne" (cited in Chartier 2013, 5). Chartier finds this duplicity of meanings in other languages, too, pointing at two different ways in which one can talk of the semiotic of representation: either as a mediating relation, where the sign points to the (absent) object, or as a relation of identity between of the sign and the object.[11] In the former case the sign "rend[re] présent quelque chose"; in the latter the sign "rend[re] manifeste vers l'extérieur une chose" (Chartier 2013, 6). In common English we find, though perhaps less obviously so, a similar range of meanings. Among the meanings for *representation*, the Oxford English Dictionary includes "presence, bearing" and also "appearance" (which, of course, can be taken as the outward form of something or its very manifestation). Thus, it would seem that the old legal meaning of *repraesentare*—to exhibit something (like a witness in court) or to manifest it and make it public—translated into many European languages. This fact underscores the polysemic nature of *representation* and of *to represent*, not just in their more technical and specialized usages but also in ordinary language. A theatrical representation, the way in which an actor represents a character on either stage or screen, is not necessarily a depiction or a mimetic rendering of something absent. It is true that, by playing a role, an actor can be said to take on someone else's identity or *persona*. In Hobbes, for instance, the theatrical metaphor is further complicated by his introduction of the idea that acting, or taking the "outward appearance of a man, counterfeited on stage," is wearing a "mask."[12] But theatrical representations and acting are also performances in their own right, or the embodiment and manifestation of a character. Nonnaturalistic forms of theater and abstract and performative art in general are clear examples of this more immediate sense of representation as exhibition, public manifestation, and embodiment. There is a difference but also a tension, as we shall see shortly, between reflective and performative senses of representation.

We may perhaps agree at this point that representation is a polysemic concept, both in its ordinary and more specialized usages, and therefore lacks any "core" meaning on which to elaborate a convincing theory of political representation or even to base a phenomenology of the practices of representation. Meanings, and the work of conceptual clarification, are important. As Wittgenstein (1963) says, "concepts lead us to make investigations, are the expression of our interest, and direct our interest" (151 [R570]). But the meanings of political concepts, like those of any concept, are part of a pragmatics of political discourse and action that is open-ended and therefore contingent and subject to change through use and new applications, even though past meanings persist as traces in new ones and make possible their articulation. C. S. Lewis (1967) offers an excellent metaphor for this process of accretion as "ramification": "we shall again and again find the earlier senses of a word flourishing for centuries despite a vast overgrowth of later senses which might have been expected to kill them" (8–9). This clearly applies to the political sense of *representation*. Denying that there are "core" meanings or that they can be used as a kind of "court of appeal" to explain what is going on in political representation, however, does not preclude deploying a particular meaning—such as that captured by the paradox of presence/absence—to articulate both descriptive and normative claims about political representation. This is what we do all the time. But here comes another interesting lesson from Hasso Hofmann's debunking of the essentialist reading of representation that he finds so pervasive in much of the German constitutional literature of the first half of the twentieth century, summarized in what Carl Schmitt presents as a "dialectic" of presence and absence: "To represent means to make an invisible being visible and present through a publicly present one. The dialectic of the concept is that the invisible is presupposed as absent and nevertheless is simultaneously made present" (Schmitt, [1928] 2008, 243).

On the face of it, this reading would seem to be in basic agreement with Pitkin's view discussed in the previous section. But the two readings differ not only in the philosophical and methodological perspectives of the authors but also in the different uses to which they put the question of presence/absence, applying it to different problems in political representation and emphasizing different aspects as its central theoretical issue. For Pitkin, and for both her followers and critics, the paradox of representation addresses the question of how much representatives must track or be responsive to the judgment of their electors and constituencies. In the standard theory, it is mainly an issue of *government*, of democratic congruency between the manifested preferences and opinions of the citizens and the political actions of the representatives. Her main critics, as we have seen in the previous section, either suggest that responsiveness is not sufficient—if not buttressed by more descriptive forms of representation—or they shift the focus to how representatives are able to *evoke* the presence of the represented, rather than mirror it. In the German constitutional debate, and particularly in the work of Carl Schmitt ([1928] 2008) and Gerhard Leibholz ([1929] 1973),[13] the problem is that of the unity of the "political form" and therefore of the capacity of the *state* to act as *representative* of the people, not as a natural entity but as an artificial, hence represented, one. As Ernst-Wolfgang Böckenförde (1998) puts very succinctly, "In Schmitt's work, representation always relates to the political unity of the people, i.e. the state; it does not mean representation of the society vis-à-vis the state or representation of interests within the society. Moreover, the subject of representation is not the people *in* the state but, rather, the politically united and organized people which is the state itself" (49). It may not surprise that this comes close to the problem of representation as formulated by Hobbes. As Pitkin (1967) says: "Hobbes set himself the problem of creating a lasting union . . . and solved it with his theory or representation" (35). But from Pitkin's perspective, Hobbes's conception of representation was "partial, formal and empty of substance" (34); therefore, his solution was mostly a "verbal game," which fails to address the "real problem of the creation of political consensus" (35). In other words, in Pitkin's parlance, the problem of Hobbes and the German constitutional lawyers is one of *authorization*,[14] which she regards as important but not crucial to (democratic) representation, where what counts above all is *how to act for* the represented.

From the point of view of modern democratic representation, separating the issue of authorization from that of consensus may not do. Indeed, as we suggest in the introduction to the volume when we talk of two faces of representation, modern political representation partakes in two separate but intertwined processes and discourses, one concerning the nature of the modern state, its authority and legitimacy, and the other concerning the form of modern democratic government, its springs and power mechanisms. It is at the conjunction of these two problems that we can better understand the inner tensions of representative democracy and of other forms of democratic representation operating in society. Although Schmitt and Leibholz are mainly concerned with how representation gives body to the political unity, what they say has implications for democratic representation itself.

Two points are worth considering. The first is that their main interest is in rejecting an indiscriminate conception of vicarious representation where substitution is reduced to standing or acting for someone else by either following their instructions or attending to their private, more factual preferences, opinions, and interests.[15] They identify this by using the German term of "*Vertretung*" or "*Stellvertretung*" in opposition to "*Repräsentation*" (Leibholz [1929] 1973, ch. 1). As Schmitt ([1928] 2008) says, "that X steps in for the absent Y or for a few thousand such Ys is still not an instance of representation" (243). For both Schmitt and Leibholz, "*Repräsentation*" only takes place where superior, spiritual entities are involved, and it belongs to the political not the private sphere. In their view, there is a clear separation between a private sphere, in which individual and groups' interests are considered through the action and the categories of civil law, and political representation in the strict sense, which instead belongs to the domain of public law, and needs publicity as one of its constituent elements. They therefore criticize the historical and legal literature, where, they argue, "the concepts 'representation,' 'vicem gerere,' 'mandatum,' 'commissio,' 'empowerment,' 'advocacy' are mixed up with one another" (Schmitt [1928] 2008, 247). They also regret that other European languages, by relying on a single word, are more easily prone to confuse the privatistic and the public law characters of these different concepts and practices (Leibholz [1929] 1973, chs. 1 and 8). When looked at from a democratic perspective, this understanding of political representation excludes that civil society organizations, private and corporative groups, or other particularist instances can participate directly in the formation of the general will through public discussion. Their interests and opinion need to be *represented* in and through the unity of the political form. Such unity consists in the state and its institutions, which *represent* the political unity of the people (or the "Nation," in the version embraced by Sieyes during the constitutional debates at the time of the French Revolution). The mediation between the private interests and their public manifestation takes place through the representatives, who act as the delegates of the *entire* people, but also through the citizens' own internalization of their role qua "citizens." Schmitt ([1928] 2008) thus suggests that even in plebiscitarian forms of decision-making, the citizen, like the representative, "must be thought of as 'independent,' as 'not bound to instructions and commissions,' and as a 'representative of the whole,' not of his private interests. At no time or place is there thorough, absolute self-identity of the then present people as political unity" (241).

The second point follows directly from Schmitt's final observation. A democratic state needs political unity, through representation, in order to act politically; otherwise it dissolves in a multiplicity of interests and wills. At the same time, for Schmitt, the democratic political form, like any other, is a mix of two principles: representation and self-identity. According to Schmitt, the "principle of the self-identity of the then present people as political unity rests on the fact that there is no state without people and that a people, therefore, must always actually be existing as an entity present at hand" (239); but as we have seen, Schmitt also admits that, at least in modern conditions, it is hardly ever possible for this principle to take place fully. This may perhaps happen, as he says, "by virtue of a strong and conscious similarity, as a result of firm natural boundaries, or due to some other reason" (239), but most of the time political unity, even in democracy, is the result of representation. It may also be, as he says later in the same text, that there is never a maximum degree of identity and homogeneity; a strong substantial similarity to the people is a fiction (248). In this sense, the two principles can be distinguished in relation to the amount of governmental power that is required to achieve political unity, and both principles to a certain degree are always required (see also Leibholz [1929] 1973, ch. 1; Duso 2003, 158–67).

Both the rejection of corporative and privatistic forms of representation as nonpolitical and the uneasy dialectic between the principle of self-identity and that of representation throw up difficulties and ambiguities.[16] Besides, on these points there are obvious differences between Schmitt and Leibholz, and between them and other German constitutionalists of the same period who embrace similar conceptions of representation. But such differences are of no particular interest in the context of this chapter. The main point is that from the dialectic of presence/absence these authors draw conclusions quite different from Pitkin's. The logic of presence that Schmitt and Leibholz identify in representation is, on the one hand, necessary to establish the form and unity of a state or people (democratic or otherwise) so that it can have the capacity to act politically; on the other hand, presence is necessary to ensure that the actions of the representative state are imputed to the people in their political capacity, with the ensuing rights, responsibilities, and obligations that come to the citizens. Note that, whatever criticisms one may wish to move toward their understanding of representation, and there may be many, none of the criticisms we identified in the previous section really applies to the meaning that they give to the presence/absence dialectic. A politics of presence is ruled out of court almost on principle, given Schmitt's and Leibholz's rejection of a pluralism of interests and the emphasis that they put instead on representation as providing the kind of embodiment needed for the unity of the political form. The constructivist critique hardly applies to Schmitt's and Leibholz's version of the dialectic of presence and absence. Indeed, they do not understand unity of the people as something natural, but the very process of *construction* of the people itself as a political agent. Rep-

resentation for them is precisely the opposite of government based on immediacy and a preexisting identity; it has instead a constitutive role, as the
constructivists maintain (and we are all constructivists in this respect). In
a similar way, the more sympathetic concerns raised by David Runciman
regarding the weaknesses of Pitkin's own version of the "paradox" do not
really apply to this version of the paradox. Runciman (2007) observes that
the "particular political difficulty with Pitkin's argument" is that "her non-
objection criterion explicitly confines representation to the representation
of individuals" (99). His own answer is to stress that there is a difference in
the ways individuals and groups can object and that this depends on an
asymmetry of status, which gives legitimacy to their objections. But the
same problem does not arise in the way in which Schmitt, Leibholz, and
others make use of the dialectic of presence and absence in representation,
for representation constructs the people as a political unity and not as a sum
of individuals. Of course, neither Schmitt's nor the more democratically inclined Leibholz's versions of this dialectic may be fully convincing or attractive. But the logic of presence in representation that they propose points
to a different set of problems than those concerning the more or less direct
representation of the interests and judgments of individuals and particular
groups in the action of government, which were at the center of the disputes
discussed in the first section. Whereas Pitkin concentrated on how the channel of representation could keep the action and judgment of the representatives in tune with those of the represented, Schmitt and Leibholz were
more interested in how representation creates the conditions for the unity
of political action and for the attribution of that very action to the people
as represented by the state. These, however, are not the only two ways in
which we can imagine democratic presence in political representation.

## Inclusion and Empowerment in the System of
## Democratic Representation

A key focus of current discussions of political representation is its relational aspects. In any of the intellectual fields where representation has
prominence, one of the more controversial issues is how to understand the
connection between its different elements—its relational character. The
two presence/absence theories we have examined point to such relational
properties, offering different ways in which representatives and represented relate to each other. Yet, as has been remarked by Young (2000,

125–28) and Plotke (1997, 27–28), this conceptualization tends to see the relation as mainly one of identity. They may not be entirely right on this. As we have seen, Schmitt, for instance, conceives representation as opposite to the principle of identity in government; only from the combination of these two principles can the political form take shape. Pitkin (1967) says that representation allows only for *some* presence, and, throughout chapter 10, where she discusses political representation in general, she paints a careful picture of the relationship between representatives and represented as one of reciprocal independence between two sets of agents both capable of action and judgment. Nonetheless, their respective uses of the dialectic or paradox of presence/absence seem to confirm what Young and Plotke suggest: that such views ultimately understand the relationship of representation as a way for the ruled to rule *through* their representatives and therefore for the represented to be identified in the actions of the representatives. Both Young and Plotke argue that to appreciate the relationship in its more dynamic aspects and to explore its democratic potential one should look at representation as a relation of "non-identity" (Plotke 1997, 28) or, as Young suggests by borrowing a term from Derrida, of "*différance*" (Young 2000, 127).

Young and Plotke both point here to an underlying difficulty in more mimetic and vicarious conceptions of representation. Without going too far into philosophical terrain, there is something irreducible in the relationship between what represents and what is represented. In the previous section, we pointed out the sense in which representation can be understood in the terms of an actual presence (a public exhibition or the very embodiment of something). In this sense, representation does not refer back to any absent thing. But, even when we conceive representation as something standing for something else, it appears to us in two different ways: as something pointing to something else, and therefore establishing some form of identity and similarity between it and the absent thing, but also as something with its own presence, and therefore something different from the one it purports to point our attention toward. Roger Chartier (2013) quotes the art critic Louis Martin, who distinguishes two dimensions through which linguistic and visual representations work. One he defines as a "transitive" dimension where the signifier, symbol, or image refers to something else. The other he takes to be a more "reflexive" dimension, in which "toute représentation *se présente* représentant quelque chose" (cited in Chartier 2013). A very similar point is made by Hans-Georg Gadamer (1979) when he discusses the status of pictorial representation and contrasts it to the way in which a mirror may reflect an image. Of the latter, Gadamer says, the "mirror throws back an image and not a copy: it is the image of what is represented in the mirror and is inseparable from its presence"; here we have a "unity and non-differentiation of representation and what is represented" (123). In the case of a picture there is no such identity: "the picture has its own being. *This being as representation*, as precisely that in which it is not the same as what is represented" (124; emphasis added). In this sense, as Gadamer goes on to say, the picture has an "autonomous reality"; there is "no longer a one-sided relationship," and "it is only through the picture that the original becomes the original picture" (124–25).

The assertion of the ontological status of the representation *as* representation, with the correlative establishment of the represented *as* represented, offers a view of the relationship not as one where the two come to be identified but, on the contrary, where they are two distinct identities. Such a conception of the work of representation has important philosophical complexities, as well as the obvious difficulties, when we translate it into the political domain. Nonetheless, it offers some interesting analytical and normative ways of rethinking democratic representation, for the main precipitate of such a conception is that we need to think of the relationship of political representation as one involving the presence or contextual formation of two or more distinct political subjects. The problem of democratic representation therefore is not so much how successfully the representatives act for, stand for, or embody the represented but how the process of political representation may aid (or impede) the establishment of meaningful practices of self-government. The forms and instruments of political representation therefore must be judged on whether they empower citizens to have some voice and control over collective decisions and whether they facilitate either democratic inclusion or exclusion.

Much of the new literature on political representation is an attempt to explore the possible connections between representation and democratic empowerment and inclusion, a task continued in this volume. Part of such a task has been to extend the analysis of the relationship of representation beyond formal and institutionalized settings but also to explore the particular dynamics of communication, contestation, and trust-building that take place between the representatives and the represented in both the social and political arenas. This view of representation makes us look anew at the established institutions of representation, their functions, and their limits. It also helps us understand better how much more complex, controversial, and diffuse the process of democratic representation is. The idea of a system of representation may here come handy. This is not entirely new. Pitkin (1967) herself has interesting things to say when she describes political representation as a "public, institutionalised arrangement" and states that "what makes it representation is not any single action by any one participant, but the over-all structure and functioning of the system, the patterns emerging from the multiple activities of many people" (221–22). In his analysis of the metamorphoses of representative government, Bernard Manin captures this more systemic aspect of political representation when he describes four institutional arrangements that embody the principles of representative government and through which one can judge how the decisions arrived at by the representatives relate to the wishes of the electorate or the citizens. Two of these arrangements refer to the partial independence of the representatives and to the recurrent character of elections in democracy. These speak more of the relationship between people and representatives and the way in which citizens can contribute to the general direction of legislation. But the other two arrangements identified by Manin, the freedom of public opinion and the trial by discussion, are more concerned with the specific role that the public, as an institutional phenomenon, distinct from both the people and the electorate, plays in representative democracy (Manin 1997, ch. 5; see also Urbinati 2006; Castiglione 2018). These features refer to the way in which the institutional system of political representation, if it is to be both empowering and inclusive, must involve the citizens in both their private and public capacities in the very process of opinion formation. Finally, besides inclusion in ruling and opinion formation, a third element belongs to the process of political representation,[17] and that is identity formation, not only in the sense of the constitution of the people as a democratic subject but also in the sense of the political subjectivity of various groups within society and how they can contribute to defining the public interest through consensus building as well as more agonistic aspects of democratic politics. In short, the construction of democratic presence in representation is not fixed by semantics but open to the political imagination.

## Notes

1. At least in the Anglo-American literature, Pitkin's is often referred to as the standard view or theory of representation. But, more generally, her account of democratic representation is supposed to capture some important elements of political representation as enshrined in the institutional practice of constitutional democracies.

2. Frank Ankersmit's contribution to this volume uses two different rhetorical tropes, both of which work, though in different ways, as symbolic substitutions that propose two distinct models of political representation. Although Ankersmit's intention is to show how different the models are, he implicitly suggests that representation is always symbolic.

3. This argument is further explored by Saward in his contribution to this volume.

4. For a rough distinction between "representative" and "constructivist" turns, see the introduction to this volume. In some of the literature, however, the two are used almost synonymously.

5. Not all criticisms of what is identified as the standard theory should be read as criticisms of Pitkin. For instance, her theory tends to construct representation as a dynamic relationship where both the represented and the representatives need to have a certain degree of independence. But while Pitkin's conceptual analysis relies on distinctions, the overall intention of her work is to deny that such distinctions are fixed. Instead, its main purpose is to suggest that the concept of representation has different perspectives (or facets), each offering a different view or aspect of political representation. Her analysis of the trustee-delegate dichotomy, for instance, is mainly intended to show that both are, in some sense, right, and so partly collapses the distinction in practice.

6. This point is discussed at some length in Mansbridge's contribution to this volume.

7. Although the kind of problem-based approach we suggest here is pitched against a concept-based approach and does not seek to specify problems across different models of democracy as Warren (2017) does, we think similarities exist between what we are trying to do here and what Mark Warren does in a different context.

8. Unfortunately, Hasso Hofmann's book is unavailable in English and not well known. Translations of the book, or parts of it, exist in only a couple of languages. For an excellent summary of its main arguments, see Mulieri 2016.

9. The following reflections on the importance of acknowledging the polysemic nature of representation, not only for its historical reconstruction but also for a theory of political representation, are indebted to the use that both Sintomer and Mulieri make of Hofmann's work.

10. As his source, Chartier makes use of Furetière's 1694 *Dictionnaire de la langue française*.

11. This duality of meanings in common usage is also present in important debates in the philosophies of language and mind, which cannot be explored in this context. To have a sense of the implications that such duality has in these other fields, see Nöth (2003) and the entry "Représentation" in the *Dictionary of Untraslatables* (Dokic [2004] 2014, 891–94).

12. Hobbes's use of *person* is rather complex, and we lack the space to discuss the intricacies and implications of his argument, including the way in which it may

relate to the important tradition of *persona ficta* and the role that this legal convention may have played in shaping ideas of representation. For important contributions, see Thomas 1995 and Scalone 2017. Pitkin (1967, 23–8) makes a number of interesting observations about the role of the "person" and personification in Hobbes, but ultimately she struggles to make full sense of it, because she starts from a democratic consent- and election-based idea of political representation as "standard." For an excellent discussion of Pitkin and Hobbes, see Mónica Brito Vieira (2009; 2017b, 29–31).

13. Schmitt's and Leibholz's use of the presence/absence definition of representation exemplified a more diffuse position in the German constitutional debate between and after the two World Wars. Their discussions of the problem helped to shape widely held convictions, and they are among the main targets of Hofmann's attempt to correct historical and conceptual confusions. Other authors who shared similar views include Ernst Fraenkel ([1964] 1991) and Eric Voegelin (1952). On the essentialist view in the German debate, see Pollak (2007b, 30).

14. In chapter 3 (on "formalistic views of representation") Pitkin outlines the main aspects of the authorization conception as a continuation of Hobbes's view. With reference in particular to Voegelin and Leibholz, she insists on the implications of the authorization conception in terms of the "attribution" of the actions of the representative and the moral responsibility to the represented that accompanies those actions: "Voegelin speaks of representatives (in the 'existential' or authorization sense) as men whose actions are attributed not to themselves but to others" (51), and later on, "the ascription of the action is what is fundamental here" (52), with reference also to Leibholz (261n43).

15. Schmitt's and Leibholz's understanding of substitution is closer to the kind of semantic meaning that Hofmann associates with the more symbolic relation that in knowledge exists between the *Urbild* and the *Abbild* (Hofmann [1974] 2003, ch. 2).

16. For the reconstruction of a neocorporativist conception of representation in postwar Germany, which denies the strict opposition between private law and public law conceptions and that sees parties and associations as part of the representative structure, see Scalone 1996.

17. On the various functions of political representation, see Pollak 2007a.

## References

Böckenförde, Ernst-Wolfgang. 1998. "The Concept of the Political: A Key to Understanding Carl Schmitt's Constitutional Theory." In *Law as Politics: Carl Schmitt's Critique of Liberalism*, edited by David Dyzenhaus, 37–55. Durham, NC: Duke University Press.

Brito Vieira, Mónica. 2009. *The Elements of Representation in Hobbes*. Leiden: Brill.

———. 2017. "Introduction." In *Reclaiming Representation: Contemporary Advances in the Theory of Political Representation*, edited by Mónica Brito Vieira, 1–21. New York: Routledge.

———. 2017. "Performative Imaginaries: Pitkin versus Hobbes on Political Representation." In *Reclaiming Representation: Contemporary Advances in the Theory of Political Representation*, edited by Mónica Brito Vieira, 25–49. New York: Routledge.

Castiglione, Dario. 2018. "Métamorphoses du gouvernement modern: par le peuple, par la représentation, par le public." In *Les défis de la representation*, edited by Dario Castiglione and Manuela Albertone. Paris: Classiques Garnier.

Castiglione, Dario, and Mark Warren. 2006. "Rethinking Democratic Representation: Eight Theoretical Issues." Paper presented at "Rethinking Democratic Representation," Centre for the Study of Democratic Institutions, University of British Columbia, May 18–19, 2006.

Chartier, Roger. 2013. "Le sens de la representation." *La vie des idées*, March 22, 2013. http://www.laviedesidees.fr/Le-sens-de-la-representation.html.

Disch, Lisa. 2015. "The 'Constructivist Turn' in Democratic Representation: A Normative Dead-End?" *Constellations* 22 (4): 487–99.

Dokic, Jérôme. (2004) 2014. "Représentation." In *Dictionary of Untraslatables: A Philosophical Lexicon*, edited by Barbara Cassin, 891–94. Princeton, NJ: Princeton University Press, 891–4.

Duso, Giuseppe. 2003. *La rappresentanza politica. Genesi e crisi del concetto.* Milano: Franco Angeli.

Fraenkel, Ernst. (1964) 1991. *Deutschland und die westlichen Demokratien.* Frankfurt: Suhrkamp Verlag.

Gadamer, Hans-Goerg. 1979. *Truth and Method.* London: Sheed and Ward.

Hofmann, Hasso. (1974) 2003. *Repräsentation. Studien zur Wort-und Begriffsgeschichte von der Antike bis ins 19. Jahrhundert.* Berlin: Duncker & Humblot.

Leibholz, Gerard. (1929) 1973. *Die Repräsentation in der Demokratie.* Berlin: De Gruyter.

Lewis, C. S. 1967. *Studies in Words.* Cambridge: Cambridge University Press.

Manin, Bernad. 1997. *The Principles of Representative Government.* Cambridge: Cambridge University Press.

Mulieri, Alessandro. 2016. "Hasso Hofmann and the Polysemy of Representation." *Redescriptions* 19 (2): 127–45.

Nöth, Winfried. 2003. "Crisis of Representation?" *Semiotica* 143 (1/4): 9–15.

Phillips, Anne. 1995. *The Politics of Presence: The Political Representation of Gender, Ethnicity, and Race.* Oxford: Oxford University Press.

Pitkin, Hanna. 1968. "The Paradox of Representation." In *Representation. Nomos X*, edited by J. Roland Pennock and John W. Chapman, 38–42. New York: Atherton Press.

Pitkin, Hanna F. 1967. *The Concept of Representation.* Berkeley: University of California Press.

———. (1972) 1993. *Wittgenstein and Justice.* Berkeley: University of California Press.

Plotke, David. 1997. "Representation Is Democracy." *Constellations* 4(1): 19–34.

Pollak, Johannes. 2007a. "Contested Meanings of Representation." *Comparative European Politics* 5: 87–103.

———. 2007b. *Repräsentation ohne Demokratie. Kollidierende Systeme der Repräsentation.* Wien: Springer.

Runciman, David. 2007. "The Paradox of Political Representation." *Journal of Political Philosophy* 15(1): 93–114.

Saward, Michael. 2006. "The Representative Claim." *Contemporary Political Theory* 5: 297–318.

———. 2010. *The Representative Claim.* New York: Oxford University Press.

———. 2014. "Shape-Shifting Representation." *American Political Science Review* 108 (4): 723–36.

———. 2017. "Performative Representation." In *Reclaiming Representation: Contemporary Advances in the Theory of Political Representation*, edited by Mónica Brito Vieira, 75–94. New York: Routledge.

Scalone, Antonino. 1996. *Rappresentanza politica e rappresentanza degli interessi.* Milano: Franco Angeli.

———. 2017. "La Potenza del diritto e il principio rappresentativo." *Quaderni Fiorentini. Per la Storia del Pensiero Giuridico Moderno.* 46 (2): 1015–25.

Schmitt, Carl. (1928) 2008. *Constitutional Theory.* Translated and edited by Jeffrey Seitzer. Durham, NC: Duke University Press.

Sintomer, Yves. 2013. "The Meanings of Political Representation: Uses and Misuses of a Notion." *Raisons politiques* 50 (2): 13–34.

Thomas, Yan. 1995. "Fictio Legis. L'Empire de la fiction Romaine et ses limites Médiévales." *Droits, Revue Française de Théorie Juridique* 21: 17–63.

Urbinati, Nadia. 2006. *Representative Democracy: Principles and Genealogy.* Chicago: University of Chicago Press.

Voegelin, Eric. 1952. *The New Science of Politics.* Chicago: Chicago University Press.

Warren, Mark. 2017. "A Problem-Based Approach to Democratic Theory." *American Political Science Review* 111 (1): 39–53.

Wittgenstein, Ludwig. 1963. *Philosophical Investigations.* Oxford: Basil Blackwell.

Young, Iris Marion. 2000. *Inclusion and Democracy.* Oxford: Oxford University Press.

PART I

# Representation as Democratic Empowerment

# CHAPTER TWO

# How Representation Enables Democratic Citizenship

Mark E. Warren

Within standard democratic theory, representation is primarily about scaling democracy onto mass societies. Through election or selection, representatives stand for, speak for, and act for those who cannot be present in places in which political decisions are deliberated and made, owing to the constraints of scale, time, complexity, knowledge, and attentiveness. In Hanna Pitkin's (1967) well-known formulation, representative processes overcome these constraints by *re*presenting: making present what is absent (9). Representation is *democratic* when those who are represented have ways and means to authorize representatives to represent them as well as to hold them accountable for their representative activities.

While the concept of democratic representation has received renewed and sophisticated attention over the last decade or so, the broad outlines of Pitkin's theoretical formulation have remained intact. Importantly, it continues to focus our attention on how and whether representative relationships serve to extend the powers of citizens (a term I use generally to refer to individuals in their political capacities) beyond limitations imposed by time, space, and complexity. We should notice, however, that the formulation focuses primarily on the activities of representatives, not the represented. The focus is part of the framing of representation as a matter of presence and absence: representatives stand in, speak, or act for the represented *in their absence*: they are *represented in* the spaces and activities where they cannot be.

In this chapter I focus on the political activities of the *represented* within representative relationships. I am not challenging the questions generated by the standard view of democratic representation but rather adding another set of questions: What are citizens *doing* when they assess representative claims; authorize representatives to stand, speak, or act for them; and then hold representatives accountable? How do representative relationships construct and enable the capacities of democratic citizenship? Representative relationships within democratic contexts, I shall argue, can and should develop the capacities of citizens by (1) inducing autonomous judgment; (2) framing individuals in their roles and capacities as members of collectivities; (3) enabling moral judgment by inducing citizens to view the world from the perspective of others; and (4) making discursive accountability possible. Along with other normative criteria, the institutions and practices of representative democracy can be judged as better or worse according to the ways they enable these capacities of democratic citizenship.

In the first section, I review the standard theory of democratic representation, noting the ways it deflects attention from activities of the represented. In the second, I examine the constructivist turn in theories of political representation. The constructivist turn moves democratic theory in the right direction by focusing on (1) the ways interests are constructed within representative relationships and (2) the conditions of contestability that reduce the possibility that the constructed interests of the represented simply reflect representatives' preferences. But the constructivist turn remains overly reactive to problems generated by the standard approach, failing to frame directly the (potential) contributions of representation to capacities of democratic citizenship. In the remaining sections, I develop the positive part of the argument by focusing on the four ways representative relationships can form individuals into democratic citizens.

## The Standard Theory of Democratic Representation

As already remarked, representation is about scaling democratic decision-making onto large societies. The standard approach asks how those who are absent can not only communicate their interests and preferences but also ensure that they are, in fact, being represented. In what ways can individuals (citizens, constituents, etc.) authorize a representative to stand for, speak for, or act for them? And in what ways can individuals hold representatives accountable for their activities as a representative? Electoral democracy empowers the authorization and accountability cycle: the vote has the dual role of authorizing a representative and subsequently empowering voters to pass judgment on the representative's performance (Urbinati and Warren 2008). Parties and advocacy groups mediate the voter-representative relationship with platforms, positions, and arguments, ideally serving to connect voters' preferences to their votes for representatives.

Much of the recent literature on democratic representation moves beyond (and challenges) the standard view by posing three additional questions (following Näsström 2011): (1) How do representative relationships constitute the interests of the represented? (2) What are the contributions of representative relationships to political judgment? (3) What kinds of representation relationships exist outside of electoral representation, and what do they contribute to democratic representation? I focus here on the first two (but see Saward [2010] and Montanaro [2012] for analysis of the third).

The first of these questions was already framed by Pitkin: the interests of the represented are not exogenous to the relationship between representative and represented. They are always constituted in some way by the representative relationship. Representatives make claims, which, when successful, at least partially define the interests of those they claim to represent (Saward 2010). The challenge to *democratic* representation is that if people do not have autonomous preferences, it is difficult to understand them as choosing and directing their representatives—authorizing them to stand, speak, or act on their behalf. Nor can they hold representatives accountable, since what people understand their interests to be are at least partially constructed within the representative relationship itself (Disch 2011, 2015; Montanaro 2012). Political elites can use their resources to manipulate those they claim to represent—and electoral politics provides plenty of incentives to do so. At some (unlikely) limit, "the people" could be fully constructed, with their assent, by political entrepreneurs, which would of course vitiate any sense in which the people could be said to rule through their representatives.

Responses to this issue tend to focus on either the representative or the represented. Those who focus on representatives emphasize role responsibilities. Pitkin (1967), recognizing that those who are represented often do not have well-formed preferences prior to articulation by representatives, argues that representatives should "act in the interest of the represented, in a manner responsive to them" (209). This formulation recognizes the constructed element of representation, distinguishes the interests people have from the preferences they hold, and defines the duties of the representative. As Disch (2011) notes, Pitkin's formulation both articulates and suspends the problem (106–8). On the one hand, Pitkin recognizes that preferences can (and often must) be formed by representatives. On the other hand, without more analysis, the formulation can tacitly legitimize paternalistic claims by representatives to know what is best for their constituents' interests, often despite their preferences. At some limit, this formulation merges with Burke's conception of elected representatives as *trustees* who substitute their (better) judgment for those of their relatively uninformed constituents. But it can also issue in the more productive question implied in Pitkin's formulation: democratically speaking, how should a representative fulfill the duties of responsiveness, given their constitutive role in representative relationships (Dovi 2007)? What is occurring within this relationship that could count as responsiveness?

The second of these questions helps to give definition to this problem of responsiveness: How is representation involved in political judgments—especially those that are responsive to constituents? Bernard Manin (1997) focuses on the ways in which representatives form decision-making bodies (legislatures, councils, etc.), within which justifications for representative claims are deliberatively structured. For this reason, representative constitution of the interests of the represented are not arbitrary; they are molded *within* discursive relationships and justified *by* arguments *to* the represented (Manin 1997). Nadia Urbinati (2006) broadens Manin's approach, focusing on the ways in which representative institutions focus public advocacy and discourse, through which interests gain articulation and constituencies are called forth (see also Disch 2011; Garsten 2009; Runciman 2007).

If we pursue this line of argument, it frames a question that has been mostly overlooked in the new literature on representation. We have focused mostly on the activities of representatives, whose judgment we have tended to see as *substituting* for citizen judgment. To a large extent, this focus follows from a spatial metaphor built into the Latin *repraesentare*, which "means to grant something a literal presence, for example ... to present a new Pope before a crowd" (Runciman 2007, 94). The spatial metaphor has stuck, so that political representation is widely understood as making present what is absent, which in turn underscores the presence of representatives and the absence of citizens. The metaphor works for, say, the far-flung empire of the Romans or forging a representative government for the original thirteen American colonies. But we should notice that the metaphor also defocuses nonspatial connections—language in particular—which do not follow the spatial logic of presence and absence. Especially in highly mediated, linguistically saturated contexts, those who are represented may be quite active, especially in their judgments as to how they should be represented and who or what should represent them. To fill out our theories of democratic representation, we shall need to ask about these activities and judgments of the represented—those that the spatial metaphor renders "absent" (see Mansbridge 2003, 2009).

Stated just a bit more analytically, any simple political representative relationship can be formulated as follows: $x$ represents $y$ with respect to their interests $z$ as involved with, or affected by, a collectivity $c$ within which $x$ serves as a representative. Within this formulation, two loci of judgment must be robust for *democratic* representation to occur:

- The representative must be responsive to the represented, which involves judgments about their interests as affected by a relevant collectivity.
- The represented must judge in what ways and how well they are represented by a representative, especially insofar as their interests are affected by a relevant collectivity.

The literature has tended to focus on the first kind of judgment, influenced by the standard view that representation substitutes the judgment of the (present) representative for the (absent) represented. But decisions about *being* represented—accepting or rejecting a representative claim; trusting, monitoring, or opposing your elected representative or governing party, and so on, are kinds of political judgments. They comprise democratic citizenship; indeed, they are among the most important kinds of political participation in a representative democracy.

Here I am interested in four further questions that follow from a focus on citizens' judgments:

- When are citizen judgments to be represented autonomously, in the sense that their judgments can be said to be their own?
- How do citizens come to understand themselves as represented in their role as members of a collectivity, such that they can be represented at the level of a collectivity and be said to be a constituent of that collectivity?
- What kinds of capacities for moral judgments—that is, judgments about duties and obligations to others—are enabled by representation?
- How do representative relationships enable relations of discursive accountability?

In formulating these questions, I am focusing mostly on individual-level effects of democratic political systems. While I will not do so here, we can judge the representative dimensions of democratic systems by the ways they enable these individual-level capacities. Political systems that enable citizens to use their powers will also be more likely to generate these powers—a point that has been fundamental to those strains of democratic theory that stress the active and vigilant features of citizenship, represented by Tocqueville, Mill, Dewey, as well as contemporary participatory and deliberative theories of democracy.

## The Constructivist Turn

Although these questions have not been put directly in the literature, they have been broached indirectly, especially by the new constructivism, which is most completely represented by Michael Saward's innovative book *The Representative Claim*. Representation, as Saward puts it, "is not just *there*, a thing. It is made, or constructed, by someone, for someone, and for a purpose" (Saward 2010, 13; see also Urbinati 2007; Disch 2011, 2015; Montanaro 2012). Saward develops a theoretical account of representation in two steps, focusing on analysis of representative claims. The "general form" of the representative claim involves these relationships: "A *maker* of representations . . . puts forward a *subject* . . . which stands for an *object* . . . that is related to a *referent* . . . and is offered to an *audience*" (2010, 36; see also Rehfeld 2006). By abstracting from institutionalized forms of representation and focusing on the speech act (the claim), Saward is able to formulate precise questions about each element. Thus, on the one hand, through their assertions, makers of representative claims seek to form their audiences relative to problems, goods, or topics. On the other hand, audiences accept or reject the claims made on their behalf. So, if a representative claim is successful, it "prompts certain constituents to recognize the status-claim, and to recognize the selective depiction of themselves—the object—within it" (2010, 47). In this way, he shows the many ways in which constituencies can be constructed by the activities of claim-makers. While Saward's approach is quite consistent with voting-based representation, he shifts the focus to the performative features of representation: elections serve to select and remove representatives, but performing *as* a representative—interacting with constituents, responding to problems and initiatives, locating oneself within a party—takes place through serially sequenced speech acts in response to specific audiences.

It is this feature of Saward's analysis that is especially salient here: he shifts the theoretical framework from *spatial* metaphors of presence and absence to *speech acts that establish representative relationships* (see also Saward 2014, 725). A *claim* is an assertion whose generic form is performative and linguistic. It follows from Saward's framing of representation as claims that the *democratic* features of representation will focus on uptake and acceptance by those subject to claims. Saward generalizes by speaking of "acceptance acts" which need not take a verbal form. Voting, for example, is a speech act only in the sense that a vote expresses a preference from a limited list of possibilities. Other kinds of acceptance acts may include (presumably) followings, memberships, verbal support, and other acts that transform representative claims into a democratic relationship (Saward 2010, 151–53). The logic, however, is that each kind of act could be justified in the form of speech: "I voted for $x$ because . . . ; I joined this group because . . ."

The constructed features of representative relationships follow this form: potential representatives make claims, which "call forth" a constituency. The representative claim forms and engages; members of a proposed constituency are challenged, as it were, to accept the claim or to offer objections. Representatives gain their democratic legitimacy by building constituencies through claiming and responding.

From the perspective of democratic representation, then, Saward's framework directs attention to the nature and status of acceptance acts. How do we know that these acts are *owned* by citizens, especially if they are "called forth" by representative claims? From a democratic standpoint, the choice to be represented should (ideally) be made *autonomously*—not outside of constructed representative relationships but rather the result of reflection on the claims to represent interests. Moreover, we should want to know how representative relationships underwrite citizens' capacities to make political judgments.

Saward is appropriately cautious. In some cases, it is reasonable to infer the autonomy of acceptance acts—for example, a party wins an electoral majority under free and fair conditions. Others may be ambiguous, complicated by repeated and shifting representative claims. Even more difficult is to infer democratic legitimacy from silence—the linguistic form of *absence*. Even in relatively robust mass democracies, most citizens are relatively inattentive to most issues most of the time. Their representatives must infer their legitimacy much of the time from (as Pitkin puts it) "non-objection" (Runciman 2007). And how do we know that nonobjection is, say, affirmative acquiescence or a considered judgment to trust (Mansbridge 2009) rather than disaffection, ignorance, or the effect of subtle forms of silencing built into marginalizations or dependencies (Saward 2010, 152)? The question of the quality of citizen judgments (in being represented) is bound up in the same question: how do we know that citizens' acceptance acts are considered, reflective, and politically robust?

Constructivists have a common answer to both questions—one that is certainly right but also incomplete: we need to look at the conditions under which judgments are formed (Mansbridge 2009, 391). Saward (2010) focuses on the differences between open and closed societies. In "relatively closed" societies, "it may be more difficult for actors and observers to impute a degree of democratic legitimacy" to representative claims. "In undemocratic or semi-democratic contexts, with, for example, limited information flows and freedoms, people may not have sufficient resources . . . to make assessments of representative claimants" (158–59). Thus, we need to ask, are the conditions "conducive to open and uncoerced choices by members of the appropriate constituency?" (Saward 2014, 733). But, since it will be difficult to judge the conditions of each kind of judgment, we should "zoom out" and ask "to what extent are conditions conducive to uncoerced and open acceptance acts across a diverse range of dyadic claims—at a systemic-governmental level or more broadly on a systemic-societal level" (2014, 733).

Along the same lines, Disch builds a "mobilization" theory of representation that focuses on the ways groups articulate the needs, identities, and interests of constituents through successive formulations. Democratic responsiveness is more likely when political systems are "reflexive"—full of places and institutions within which claims are considered and reconsidered from differing perspectives. What induces reflexivity, Disch argues, is competition among claims. And competition is good because it "may activate citizens' judgement" (Disch 2011, 112).

We find the same kind of approach offered by Runciman (2007), whose key concern is with Pitkin's nonobjection principle. Because of the absence that is definitive of *re*presentation, representatives must speak and act in the name of those they represent, usually as groups, in spite of their absence. Following Pitkin, Runciman suggests that *democratic* legitimacy can be constructed from the "non-objection criterion": "presence comes from the ability of individuals to object to what is done in their name" such that "representation takes place when there is no objection to what someone does on behalf of someone else" (95). Thus, "the non-objection criterion allows a kind of latent presence for the represented, such that their *silence* can be taken as a form of assent. However, it also means that where that silence is broken, and explicit objections are voiced, representation starts to break down" (95). When does an objection to a representative claim terminate representation? It cannot simply be that individuals object *qua* individuals. Rather, objections must be registered on behalf of a group. Thus, objections capable of terminating representation must be made from a second-person, not first-person, vantage point: "For these objections to count, they must be voiced not on behalf of the crowd, speaking for themselves, but by a crowd making a claim to speak in the name of the people" (107). And the conditions for this kind of process involve competition among claims. "Political representation is best understood not in the language of veto but of competition. Objections to the actions of representatives can prove decisive when they constitute a plausibly competing claim to speak in the name of the person or thing being represented" (106–7).

Finally, Garsten (2009) offers a libertarian version of a similar logic, arguing that "a chief purpose of representative government is *to multiply and challenge governmental claims to represent the people*" (91). Representative institutions should "prevent any one interpretation of the popular will from claiming final authority" (91), accenting "the negative function of popular sovereignty" (107). If we extend Garsten's logic to the individual level, however, what such institutions accomplish is to induce reflexivity though competitive claim-making.

## Can Representation Underwrite Democratic Citizenship?

We can now put the central question for this chapter directly: In what ways can representative political systems support and develop capacities for democratic citizenship? A premise of this question is that decisions *to be represented* are an important kind of political judgment in democratic political systems. As Pitkin (1967) notes (presciently but without developing the idea), "the represented" need to be conceived as entities "capable of action and judgment" (155). How do the judgments of the represented contribute, in principle, to capacities of democratic citizenship?

I suggest we can identify at least four kinds of potential contributions. Democratically representative political systems can contribute to (1) citizen autonomy, (2) citizens' views of themselves as members of collectivities, (3) citizens' moral/ethical capacities, and (4) citizens' capacities for discursive accountability. As we shall see, the literatures of political theory discuss each of these capacities. But they have been discussed only tangentially as normatively desirable consequences of democratic representative relationships.

## Autonomy

The term *autonomy* has Kantian origins and describes the capacities of individuals to form views in ways that reflect not simply impulses or desires but rather considered positions that can be justified with reasons to others. Autonomy in this sense is a capacity that individuals gain through their participation in discursive relationships. From a democratic perspective, autonomy is essential to self-rule within the context of collectivities. On the one hand, autonomous judgments are the results of self-reflection that can be said to be *owned* by individuals (that is, they are not the result of manipulation, propaganda, etc.). As Nedelsky (2011) puts it, autonomy is the idea that "acts can arise from the actor rather than being determined by something else" (45) On the other hand, autonomy is enabled *through* discursive interactions with others, particularly through interactions that involve mutual justification through the offering and receiving of reasons (45–49).

The possibility of autonomy responds directly to the primary problem for most constructivists—the endogeneity of preference formation within representative relationships. As we saw above, the constructivist response is that representative systems should underwrite reflexivity through openness to multiple and competing representative claims. The implication is that where individuals are subjects of multiple competing claims they will be induced to judge simply by competition among them, thus tending to transform preferences into choices that can be articulated and justified. Thus, autonomy is, at least in part, a consequence of considered individual decisions to be represented in one way rather than another.

It is possible, of course, to describe electoral representation in these terms. While political scientists have put enormous energy into understanding voting behavior, it has been remarkably unusual to view voting decisions as anything more than, say, selection or removal of representatives based on their promises relative to pocketbook voting or ideological framing. In contrast, Mansbridge's 2003 article "Rethinking Representation" was innovative because she identified representative relationships that go well beyond this "promissory" relationship. Representatives may anticipate constituent's needs and interests; they may function as moral "gyroscopes" that voters select for their moral trustworthiness, and they may represent causes outside of their districts as "surrogates." Each of these roles requires some level of deliberative interaction with constituents, which helps to redirect our attention to citizens' participation in representative judgment. When competition and multiplicity in representative claims induce these kinds of judgments, we can go one step further, and describe one ideal function of representation as the development of autonomy.

### Citizens as Members of Collectivities

One of the oldest questions in democratic theory—indeed, political theory—is the question of how individuals come to see themselves as belonging to collectivities for purposes of collective self-rule. How do individuals come to understand themselves as part of a *people* that can self-rule? There are ways of dissolving the problem by speaking of nations, communities, and other collectivities to which individuals are attached in prepolitical ways. But in modern societies collectivities are multiple and fluid, and individuals belong to multiple collectivities for different goals and purposes. Political collectivities are more challenging than many other kinds in that they are usually not chosen; individuals find themselves as codependents entangled with others, sharing fates, injustices, or relative advantages, as well as sharing collective action problems for the provision of collective goods.

It is within this context that political representation can and should function as a pivot between individual self-understanding qua individual and individual self-understanding as a member of a collectivity, people, or public. Without representation, there is no "people," with perhaps the exception of small, inclusive, face-to-face contacts where each is involved in crafting a collectivity. Focusing on the aesthetic functions of representation, Ankersmit (2002) aptly comments that "without political representation we are without a conception of what political reality—the represented—is like; without it, political reality has neither face nor contours.... Political reality only comes into being after the nation has unfolded itself into a represented and in a representation representing the represented. Without representation, no democratic politics" (115).

If we combine Ankersmit's point with the constructivist ideal of the representative environment as composed of multiple competing claims, then we can see that these claims amount to differing accounts of collective membership. Representatives assert their claims in the form of *we* (and, too often, *they*), each with their accompanying identities, demands, benefits, burdens, and responsibilities. Importantly, Ankersmit argues, representation opens a distance between representative and citizen (118). In doing so, the representative enables citizens to objectify the claims—to distance the claim from the self—to decide whether to try it on, and to judge its fit with the multiple collectivities within which each individual is always already embedded. When issues are significant enough to have representative claims attached, individuals are presented, in effect, with a pallet of possible memberships: Canadian, woman, taxpayer, middle-class, entitled, disenfranchised, trustee of nonhuman beings, caretaker of the Earth, parent of children, youth, employee, retiree, Christian, aggrieved, exploited, subject of injustice, crime-threatened, and so on. In democracies, representatives are continually trying out these identities, along with the groups they identify with their associated goods, risks, and boundaries. Sometimes claims build on existing communities; sometimes they build on reactive fears; sometimes they challenge individuals to assume responsibilities for as-yet-unacknowledged shared fates (Williams 2003).

Although Ankersmit makes this point by reference to the aesthetic dimensions of representation, the same point can be made through its discursive dimensions. Indeed, the point is better made in discursive terms, since it is language that transforms representations (visual or verbal) into propositions—claims—to which individuals can assent or object.

Runciman (2007) arrives at a parallel formulation in working through the question of what it could mean for a *group* to object to the way in which it is represented. While a group cannot typically object *as a group* (unless the group is small enough to speak with one voice), individuals can object to representations that are made "in our name" if they have formulated their positions in a public form to which a constituency is attached: "As an *x*, I object to *y*." That is, a representative claim identifies a public that exists in the form of public opinion by naming and claiming, giving it an existence sufficient for discursive assent or objection. To make this point, Runciman draws a distinction between

> the public on whose behalf political representatives act, and the public whose opinions of the actions of those representatives determine whether or not they can plausibly claim to be representing the people as a whole. The first of these publics is an abstraction … an incapable object at the mercy of competing claims of its representatives and the separate individuals who retain the right to object to what is being done in its name. The second public—the public of

"public opinion"—is not an abstraction as such, since it is constituted by agents capable of acting their own right. (106)

This "second public" gains its identity through the process of being identified and represented. This said, Runciman's formulation is ambiguous on the crucial question of whether public opinion preexists the representative process. A clearer theoretical formulation would be that acts of representation give public opinion form, such that individuals can assent or object to the collectivity and positions framed by that opinion. Many empirical variations will exist, of course: some publics are old, stable, and established; others may coalesce around an issue or problem that calls it into existence. Urbinati's emphasis (2000, 2005) on the ways in which advocacy brings publics into existence follows similar lines of thinking. When we view this idea from an individual perspective, it highlights a shift in register from individuals speaking (or judging) *as* individuals to individuals speaking (or judging) *as members of collectivities*—that is, as citizens.

### Perspective-Taking and Moral Thinking

We are now at a point, conceptually speaking, at which the potential moral (or ethical) functions of representation come into view. To develop this possibility, I turn to another literature, this one having to do with the moral or ethical representations of broad communities. The conceptual transition is not a big one. Once being represented introduces the perspective of being part of a people (public, constituency, etc.) within the context of representative claim-making, the theoretical infrastructure is in place to view citizens in their capacities for perspective-taking—that is, viewing a situation, issue, or train of effects from the perspective of another. Perspective-taking in this sense is the core capacity in all moral and ethical judgments. Representation plays a pivotal role in enabling this kind of capacity.

This idea that representation and moral competency are intertwined can be found in two early arguments for representative government. The first can be found in Madison's well-known discussion of the problem of faction in *Federalist* 10 (Hamilton, Madison, and Jay [1787] 2003). Here Madison argues against "democracy"—by which he idiosyncratically means direct, assembly democracy—in favor of a "republic," by which he means "a government in which the scheme of representation takes place." The problem to which representation is the solution is that of citizens' judgment: because it is direct, a "democracy" unites judge and cause, which is likely to undermine good judgment. "No man is allowed to be a judge in his own cause, because his interest would certainly bias his judgment, and, not improbably, corrupt his integrity. With equal, nay with greater reason, a body of men are unfit to be both judges and parties at the same time." Madison notes that, in matters of justice, the judge clearly cannot be an interested party if justice is to be served. In matters of legislation, however, parties to a judgment are almost always interested. It is not possible to remove interests, but it is possible to structure a scheme of representation that increases the likelihood that collective judgments will be good judgments. Famously, Madison's solution is twofold. First, representative relationships separate the sites of cause and judgment, locating the latter within small, deliberative bodies such as legislatures that represent broader publics. Second, the scale of constituencies should sufficiently encompass interests so that no single set of interests (including "majority factions") can dominate the body. Interestingly, Madison sees breadth of inclusion as serving a communicative checking function as well: "Besides other impediments, it may be remarked that, where there is a consciousness of unjust or dishonorable purposes, communication is always checked by distrust in proportion to the number whose concurrence is necessary."

We should notice two features of Madison's framing of the problem that are generalizable. First, Madison's dictum that "no one should be judge of their own cause" highlights the psychological circumstance that people often lack perspective on their own lives, including the claims they make on others, no matter how well motivated. Narcissism—or, less unkindly, partiality—is built into the first-person perspective through which we view ourselves. This existential circumstance becomes a moral failing if not checked with the perspectives of others. Madison's twofold solution positions the perspective gained by separating judge and cause through representation against that gained by multiplying the interests included in a representative body. It is not just that this kind of political design counterbalances interests through competing perspectives—although it does do that. It is also that representative structures induce broader perspectives, as representatives must couch their claims in terms of an inclusive *we*. The effective extent of inclusions—how they are expressed and tested—depends crucially on how incentives for representative claims are built into representative institutions.

We find a similar kind of argument in Kant, who argues that the primary consideration in political institutions is whether judge and cause are unified or separated. Unified structures amount to "despotism," whether the polity is a monarchy, aristocracy, or democracy. Similar to Madison, "republican" governments build in the separation of judge and cause through representation. While Kant's constitutional thinking is not remarkable in itself (Madison's thinking is much more sophisticated), he does combine these recommendations with a philosophy of right (*Recht*) that mirrors the ethics (*Moralität* or *Sittlichkeit*) he develops in the *Critique of Practical Reason*. The general formulation for Kant's ethics is, of course, the categorical imperative: *act in such a way that the maxim of your conduct could become a universal law*. The parallel formulation of right is "the sum total of those conditions within which the will of one can be reconciled with the will of another in accordance with a universal law of reason." The imperative for individuals is to "let your external actions be such that the free application of your will can coexist with the freedom of everyone in accordance with a universal law" (Kant 1991 [*Metaphysics of Morals*]; see also Arendt 1989).

While it has long been fashionable to dismiss Kant's ethics as overly rationalistic, two key features that relate representation to citizen judgment remain important. First, Kant prescribes no particular action but rather a "law of reason" that individuals should apply to their potential actions. That is, Kant's ethics is not prescriptive or paternalistic; it asks for judgment from *each* individual. Second—and this is the important link to theories of political representation—Kant's law of reason asks individuals to consider whether they could live in a world in which other individuals acted in ways they are considering. The categorical imperative asks each individual to imagine the community of people linked through their (potential) actions and their effects. These communities must be *represented* in the imagination for individuals to exercise practical reason. The imagination, in Arendt's (1989) evocative commentary on Kant's political philosophy, must go "travelling." The concept Kant chooses for these purposes, following Rousseau, is "the General Will." The concept is far too abstract in itself. But interpreted as a concrete guideline for judgment it directs individuals to consider potential collective decisions from the standpoint of every other individual. The imperative borne by each individual as a rational being is to represent, if only in the imagination, the community constituted by the effects of proposed laws and legislation. The objects of representation are those linked by *effects*. Indeed, this principle is so central to Kant's thinking that he should be considered an early proponent of the "all-affected interests" principle in contemporary democratic theory (Fung 2013).

Rawls (2001) develops this line of thinking more explicitly. Building his theory of justice within a broadly neo-Kantian framework, he suggests the "original position" as a "device of representation" aimed at restricting reasons for principles of justice to those that apply only to persons as free and equal beings endowed with capacities to self-govern under fair terms of cooperation (17–18). It is somewhat curious that Rawls refers to the original position as a "representative" device, although he uses the term in the old philosophical sense in which concepts were considered to be mental representations. But there is an obvious translation into a *political* concept that does not suffer from abstract universalism. If we consider the original position as a representative claim (specifically, a claimed moral imperative), it amounts to a demand that each individual view the impacts of collective decisions (legislation, policies, etc.) on everyone else, admitting justifications only insofar as they work from the perspective of everyone else. Universalization is embedded in acts of judgment relative to the impacts of collective actions on individuals viewed as beings capable of self-government and embedded in relationships of codependency. Because this is precisely what moral reasoning requires, representative claim-making that assumes the form of the original position is, in effect, a capacity for moral judgment by individuals in their capacity as citizens.

These formulations may seem unduly abstract. There is a point, however: they bring into focus an important relationship between representations of universal perspectives and democracy. Madison and Kant imagined that representatives would look inward, toward the institutions in which they are embedded, while citizens would remain subject to their individual or group desires. But the distancing between judge and cause can occur through public discourse, where that discourse is structured by representative claim-makers, the key conduits of voice within mass democracies. The means through which individuals can develop their moral capacity is by listening and attending to the (represented) perspectives of others—and listening to (understanding, empathizing with) the perspectives of others.

Hannah Arendt has a particularly nice description of the relationship between representation and the capacity for perspective that is at the heart of moral thinking:

> Political thought is representative. I form an opinion by considering a different issue from different viewpoints, by making present to my mind the standpoint of those who are absent; that is, I represent them.... The more people's stand-

points I have present in my mind while I am pondering a given issue, and the better I can imagine how I would feel and think if I were in their place, the stronger will be my capacity for representative thinking.... (It is this capacity for an "enlarged mentality" that enables men to judge; it was discovered by Kant ...). (237)

Following Arendt, the way to avoid abstract universalization is not to give up on generalization but rather to generalize by adding more perspectives, to ask others, to understand their places, problems, and lives up to the point that the chains of affectedness that link the circumstances of one to another are reasonably exhausted. Representation within the context of an open democratic society is what makes this possible: claim-makers propose impacts, which are, in turn, discursive claims that can be accepted, modified, rejected, or simply ignored. Claims of these kinds provide the substantive structure of political deliberation, which in turn should pull individuals out of their existential narcissism, providing them with discursive context that enables ethical judgments—that is (following Kant and Rawls), judgments that consider multiple circumstances and vulnerabilities. The best description of the supporting ethical theory is *discourse ethics*: that is, ethics that produces judgment through the give and take of reasons—often embedded in representations—among those affected or potentially affected by situations, possibilities, fates, and proposals (Habermas 1990, 43–115). Political representation makes it possible for citizens to generalize their judgments though hearing, contesting, debating, and understanding their impacts on others. Representatives can provide the pathways for such voices just to the degree that a political system and society provides protection and standing for representative claims (see also Young 2000, chap. 4; Benhabib 2002, chap. 2). The context that enables representative claim-making to assume these kinds of moral/ethical functions is, of course, exactly that of a deliberative democracy.

## Discursive Accountability

The final citizenship capacity enabled by representation is accountability. There is, of course, the obvious sense in which representative democracy enables accountability by empowering citizens with votes with which they can hold elected officials accountable for their performance in office. As Mansbridge (2003, 2009) has argued, these relationships are more complex than their stylizations in much of the literature on voting and elections.

And, of course, the power of the vote to hold accountable is highly contingent upon constitutional design, electoral system design, and the overlap between issues and residence-based constituencies.

Here, however, I want to return to a somewhat more generic question: What is the relationship between a representative *act*, especially the act of *speaking for*, and citizens' capacity to hold representatives accountable? I want to focus on a relatively simple answer: accountability relationships are intrinsic to speech acts. They must therefore be intrinsic to acts of representative claim-making. This meaning of accountability is both obvious and widely overlooked—probably because within theories of representative democracy the problem of accountability is usually framed as a problem of enforcement or sanction. Voters hold representatives accountable by selecting or deselecting them for office in regular, competitive elections. Constructivists converge on competition among claims as enabling accountability: citizens can hold accountable when they can choose among the claims on offer. These analyses are not wrong. Conceptually speaking, however, they start downstream of accountability relationships that are constituted by speech acts.

This feature of representation is better captured by the idea of *discursive accountability*: to hold to account is always, at least in part, to ask for an account—that is, a justification of an act—here a representative act, such as *speaking for* (Warren 2014). This concept is now widely used, and I simply wish to elaborate its enabling features within the context of representative claim-making.

The most generic problem of accountability in representative relationships is the question of agency: *who* is accountable to whom for what? It is basic to speech acts that they constitute speakers as agents by tying the content of a speech act to a performance. Representative claims that involve *speaking for* have a relatively simple structure that identifies agency through promises and commitments: "If elected, I promise . . ." "As an *x*, I will fight for *y* on your behalf." "As party *x*, we will protect your *y*." And so on. In each case, the promise gives the audience license to view the speaker as an agent responsible for a claim. Speech acts *by their very nature* leave behind what Robert Brandom (2000) calls chains of "deontic scorekeeping." That is, speaking reveals an agent but also commits agents to actions relative to others. Simple commitments among individuals coordinate actions: "I'll meet you at seven"; "I'll get the groceries on the way home." Thus, when I speak or act, I entitle you to expect from me that which is implied by my claim or action. I take on this obligation with respect to you.

You may respond explicitly, or you may simply register the commitment and organize your actions accordingly. Deontic scorekeepers "are licensed to infer our beliefs from our intentional actions (in context of course), as well as from our speech acts" (Brandom 2000, 93; see also Arendt 1958, chap. 24). Speaking involves, in Brandom's terms, a "default entitlement" in which the speaker is assumed to be trustworthy unless and until they prove otherwise. In these ways, then, speech acts *generically* constitute agents and establish responsibilities, for which agents can then be held accountable.

In the simplest cases, the agent is an individual. Representative claim-making usually involves more complex forms, since the claim is often on behalf of a collective agent, such as a party with a platform, a government, an opposition, or an organization with a leadership and mission. In the politically interesting cases, representative claims function to constitute collective agents. Without this agent-constituting moment, there can be no accountability, for citizens have no agents to hold accountable.

Lest this point seem too abstract, note that one of the reasons that people dislike politics (or so they will often say) is that the collective agents implied in claim-making too often disappear. Campaign promises become fuzzy or lost. Interpolated agents never fully materialize. From the perspective of disaffected citizens, speech fails to do what it should: reveal an agent who can become the locus of accountability. It can work the other way around, too: representatives can infer their constituencies (and their positions) from their silence, taking it for nonobjection—and then find that their silence was evidence of disaffection or lack of interest rather than authorization.[1] In contrast, political arrangements that result in collective agents enable citizens to use their votes to extract accountability, to engage in other kinds of political participation that has both locus and focus. When these conditions are in place, citizen participation is enabled because it has an object. But where representative claim-making fails to constitute responsible agents, the reasons for political participation drift away into disaffection.

Constituting collective agents of a kind that can be held accountable by citizens is thus one of the most important functions of representative political institutions. The problem is relatively easy for mission-based organizations, as they can align words and deeds through self-selection. In contrast, inclusive political institutions internalize conflict (that is what they are for), meaning that their agent-constituting functions will often conflict with political brokerage, which is also an essential function of democratic institutions. Westminster systems, for example, excel at constituting collective agents based on strong parties with relatively clear platforms. Elections constitute governments that unify powers so that agency is relatively clear from the campaign through actual governing. But Westminster systems achieve these effects by giving up on political negotiation and deliberation once governments are formed: unified powers enable governments to externalize conflict. In contrast, the US system of separated powers buys political brokerage at the cost of collective agency: often no one appears to be in charge. Individual politicians can make wildly irresponsible claims and promises, knowing they can blame "Washington insiders" or other scapegoats when their promises come to naught. Citizens seldom know whom to hold to account and, so, find it difficult to use their votes and voices well. The northern European unified power parliamentary systems based on proportional representation probably do a better job of splitting the difference between strong collective agency and the necessary political work of deliberation and negotiation. Ideally, representative institutions should close the loop between sanction-based accountability based on elections and discursive accountability based on reason-giving. When they function in this way, they develop citizens' capacities for discursive accountability.

## Conclusion

I have been arguing that representation builds and maintains capacities for democratic citizenship by performing four functions: enabling autonomous judgment; granting individuals roles and capacities as members of collectivities; enabling moral development through perspective-taking; and making discursive accountability possible. While I have been primarily concerned with the question of what representation does—how it works— the argument is also straightforwardly normative. These are functions that representation *should* accomplish insofar as it contributes to democracy generally but more particularly to the capacities that constitute democratic citizenship. In making this argument, my focus has thus been on individuals rather than social structures and institutions, mostly because individuals—as the represented—have often been framed out of consideration as requiring *re*presentation by virtue of their absence. It should also be clear, however, that institutions and their encompassing societies should structure representative relationships in ways that enable and empower democratic citizenship.

## Notes

1. Thank you to Sean Gray for this formulation.

## References

Ankersmit, Frank. 2002. *Political Representation*. Stanford, CA: Stanford University Press.

Arendt, Hannah. 1958. *The Human Condition*. Chicago: University of Chicago Press.

———. 1968. *Between Past and Future*. New York: Penguin.

———. 1989. *Lectures on Kant's Political Philosophy*. Edited with interpretive essay by Ronald Beiner. Chicago: University of Chicago Press.

Benhabib, Seyla. 2002. *The Claims of Culture: Equality and Diversity in the Global Era*. Princeton, NJ: Princeton University Press.

Brandom, Robert B. 2000. *Articulating Reasons: An Introduction to Inferentialism*. Cambridge, MA: Harvard University Press.

Disch, Lisa. 2011. "Toward a Mobilization Conception of Democratic Representation." *American Political Science Review* 105 (1): 100–114.

———. 2015. "The 'Constructivist Turn' in Democratic Representation: A Normative Dead-End?" *Constellations* 22 (4): 487–99.

Dovi, Suzanne. 2007. *The Good Representative*. Oxford: Blackwell.

Fung, Archon. 2013. "The Principle of All-Affected Interests: An Interpretation and Defense." In *Representation: Elections and Beyond*, edited by Jack H. Nagel and Rogers M. Smith, 236–68. University Park: Pennsylvania State University Press.

Garsten, Bryan. 2009. "Representative Government and Popular Sovereignty." In *Political Representation*, edited by Ian Shapiro, Susan C. Stokes, and Elisabeth Jean Wood. New York: Cambridge University Press, 90—110.

Habermas, Jurgen. 1990. *Moral Consciousness and Communicative Action*. Translated by Christian Lenhardt and Sherry Weber Nicholson. Cambridge, MA: MIT Press.

Hamilton, Alexander, James Madison, and John Jay. (1787) 2003. *The Federalist Papers*. New York: Signet Classics.

Kant, Immanuel. 1991. *Political Writings*. Edited by Hans Reiss. Cambridge: Cambridge University Press.

Manin, Bernad. 1997. *The Principles of Representative Government*. Cambridge: Cambridge University. Press

Mansbridge, Jane. 2003. "Rethinking Representation." *American Political Science Review* 97 (4): 515–28.

———. 2009. "A 'Selection Model' of Political Representation." *Journal of Political Philosophy* 17 (4): 369–98.

Montanaro, Laura. 2012. "The Democratic Legitimacy of Self-Appointed Representatives." *Journal of Politics* 74 (4): 1094–107.

Näsström, Sofia. 2011. "Where Is the Representative Turn Going?" *European Journal of Political Theory* 10 (4): 501–10.

Nedelsky, Jennifer. 2011. *Law's Relations: A Relational Theory of Self, Autonomy, and Law*. Oxford: Oxford University Press.

Pitkin, Hanna F. 1967. *The Concept of Representation*. Berkeley: University of California Press.

Rawls, John. 2001. *Justice as Fairness: A Restatement*. 2nd ed. Cambridge, MA: Belknap Press.

Rehfeld, Andrew. 2006. "Toward a General Theory of Political Representation." *Journal of Politics* 68 (1): 1–21.

Runciman, David. 2007. "The Paradox of Political Representation." *Journal of Political Philosophy* 15 (1): 93–114.

Saward, Michael. 2010. *The Representative Claim*. New York: Oxford University Press.

———. 2014. "Shape-Shifting Representation." *American Political Science Review* 108 (4): 723–36.

Urbinati, Nadia. 2000. "Representation as Advocacy: A Study of Democratic Deliberation." *Political Theory* 28 (6): 758–86.

———. 2005. "Continuity and Rupture: The Power of Judgment in Democratic Representation." *Constellations* 12 (2): 194–222.

———. 2006. *Representative Democracy: Principles and Genealogy*. Chicago: University of Chicago Press.

Urbinati, Nadia, and Mark E. Warren. 2008. "The Concept of Representation in Contemporary Democratic Theory." *Annual Review of Political Science* 11: 387–412.

Warren, Mark E. 2014. "Accountability and Democracy." In *Oxford Handbook of Public Accountability*. Edited by Mark Bovens, Robert E. Goodin, and Thomas Schillemans, 39–53. Oxford: Oxford University Press.

Williams, Melissa S. 2003. "Citizenship as Identity, Citizenship as Shared Fate, and the Functions of Multicultural Education." In *Citizenship and Education in Liberal-Democratic Societies: Teaching for Cosmopolitan Values and Collective Identities*, edited by Kevin McDonough and Walter Feinberg. Oxford: Oxford University Press, 208–47.

Young, Iris Marion. 2000. *Inclusion and Democracy*. Oxford: Oxford University Press.

# CHAPTER THREE

# Judgment Alone

## *Cloven Citizenship in the Era of the Internet*

Nadia Urbinati

Political representation is both a practice and an institution.[1] This dual nature is what makes it permanently exposed to criticism and dissatisfaction; it is also the inevitable condition that allows modern democracy to exist and persist through time. Political history shows that representation and democracy emerge and decline together and that citizens' dissatisfaction with how the former works always translates into some kind of distrust of the legitimacy of democratic institutions. The electoral abstention we observe and lament today is not a marginal phenomenon but citizens' silent denunciation of a severing of representation from participation; this disconnect is primed to leave citizens with voice and judgment but no well-distributed power that can condition the elected. In paraphrasing the incipit of Michael Saward's chapter in this book, I argue that in politics representation is *not* simply what representation does. The unsympathetic relation of democratic citizens to representation derives precisely from the fact that no matter how they structure it, representation produces things in their lives and the life of their community because it *is* engrafted in state institutions. The phenomenology of representation as the making of claims that represent what we are and want is thus only one part of the representative game; the other part is the process of decision-making that our vote initiates.

I have elsewhere associated representation with the making of modern democracy, which I define as a diarchy of will (decision) and judgment (Urbinati 2006, 2014). Democracy involves both a public form of citizen presence and a form of government as well; it involves both the formation and manifestation of ideas and opinions and the selection and appointment of those who are *pro tempore* in charge of actualizing them. Representation is the name of a complex participation composed of both direct and indirect action, freedom as the first-person decision and indirect freedom (allowing others to do things while monitoring and judging them), thus freedom as the exercise of influence over others and the system at large (Sen 1983). It is no exaggeration to say that representation activates a rich and multi-faceted participation, which we devalue if we focus only on one half of the diarchy. Taken in its completeness, representation mobilizes citizens well beyond decision (voting in elections, referenda, and plebiscites). It also encompasses the quotidian work of reflection, contestation, and organization, or what I list under the broad and capacious term of *political judgment* as not identical to the will (decision) although capable of inspiring and furthering it. Representation and voting together—that is, claim-making in view of obtaining decisions of some kind—are the pillars of our political identity as citizens and of our constitutional democracy.

"The conceptualization of representative democracy as diarchy makes two claims: that 'will' and 'opinion' are the two powers of the sovereign citizens, and that they are different and should remain distinct, although in need of constant communication" (Urbinati 2014, 2). Clearly diarchy entails tension rather than harmony. The two halves composing it prove that democracy has an endogenous disposition to generate dissent and conflict along partisan lines that voting regulates but is never supposed to resolve (White and Ypi 2016). Before and after an election—in fact, just after the counting of votes—we always witness the growth of criticism and contestation, not only among the losers (in their attempt to assess responsibilities and understand what went wrong) but also among the winners (the elected in particular) who are tempted to deviate from their promises. Said briefly, political representation is the structural domain in which decision and deliberation interact and impact each other: a sophisticated exercise of power that relies on intermediary means, some human and some technical, and that is not a mere act of testimony or claim-making because it is performed in view of obtaining results of some kind, be they linked to judgment or to decision (Brito Vieira and Runciman 2008, 55–62).[2] Hence, contemporary societies are democratic "not simply because they have free elections and the choice of more than one political party, but because they permit effective political competition and debate" (Hirst 1990, 33–34).

Equal political power is critical and fundamental in both accounts. It is true that arithmetical equality (one person/one vote), while empowering

citizens by diffusing power, has serious limits in guaranteeing accountability (Manin 1987; Dunn 1999; Rubinstein 2007; Warren 2014). But the
many analyses of the mechanisms for inducing the elected to respect their
promises to the voters (Manin, Przeworsky, and Stokes 1999; Mansbridge
2014) confirm that in the end, and although very deficient, only the threat
of losing power or of failing to win it appears to be an effective strategy
of representative accountability. The negative power citizens gain through
their judgment and civic presence is essential in making accountability
more than a rhetorical claim. It is thus when we turn to the world of politics
outside its institutions that we sense the effective power of citizenship, the
relationship between enjoying equal rights and performing them. Equal
political liberty and, particularly, civil rights are paramount, as they exalt
representation's discursive and adversarial potential, make it exceed its
institutional form, and allow citizens to connect with and distance themselves from the elected by pressing, checking, and influencing them endlessly. It is because citizens have equal voting power that they develop a
sense of equal dignity with the elected and do not feel subjected when
obeying laws that they did not make and with which they often disagree.
This is the reason why they seek endlessly to promote equality by removing the obstacles (economic and cultural) that jeopardize it. This endless-
ness suggests that we interpret the claiming of equality and equal rights in
democratic constitutions as saying that, although equal as electors, citizens
are not and perhaps will never be equal in their social conditions and the
opportunity to actualize their plans (Przeworski 2007). The engine ("the
spirit" in Montesquieu's sense) of the tension between the two halves of
democratic diarchy is thus equality, the fact that "achieving membership
within a political community is not necessarily the same thing as achieving
*equal* membership" (Bybee 1998, 12; Näsström 2015).

Equality is thus the principle identifying representative democracy,
both in the domain of institutions and in that of political action outside
them; this makes for the diarchic structure of democracy as the normative frame within which representation must be understood and judged.
Equality will be my guide both in the analysis of current interpretations of
political representation and in the evaluation of the transformations that
the use of the internet may have on the diarchic structure of democratic
representation by exacerbating the divorce of judgment from the will.

The chapter proceeds as follows: I show how representation displays
different conceptions of democracy, which I group into two broad fami-
lies, both procedural, one in a traditional (minimalist) sense and one in a

deliberative sense. This parallel analysis brings me to argue that the idea of representation as a practice of informal participation (claim-making in all its complexity) and as a process that partakes in lawmaking (electorally based) leads us to disengage democracy from that dualism and adopt a diarchic conception instead, in which the domain of procedures and institutions and the domain of opinion and partisan participation are thought jointly and unavoidably interconnected. The goal of this parallel analysis is to prove that representation is neither a mere practical solution to a problem of functionality in large states nor an astute strategy for expelling people from power. Whatever the intention of the political leaders who have constructed and interpreted it, political representation is essential to democracy precisely because of the complex forms of participation it engenders. Starting from this premise, in the final part of the chapter I advance a critical assessment of the implications for democratic citizenship of a view and a practice of representation (facilitated by the internet) that breaks down the diarchy of claim-making and decision-making, perhaps on the assumption that the former enriches democratic citizenship action while the latter constrains it. This results in a cloven form of democratic citizenship, privileging the articulation of claims over the power of decision-making. Yet judgment alone is not enough for democratic representation.

## Representation in Democratic Theory

Scholars of representation divide along the line of democratic theory's broad bifurcation between a minimalist interpretation of the democratic process and a deliberative one, a distinction that some authors have rendered as between a realistic as formalistic view and a normative as perfectionist view (Kelsen [1929] 2013; Sartori 1987; Manin 1997; Habermas 1996, chap. 7). I am aware that conceptual distinctions may risk abstraction and ontologization. Yet a distinction within the broad horizon of contemporary democratic theory is needed to map the field and orient our understanding of actual political processes. Although contemporary theories acknowledge electoral representation as constitutive of the government of the moderns, none posits that representation makes democratic participation richer and more valuable.

## Election Makes Democracy

A traditional procedural interpretation of democracy (which started its journey along with both democratization and its critics) (Maine 1909) views the voting act as that which legitimates legislative power and makes obedience to laws authored by others more bearable. Proceduralism is of course not monolithic, as procedural visions can span from formalistic (Kelsen [1929] 2013) and minimal (Schumpeter 1942) renderings to more condition-based versions that demand the rules be connected with the social and economic circumstances and the resources of participation (Dahl 1973; Bobbio 1987). Yet, as Adam Przeworski (1999) writes, although attractive, these goals and desiderata do not give us any workable definition of democracy, because the assumption that the latter is capable of delivering its promises (political equality, representativeness, and social justice) is the product of a perfectionistic vision of democracy whose actualization is always deficient. Democracy makes only one realistic and reckonable promise: to solve political conflicts over seeking, holding, and transferring power in a nonviolent way—that is, casting "paper stones" rather than real stones, counting votes rather than breaking heads.

The democratic rules of the game deliver what they promise because they consider democracy essentially and only a set of procedures and institutions and dismiss all content-based desiderata. As a matter of fact, extant democracies show that this form of government is hardly capable of delivering what its principles declare. Thus, to make democracy safe, we should deflate its idealism and remain content with a realistic rendering of it, according to the guidelines offered by Joseph A. Schumpeter, who wrote in a time of despotic mass regimes backed by substantive ideologies. In sum, as traditional proceduralists claim, the argument is not that democracy is good because it can be improved (i.e., that it fulfills some of its promise) but that it is worth defending even if it cannot be improved. Its value resides in allowing us to peacefully solve our disagreements and be governed by periodically changed and elected majorities, which means that liberty and the equal chance to be the majority are recognized *ex ante* as conditions for civil peace.

Within this approach, the issue of representative politics and even the discussion of the nature of representative democracy make little or no sense at all. "Our institutions are representative. Citizens do not govern" (Przeworski 2010, 15). Representation is a condition that relies upon the fact that we have civil rights (to freely speak in public and organize

ourselves for electoral competition) and that the government is institutionally divided. Technically speaking, representation is an institution that the
adoption of universal suffrage has neither changed nor altered: the government it makes possible is a mixed one, in which the democratic element
consists essentially in renouncing direct self-rule by electing lawmakers
(Manin 1997, chap. 4).[3]

On this reading, democracy can be implemented only in a direct way.
This means that elections are what make a representative democracy an
oxymoron since they expel the citizens from the assembly that decides on
laws. Elections make the citizens voluntarily release their power to rule.
Then, of course, we may have a society made of vibrant movements or in
which parties are deliberative and inclusive rather than narrow clubs of no-
tables; yet all these factors, important as they are, do not change the basic
characteristic of representative government as one in which an elected
few rule with the consent of the many. At the most, they are phenomena
that confirm the contextual differences between democratic societies—
differences in political ideology, cultural and social relations, electoral systems, and institutional arrangements, differences that pertain to the historical context not to the basic workings of democracy. According to this
view of government, voting is what counts and is the site of power, and this
is identical everywhere democracy is in place.

A government is not more democratic because citizens have the perception that they are well represented—a vague and fluctuating perception
that may depend on the rhetorical ability of the politicians to make people
feel that their views or interests are represented. Thus, the question of representation concerns the domain of ideology and the kind of persuasive (to
use Jane Mansbridge's word, "gyroscopic") narrative a party uses to make
its identity strong—in relation to its members and sympathizers and to
others—and finally to achieve a majority and govern (Mansbridge 2003).
Representation is the ideological game that actualizes the game rules and
makes them acceptable.

Clearly, if its domain is ideology or claim-making, and if it inhabits the
sphere of opinion, then what we call democratic representation cannot be
translated into norms and procedures. When not simply the description of
an elected lawmaker's function, representation expresses the free activity
of the citizens; it is a phenomenon that accompanies discussion within a
democratic society, and while it can be the object of political history it provides no solid ground for theorizing the norms of democracy. One reason
for this is that representation can expose states' institutions to partisan

manipulation or subject them to what Jeremy Bentham called "sinister" or organized factional interests. In addition, when mass parties enter the domain of democratic theory, democracy risks becoming a means for actualizing specific projects or models of society—that is, a means for the actualization of some supposed good. Thus, to be respectful of the competition between visions or ideologies—that is, to be pluralistic—procedural democracy ought not be enriched with the inclusion of representative promises and practices. Minimalist rules allow for the richness of the game the actors play. This has been the argument developed by formalist proceduralists against substantive theories of democracy (Bobbio 1987).

To return to square one, elections alone make a representative, not the substance of the ideas she stands for; and legal and constitutional order alone defines her identity and role, not her relation to her constituency. *Representation* is a confusing term if rendered as more than an institution—if its identity is expanded beyond its juridical status, beyond what Hanna Pitkin classified as "standing for" (Pitkin 1967, chap. 4). When we want to give representation some content and analyze it from the perspective of its "acting for" dimension, we exit this rules-based domain and enter the messy world of practical politics, which is an object of interpretation, of social- and political-scientific analysis.

The minimalist approach has some interesting implications, as it does not prevent us from *seeing* "representation as a dynamic process of claim-making" instead of "a static fact of electoral practices" (Saward 2010, 3). It simply makes us aware that this dynamic process belongs in the informal world of opinions and political judgment; representation is a political construction that is freely developed by citizens through their associations and political movements. We may say that representation is claim-making, a mobilization from below, or an ideological construction unifying different citizens under a narrative; whatever we think and say, however, has no effect on the rules in which the democratic game consists. The minimalist theory thus stresses one pole of democracy's diarchy, the one comprising decision-making processes and state institutions. Although it acknowledges the existence of the other pole (the rich panoply of participation that makes for the sphere of opinion and political judgment), minimalism does not make it internal to the conception of representative democracy. It makes it instead an expression of civil rights, consistent with the liberal aspect of constitutional democracy. As we shall see, this liberal reading is key to making sense of the role and the place of representation as claim-making.

## Deliberative Practices Make Democracy

Deliberative theory is the other interpretation of democracy that inspires and shapes today's conception of political representation. Its rendering of the democratic process is no less attentive to procedures than the minimalist approach, and it promises to be strictly procedural, not substantive or ideological. Yet procedures are conceived in this case as norms intended to shape citizens' participation in ways consistent with democracy's moral norms: equal consideration; reciprocity; respect for autonomy and transparency; and the sincere, open exchange of reasons, not rhetoric and ideological partisan views (Cohen 1997; 2010, 260–315; Christiano 2008). Without these moral and legal premises shaping mental and political behavior, there cannot be deliberative democracy to begin with, only the most instrumental bargaining and bloc voting. Moreover, since this form of government requires and rests on people's consent, the way consent is formed, articulated, and expressed is part of the process and its norms, not an external or variable factor. Free speech and freedom of association, religious tolerance and ideological pluralism are not empirical facts that may or may not be in place but norms that need to be reinforced through political behavior. Schumpeter and the minimalists who follow him would agree of course with these liberal conditions of democracy. But only the deliberativists make the claim that these conditions are not simply individualistic rights external to the democratic process that allow citizens to express their preferences; they are instead conditions of political participation that govern the public relations among citizens and between them and the institutions in a way that citizens choose and express not only freely but in manners consistent with those principles (Mackie 2011). Democracy is the name of a self-encompassing world in which practices and norms are intertwined in citizens' ordinary public behaviors and institutions.

Rights and the social conditions of equal participation sustain citizens in their deliberative process, which orients them toward not only forming their opinions but also changing them to make them cohere more consistently with democratic principles or norms. Procedures and institutions predispose politics to actualize this desideratum, as they make it a criterion of judgment that citizens and their representatives can use to challenge the *status quo* and make a democratic society permanently open to self-revision or further democratization. Looking at the constitution and the formal rules of the game is highly insufficient (as we know, the 1936 constitution of the Soviet Union was the most advanced constitution on paper). The formality of procedures is not supposed to blind us to the practices those procedures inspire and shape, and in this sense the dualism between ideal and real is hardly tenable; and an ideological definition of democracy is equally untenable, as we see in Habermas's (1996, chap. 7) critique of Robert Dahl.

To deliberativists, in sum, democratic norms are within the practice of politics as its shaping structures. They are not a superimposed order that gives "form" to a brute political "matter." Deliberativists in the tradition of Habermas are close to pragmatism as they resist the dualism between ideal and real as much as that between form and matter, norm and content. Their democratic politics is a *public practice* that guides the citizen's mind toward making reflective judgments and taking action and that transforms reality and mentality (Dryzek 1990). Thus, deliberative democracy also consists in permanent self-monitoring. The citizens, through their free and audible presence in the public sphere, perform this monitoring along with the institutional and legal order. Indeed, institutional control and the formal enjoyment of the suffrage right are only one part of the game as, clearly, the personnel serving in the institutions can be smartly chosen by insiders (parties and lobbies), and, although they act according to the rules and with electoral consent, their power is never sufficiently safe for a democracy. This means that the presence of the citizens is not optional, and not a fact external to the procedures either, but central to their very survival.

Of course, the deliberativist camp is no less complex and pluralistic than the minimalist one and is hardly identifiable with one stream of interpretation (Dryzek 2000). Some deliberative theorists are more attentive to elections, while others are more concerned with the epistemic rendering of democratic procedures; yet all of them show a common dissatisfaction with electoral democracy, for it puts an end to the deliberative trial with majority counting (Bohman 2000). After all, their stress on deliberation derives from the assumption that merging toward a shared perspective on some issues is not only possible but necessary, insofar as the principles orienting citizens' judgment are the working rules of the procedures. Somehow, when a process of deliberation ends with voting and counting this looks to deliberativists like a confession of citizens' impotence to achieve a result that is more in conformity with democratic principles and thus more comprehensive than a simple majority. It shows that modern society is inhabited by loci of powers, economic and social, that contain rather than facilitate democratic citizenship, because they subject public behavior to interests that are stubborn and deaf to impartial reasoning.

While minimalists focus essentially on voting (the "paper stone" that has the power to make decisions that condition other decisions), deliberativists (although not all of them in the same way) focus on the conditions for deciding well and achieving good deliberative results and less on voting, counting, and the electoral cycle. Quantity and quality are somehow disjoined here. Again, not all deliberativists are equally refractory toward voting, and not all are equally indifferent to or suspicious of the party politics that elections (voting and counting) produce (see respectively Dryzek 2000; Dryzek and Niemeyer 2008; Goodin 2003). Yet, in point of principle, they want to distance deliberation from "aggregation" of votes and ask something more of democracy than the formal conditions of regular elections or peaceful conflict management. Attention to good deliberation induces them to turn their interest to localized participatory events like citizens' assemblies and away from national institutions like parliaments, which they seem to devalue, although acknowledging their democratic function (Fung and Wright 2003).

Deliberativists are also dissatisfied with participationists; deliberativists' goal is to have people participate not directly but indirectly and well: reflecting upon their preferences, exchanging their opinions, and being ready to change their minds to be more in agreement with the deliberative process (Goodin 2003). Deliberative democracy is a celebration of indirectness and reflexivity, of judgment and self-questioning in the way that citizens should reason as democrats. For deliberative democrats, the quality of participation is what counts, not participation per se.

## The Place of Representation

Both minimalism and deliberativism confirm the ambiguity of representation in relation to democracy and more generally of indirectness in politics. They seem also to confirm by default that the pivotal value of directness resides primarily in its removing that ambiguity, either by permitting an unmediated translation of people's will into decisions (voting) or by refining people's will until it becomes an uncontested expression of the general interest. Although for quite different purposes, Rousseau's paradigm—a directly sovereign and uncontested general will—lies at the horizon of both conceptions of representative government. This explains *a contrario* the nature of representative democracy—a regime of indirect practices and translators that gives birth to a complex domain of political activity

filled with a variety of intermediary bodies and discourses, in which decision seldom stops. Representation lives on rhetoric, as it were, because
it must construct the interpretation that makes the constituency, and it
preserves and expands consent by attracting new people and developing
new claims.

Wishing to recover representation's reputation, scholars have had to
amend its exclusively institutional conception and acknowledge representation's complexity. This was one of the most seminal contributions of
Hanna Pitkin's *The Concept of Representation* (1967), in which representation was conceptualized for the first time as not only electoral appointment ("standing for") but also discursive advocacy ("acting" or "speaking
for"). Pitkin reinstated representation in political theory by interpreting it
as political creation, not only against those who deemed it "by definition"
"anything done after the right kind of authorization" but also against those
who regarded representation as alienation of the political will to the few
(39). The most recent achievement, which develops from a critical revision of both Pitkin's "speaking for" approach and the now preponderant
deliberative approach, holds representation to be a process of collective
subject construction through the making of claims (Saward 2006, 2010).
This approach has the ambition of overcoming all residue of prepolitical
ontology and of questioning the adoption of criteria of validation that are
external to political activity itself—thus both the "speaking for" approach
(as if political subjects existed prior to their representative's appearance)
and the normative attitude of deliberative democracy (its taming of claims
in the attempt to adapt them to reflexivity and a principled rationality).[4]

Representation acquires a new capacity—that of making possible the
full-fledged political appearance of claimants in the forum. Adapting and
democratizing Thomas Hobbes's famous argument for the construction of
the sovereign, contemporary constructivists argue that prior to the articulation of claims there are no political actors and no "people" to begin with
(Ochoa 2011). Iris Marion Young (1997, 2000) and Ernesto Laclau and
Chantal Mouffe (1985) contributed importantly to this movement, which
now finds its most complete theoretical rendering in Michael Saward's idea
of representation as claim-making: it is only through "a multisided process
of claim-making and the reception and judgment of claims" that citizens
and persons become political actors (Saward 2010, 42). Although it can
have an institutional frame and still derives its formal democratic legitimacy from universal suffrage, representation here is a form of political
creativity autonomous from voting and the representative lawmaking

function. It is synonymous with politics itself as the varied activities that people stage in the public sphere when they stand against or for something and, in so doing, express themselves as political actors to modify or affect the political discourse of their society.

Representation as claim-making is the most mature fruit of the "representative turn" in political theory and particularly in democratic theory, which has coincided with the acknowledgment of this complexity and of the central role played by opinion and ideological construction in the making of representative claims (Disch 2015, 2–3). This turn has signaled a break with the prioritization of direct forms of participation (thus also authorization via voting) and considers representation "an intrinsic part of what makes democracy possible" (Urbinati and Warren 2008, 395). The electoral appointment per se is not the object of interest (although electoral techniques are not irrelevant in determining the degree of responsiveness of the representatives to the electors) but rather representation as a political practice. Begun by elections, representation opens a spectrum of activities that exceed the (nevertheless) crucial moment of voting. Representation stimulates citizens' participation by other means. This is the terrain upon which the democratic tenor of representation takes shape. Scholars have thus searched in the phenomenology of representation for the sources of the spontaneous movement of claim-making and the construction of collective subjects that occurs within and enriches the public arena without being subordinated to either the terminal moment of voting or to the quality of deliberation.

As Saward explains in *The Representative Claim*, the democratic character of participation resides in its being a form of claim-making not in generating elected representatives and not even in polishing claims of their partial interests or idiosyncratic visions. This approach, of course, has an impact on the way the sovereign demos is conceived. Assuming representation has essentially only an institutional identity, as both of the abovementioned conceptions of democracy suggest, it entails holding a juristic conception of sovereignty that connects the legitimacy of constituted politics to a formal act of designation regulated through a legal norm like voting. Representation as claim-making does away with the primacy of sovereignty and can be considered as the most radical expression of a postjuristic conception of sovereignty, an avenue that the deliberative theory has opened without consistently pursuing. This line of thought can be considered the most radical legacy of Claude Lefort, whose work contains the clearest attempt to include representation in democratic theory.

Lefort argued years ago that the lack of a clear definition of the people (the impossibility of giving it substance, as with a body) marks the value and worth of representative democracy; dispersion of power and the openness of all decisions to change qualify this form of government as a perpetual redescription of social relations, which no institution or person or decision can ever claim to embody or even represent. Not even suffrage and the institutions that spring from it, like the Parliament, are legitimated in claiming to embody democratic sovereignty. Thus, in representative government, the locus of democracy exceeds the right to vote and the institutional organization of decision-making to include advocacy groups and forms of participation in the public arena, from parties and movements to petitioning and media (Lefort 1986; Disch 2011). Representation as claim-making is a radical development of postjuristic sovereignty and brings representation fully into the democratic practice, but at the cost of keeping it disconnected from the status of citizenship, which has the right to suffrage or political equality at its core.

## Consent and Audience-philia

The argument around which representation as claim-making pivots obtains full expression only in democracy, not because decisions acquire validity by suffrage or by a broad process of discursive deliberation but because representation occurs wherever persons intervene in the public sphere and in whatever moment they decide to have a voice, merge their claims, and recognize a popular figure who speaks for them and makes their claim visible to an audience, which is not circumscribed by a nation or a juridical system of ruling power. The event of representation happens outside both the minimalist and the deliberative conception of democratic legitimacy and is disentangled both from formal legitimacy and from any normative approach that prioritizes some would-be criteria of judgment. Unlike both minimalism and deliberativism, Saward (2010) argues, "it is the judgments of appropriate constituencies, not independent theoretical judgment, that matter to democrats" (159). The basis for legitimacy (and democracy) is mainly consent in the public sphere of opinion: "in principle the representative claim is neither good nor bad. Representative claims can activate and empower recipients or observers, even if that is not the intention of the makers" (55). Consent and the direct expression of support by the people (those who identify with claims and those who express judgment on them) are prerequisites for representation as empowerment insofar as they make claims public; they make people feel that their claims went public and attracted a large audience, even though their claims would perhaps never be formally recognized within a legal system. It is the act of alerting the public and receiving attention from an audience that gives claim-makers a sense of acting legitimately. The problems generated by the centrality of consent and the audience are several and require some inspection.

First, consent alone may not comply with democracy if the claim-makers are not equal players, if they are excluded from the demos and depend on the included for attention and consideration, or if they do not choose those who speak for them. This set of problems internal to the theory of representation as claim-making deserves a more careful analysis than this short section allows. Briefly, the theory argues that political representation is a discursive dynamic by which means persons (not necessarily or not only citizens) converge in various ways thanks to the advocacy of a speaker (the maker of the representative claim). The speaker speaks for the represented by portraying claims (the subject of representation) validated by the judgment of both the represented (the constituency) and the public at large (the audience). The maker, the claim, the constituency, and the audience are the four components of the event of representation, regardless of whether voting occurs. What makes it political is the free work of rhetorical construction by a speaker and the group of persons represented by making claims. The representative construction is a purely ideological creation and, in this sense, an expression of freedom first and foremost.

Representative claim-making certainly complies with a constitutional state based on civil rights and individual liberty, but it has a less certain linkage with equal political liberty (and the right to vote), although the latter is an essential condition for the actualization of claims. Representation is the name of opinion-making movements, which bring claims to the public forum that may or may not result in democratic achievements. Outside state institutions and disconnected from suffrage, representative claim-making is an expression of freedom of association and the formation and open discussion of ideas; it is not necessarily or directly an expression of democratic empowerment, which may or may not occur. Based on this, I surmise that its democratic legitimacy is evaluated essentially in relation to the free expression of the speakers (the actor, the represented, and the audience) and their freedom of association, rather than the self-governing process of the citizens (lawmaking decisions) or the equal share in power between speakers and represented (intra-claim-making democracy).

Representation so conceived is a form of voluntary public presence in the social through voice, yet not necessarily a political process that partakes in government or makes claims that aim at some political resolution. In relation to voting and governing institutions and to power relations among political actors that constitute the representative event (i.e., in relation to the two domains in which questions of democratic legitimacy are pivotal) representation as claim-making is silent. Claim-making surely is or can be an expression of contestation against conditions of exclusion, injustice, and discrimination—in this sense we can consider it a chapter in the negative power of contestation and surveillance that democracy embodies (Rosanvallon 2008). But its discursive and judging nature does not require that representation as claim-making enter the electoral competition and translate claims into new laws. Hence, the only sources of authority or legitimacy that claim-making presumes and demands are either informal consent or the expression of political judgment by the people who identify with the claims through the speaker and by the audience that approves or disapproves them. Power in government and equal political power are peripheral, while power of opinion and power as symbolic presence are central.

Connected to this is the issue of the role of the audience. The audience is part of representation as much as are the work of persuasion performed by the speaker and the claims that realize the otherwise hypothetical status of the represented. "Credibility" and "acceptability" are key words here as synonyms of a kind of legitimacy that depends on "the perception of legitimacy," a created "event" that may arouse sympathetic adhesion to or emotional identification with the claimants and the performance of the speaker (Saward 2010, 145). The role of the audience becomes paramount, and, as we know, the "job of an audience is to watch and listen, not to contribute or take part" (55). Without the attention or the positive judgment of an audience, the entire process of representative claim-making risks becoming useless, since it is only an empowering process in the perception of the claimants and in the echo it may have on the stage of opinion.

Furthermore, once we disjoin the dynamic of representation from voting and institutions, the issue of the political success of a claim is essentially audience dependent, and this fact highlights a contradiction with democracy. Indeed, while representation gives public visibility to claims and their recipients, it also exalts the role of the speaker, whose ability to win consent confirms the traditional tension of representation with equality (Green 2010). Ronald Dworkin raised this problem years ago when he argued that ascriptive representation makes no sense at all, because if the speaker is to make claims in favor of some people she will be chosen on the grounds not that she resembles the people she represents but that she performs effectively for them. Thus, the very moment we render representation as claim-making we advance two assumptions at once: that all people are morally equal (as persons claiming visibility and as members of the audience) and that they are unequal in how they perform politically and in public; in sum, some have more ability or more passion than others and thus more of a chance to achieve consent and attract an audience (Dworkin 1987).

One might say that making representation democratic on the sole claim-making performance deepens the democratic deficit, as it narrows the egalitarian ambition of democracy, exalts the role of the representative leader upon whose skill the efficacy of representation depends, and finally induces the claimants to think that being heard and openly expressing their judgment is what makes them democratic actors (Severs 2012). This is not the appropriate place to analyze the meaning of democratic legitimacy and the constraining power (aside from the classical threat of voting withdrawal) that the represented are able to exercise on the speakers. Yet it is worth mentioning that the role of the audience comprises one of the two halves of the democratic diarchy, pertaining to the informal or indirect power of opinion in proving a leader's success or failure and his reputation. The power of the audience is highly dependent on the persona (her symbolic identity or her rhetorical skill or reputational performance) who is truly the leading protagonist of the representative process. Sofia Näsström (2015) has observed that talking in the name of the people or being a good advocate of some people's claims does not itself "qualify as a democratic form of representation"; it is not, after all, the represented who start the game or decide on the claim in that they do not exist before and apart from the making of the claims that qualify them (2). We thus return to the basic observation: disjoining representation from institutions and electoral accountability entails making it de facto a liberal expression of freedom of speech more than an expression of democratic empowerment. Indeed, a democratic form of representation claims that people not only have voice but that they have voice on equal terms and that their voice produces effects on the terrain of political decisions. Expressing one's claim and being heard is one half of the democratic diarchy.

## Constant's Prophecy in the Age of the Internet

The conception of representation as claim-making promises to be a fertile guideline to understand (and critically assess) the impact that the internet has on political participation, as it projects the latter less toward elections and institutions and more toward developing judgments and conquering audiences. Some scholars have recently stressed the positive role new media can play in democracy as "the rigid division between producers and audience evaporates, [and] opportunities for self-presentation become more realistic. Citizens are no longer content with the role of just being passive spectators" (Coleman 2005, 210). New media, according to this reading, help democratize representative claim-making as they deflate the role of the speaker and horizontalize voice and thus allow citizens to overcome all intermediation between them, their claims, and those who propose themselves to represent them.

In *Siamo in guerra* (*We Are at War*), Roberto Casaleggio and Beppe Grillo (2011), the founders of the Five Star Movement (M5S) claim a war exists between the "old world" and the "new world." The old world stands for party democracy and political representation, while the new stands for free citizens connected horizontally through the internet, without intermediary organizations or divisions between "inside" and "outside." "The Net does not want middlemen," and political parties and traditional media are doomed to disappear. Established parties and accredited media are depicted as obstructions to democracy that citizens can get rid of thanks to the internet. What makes M5S's claim so radical is not so much the reasonable desire of making the internet a means for deepening participation but the argument against the establishment and the quest to eliminate partisan competition and political deliberation among parties. This is the argument that makes the M5S a "non-party party" (as its charter claims) in agreement with populism's dualism between "folk democracy" and "established democracy"; M5S aims to reunite the "inside" and the "outside" of the state on the new ground that the internet allows, against political parties and traditional media.

I have elsewhere discussed this form of horizontal "directness" that internet technology seems to inject into politics when it demystifies the power of the two intermediary bodies that have historically made representative government possible—the political party and professional journalism (Urbinati 2015). I have characterized this internet claim-making

process as a form of *direct self-representation*; it can be an advanced fron-
tier of representation that blurs representative politics' indirectness. Some
authors stress the balkanizing effects of internet practice and highlight the
paradox of a horizontal means of communication that creates niches of
identity visions that cultivate sameness rather than expanding and opening
the conversation among different visions and claimants (Ess and Sudweeks
2001; Sunstein 2006). It is still hard to say that this will entail an increase of
citizens' power (Morozov 2011). Here I would simply like to call attention
more specifically to the *audience-philia* that new media favors and how
this radical claim-making changes representative politics and deepens its
dissociation from voting.

The impact of self-representation through the internet on democratic
politics can be elucidated by the paradoxical move that Peter Mair (2013)
has highlighted: on the one hand, the decline of electoral participation
(citizenship as autonomy in the classical sense) and, on the other, the increase of participation through voice along with an exponential growth of
the power of judgment (2–16). These two diverging phenomena—decrease
of the will and increase of judgment—seem to be a confirmation not of
more democracy but of more liberalism, a validation of the argument according to which citizens in representative government do not need to
practice political autonomy to enjoy their liberty. What citizens need to
have, as Benjamin Constant argued in 1819, are rich and varied loci in
which they can publicly interact, exchange, form, and express their opinions on the many issues that affect them, while also using the free press and
freedom of association to monitor the work of the politicians (Constant
1988). The rights of association and free speech are the pillars of this new
form of participation based on the role of judgment; this was for the liberal
Constant the paradigm of the political liberty of the moderns versus that
of the ancients.

Today, the profusion of blogs, social networks, and sites of discussion
and representation of issues and claims seem to confirm Constant's intuition, as they make citizens active, if they so choose, although their voluntary engagement in public issues is somehow distant from the agents of
state politics, such as organized parties and their elected representatives,
and not necessarily capable of impacting the lawmaking process. E-citizens
are hyperactive in commenting, questioning, and judging; do not feel compelled to act in the domain of decision-making; and moreover are not
certain that their voice has the power to orient the behavior of the politicians, as in electoral democracy. On the other hand, however, since their

claim-making reaches the audience, e-citizens may feel empowered and truly protagonists, regardless of whether they directly participate in representing their claims or are more distant than ever from the institutions of their government.[5]

This seems to suggest that claim-making is a form of political practice that denotes a change in the relation to both the sphere of political autonomy and the sphere of informal participation. Again, this seems a further fulfillment of Constant's prophecy about the political liberty of the moderns, which unlike that of the ancients does not have lawmaking (or the will) at its core but instead judgment and opinion making—that is, not voting but claim-making. As a matter of fact, as Constant wrote in his lecture, modern citizenship consists more in a rich activity of talking and commenting on the questions pertaining to citizens' life and the affairs that government discharges than in participating for sake of decision. As confirmation of this change, in today's democracies, although the many only judge and comment on what the few do, this does not translate into less individual liberty. People exercise their right to vote less and tend to concentrate their participation in the manifestation of their views online. One may even argue that electoral democracy is futile and anachronistic, a phenomenon historically specific but with no normative value of its own and, finally, with no efficacy. The massive indifference to conventional politics by ordinary citizens, Mair has observed, pairs with a new scholarly interest in noninstitutional and nonelectoral forms of participation.

The new energy that the internet gives political discourse seems to support this trend if we consider that this pervasive technology of communication is marked by a natural overproduction of claims, judgments, and opinions on all possible issues. The effects of this hyperproductivity of judgments on the practice and conception of democracy seem to be twofold: first of all, as mentioned, has been the delegitimization and overcoming of the two pivotal intermediary bodies—the political party and journalism—that made possible the functioning and consolidation of representative democracy in an age in which voting was central; second has been the decline of the importance of suffrage along with the incremental expansion of the activity of judgment as a surrogate for political autonomy. I would like to conclude this chapter by calling attention to the following scenario: citizens who desert voting booths (as well as political associations that are functional to conquering seats in parliaments) and abandon traditional media (in favor of self-made information and opinion making) seem to do so not to achieve more power in decision-making but to reclaim a controlling judgment over those who exercise power. They do not contest the political division of labor and do not claim direct involvement in decision-making—in this sense, they do not make a claim for direct democracy over electoral democracy. They reclaim instead the role of guardianship or surveillance, the negative power of denunciation more than the positive power of actualization; they show that they regard electoral power as an "empirical convention" not constitutive of democracy (Rosanvallon 2011, 220–21). Independent of this hyperproduction of judgment is the question of whether their claims are heard by those who exercise power. The problem is that this question looks peripheral if we assume expressive participation to be disconnected from voting and if we deem nonelective representation to be the mark of a less compulsory politics because it is deinstitutionalized and more open to creativity.

## Conclusion

The idea that representation achieves a democratic character by being an exercise of claim-making has its basis in a diarchic view of democracy; this means to be a critique of both the minimalist and the deliberative theory and a reminder that democracy is both a decision-making order and an articulation of public judgment. By voting and monitoring and evaluating, free citizens interpret and question their power relations in society. Yet representation as claim-making utilizes the diarchic perspective to make a case for an autonomous role of judgment in representation as the making of a constellation of views, opinions, and interests that unify a certain number of persons in a recognizable group; this role is itself a form of democratic participation. This rich symbolic form of public action may or may not translate into the "the will" (namely, voting as authoritative decision), which thus falls outside the definition of political representation. This approach advances two arguments that disentangle representation from normative issues: first, that the norm of suffrage is external to representation; second, that any normative theory of democracy risks displacing the actual claims people make by prioritizing some would-be criteria of judgment, while "it is the judgments of appropriate constituencies, not independent theoretical judgment, that matter to democrats" (Saward 2010, 159). The movement that representation as claim-making puts into action is an exquisite example of informal consent formation, vindication, and mobilization. Consent does not, at this stage, need to pass through voting and can very much remain what it is: a free process of "invocation" (4) of issues before the public that judges them. The validation or refutation of a claim, the acceptance or rejection of its maker—both by the persons who recognize themselves in the maker's claim and by the audience at large (local, national, and global)—these actions confirm that claim-making aims at a strong manifestation of consent and belongs in the domain of opinion movements. It expands outside institutions and enjoys the civil rights of free speech and freedom of association.

Although endowed with no authoritative power, consent carries clout, and the maker who seeks and embodies it may have a strong impact on people's imaginary, state institutions, and finally voters and decision makers. A claim-making movement may have more impact on opinion at large than a political party; it may induce decisions by electors or institutions without intentionally partaking in the decision-making process. It is thus precisely its informality that challenges us to interrogate consent from the point of view of democratic legitimacy, because we assume not only that voting procedures are a form of power but that the extrainstitutional world of opinion and claim-making is as well. In conclusion, the phenomenology of representation is certainly a creative manifestation of free action. However, since it rests greatly on leaders, and since claim-making conditions lawmaking, political representation cannot be solely a form of free and voluntary association that seeks audience and visibility. Thus, further inquiry must be made into the role that citizens and democratic procedures play in claim-making and how they can determine the power of their claims. This step consists in the acknowledgment that political representation is the site of two interrelated authorities, the will and opinion; this is needed because effective claimants and a judging audience occur within a horizon in which decisions and institutions are implicated. Political representation seeks not to be solely a testimony of claims made by actors before an audience on behalf of a group of recipients with no political authority. "For without recourse to election as a source of legitimacy, how do we know that such representation is democratic?" (Näsström 2015, 1).

## Notes

1. I would like to express my debt of gratitude to Dario Castiglione, whose comments have been essential to the completion of this chapter.

2. Sintomer (2013) provides an overview of the several conceptions of representation.

3. The view of representative government as *"un régime aristocratique"* which *"a donc pour but une sélection"* was eloquently conceptualized by Carré de Malberg (1922, 2:208).

4. As Bernard Manin (1987) pointed out, in Jürgen Habermas's theory of democracy inclusion in the deliberative process is intended to develop "rationally motivated" forms of participation (367).

5. The European case of weak citizenship status with strong representative expressiveness (proved by the existence of a large number of lobbies) is an example of citizenship as expressivity or as "acts of citizenship: claims to multiple legal and political forms of access to rights, or recognition, made by a myriad of actors, be they formal EU citizens or not" (Isin and Saward 2013, 2).

# References

Bobbio, Norberto. 1987. *The Future of Democracy: A Defence of the Rules of the Game.* Translated by R. Griffin. Edited by Richard Bellamy. Minneapolis: University of Minnesota Press.

Bohman, James. 2000. *Public Deliberation: Pluralism, Complexity, and Democracy.* Cambridge, MA: MIT Press.

Brito Vieira, Mónica, and David Runciman. 2008. *Representation.* London: Polity Press.

Bybee, Keith J. 1998. *Mistaken Identity: The Supreme Court and the Politics of Minority Representation.* Princeton, NJ: Princeton University Press.

Carré de Malberg, Raymond. 1922. *Contribution à la Théorie générale de l'État.* 2 vols. Paris: Librairie Recueil Sirey.

Casaleggio, Gianroberto, and Beppe Grillo. 2011. *Siamo in guerra: Per una nuova politica.* Milan: Chiarelettere.

Christiano, Thomas. 2008. *The Constitution of Equality: Democratic Authority and Its Limits.* Oxford: Oxford University Press.

Cohen, Joshua. 1997. "Deliberation and Democratic Legitimacy." In *Deliberative Democracy: Essays on Reason and Politics,* edited by James Bohman and William Rehg, 67–91. Cambridge, MA: MIT Press.

———. 2010. *The Arc of the Moral Universe and Other Essays.* Cambridge, MA: Harvard University Press.

Coleman, Stephen. 2005. "The Lonely Citizen: Indirect Representation in an Age of Networks." *Political Communication* 22 (2): 173–91.

Constant, Benjamin. 1988. "The Liberty of the Ancients Compared with That of the Moderns." In *Political Writings,* edited by Biancamaria Fontana, 307–28. Cambridge: Cambridge University Press.

Dahl, Robert A. 1973. *Polyarchy: Participation and Opposition.* New Haven, CT: Yale University Press.

Disch, Lisa. 2011. "Toward a Mobilization Conception of Democratic Representation." *American Political Science Review* 105:100–114.

———. 2015. "The Constructivist Turn in Democratic Representation: A Normative Dead-End?" *Constellations* 22 (4): 487–99.

Dryzek, John S. 1990. *Discursive Democracy: Politics, Policy, and Political Science.* Oxford: Oxford University Press.

———. 2000. *Deliberative Democracy and Beyond: Liberals, Critics, Contestationists.* Oxford: Oxford University Press.

Dryzek, John S., and Simon Niemeyer. 2008. "Discursive Representation." *American Political Science Review* 102 (4): 481–93.

Dunn, John. 1999. "Situating Democratic Political Accountability." In *Democracy, Accountability, and Representation*, edited by Adam Przeworski, Susan C. Stokes, and Bernard Manin, 329–44. Cambridge: Cambridge University Press.

Dworkin, Ronald. 1987. "What Is Equality? Part 4: What Is Political Equality?" *University of San Francisco Law Review* 22: 1–30.

Ess, Charles, and Fay Sudweeks, eds. 2001. *Culture, Technology, Communication: Toward an Intercultural Global Village.* Albany: State University of New York Press.

Fung, Archon, and Erik O. Wright. 2003. *Deepening Democracy: Institutional Innovation in Empowered Participatory Governance.* London: Verso.

Goodin, Robert E. 2003. *Reflective Democracy.* Oxford: Oxford University Press.

Green, Jeffrey Edward. 2010. *The Eyes of the People: Democracy in the Age of Spectatorship.* Oxford: Oxford University Press.

Habermas, Jürgen. 1996. *Between Facts and Norms: Contribution to a Discourse Theory of Law and Democracy.* Translated by William Rehg. Cambridge, MA: MIT Press.

Hirst, Paul. 1990. *Representative Democracy and Its Limits.* Cambridge: Polity Press.

Kelsen, Hans. (1929) 2013. *The Essence and Value of Democracy.* Translated by Brian Graf. Introduction by Nadia Urbinati and Carlo Invernizzi Accetti. Lanham, MD: Rowman & Littlefield.

Isin, Engin F., and Michael Saward, eds. 2013. *Enacting European Citizenship.* Cambridge: Cambridge University Press.

Laclau, Ernesto, and Chantal Mouffe. 1985. *Hegemony and Socialist Strategy.* New York: Verso.

Lefort, Claude. 1986. *The Political Form of Modern Society: Bureaucracy, Democracy, Totalitarianism.* Edited by J. B. Thompson. Cambridge, MA: MIT Press.

Mackie, Gerrie. 2011. "The Values of Democratic Proceduralism." *Irish Political Studies* 26 (4): 439–53.

Main, Henry Sumner. 1909. "Nature of Democracy." In *Popular Government: Four Essays*, 56–126. London: Murray.

Mair, Peter. 2013. *Ruling the Void: The Hollowing of Western Democracy.* London: Verso.

Manin, Bernard. 1987. "On Legitimacy and Political Deliberation." *Political Theory* 15: 338–68.

————. 1997. *The Principles of Representative Government*. Cambridge: Cambridge University Press.

Manin, Bernard, Adam Przeworsky, and Susan C. Stokes. 1999. "Elections and Representation." In *Democracy, Accountability, and Representation*, edited by Adam Przeworsky, Susan C. Stokes, and Bernard Manin, 29–54. Cambridge: Cambridge University Press.

Mansbridge, Jane J. 2003. "Rethinking Representation." *American Political Science Review* 97: 515–28.

————. 2014. "A Contingent Theory of Accountability." In *The Handbook of Accountability*, edited by Mark Bovens, Robert E. Goodin, and Thomas Schillemans, 55–68. Oxford: Oxford University Press.

Morozov, Evgeny. 2011. *The Dark Side of Internet Freedom: The New Delusion*. New York: Public Affairs.

Ochoa, Paulina Espejo. 2011. *The Time of Popular Sovereignty: Process and the Democratic State*. University Park: Penn State University Press.

Näsström, Sofia. 2015. "Democratic Representation beyond Election." *Constellations* 22 (1): 1–12.

Pitkin, Hanna F. *The Concept of Representation*. Berkeley: University of California Press, 1967.

Przeworski, Adam. 1999. "Minimalist Conception of Democracy: A Defense." In *Democracy's Value*, edited by Ian Shapiro and Cassiano Hacker-Cordón, 23–55. Cambridge: Cambridge University Press.

————. 2007. "Democracy, Equality, and Redistribution." In *Political Judgement: Essays in Honour of John Dunn*, edited by Richard Bourke and Raymond Geuss, 281–312. Cambridge: Cambridge University Press.

————. 2010. *Democracy and the Limits of Self-Government*. Cambridge: Cambridge University Press.

Rosanvallon, Pierre. 2008. *Countre-Democracy: Politics in an Age of Distrust*. Translated by Arthur Goldhammer. Princeton, NJ: Princeton University Press.

————. 2011. *Democratic Legitimacy: Impartiality, Reflexivity, Proximity*. Princeton, NJ: Princeton University Press.

Rubinstein, Jennifer. 2007. "Accountability in an Unequal World." *Journal of Politics* 69: 616–32.

Sartori, Giovanni. 1987. *The Theory of Democracy Revisited. Part One: The Contemporary Debate Revisited*. Chatman, NJ: Chatman House.

Saward, Michael. 2006. "The Representative Claim." *Contemporary Political Theory* 5: 297–318.

————. 2010. *The Representative Claim*. Cambridge: Cambridge University Press.

Schumpeter, Joseph A. 1942. *Capitalism, Socialism and Democracy*. New York: Harper Torchbook.

Sen, Amartya. 1983. "Liberty and Social Choice." *Journal of Philosophy* 80 (5): 5–28.

Severs, Eline. 2012. "Substantive Representation through a Claim-Making Lens:

A Strategy for the Identification and Analysis of Representative Claims." *Representation* 48 (2): 169–81.

Sintomer, Yves. 2013. "Les sens de la représentation politique: Usages et mésusages d'une notion." *Raison Politique* 50 (2): 13–34.

Sunstein, Cass R. 2006. *Infotopia: How Many Minds Produce Knowledge*. Oxford: Oxford University Press.

Urbinati, Nadia. 2006. *Representative Democracy: Principles and Genealogy*. Chicago: University of Chicago Press.

———. 2014. *Democracy Disfigured: Opinion, Truth and the People*. Cambridge, MA: Harvard University Press.

———. 2015. "A Revolt against Intermediary Bodies." *Constellations* 22: 477–86.

Urbinati, Nadia, and Mark Warren. 2008. "The Concept of Representation in Democracy." *Annual Review of Political Science* 11: 387–412.

Warren, Mark. 2014. "Accountability and Democracy." In *The Handbook of Accountability*, edited by Mark Bovens, Robert E. Goodin, and Thomas Schillemans, 39–54. Oxford: Oxford University Press.

White, Jonathan, and Lea Ypi. 2016. *The Meaning of Partisanship*. Oxford: Oxford University Press.

Young, Iris Marion. 1997. "Deferring Group Representation." In *Ethnicity and Group Rights: Nomos XXXIX*, edited by Ian Shapiro and Will Kymlicka, 349–76. New York: New York University Press.

———. 2000. *Inclusion and Democracy*. Oxford: Oxford University Press.

# CHAPTER FOUR

# Political Parties and Conflict Handling

John Erik Fossum

More than seventy years ago, Elmer E. Schattschneider ([1942] 2009) labeled political parties "the orphans of political philosophy" (16). Reflecting on the statement's relevance today, Nancy Rosenblum (2008) notes that "if parties are the orphans of political philosophy, they are the darlings of political science" (3). Political scientists' fascination with political parties reflects the central role of parties in modern systems of governance.[1] At the same time, parties are widely held to be facing decline or increasing irrelevance, and publics' appreciation of parties is anything but unconditional.[2] Democratic theorists discuss parliaments and other representative bodies but jump nimbly over political parties. One way of putting this is to say that "political theory harbored no great political expectations parties could disappoint" (Rosenblum 2008, 5).

In her important attempt at addressing this, Nancy Rosenblum (2008) undertook a systematic search for normative justifications for political parties in the works of key political philosophers. Key among the defenses she found was political parties' central role in conflict handling, especially in *civilizing* conflicts. Nevertheless, one effect of the disconnection between political science and political theory is that little systematic effort is expended discerning *how* political parties handle and civilize conflicts and what the implications are for parties' role in representing citizens. The purpose of this chapter is to address this disconnection by focusing on how political parties handle and civilize conflicts.

If we start with the assumption that responsiveness lies at the core of democratic representation (the standard account of representation's core norm) then we would assume that parties strive to "take citizen preferences as the 'bedrock for social choice'" (Disch 2011, 100). Political parties seek to incorporate citizens' preferences; when these diverge, parties are pitted against each other. Each party then faces the challenge of reconciling the need for responsiveness to its members and voters with the need for settling conflicts and disagreements with the other parties. The bedrock norm thus posits that parties face a trade-off between responsiveness and conflict management/reduction. The more divided the populace along ideological, religious, or other lines, the more difficult it is for parties to deal with this dilemma. And since responsiveness is so crucial to democracy, conflict handling will always be a democratic problem.

How fitting is this depiction of the plight of parties? I will discuss it with reference to the various mechanisms that parties have for handling conflicts. No such survey has thus far been undertaken; the chapter breaks new ground in doing so. An assessment that confines itself to the role of mechanisms will however not be complete. We also need to question the veracity of the bedrock assumption of responsiveness. The assessment of the mechanisms will therefore contrast the standard account of representation (from which the bedrock norm derives) with a conception of representation steeped in the constructivist turn to representation. These two sets of examinations yield new insights into how parties relate to the conflicting demands of those they represent and how parties' acts of representation shape their conflict handling.

In the following, I start by defining conflict handling. Thereafter I discuss the two different conceptions of representation and apply these to political parties. In the subsequent section I outline and discuss the different mechanisms that parties have for conflict handling. The final section offers conclusions.

## What Do We Mean by Conflict Handling?

Before we discuss parties and representation it is necessary to specify what we mean by conflict handling. Analytically speaking, we may distinguish between three types of conflict: solvable, manageable, and unsolvable (and unmanageable). The lines between these categories vary considerably across countries and issues. Of crucial importance is that conflict handling is not the same as conflict solving, because those conflicts that require handling will lack ready-made solutions. That does not mean that they cannot at a future point in time be solved or disappear, but the gist of conflict handling is the ongoing effort to live with and to manage the effects of a conflict or a division that does not go away. When parties frame and relate to conflicts to make them amenable to handling by the political system (thereby preventing system breakdown, violence, or other patholo-gies), we say that parties *civilize* conflict. Conflict handling thus refers to a situation where parties face issues or questions that pit them against each other and where no easy solution exists. Conflict intensity will vary depending on a range of factors. The following conditions will likely apply: (a) high stakes (substantive, symbolic, or both); (b) a divided population (between political parties, within parties, or both); (c) intense conflict with a high likelihood of creating disruption; and (d) a zero-sum game with binary positions and no apparent win-win scenario. Conflicts marked by such conditions must be *handled*. If not, the political system may face a stalemate or, in the worst case, break down. Such conflicts can manifest in distinct societal cleavages or divisions (Lipset and Rokkan 1967); between ideological, religious, or other overarching worldviews; in insoluble or not easily negotiable questions pertaining to race, ethnicity, class, nationality, gender, and other forms of identification, belonging, and social structuring.

An empirical illustration of a deeply divisive political conflict where political parties have been the main handlers is the issue of Norwegian EU membership. This issue has figured as one of the most politically divisive issues in Norway since the Second World War. The EU membership issue widened old and entrenched cleavages in Norway (Valen 1999); it pitted regions against each other; it caused a significant rural-urban split; and it caused deep divisions between and within political parties. Two popular referenda have added to the conflict by further mobilizing the populace. The first EU membership referendum was held in 1972, and the *no* side won with a small margin after a deeply divisive debate. When Sweden and Finland decided to become EU members in 1994, a new referendum was arranged, and the *no* side again won with a small margin.[3] Even before the referendum, however, Norway had become a member of the European Economic Area Agreement. Through this highly dynamic agreement and a range of other agreements with the EU, Norway now adopts roughly three-quarters of the EU's regulations and directives (Norway 2012, 790). It is an associated member of the Schengen Area, which locates Norway within the EU's external borders, giving it responsibility for EU external border controls. The period since the 1994 referendum has produced an ever-closer EU affiliation without formal membership. The political parties are central to this form of conflict handling: they have forged and maintain the political compromise of nonmembership coupled with rapid and dynamic EU adaptation. The example is telling for how a consensus-oriented party system can relate to an intense and lasting conflict with no obvious solution that all will agree to. People are constantly reminded of Norway's EU association because so many of their daily activities are de facto EU-regulated. Since the EU membership issue cannot be resolved, the option left for the parties is to manage the situation so that the tensions it creates do not spiral out of control. I will revisit this example when discussing the mechanisms that parties avail themselves of when handling conflicts.

In the next section, the standard conception of representation will be presented and contrasted to the new constructivist notion of representation.

## Contending Conceptions of Representation

With the norm of responsiveness at its core, the standard account of representation consists of the following four elements (Urbinati and Warren 2008, 389; see also Castiglione and Warren 2006):

1. a principal-agent relationship, in which the principals—constituencies formed on a territorial basis—elect agents to stand for and act on their interests and opinions, thus separating the sources of legitimate power from those that exercise that power;
2. a space within which the sovereignty of the people is identified with state power;
3. electoral mechanisms that ensure both some measure of responsiveness of the representatives to the people and a place for political parties that speak and act in the people's name;
4. an important element of political equality endowed to electoral representation by the universal franchise.

The standard account understands representation as a principal-agent structure where the represented (the principal) authorizes and holds the representatives (the agents) to account. The focus is on *elected* representatives, in other words, democratic representation. The strong emphasis on responsiveness makes the representative relationship quite unidirectional: from the represented to the representative.

The constructivist turn to representation challenges several of the core assumptions of the standard account.[4] To begin with, the representative relationship starts from the side of the representative: a representative does not simply stand for or act for a preconfigured constituency; the representative plays an active role in socially constructing those that he or she claims to represent. They in turn choose whether to accept or reject these representations of themselves. The most explicitly articulated alternative to the Pitkin-inspired standard account[5] is the model of representative claim-making associated with Michael Saward (2006, 2010).

Drawing mainly but far from exclusively on Saward's representative claim-making approach, we can discern five important differences from the standard account. First is that representation is *constitutive* of the representative relationship. Representatives play an important role in defining the terms of the representative relationship in the sense that they *construct* the represented, which refers to the ways in which they depict and address them. Second, representation is dynamic; it is a matter of an ongoing communication and interaction between representatives and represented.[6] That has bearings on a third feature, namely preference endogeneity; preferences are altered through communication and interaction. Fourth is that there is an important cultural and symbolic aspect to representation. When representatives depict those that they claim to represent, they do so within a context of cultural norms.[7] Fifth, constructivists underline that representation is performed by not only elected but also nonelected representatives. In addition, representation unfolds within state-based contexts *as well as* within transnational and international realms. This often makes it necessary to specify who the constituency is; we cannot take it for granted that we know precisely who will be addressed or who will respond.

Constructivists do not abandon responsiveness but understand it as situated within a dynamic structure of representation. How this unfolds requires close attention to concrete instances of representation. These two conceptions of representation—the standard and the constructivist—provide us with different takes on political parties, which I will specify in the next section. One interesting issue that cannot be systematically assessed here is whether the two perspectives differ in how they conceive of parties or whether they refer to different types of parties.[8]

The next section spells out the nature and functions of political parties and shows how these two conceptions of representation conceive of political parties.

## Political Parties and Representation

In his classic book *Parties and Party Systems*, Giovanni Sartori defines a political party as *"any political group that presents at elections, and is capable of placing through elections, candidates for public office"* (Sartori 2005, 56; italics in original). Nancy Rosenblum's (2008) definition is more specific: "a party is a group organized to contest for public office; it is avowed in its partisanship and operates not conspiratorially but in public view; it is not an ad hoc coalition or arrangement for vote trading and compromise on a specific issue, but an institution formed for ongoing political activity; and it can claim a substantial number of followers, in current terms, a partisan 'base'" (20).

Parties have developed into central components of modern representative democracies. They play a vital role at the level of *input* by aggregating and articulating voters' and members' views to the political system. They play a key role at the level of *throughput* (for this notion see Eriksen 2005; Schmidt 2013) by orchestrating and performing the work of parliaments and governments; they seek out compromises and arrangements to reach decisions; they give content and direction to political action programs; they recruit leaders, and they furnish political leadership. Parties also play a role at the level of *output*, especially in situations where government ministries act as political secretariats or where public administration bears a strong partisan imprint (as in the spoils system in the United States). Parties play a key role in terms of societal *feedback*. The party system is really the only organizational category that is present in all of these parts of the political cycle. The late Peter Mair (2014) put it succinctly: "The same organization that governed the citizenry also gave that citizenry voice, and the same organization that channeled representation also managed the institutions of the polity" (581–82).

All of these tasks that political parties undertake are relevant to conflict handling. But since parties are involved in basically all stages of the democratic decision-making process, they relate to conflicts differently depending on the stage in question. It follows that the range of conflict-handling mechanisms is very wide. A further source of complexity is that party scholars distinguish between partisanship, the party as organization, and the party system. Each of these categories implies a distinctive take on conflict handling. It is virtually impossible to develop an approach to parties and conflict handling that encompasses all the things that parties do (at the input, throughput, output, and feedback stages) that at the same time pays sufficient attention to the three dimensions involved: partisanship, party, and party system.

Our concern here is accordingly narrower: the relationship between partisan representation and conflict handling. The best way of conceiving that relationship is to consider the two main conceptions of representation outlined above, with emphasis on the input side. This will shed proper light on the dilemma of responsiveness and conflict handling.

The most widely held views of political parties are rooted in rational choice perspectives, which see parties variously as office-seeking instruments (Schlesinger 1991), as vote seekers, or as policy seekers (Strøm 1990). Rational choice conceptions of parties typically cast them as instruments and as strategic actors. Parties handle conflicts—internally or externally— through powering, bargaining, and persuasion. Rational choice conceptions of parties are steeped in the bedrock assumption of responsiveness because rational choice sees parties' preferences as exogenously given. Party officials develop strategies that guide the party, but they are constrained by the preferences of the party's voters and supporters. The specific constellation of actors and interests within and without the party is an important determinant of the nature and intensity of conflict and the scope for handling conflict. It is apparent that rational choice–inspired conceptions of parties place the accent on parties and party systems, not on partisanship. This reflects the relative disinterest in normative issues among party scholars. In sum, we see that the mainstream view of parties takes as its point of departure the standard conception of representation and adopts the conventional view of a clear trade-off between responsiveness and conflict handling.

In recent years a growing body of scholarship has focused on the meaning of partisanship, sought normative justifications for parties, and operated with conceptions of representation that resonate with the constructivist turn to representation. One recently developed position is formulated by Jonathan White and Lea Ypi (2010, 2011, 2016), who establish a close association between partisanship and deliberative democracy. They argue that: "partisanship ... is indispensable to the kind of political justification needed to make the exercise of collective authority responsive to normative concerns" (2011, 381). Partisanship is critically important for collective decision-making in the sense that it supplies normative, motivational, and executive resources. Partisanship is clearly relevant to conflict handling, but White and Ypi understand partisanship's merit to extend beyond mere conflict *handling*. They argue that partisanship "involves citizens acting to promote certain shared normative commitments according to a distinctive interpretation of the common good" (382). This in no way detracts from the partisan nature of the political party; instead it underlines that the party seeks to justify its proposals "in the name of the whole." While the party represents a mere part of the whole, it must nevertheless take a non-partial approach to the whole. White and Ypi thus operate with a far more sophisticated approach to partisan responsiveness than the standard one, since their approach pays attention to preference endogeneity and sees representation as a dynamic process. In addition, White and Ypi underline that parties as representative bodies play an important constitutive role in representation. Parties foster world disclosure through deliberation; and they stake out alternatives, render explicit what is at stake, and clarify the premises for justification. Partisan forums serve as "learning platforms for citizens, offering them the intellectual resources to deepen their knowledge of complex political arrangements and the opportunity to benefit from exchanges with political leaders and activists" (387). The important creative role that political parties play in society aids their world-disclosing and justificatory roles: they expose normative choices, values, and interests. This ideal model of partisanship presupposes that actors are willing to listen to and understand the views and positions of others, which appears most likely in situations where few fundamental conflicts pit groups and collectives against each other.

Nancy Rosenblum and Russell Muirhead depict partisanship as a distinct "political identity." Two core dimensions of this notion have direct bearing on parties' conflict handling. On the one hand, viewing partisanship as political identity emphasizes attachment and *identification with* the party. As Muirhead (2014) notes, "Partisanship . . . is spirited, or prideful. It originates in the desire for recognition, is sustained by the way being disagreed with is experienced as an insult, and is not without a noble willingness to fight (in a sense) for the sake of the common good" (x). The onus on partisan identification is an essential ingredient in the political party's ability to foster political mobilization. The party depends on a dedicated cadre of activists who are willing to devote their time and effort to the values and policies that the party espouses. The loyalty and attachment that stems from persons' positive identification with the party is vital to the party's existence over time. It is also a major source of internal and especially interparty conflict, and this has direct bearing on the other aspect of partisanship, namely that partisanship is about pluralism and partiality.

Partisanship entails acknowledging that one's positive form of identification is one among several possibilities, and that other forms may be distinctly different, even opposite one's own. Partisanship is therefore an acknowledgment of pluralism, partiality, and the constraints that this acknowledgment brings with it. In this conception, partisanship is, so to speak, located in the political party as an institutionalized organization imbued with a distinct set of values, organizational culture, persistence over time, and "organizational memory" (for the classic take on the organization as an institution, see Selznick 1957). The political party socializes persons into the political arena as political actors, as politicians capable of propounding partisan values and programs of action, and as persons equipped to engage in political contestation. As such, they are taught the rules of the political game and what constitutes appropriate partisan behavior, including how to handle conflicts.[9]

We see from this that Muirhead and Rosenblum do not operate with a conception of partisanship as situated in the bedrock norm of social responsiveness. They see the party on the one hand as an institutionalized organization that plays a central role in fostering and ensuring a sense of loyalty among its members and supporters; on the other hand they see it as a bearer of the norm of responsibility in the sense of exercising self-restraint. This system-preservation norm is of central importance to how parties understand responsiveness.

Parties can balance their concerns with responsiveness and responsibility because they are creative organizations. They "create, not just reflect, political interests and opinions. They formulate 'issues' and give them political relevance. Party antagonism 'stages the battle,' parties create a system of conflict and draw the lines of division. . . . Modern party politics is the ordinary not (ordinarily) extraordinary locus of political creativity" (Rosenblum 2008, 7). When discussing how parties handle—and civilize— conflicts, we must pay attention to this important *shaping* role of parties and party systems.

The constructivist perspective underlines that the privileged role for the party (system) in modern democracies is not that of receivers but that of shapers of ideologies, decisions, and broader patterns of societal and systemic learning. Parties formulate worldviews and foster world disclosure; they stake out alternatives: framing and imprinting them (individually or in collaboration) by amplifying those aspects that they like or support and filtering out those that they dislike. Parties structure opinion- and will-formation processes, and they mobilize the party cadre and the citizenry.

They undertake these tasks under the auspices of the norm of responsibility; parties are concerned with striking a viable balance between responsiveness and responsibility.

Parties are institutionalized organizations that persist over time and have developed an organizational culture and a structured view of the world that serve as vital influences on how the party undertakes such balancing acts. The constructivist perspective associated with Saward has thus far paid little attention to how the features of parties as institutionalized organizations condition their claim-making, socially constructive, and dynamic aspects. Even Rosenblum and Muirhead, who focus on partisanship as a political identity, have not taken the next step, namely to spell out the implications for the party as an institutionalized organization and the party system as a distinct institutional order.

In the next section I develop a set of analytical categories that enable us to spell out the repertoire of conflict-handling mechanisms and discuss the mechanisms relevant to the two conceptions of representation.

## Mechanisms of Conflict Handling in a Representative Setting

This section develops a systematic approach to the identification of the mechanisms that parties may employ in conflict handling. Focusing on the relationships both between parties and voters/supporters (responsiveness) and among parties (conflict handling), we need analytical categories that enable us to capture these dimensions. I draw on Hirschman's (1970) framework of *exit*, *voice*, and *loyalty*, which I supplement (as Stein Rokkan [1975] did) with *entry*. Hirschman devised these categories to capture how persons and consumers relate to their relevant organizations. The concepts are useful for discerning a broad repertoire of mechanisms that parties have for handling conflicts. Examining this repertoire reveals how the standard and the constructivist approaches seek to reconcile conflict handling and responsiveness, as well as the limits of responsiveness as the bedrock norm.

Among Hirschman's terms, *voice* and *loyalty* are also useful because they resonate with the two conceptions of partisanship cited above (associated respectively with White and Ypi and Rosenblum and Muirhead). When applied to parties and discussed in relation to the two conceptions of representation outlined here, these terms depict how parties receive inputs from citizens, voters, and members (in a bottom-up fashion); they will be considered from a constructivist perspective to view how parties socially construct, frame, and seek to shape the views and interests of those they claim to represent (in a dynamic, even top-down manner).

Parties relate to conflicts or contentious issues by being advocates of the common good (voice) or structures of identification (loyalty) relating to the very essence of partisanship, by being organizations with privileged access and a mediating role between state and society; and by forming party systems with distinct interparty relations and interaction logics.

The categories of voice and loyalty operate at a different level than the categories of entry and exit, which refer to what parties *do*. The latter two terms help us to understand how parties include or incorporate conflicts or contentious issues as a basis for political mobilization and influence; they amplify issues or concerns and as such raise the overall level of conflict in society (entry); they tone down conflict by various forms of conciliatory stances and behaviors; and they remove conflicts or contentious issues from the political agenda or from voters' attention (exit). There are many ways in which these dynamics unfold, and they need to be spelled out. My main concern is not with the specific meaning of voice, loyalty, exit, and entry but with their evocative and *directive* potential: as distinct ways of directing us to a range of mechanisms appropriate to the same dimension or category.

To enable us to contrast the standard conception of representation to the constructivist one, the framework must capture the fundamentally dualistic role of parties' relation to conflict (they both increase and lower levels of conflicts).

## Voice

This category refers to giving voice to or expressing something on behalf of someone, in line with the standard notion that parties are vehicles for picking up and channeling voters' voice(s) to the political system. The most obvious version is that parties consider that their voters/supporters/members should determine what stance the party should adopt on a given issue. Parties then concentrate on ensuring that their actual positions remain in line with those of their constituency and seek to persuade other parties to go along with that. Another form of voice that is also consistent with the standard conception of representation is that parties seek to elicit citizens' voices through a popular referendum. This is a strong version of responsiveness insofar as parties commit themselves to respect the majoritarian position in the referendum. The difference between the two versions is that in the former conflict handling takes place in the interaction among parties; in the latter case it is mainly dealt with internally in the party and pertains to finding a way of living with the referendum result.

From a constructivist perspective, parties spell out who the relevant constituency is, and they attribute views and self-conceptions to the constituency that they claim to stand and act for. In other words, parties as organizational collectives actively frame and shape partisan voices. The party's views are forged by the creative acts of the party's leaders and officials; party ideology and worldview; the institutionalized values of the party; and the party's historical experiences. The constructivist position adopts a dynamic view of voice as shaped and conditioned by the manner in which parties relate to the world around them, the ongoing interaction among parties and voters/supporters, other parties, and the political system. Consider how so-called populist parties seek to distinguish between themselves and the other established parties, which they claim belong to "the elite" in contrast to the populists who posit themselves as the authentic expression of "the people" (Müller 2016); they then draw on this opposition to harness the symbolic resources of "the nation." Populists posit themselves as the defenders of the nation in contrast to the other parties, which they claim betray the nation for the EU, for the UN, for global capitalism, and so forth. These are forms of strategic voice manipulation that populist parties use to realign the patterns of division in modern society, patterns of division that are more amenable to them and their favored constituencies.[10]

Conflict handling is an intrinsic part of this process of framing/constructing lines of division. Parties sort out which issues they seek to resolve, which issues they compete on, and which issues they try to ignore. These relations can be conducted through communicative or through strategic action. Parties employ spin doctors and other ways of (re)framing or manipulating public opinion. An important question pertains to the effects of these different approaches: to what extent do parties render conflict handling *more intractable* by programming action in strategic than communicative terms?

We see from this brief survey that partisan voice is not merely a matter of parties responding to a preset constituency or a relatively fixed set of preferences; it is a far more dynamic and interactionist process where the features of the party—type of party, partisan composition and history, and other contextual variables matter a lot.

*Loyalty*

The most obvious way of thinking about loyalty in the context of the party is in terms of the familiar notion of party loyalty; that is, voters do not only vote for parties, but they develop a deeper sense of attachment to "their" party because they identify with it. As such loyalty is closely associated with a distinct reading of party and partisanship, namely the notion listed above of partisanship as a political identity and parties as institutionalized organizations. This has direct bearing on parties' roles in conflict handling because it pertains to parties as carriers of mentalities that are often hard to reconcile.

The fact that a party's leaders can count on a portion of the electorate being loyal serves as a kind of license for the party leadership to pursue certain policies if and insofar as these voters see the party as responsive to them. In that sense voter loyalty provides a political party with a buffer that it can use when seeking compromises with other parties, in particular when such compromises are necessary to handle highly conflictual issues. The buffer is based on a conditional (trust) license: the more willing to strike a compromise with other parties a party is the more likely it is to jeopardize the loyalty voters feel to the party. Thus, this notion of loyalty refers back to the dilemma at the heart of the standard conception of representation, namely that a party's role in conflict handling (by entering into compromises with other parties) is inversely related to its role in ensuring voter loyalty.

When we consider loyalty from a constructivist perspective, we find that it is necessary to look more closely at the party as an institutionalized organization and how that shapes the loyalty relationship. Like any organization, the party seeks to structure and control its environment and especially its constituency of loyal supporters. One way of harnessing this relationship is to systematically espouse certain issues and issue frames that serve as points of identification: "This is what partisans do: they remember. What they remember and the way they carry what they remember to the present is what defines the *party-in-the-electorate*" (Muirhead 2014, 134). This has to do with specific issues or incidents but no less importantly with how they are framed: some parties are associated with antiimmigration or Euroskepticism; this is what the partisans remember and how the party-in-the-electorate appears. As Moffitt (2016) has underlined in relation to modern populism, this is precisely what populist leaders systematically seek to establish through the distinctive political style that they have adopted. For the party's constituency that helps to lock in their support. That in turn also constrains the party's realm of action: party members' and electors' expectations are so fixed on certain issue stances that deviations will be considered betrayals.

Constructivists would direct us to consider whether the fidelity that party leadership feels to a particular policy or stance or to a given procedure or mode of consulting the electorate could be of their own making. Parties frame issues, shape constituencies, and generate expectations. Over time the efforts expended by party leadership to foster certain issues or considerations that they hold up as designative of the party will—through constant reminder and socialization—come to be associated with the party. The party leadership must then also pay heed to these issues and considerations if they want to appear loyal to the party's most ardent supporters. Conflict handling from this angle then pertains to the type of leverage that the party leadership considers itself to have in terms of issue framing and the extent to which they opt for an exclusive or inclusive strategy. The representative claims framework is useful in capturing this in the sense that it directs us at how the partisan representatives cast themselves to the constituency that they single out as loyal supporters—loyal proponents of the common cause or more conciliatory handlers of thorny issues—and how the constituency responds to this framing.

When the party leadership focuses on internal loyalty preservation, conflicts with other political parties may ensue or be amplified. A political party can use loyalty as a means of *self-binding* through procedures that protect a certain partisan stance or policy. On the face of it, the two aspects of the loyalty relation, party-internal and interparty, suggest that loyalty may not be a very reliable mechanism for ensuring conflict handling.

Such a conclusion however would underestimate the role of loyalty or at least its cognate responsibility in modern politics. Loyalty is as noted intrinsic to the notion of partisanship, through the manner in which partisanship links to political identity (Rosenblum 2008; Muirhead 2014). The distinctive political identity that marks political parties comes with what we may term a systemic responsibility ethos. One important facet of the responsibility ethos associated with parties' monopoly in furnishing political leaders includes acceptance of the key tenet of regulated rivalry: "The innovation of regulated rivalry, in practice and conceptually, was to safely add organized opposition *within government* to political criticism and opposition outside government. . . . Regulated party rivalry entails political self-restraint, and the true discipline is rightly described as mental and emotional" (Rosenblum 2008, 121, 124). "Party conflict entails political self-discipline—institutionalized, eventually legalized, internalized, and made moral habit" (125). The notion of a "loyal opposition" is intrinsic to this. Political parties and the party system thus serve to uphold certain basic norms and values that are not only deeply entrenched in modern democratic political culture but vital to conflict handling.

From the political system's perspective, political parties serve as shock absorbers in the sense that they regulate conflict in society and channel contentious issues in a shape and a form that will enable the political system to handle them; parties work out ways of reconciling contending interests and applying relevant knowledge to the cases at hand. Drawing on Urbinati's (2006) terms, "advocacy" and "representativity," parties' advocacy as "the representative's 'passionate' link to the electors' cause" is tempered by a cross-partisan culture of political self-restraint. That political culture in turn also represents a vital precondition for ensuring "the representative's autonomy of judgement."

In modern democracies the fundamental partisan aspect is so entrenched that we almost take it for granted, but across time and space we have seen various antisystemic parties on the left and the right of the political specter (such as revolutionary parties, fascist, neo-Nazi, and to some extent also extreme populist parties) with at times devastating consequences.

This brief section on the mechanisms associated with loyalty shows us that the loyalty we associate with political parties is not confined to supporters; the central role that parties have played in civilizing conflicts stems from the fact that they have actively fostered a culture of self-restraint or a systemic responsibility ethos. Without it they could never have worked out viable ways of balancing responsiveness to voters/supporters in a context where parties are actively espousing rival worldviews and ideologies. Some of this is of parties' own making; their active role in structuring the representative relationship naturally places them in a central role here. The constructivist perspective is best suited to bringing out this vital aspect: the norms and rules that parties have developed to ensure the *civilizing* of conflicts.

*Exit*

The term *exit* generally refers to leaving, moving out of, or departing from a given context or decision situation. The main way in which we understand *exit* from the vantage point of the standard conception of representation is as a party's move to exit the representative relationship or seek to somehow move out of the representative relation to deal with controversial issues. Parties can remove controversial issues from citizens' attention. Or they can devise measures that ensure that citizens do not need to make up their minds or take decisions. One means is for individual parties or the entire party system to *collude* to keep controversial issues off the political agenda. Or they may rely on less apparent or explicit means of keeping issues off the agenda, such as *nondecisions* (Bachrach and Baratz 1962). Parties may shut out the voters and decide issues among themselves in closed forums. A special version here is *consociationalism* (Lijphart 1977). Parties can remove issues through permitting various forms of independent bodies to take decisions. Governing parties may for instance hive off tasks to commissions of inquiry or set up special bodies of experts to improve the knowledge base (and possibly enable them to postpone making controversial decisions). All these instances entail handling conflicts through sacrificing or toning down responsiveness. The standard account would therefore tend to see them as democratically problematic.

A constructivist approach would adopt a somewhat different take on the nature and range of exit mechanisms. For instance, we could argue that a redefinition of the terms of the representative relationship from responsiveness to responsibility constitutes a form of exit from the bedrock norm of responsiveness. Mair (2014) argued that such a change in the party system took place with the transition from traditional socially rooted mass parties to so-called cartel parties (parties that have become closely associated with the state) (Katz and Mair 1995). The change in party system reflects the altered context of norms and rules regulating partisan interaction in a heavily globalized context marked by a dense network of norms and rules that hem in partisan political action.

The constructivist approach underlines that the representative relationship is dynamic and that we therefore need to consider conflict handling as part of the interaction between representative and represented. The question is what range of mechanisms parties have for that. One possible mechanism that under certain circumstances can fill that role is gag rules. Gag rules are generally used to introduce barriers to decisions or to put a lid on a debate (Holmes 1995). Some gag rules are instituted to stymie or prevent debate; others are intended to block a body from taking a decision. Stephen Holmes lumps formal provisions, regulations, and tacit understandings under this category. Holmes notes that gag rules have generally been considered alien to democracy. When considered from a deliberative democratic perspective they can readily be construed as forms of strategic manipulation that rely on withholding information, removing issues from public attention, and diverting attention from salient and controversial issues. But they can also serve democracy: precisely by removing the most controversial issues from the public agenda, gag rules can preserve peace, foster agreement and consensus, and make democracy workable. Norwegian political parties have used gag rules to keep the controversial EU membership question off the political agenda (Fossum 2010). This has enabled the system to live under the present compromise of nonmembership coupled with dynamic adaptation. The Norwegian situation is patently undemocratic (Eriksen and Fossum 2015) and testifies to the difficulties of tailoring such mechanisms to democratic ends.

This brief discussion has shown that, even if exit is about issue removal, parties need not necessarily "exit out of the representative relationship." The dynamic constructivist approach to representation would consider whether the mechanisms leave scope for the represented to engage with how representatives address thorny issues. In that sense gag rules that stymie debate may be more conducive to representation than those forms of elite negotiations in closed forums that we generally associate with consociationalism (Lijphart 1977). Gag rules and consociational arrangements are hardly coterminous; the former can be a matter of avoiding discussion of a thorny issue precisely to ensure that the political system continues to function, whereas the latter generally entails that a select number of persons make decisions and settle issues in closed forums. With regard to consociational arrangements, from a democratic perspective it matters what procedures for authorization there are, as well as whether such arrangements can be compatible with the norms that Chambers (2004) establishes regarding secrecy in deliberation. The constructivist perspective underlines that the standards for assessing how conflict handling interferes with representation must take into account the dynamic nature of representation. The democratic quality of conflict handling arrangements—even those bent on exit—must be considered from that vantage point.

*Entry*

The term *entry* is used to capture another dynamic dimension of how parties handle conflict. The standard approach to representation understands entry from the perspective of increased responsiveness, in a typical bottom-up manner. The political system's responsiveness would increase if views or interests that were excluded in society could be included through the formation of new parties or if established parties would adopt the views of excluded groups or incorporate new issues and values. The rise of Green Parties could for instance be considered as a reflection of society's increased concern with environmental issues or a broader societal transition to postmaterial values (Tranter and Western 2009). Such increased responsiveness may raise or lower overall levels of conflict in society. A new party may bring new conflictual issues to the political arena. Or the entry of a new party can *diffuse* conflict through breaking up established lines of division or stalemates. Established parties may seek to increase responsiveness through bringing new issues to the public agenda with the aim of politicizing them, in which case the effect is of course to heighten rather than reduce conflict. Governing parties may co-opt a recalcitrant opposition party by including it in government, hence most likely reducing conflict.

A strong case of responsiveness is when parties leave it to voters or supporters to determine the party's stance on an issue. That suggests a way of handling conflicts that is very democratic. But even such a form of inclusion can be used strategically to deflect partisan responsibility and prevent issues from entering the political agenda, such as setting high bars to issue activation. This was the case with the Norwegian Progress Party that refused to take a stance on the contentious EU membership issue because it knew that its constituency was divided on the issue. Its official policy was that voters would decide this issue in a popular referendum. The provisions were rigged in such a manner that the popular consultation process would protect the party from taking a stance. An apparent entry mechanism was therefore devised to keep a contentious issue off the partisan agenda (Fossum 2010). This example shows that we need to consider *how* mechanisms are used in a given case to determine democratic quality.

The Progress Party example directs us to the constructivist position, which highlights partisan strategies and partisan creativity, in other words how parties use top-down strategies to affect and shape their constituencies. Parties of course do far more than use their creativity strategically. They genuinely open up intellectual space through introducing new ideas and policy solutions. Parties *facilitate entry* by soliciting others' views, values, and interests, creating space for certain conflict dimensions and issue frames. A constructivist perspective would underline that we cannot confine entry to aspects of entering and gaining access but must cast it more broadly to encompass ideas, values, worldviews, and frames.

Parties bring in new values and ideas, including ideas about governing (the diffusion of neoliberal ideas across the Western world is a case in point). Parties can actively seek to alter the composition of society in a manner favorable to them through tailored immigration policies or by targeting specific groups of immigrants in order to bolster their support (as was the case with the Harper Canadian Conservatives).

Entry affects how parties redefine the representative relationship. An established party (or group of parties) may include a populist party in government to give it a sense of responsibility as a means of civilizing conflicts. As we see in several instances in contemporary Europe, it is far from certain that such a strategy produces the desired results: populists in power may succeed in pursuing their own agenda, for instance on immigration, as we see in Norway, where the Progress Party oversees the ministries dealing with immigration and asylum policy. The result has been a stricter and more exclusivist policy.[11]

## Conclusion

This chapter's point of departure was the gap between the importance that political scientists and political philosophers attribute to political parties. There is a move by political theorists to close the gap, with one important body of work underlining the role of parties in civilizing conflicts. Today's disconnect between political philosophers and political scientists manifests itself for instance in the lack of systematic attention to the types of mechanisms that political parties use for handling conflicts. The purpose of this chapter was to provide an overview of the mechanisms that parties have for handling persistent conflicts and to examine what these mechanisms tells us about the representative role of parties. The standard conception of representation sees a difficult trade-off between responsiveness and conflict handing. I assessed that dilemma and compared the mechanisms from two approaches to representation.

First, the assessment has shown that the standard account's conception of the dilemma depends on how we conceive of parties. If we think of parties mainly as instruments of voice, then the elements that enter the equation differ from those that mark accounts of parties from the perspective of loyalty. Second, partisan responsiveness varies with function, and activates quite different mechanisms depending on whether the parties face challenges under the rubric of entry or exit.

Third, the constructivist approach shows that there are clear limits to responsiveness as the bedrock norm, especially when it comes to the manner in which political parties handle conflicts. An important reason is that parties must pay heed to the critically important norm of responsibility. Parties are concerned with the ongoing operation of the political system, which requires that they balance responsiveness with responsibility. Different party types and party systems develop different trade-offs, as reflected in the transition from socially embedded mass parties (which were by nature very concerned with responsiveness) to today's cartel parties that are more geared toward responsibility. The latter find themselves challenged by the rise of populist parties that adopt extreme versions of responsiveness in their efforts to restructure the main dividing lines in society.

Fourth, the constructivist approach underlines that parties are creative, and this shapes how they relate to those they represent and to the conflicts they confront. This creative role has bearings on how we understand responsiveness because parties play an important role in defining its terms, including the who, the how, and the what of responsiveness. From a democratic perspective, the creative role of parties increases uncertainty, because while parties may use their creativity in ways conducive to democracy they can also do the opposite.

Fifth, the constructivist approach underlines the dynamic nature of representation, as discussed in the overview of mechanisms. The general view of dynamism pitches it in vertical terms, along the lines of responsiveness. The scheme I developed here shows that we need to include the dynamism that emanates from all those aspects of entry and exit that parties experience as central conduits of conflict handling and representation.

Finally, this chapter has shown that political theory needs to take more seriously and develop further the notion of political parties as institutionalized organizations. This dimension has yet to be properly incorporated in the main body of constructivist thought.

The chapter shows that it is difficult to pigeonhole parties as either democratic or undemocratic. It is quite easy to point to democratic deficits or representative shortfalls in the actions that parties undertake. That does not however render parties deficient as such. One hallmark of parties is that they must balance different considerations, often with different democratic expectations or assumed democratic salience. Another important point is that conflict handling is at times a matter of system stability. That raises two further questions. One pertains to the normative salience of stability, the other to the need for proper sorting mechanisms: under what conditions is the system's stability at stake and under what conditions is it not? Parties play a vital function in modern societies, but they need to be kept in check by watchful eyes.


## Notes

1. As James Bryce (1921) noted: "parties are inevitable. No one has shown how representative government could be worked without them" (119, cited in Dalton and Weldon 2005, 931).

2. A recent survey of partisan images noted that "contemporary publics appear to view political parties as democracy's necessary evil—needed for running elections and organizing government, but with doubts about how political parties represent their interests within this process" (Dalton and Weldon 2015, 937).

3. In 1972 53.5 percent voted against membership and 46.5 percent voted for, and in 1994 52.2 percent voted against, whereas 47.8 percent voted in favor.

4. The main persons associated with this turn are Lisa Disch, Jane Mansbridge, Michael Saward, Nadia Urbinati, and Mark Warren.

5. It is quite common to attribute this standard account to Hanna F. Pitkin's seminal book *The Concept of Representation*. But, as several analysts have noted, there is more to Pitkin's work than that. See Castiglione 2012; Disch 2011.

6. Nadia Urbinati depicts this dynamic relationship by means of two core notions, advocacy and representativity. By advocacy is meant "the representative's 'passionate' link to the electors' cause and the representative's autonomy of judgement." The relation "leave[s] room for autonomous activity on the part of both representatives and constituents while still ensuring some connection between their respective (autonomous yet interdependent) actions" (Urbinati 2008, 45). Representativity underlines "reflective adhesion (perspectival similarity) [and] is the most consistent expression of the dialogue between society and the state that democracy activates and requires" (51).

7. This is what Saward means when he distinguishes between object and referent: the former is the representative's social construction of those the representative claims to represent; the latter is the actual existing context, including the social norms and conventions. These set the boundary of what is socially and culturally acceptable and can be examined to establish which object depictions are likely to be accepted.

8. Saward (2008) shows how claim-making can be used to analyze different types of parties. The interesting point about the traditional mass party is that it is deeply socially rooted; hence we tend to take the claim-making activities for granted. That is far less the case with other forms of parties, such as the catchall and cartel parties and especially issue-specific parties that are less socially rooted and where the scope for performativity is much greater. Saward would therefore

not associate a given type of party with a given perspective of representation; instead he shows how partisan differences shape claim-making activity.

9. For the notion of appropriateness, see March and Olsen 1995.

10. Benjamin Moffitt (2016) underlines this active shaping role of contemporary populism, which (drawing on the work of Saward among others) Moffitt understands as a distinct political style.

11. A lower-level Norwegian court has unprecedentedly ruled that the policy of incarcerating children seeking asylum violates the European Convention on Human Rights article 3.

## References

Bachrach, Peter, and Morton S. Baratz. 1962. "Two Faces of Power." *American Political Science Review* 56, no. 4: 947–52.

Bryce, James. 1921. *Modern Democracies.* 2 vols. New York: Macmillan.

Castiglione, Dario. 2012. "Giving Pitkin Her Due: What the 'Representative Claim' Gets Right, and What It Risks Missing." *Contemporary Political Theory* 11, no. 1: 118–22.

Castiglione, Dario, and Mark Warren. 2006. "Rethinking Democratic Representation: Eight Theoretical Issues." Paper presented at "Rethinking Democratic Representation," Centre for the Study of Democratic Institutions, University of British Columbia, May 18–19, 2006.

Chambers, Simone. 2004. "Behind Closed Doors: Publicity, Secrecy, and the Quality of Deliberation," *Journal of Political Philosophy* 12, no. 4: 389–410.

Dalton, Russell J., and Steven J. Weldon. (2005) "Public Images of Political Parties: A Necessary Evil?" *West European Politics* 28, no. 5: 931–51.

Disch, Lisa. 2011. "Toward A Mobilization Conception of Representation," *American Political Science Review* 105, no. 1: 100–114.

Eriksen, Erik O., ed. 2005. *Making the European Polity — Reflexive Integration in Europe.* London: Routledge.

Eriksen, Erik O., and John E. Fossum, eds. 2015. *The European Union's Nonmembers: Independence Under Hegemony?* London: Routledge.

Fossum, John E. 2010. "Norway's European 'Gag Rules.'" *European Review* 18, no. 1: 73–92.

Hirschman, Albert O. 1970. *Exit, Voice, Loyalty.* Cambridge, MA: Harvard University Press.

Holmes, Steven. 1995. *Passions and Constraint.* Chicago: University of Chicago Press.

Katz, Richard, and Peter Mair. 1995. "Changing Models of Party Organization and Party Democracy—The Emergence of the Cartel Party." *Party Politics* 1, no. 1: 5–28.

Lijphart, Arend. 1977. *Democracy in Plural Societies: A Comparative Exploration.* New Haven, CT: Yale University Press.

Lipset, Seymour M., and Stein Rokkan. 1967. *Party Systems and Voter Alignments: Cross-National Perspectives*. New York: Free Press.

Mair, Peter. 2014. *On Parties, Party Systems and Democracy—Selected Writings of Peter Mair*. Colchester: ECPR Press.

March, James G., and Johan P. Olsen. 1995. *Democratic Governance*. New York: Free Press.

Moffitt, Benjamin. 2016. *The Global Rise of Populism: Performance, Political Style and Representation*. Stanford, CA: Stanford University Press.

Muirhead, Russell. 2014. *The Promise of Party in a Polarized Age*. Cambridge, MA: Harvard University Press.

Müller, Jan W. 2016. *What Is Populism?* Pittsburgh: University of Pennsylvania Press.

Norway. 2012. *Outside and Inside: Norway's Agreements with the European Union*. Official Norwegian Report NOU 2012:2. Delivered to the Norwegian Ministry of Foreign Affairs, January 17, 2012.

Pitkin, Hanna F. 1967. *The Concept of Representation*. Berkeley: University of California Press.

Rokkan, Stein. 1975. "Dimensions of State Formation and Nation Building: A Possible Paradigm for Research on Variations within Europe." In *The Formation of National States in Western Europe*, edited by Charles Tilly, 562–600. Princeton, NJ: Princeton University Press.

Rosenblum, Nancy. 2008. *On the Side of the Angels: An Appreciation of Parties and Partisanship*. Princeton, NJ: Princeton University Press.

Sartori, Giovanni. 2005. *Parties and Party Systems: A Framework for Analysis*. Colchester: ECPR Press.

Saward, Michael. 2006. "The Representative Claim." *Contemporary Political Theory* 5, no. 3: 297–318.

———. 2008. "Making Representations: Modes and Strategies of Political Parties," *European Review* 16, no. 3: 271–86.

———. 2010. *The Representative Claim*. Oxford: Oxford University Press, 2010.

Schattschneider, Elmer E. (1942) 2009. *Party Government*. New Brunswick, NJ: Transaction.

Schlesinger, Joseph A. 1991. *Political Parties and the Winning of Office*. Ann Arbor: University of Michigan Press.

Schmidt, Vivien A. 2013. "Democracy and Legitimacy in the European Union Revisited: Input, Output and 'Throughput.'" *Political Studies* 61, no. 1: 2–22.

Selznick, Philip. 1957. *Leadership in Administration: A Sociological Interpretation*. Evanston IL: Row, Peterson.

Strøm, Kåre. 1990. "A Behavioral Theory of Competitive Political Parties." *American Journal of Political Science* 34, no. 2: 565–98.

Tranter, Bruce, and Mark Western. 2009. "The Influence of Green Parties on Postmaterialist Values." *British Journal of Sociology* 60, no. 1: 145–67.

Urbinati, Nadia. 2006. *Representative Democracy: Principles and Genealogy*. Chicago: University of Chicago Press.

Urbinati, Nadia, and Mark Warren. 2008. "The Concept of Representation in Contemporary Democratic Theory." *Annual Review of Political Science* 11: 387–412.

Valen, Henry. 1999. "EU-saken post festum." In *Velgere i 90-årene*, edited by Bernt Aardal, Hanne Marte Narud, and Frode Berglund, 106–19. Oslo: NKS Forlaget.

White, Jonathan, and Lea Ypi. 2010. "Rethinking the Modern Prince: Partisanship and the Democratic Ethos." *Political Studies* 58: 809–28.

———. 2011. "On Partisan Political Justification." *American Political Science Review* 105, no. 2: 381–96.

———. 2016. *The Meaning of Partisanship*. Oxford: Oxford University Press.

CHAPTER FIVE

# Populist Twist

*The Relationship between the Leader and the
People in Populism*

Paula Diehl

This chapter examines the shift of political representation occurring in populism. Populism establishes a very particular relationship between leaders and followers, twisting democratic representation. For this reason, turning attention to the relationship between populist leaders as representatives or "claim makers" (Saward 2006) and their followers can help clarify many ambiguities of both populism and democracy.

Even if scholars' definitions of populism often diverge,[1] the majority agree on the centrality of the relationship between the leader and the people. According to Yves Mény and Yves Surel (2000), populist movements have one common feature: the fundamental importance of the leader (104). Whether one accepts that populist movements can arise without a leader, as Paul Taggart (2000, 5–6) asserts, or that populism is a "mode of articulation" and discourse, as Ernesto Laclau (2005b, 34) claims, a look at populist phenomena since the beginning of the twentieth century makes it impossible to deny the role of leaders as catalysts for mobilization. This seems to be one of the most important differences between nineteenth- and twentieth-century populism.[2] Scholars interested in understanding the mechanisms of political mobilization are particularly attentive to the role of charismatic leadership in populism. Although populism is based on a mobilized popular sector, a populist movement is not autonomously organized (Di Tella 1997, 196). The adjective *popular* describes the self-articulation of the people as a political actor. In contrast, the word *populism* focuses on the shift from self-articulation to the exploitation of people's political passions (Lits 2009).[3] In light of this distinction, movements like los indignados in Spain or occupy in the United States cannot be classified as populist; instead, they should be called popular since they are self-organized.

In order to remain cohesive, most populist movements require a charismatic leader who is "able to establish a personalized link between him and the led" (Di Tella 1997, 196). Recently, populist leaders have become increasingly important as they are effectively "able to exploit existing social conditions of anxiety and availability" (Pasquino 2008, 27). Alternatively, if the same social conditions exist, but there is no populist leader able to capitalize on the situation, no populist movement occurs. I argue that the relationship between the leader and the people is a key element in understanding the effects of populism on democracy and, more importantly, that this relationship causes a twist in democratic representation.[4] Many scholars have studied the role of leaders in populism (Akkerman, Mudde, and Zaslove 2014; de la Torre 2013; Jansen 2011), but surprisingly the mechanisms responsible for twisting the relationship between leaders and the people have been ignored. In what follows, I examine these mechanisms and their consequences for democracy.

This chapter investigates how populist leaders deal with the tension between verticality and horizontality within democratic representation and how these leaders relate to the democratic notion of equality between representatives and their constituencies while simultaneously advancing their own claims to guide the people. This brings one salient feature of democracy into focus: the balance between accountability and authorization in democratic representation. In a representative democracy, representatives must maintain this balance to (a) decide what is best for their constituents and (b) inform constituents of their activities and allow them to supervise what the representatives do. If authorization is a necessary component of representation, then holding representatives accountable to their constituents is the core element that makes representation work in a democratic manner (Pitkin 1972, chs. 2 and 3; Urbinati and Warren 2008). There is an intrinsic tension between authorization and accountability. This tension is an essential condition for democratic representation, in which accountability and authorization are both mutually complementary and competitive features. As such, democratic representatives must establish a balance between the two.

Populism uses a very sophisticated method to cope with this tension. The relationship between the populist leader and the people is characterized by a twist that proceeds in two nearly concurrent steps. First, populist leaders radicalize the tension between verticality and horizontality by demanding more popular power (horizontality) and simultaneously promoting strong leadership (verticality). Second, populist leaders emphasize the ostensible similarity between the leader and the people, thus legitimizing unquestioned trust in the leader and obscuring any tension within the relationship. Following the populist logic, if leaders and followers share a mimetic relationship, and the people trust the leader without question, why must the people exercise their right to sanction bad behavior or demand transparency and accountability? Upon examination, it is not difficult to find that in populism democratic accountability has been suppressed but not eliminated. As I argue, this twist has consequences for democratic representation and can threaten democracy. If populist leaders overemphasize the verticality of their relationship to the people, authorization is reinforced and accountability eclipsed. This dynamic can provide the ideal conditions for the emergence of authoritarian or totalitarian power.

I begin by defining the concepts of *populism* and *leadership*, pointing out the ambivalences within populism concerning democratic representation. Hanna Pitkin's work on the concept of representation is the starting point for my observations about how populism negotiates authorization and accountability. Since authorization and accountability contribute to making representative democracy work, they are connected to the tension between verticality and horizontality implicit in the democratic relationship between representatives and constituents. By exploring the populist structure, I analyze three important features responsible for these mechanisms: (1) the populist construction of "the people" as a unity, (2) the apparently unmediated relationship between the leader and the people, and (3) the anti-elite attitude found in populism. These features are closely connected to the populist narrative of the people's betrayal by the elites and by the political establishment. Analyzing these features will help evaluate the populist twist and elucidate how it changes democratic representation. The chapter concludes by discussing possible negative effects of populism on democracy.

## Defining Concepts

Since there are multiple definitions of the term *populism*, it is necessary first to specify the definition used in this article. It is true that populism is a phenomenon of the Right *and* of the Left and that centrist politicians and parties in recent years have increasingly relied on populist strategies. One can indeed agree with the idea of populism being a "thin ideology," a sort of mediating structure for other "more consistent" ideologies that appeal to the idea of popular sovereignty (Canovan 2002, 30–31; Mudde 2004, 554). In this regard, there are good reasons to think that populism is also a "form," a logic, or a political structure of actions, discourses, and symbols that influences political content but is sufficiently flexible to encompass strongly divergent ideologies (Diehl 2011).

## Populism as a Multilevel Concept

In a previous study, I observed that "especially in empirical research, scholars operate with varied criteria, privileging different dimensions of the phenomenon" (Diehl 2011, 273). This leads them to very different conclusions, sometimes even regarding the same case. The analysis of Silvio Berlusconi's populism is a typical example of these misunderstandings. From the political-communication point of view, Berlusconi is a prototype of a populist leader. But looking at Berlusconi from the ideological perspective makes it more difficult to categorize him as populist, since he does not emphasize popular sovereignty. The reason for this discrepancy in observations is that scholars analyze different dimensions of political practice. In light of this problem, I have proposed a complex concept of populism that takes the different dimensions of political practice into account.

I define populism as a specific kind of political practice that is observable in different dimensions, such as the communicative, ideological, or organizational (the social organization of a movement or party). The populist practice follows a specific structure but is never absolute since its intensity varies according to the political actor claiming to represent popular demands (Diehl 2011). As Ben Stanley (2008) points out, certain parties and movements—and I will add political leaders—"can be 'more populist' than others" (108). From this perspective, populism has a specific structure that may be more or less prominent depending on the case.

I proceed by building an ideal type definition of three dimensions of the populist structure that combines elements described by different authors in the field. Following Max Weber, I do not expect to have a definition that fits perfectly with reality. Instead my ideal type definition should set criteria for analyzing and comparing phenomena from the point of view of the populist structure in a multidimensional analysis. Having said that, I do not pretend to give an exhaustive explanation of the definition of populism, as I have in an earlier article. Here I provide the reader with brief descriptions of the three dimensions of the conception of populism I have adopted.

## Ideological Dimension of Populism

A good point of departure for defining the ideological dimension of populism has been provided by Cas Mudde. According to Mudde (2004), populism is "a thin-centred ideology that considers society to be ultimately separated into two homogeneous and antagonistic groups, 'the pure people' versus 'the corrupt elite,' and which argues that politics should be an expression of the *volonté générale* (general will) of the people" (543).[5] The first feature of this conception of populism is the belief that political power belongs to the people. This connects populism to democracy. Yet, the people in populism are not only the unique source of political legitimacy; they are also idealized and conceived of as a unity (Canovan 1999, 3–5; Taggart 2000, 92–97). Populism fuels anti-elite resentments, and it builds a dichotomy between friends (the people and the leader) and foes (corrupt elites and established representatives). Populism constructs a privileged and intimate relationship between the people and the leader, one that avoids institutional mediation (Taggart 2000, 98).[6] In populism, elites are usually portrayed as corrupt, incompetent, and disconnected from the everyday lives of ordinary people (Mudde 2004, 543). In populist ideology the leader is central, believed to be the voice of the people and the expression of their will. Together with the people, the leader constitutes a common block (Laclau 2005a) against elites and established political parties, who are accused of abusing the trust of the people.

## Communicative Dimension of Populism

On the communication level, populism is expressed by multiple features (Diehl 2011, 282–87). An extensive list cannot be given here; instead I present the core features necessary for the understanding of the populist twist: Particularly noticeable are the strong invocation of the people, the appeal to common sense, and words suggesting collectivity and dichotomy: "We" against "the others." As Martin Reisigl (2002) has pointed out, populist discourse generates a vertical perspective from the bottom (people) to the top (elite). Populist rhetoric is characterized by short and simple sentences, oversimplifications of both arguments and their contexts, and by

Manichaeism, antagonism, dramatization, and strong emotional appeals. Taboo-breaking and scandal are equally important here. Concerning the populist leader, two features play a crucial role: a strongly personalized presence and body performances and verbal language that stress a similarity between leader and led (Diehl 2017). This feature is the object of analysis in the further sections.

### Organizational Dimension of Populism

As Peter Mair (2002, 89) stresses, populism develops an organizational form that does not depend on a party or a strong institution. Indeed, when the populist structure manifests itself in the organizational dimension of the political practice, political actors tend to reject institutional mediation by privileging the direct mobilization of their followers (and plebiscitary decision-making) instead of deliberative and more participative mechanisms. From the organizational point of view, leaders build hierarchical and direct relationships with followers (Diehl 2011, 287–89).

### The Gradual Concept of Populism

Populist structure may be more or less pronounced depending on the political actor who claims to represent a movement or a popular instance. Thus, populism is not a clear category but rather a phenomenon observable in varying degrees (Diehl 2011, 277).[7] This can explain the populism of mainstream parties (Mudde 2004, 542). In addition, the populist structure does not necessarily manifest itself in equal intensity with regard to the three dimensions described above. This is the reason Berlusconi's communication practice can be seen as populist: it is oversimplifying, dramatizing, personalizing, highly emotional, creating scandals and taboo-breaking. Berlusconi's body performance is based on similarity with his followers, as the "bandana" episode shows. During a visit from the British prime minister Tony Blair, Berlusconi wore a bandana, a head covering very common in popular milieus. Doing so, he emphasized his popular appeal and broke with diplomatic protocol. But the ideological aspects of Berlusconi's practices are less obviously populist. Berlusconi built a direct relationship with his followers and intensified his role in speaking for them, but he never suggested that the power should be returned to the people. He promoted certain anti-elite resentments, which were not directed at the country's economic elite but rather at its educated people and intellectuals.

The enemy was constructed as the communists and politicians of the left (including established parties) rather than the professional political elite as a whole. The example of Berlusconi shows that, depending on the case, the populist structure can manifest itself with varying intensity across the three dimensions of political practice.

While this explanation cannot answer every question about how the populist structure operates, my general definition should provide a framework capable of advancing my analysis of the populist twist. Many of the features mentioned above play a crucial role in the populist twist of democratic representation and will be an object of analysis later in the chapter.

## Leadership

The second fuzzy concept is leadership. Since leadership can be described in very different ways, this chapter relies on a minimal definition given by Orazio M. Petracca. According to Petracca (1983), leaders are those who (a) act within a group, (b) hold a position of power that gives them significant influence over strategic decisions within the group, and (c) actively exercise power. Moreover, leadership is not unilateral; instead, it requires the action of followers. Leadership is thus also (d) connected to the expectations of the group that confers legitimacy on the leader, making the relationship between the leader and the led crucial. In addition, Petracca distinguished three types of leaders according to their types of relationship with their followers. In the first case, leaders are "seducers of the masses" (*trascinatori della folla*) and are able to impose themselves on the masses. In the second, leaders claim to be interpreters of the masses and are able to understand and give shape to the masses' vague wishes. The last type of leaders are representatives of the masses who express only widely accepted opinions and widely shared sentiments. In reality these ideal type categories often mix, and leaders may move between all three forms. This minimal definition has two advantages: on the one hand, it stresses the dimensions of authority and verticality present in Max Weber's definition of leadership; on the other, it is applicable to different types of leadership. This minimal definition should help us to analyze the relationship between the populist leader and the people.[8]

## Populism and Democracy

The relationship between populism and democracy is quite complex. Like democracy, populism invokes the principles of popular sovereignty and equality. It demands an increase of popular power, and it denounces the government's lack of accountability to citizens, the elites' alienation from the people, and the politicians' failure to represent the people and their interests. According to the populist structure, the people are the sole legitimate sovereign, and politics must be the expression of the popular will. This explains why populism can be located within democracy (Mény and Surel 2000; Canovan 1999; Laclau 2005a; Mudde and Rovira Kaltwasser 2012). Both left-wing populist leaders such as deceased Venezuelan president Hugo Chávez (United Socialist Party of Venezuela, PsUv) and right-wing populists like Heinz-Christian Strache (Freedom Party of Austria, FPÖ) take up democratic discourses.[9] For populists, the established political class and the elites are illegitimate because their actions do not correspond to the interests of the people. Hence, they cannot be recognized as "real" representatives of the people. Consequently, populists insist on putting the principle of popular power into practice. In that sense, they do more than postulate popular sovereignty (Canovan 2005, 30); they further reinforce its importance.

From this perspective, populism can operate as a corrective to democracy by claiming the unrealized promise of popular power. Benjamin Arditi (2005) offers a useful metaphor to illustrate this situation. According to Arditi, populism behaves like a drunken guest at a dinner party: "He is bound to disrupt table manners and the tacit rules of sociability by speaking loudly, interrupting the conversations of others, and perhaps flirting with the wives of other guests" (90). Populism breaks taboos, disrupts established rules of communication, and states unpleasant truths that, up to that point, had been successfully avoided. Calling attention to these suppressed truths may help shake things up within representative democracy and facilitate popular questioning of power (Mény and Surel 2000, 38–40). Therefore, populism carries the potential to mobilize citizens and to foster a critique of established procedures that can have a positive impact on democracy.

Nevertheless, populism's relationship to democracy is ambivalent and bears several risks. The most important factors of these risks are the specific populist relationship between leader and people and the way populist leaders deal with the tension between verticality and horizontality within democratic representation.

## The Tension between Horizontality and Verticality

The tension between horizontality and verticality is not only a characteristic of populism. It also marks, though less intensely, the relationship between representatives and constituents in representative democracies. Representatives[10] must behave according to the democratic idea of political equality between the members of society (Urbinati and Warren 2008). Since they are also citizens, they are in principle equal to their constituents. This sets up a horizontal relationship between all citizens, including representatives themselves. But if constituents and representatives have a horizontal relationship in principle, this is counterbalanced by the mechanism of authorization. As Bernard Manin (1997) points out, there is a "vertical relationship between the governed and the government" (170) since representation always involves authorization. Constituents authorize their representatives to make decisions and act in their place. They transfer their power to their representatives. Representative democracy implies a division of labor[11] that necessarily shifts decision-making power to the representatives and that hence constitutes a vertical relationship between those who represent and those who are to be represented. In modern democracies, the free mandate allows representatives to make decisions according to their own conscience, even if they are doing it in place of their constituents. This necessarily reinforces the verticality of democratic representation relationships in contrast with the horizontal principle of equality.

It is now easy to recognize the tension between vertical decision-making and horizontal equality inherent in democratic representation. Democratic representatives have to manage this tension effectively: they must act in accordance with the principle of equality, but they also must be able to make decisions in the name of those whom they represent.

## Authorization and Accountability and the Tensions of Democratic Representation

Hanna Pitkin recognizes two crucial conditions for political representation in modern democracy: authorization and accountability. Authorization is a necessary formal condition that precedes the act of representation and enables representatives to act in place of their constituents (Pitkin 1972, ch. 3). Authorization occurs in the trust that representatives will not only act on their constituents' behalf but also make decisions according to their constituents' interest. In order to be democratic, however, authorization also needs to be limited. If representatives have the right to act in the place of their constituents but have no obligation to them, the Hobbesian problem can easily occur: representation becomes "a kind of 'black box' shaped by the initial giving of authority, within which the representative can do whatever he pleases" (Pitkin 1972, 39). This kind of representation is incompatible with democracy where sovereignty is located in the demos. In order to reduce this risk, representatives must be held accountable to their constituents.

Pitkin relies on accountability to better delineate the limits of representatives' power in democracy. Representatives' acts should be overseen and checked by those who authorized them to act on their behalf. Pitkin clearly both defines accountability as a postrepresentation mechanism and classifies it as a formal representation feature. However, on closer inspection, one can identify several different mechanisms operating within accountability. Representatives must inform the constituency directly or indirectly of their acts; they must justify their decisions, and they are the object of sanctions if they do not behave as they should (Schedler 1999; Borowiak 2011). There are also many opportunities for constituents to influence representatives' behavior since the former can demand their representatives provide information and justification for their acts during the political process itself. Even if sanctions can only operate after an act of representation, well-informed and active citizens are able to affect representatives' behavior. Conceptualizing accountability as a relationship, Guillermo O'Donnell (1994) distinguishes between two types of accountability: The first type occurs when constituents can hold their representatives accountable. It presupposes a hierarchical difference between governed and governors that leads O'Donnell to call it "vertical." This is especially the case with elections. Since there is no mediation in this case, I would call it *direct accountability*. The second type describes the relationship between equals ("horizontal accountability"), where accountability "runs ... across a network of relatively autonomous powers (i.e., institutions)" (O'Donnell 1994, 61). From the popular sovereignty perspective, the second type is a *mediated accountability*. Using the terms *direct* and *mediated* to describe accountability will help provide clarity concerning the relationship between the leader and the people.

Both authorization and representation are essential aspects of representative democracy and engender an intrinsic and fundamental tension within the representational relationship. "Representation entails accountability: somehow representatives are held responsible for their actions by those they claim to be entitled to speak for" (O'Donnell 1994, 61). Democratic representatives and especially holders of executive offices have been authorized by the people and are thus in a vertical position over their constituents, but representatives are at the same time equal in principle to other citizens and are accountable to their constituents. One consequence of this tension is that in representative democracies (as opposed to authoritarian regimes), leadership is embedded in judicial and political institutional mechanisms of control. The power of leaders is also limited by political parties, the "classic government-opposition dynamics," which vary depending on the type of political system, public opinion, and political culture (Helms 2012, 10). Democratic institutions make political leadership possible while simultaneously helping to limit the scope of this leadership and reducing the tension within democratic representation. In practice, democratic representation involves actions enabling representatives to both make decisions in the name of constituents and remain accountable to citizens. Transparency of decision-making, liability of the government vis-à-vis the governed, mechanisms for citizens to monitor their governors, and political messaging that makes clear that representatives are committed to citizens' interests are vital features of accountability.

Political accountability is central to preventing and redressing abuses of power, but it does not eliminate power. There are two important dimensions of accountability that influence political practice: answerability (impelling representatives "to inform about and to explain what they are doing") and enforcement (for instance, "the use of sanctions" in cases of bad behavior) (Schedler 1999, 14–16). While answerability demands information and justification regarding representatives' acts, enforcement enables constituents to "eventually punish" representatives in case of improper conduct. Transparency, obligation to justifying acts, and sanction are crucial for holding representatives accountable. These elements become instruments of democratic representation when they are connected to the demos. Democratic accountability presupposes first that the people are the source of sovereignty; second, that the constituents should exert control over their representatives; and, third, that formal governmental institutions are central for realizing democratic accountability. Institutionalized mechanisms of monitoring and sanction are instruments to render representatives accountable and limit authorization, thus balancing the verticality and horizontality inherent in democratic representation (Schedler 1999, 16).

## Twisting Representation

Populist leaders deal with these constraints by twisting democratic representation. First, the populist twist invokes people's powerlessness in the face of bad representation by established politicians, parties, and elites. Like the drunken guest at the dinner party, populism reveals the shortcomings of popular power, including the lack of accountability. Populist leaders promise their followers that this situation can be changed and that power can be given to the people. In doing so, they stress popular sovereignty and build a horizontal relationship with the people, demanding more accountability from established politicians and parties. But populist leaders simultaneously insist on their own leadership role and stress the verticality of their relationship to the people; the populist leader is a "political figure who seeks to be at the same time one of the people and their leader" (Panizza 2005, 22). In doing so, they neglect their original demand for greater popular power and democratic accountability. It is easy to identify the first radicalization of the tension between the horizontality implicit in the principle of equality and the idea of popular belonging on the one hand and the verticality inherent to the appeal for strong leadership on the other. The twist here consists in the rapid eclipse of this tension, which is possible only because populist leaders present themselves as "one of the people." Similarity between leader and people is used to legitimate the leader's power and establish personal trust in the leader, suggesting that he or she can act without being bound by any procedure, institution, group, or person. Since the leader is "one of us," according to populist logic, he or she is the only one who can speak as the voice of the people.

During a television interview in 1973, Juan Domigo Perón gave the most concise explanation of the populist concept of leadership: "To lead is not to command. To command is to force. To lead is to persuade." For Perón, the leader should foster, conceptualize, and ultimately enact the will of the people. "The political leader is the one who does what the people want."[12] Describing populist leadership in this way, Perón stresses the horizontality between leader and people. But by parsing more carefully his description of the leader's role, one can identify a problem for democracy under populist leadership: the current will of the people should not simply be expressed by the populist leader; instead, the leader should be able to persuade, "foster" and "promote" (*promover*), "conceive" (*concebir*), and "launch" (*lanzar*) the people's will. In doing so, the leader becomes more than the voice of the people; the leader shapes and defines the people's will. In the same interview, Perón also gives advice to young politicians, insisting that the best method for getting one's way is not to impose it on others but to make others think that one's preferred course of action is their own independent decision. This is no more than manipulation used to make the leader's decisions appear legitimate.

Certainly, political debate is always affected by rhetoric and manipulation. Though populism is also characterized by manipulation and rhetoric, it cannot be reduced to them. In order to analyze the populist twist more effectively, we return to the structure of populism and look deeper at the three features mentioned above: (1) the idealization of the people as a homogeneous unity, (2) their apparently direct and unmediated relationship to the leader, and (3) the anti-institutional and anti-elite attitudes of populism. These features are embedded in the narrative of the "betrayal of the people" used by populist movements (Taggart 2000, 28). In containing artifices that simultaneously exacerbate and sidestep the tension between verticality and horizontality, they enable the populist twist.

## The Populist Construction of the People

Populism is people-centered. Populist leaders claim to represent the people and to realize popular self-determination. To this end, they construct an image of the people as a political subject—a process that is also necessary for democracy but done here in a very specific way. The people of populism are idealized as harmonious and upright; they are presented as the source of society's morality and virtuousness, "the good common people," and the basis of the community (Kazin 1995, 3; Panizza 2005, 27; Mény and Surel 2000, 181–85). Populists imagine the people as belonging to an idealized and highly emotional place (the "heartland"). Paul Taggart defines this place as "embodying the positive aspects of everyday life. . . . Heartlands owe their power to the heart, to the evocation of sentiments that may not be necessarily either rationalized or rationalizable" (Taggart 2000, 95). In order to construct the people as a unity, populists ignore any particularity or diversity in society. Their vision of the people is monolithic and "identified with the majority" (Canovan 2002, 37; Müller 2014). Because of this idealization, the people are held up as the moral source of legitimacy.

There are two serious political implications for democratic representation here. Populist idealization first denies the heterogeneity of civil society and second blurs two different concepts of the people: the people as an ideal of democracy (*peuple idéel*) and the people as a social reality (*fait social*), the sum of all citizens, who manifest themselves in majority preferences. Pierre Rosanvallon calls attention to the fundamental and constitutive difference between the ideal and the social dimension of the people in democracy and demonstrates that the two cannot be reconciled. Furthermore, he claims that this difference is fundamental to democracy since it constitutes two dimensions of the people as a political subject: the first is necessary to maintain the idea of popular sovereignty; the second is crucial for political practice and manifests itself especially in elections (Rosanvallon 2000 and 2006).[13] If the *volonté générale* resides with the ideal people, the sociological people always express the instantaneous *volonté de tous*. The equation of these two dimensions of the people dissolves the distinction between general will and the will of the majority. This is precisely what populism does. It presents the will of the majority as identical to the general will and ignores plurality within the society.

Populist discourse draws on a permanent outward demarcation of the popular identity ("we") vis-à-vis those who are not the people, typically society's elites and, in the case of right-wing populism, also foreigners and other minorities. Even if the definition of the people itself remains formally open (Laclau 2005a, 96; Panizza 2005, 16), the demarcation of its enemies allows for the concealment (*Verdrängung*, see Freud 1922) of all cultural, religious, ethnic, gender, class, or political identities and interests within the group. Populist leaders claim to represent the people descriptively as an idealized majority (Mény and Surel 2000, 76–80), but in so doing they presuppose a picture of a homogeneous society. This can be a threat to democratic representation: if heterogeneity in a plural society is banished in favor of a homogenous vision of unity, society can turn antidemocratic.

The construction of the people as an idealized unity and the equation of the general will with the will of the majority constitute further conditions for a radicalization of the tension between the verticality implicit in leadership and the horizontality inherent to equality.

## The Apparently Unmediated Relationship to the Leader

Once the people's identity is constructed, a crucial question emerges: how do the people come to know their will? Precisely at this point, one important populist artifice creeps in. Following the populist narrative, even though the people allegedly know the truth, they are unable to articulate their will properly. They need a voice to speak as one, and they borrow it from the leader. This requires a direct and unmediated relationship with the leader. Yet populist leaders do not simply give a voice to the people. As Perón argues, it is the duty of the leader to serve as the voice of the people, but he sees the leader as a "shaper" of the popular will, which he is entrusted to defend. Now it is clear that populist leaders do not perceive themselves merely as a medium for expressing the popular will; they rather claim to be the ones who decide what the people want in the first place. Despite the horizontal rhetoric of popular power, populist leaders pursue a strongly vertical relationship with their followers. The twist movement consists here in presenting the leader's formation of the popular will as a simple practice of popular expression, thereby eclipsing procedures of direct accountability.

The leader of the Italian Movimento 5 Stelle (Five Star Movement), Beppe Grillo, provides us with a very good example of this twist. He defines his role as follows: "Folks, it works like this: You let me know, and I play the amplifier" (Vignati 2013, 43). But, in practice, Grillo is a very centralist and vertical decision-maker who uses his power to expel members of the Five Star Movement when they express disagreement with the leader.[14] In reality, he is not the amplifier for the will of the people but rather controls his followers by establishing a centralistic and authoritarian power structure within the movement. With good reason, the participants of the Five Star Movement call themselves *grillini* (the followers of Grillo). Even if populist movements are not so strongly controlled by the leader as the Five Star Movement, a clear centralistic tendency in populism can become authoritarian or even totalitarian.[15]

### The Anti-Elite and Anti-Institutional Attitudes of Populism

The apparently unmediated relationship with the leader is closely linked to the next element of the populist structure: the anti-elite and anti-institutional attitude. Established parties and politicians are equated or associated with the elite, which populist rhetoric reproaches for ignoring the people and, even worse, avoiding them. From the populist perspective, political institutions are the elite's instruments to impede the people from using their own power. This makes established institutions incapable of legitimately representing the people. "Populists always attack the power elite of politicians and bureaucrats for their privileges, their corruption, and their lack of accountability to the people" (Canovan 2002, 32). In doing so, they reject the mediated accountability provided by institutions and procedures while simultaneously demanding more direct answerability.

In their critique of the establishment, populists generally reinforce popular power (Mény and Surel 2000, 74). Venezuela's former president Hugo Chávez used to accuse capitalists of corrupting the representative system and dominating the economy and politics. In doing so, he advocated for returning power to the people. The leader of the Freedom Party of Austria (FPÖ) Heinz-Christian Strache also presents himself as handing power back to the people. His May 1, 2012, speech started with the slogan "Dem Volk sein Recht!" (Give the people their right!). With this pronouncement, Strache claimed to denounce the "arrogance of those in power" and the political class who would "govern against the interests of the population." For Strache, established parties, "the red and black bunch of slobs," are "self-enriching stooges of the economic and European elites."[16]

The anti-elite and anti-institutional attitude of populism has further consequences for the relationship between the leader and the people. First, leadership becomes completely decoupled from the elite, which can indeed be interpreted as an increase in popular power and underlines the horizontality of the people-leader relationship. Second, populist discourse constructs an antagonism between the people and the elite. In doing so, it divides society in two camps: on one side the elite and the consolidated power structure and on the other the block constituted by the populist leader and the people.[17] Following this logic, the leader claims to be an outsider or a maverick (Barr 2009). This putatively guarantees his or her incorruptibility.

This brings us back to the people's apparently unmediated relationship with the leader. Populist leaders do not trust the establishment; they prefer direct contact with the people. Institutionally, the presentation of the leader as part of the people implies the rejection of any mediation between them (Taggart 2000, 71–79). This is why populists nourish an anti-institutional attitude (Taggart 2000, 96–98; Pasquino 2008, 28). In that sense, one could presume an increase in popular power and an emphasis on the equality between the leader and the people. But here, then, the populist twist operates behind the demand for more popular power: in rejecting institutions, populists also reject mediated accountability, which is an important instrument to delimit the power of the leader (O'Donnell 1994, 61). And, by opting for acclamation, populism circumvents deliberation (Urbinati 1998, 119). Populists are not interested in participation *per se*; they rather privilege pseudoparticipation while mobilizing their followers.

As long as the demand for popular participation in political organization and decision-making prevails, populism can have revitalizing effects on democracy. But, as soon as populist leaders present acclamatory and pseudoparticipative behavior as evidence of participation, democratic representation can be distorted or even destroyed. The more deliberation and accountability disappear, the greater the verticality of the relationship between people and leader.

## The Narrative of the Betrayal of the People

The features described above twist the democratic relationship between the people and the leader. But they would not be so powerful if they were not part of a persuasive explanatory narrative (Diehl 2011, 281). This is the story of the people betrayed by the elites and cheated by the established politicians (Tagguieff 2007, 28). In this story, the people constitute a "silent majority" (Taggart 2000, 93) that goes through a process of collective self-awareness, self-organization, and popular mobilization. Following the populist narrative, the people (in the singular) reclaims its own identity and, with the leader's help, is able to fight for the reconstitution of popular sovereignty. This narrative provides populism with a fairy-tale-like logical structure in which the hero is the charismatic politician who aims to liberate the people from the power of the elites. However, while the populist leader portrays him- or herself as emerging from the people, like all charismatic leaders he or she is surrounded by an aura of extraordinariness, which predestines the leader to lead the people on the path toward emancipation. Hugo Chávez's speeches provide an especially paradigmatic example of this mechanism. Drawing on Latin America's cultural background, Chávez ascribed the personal qualities of the continent's liberator Simon Bolívar to himself, identifying himself with the popular myth of Bolivar (Ellner 2012, 151). This allowed Chávez to construct his image as the new liberator of Latin America and strengthen an almost organic unity between himself and the people.

The narrative structure of populism enables three crucial mechanisms within the relationship between the leader and the people: (1) the people's identification with the leader, (2) the legitimation of leadership by presupposing similarity between the leader and the people, and (3) a strong emotional bond that provides unquestioned trust in the leader. These mechanisms are interconnected and twist the democratic relationship between the leader and the people.

## Identification with the Leader

In populism, the leader is an ideal figure for the projection of wishes. Indeed, as Laclau and Panizza have pointed out, the populist leader works as an "empty signifier" (Laclau 2005a, 161–62). When identifying with a leader, followers can project different meanings onto him or her. Two crucial levels of identification can be recognized in this process: the first is political. Followers recognize the populist leader as the people's voice, the one who confers their political identity by engaging them in the process of "naming" (Panizza 2005, 3)—that is the establishment of an "empty signifier" able to unify the heterogeneity of the people. At this point, the populist discourse establishes the enemies of the people and, consequently, the people itself.[18] The leader serves as the interpreter of the people's will (Arditi 2005, 82) and is the medium for establishing the people's identity as a single political subject. "If populism can be redefined as a process of naming that retroactively determines what is the name of 'the people,' the name that best fills the symbolic void through which identification takes place is that of the leader himself" (Panizza 2005, 19). Hence, leading the people subtly shifts to inventing the people.

Populist identification is more complicated than it initially appears, since the one who invents the people is, paradoxically, supposed to be one of the people. This supposition places the leader in a double perspective in the eyes of the people: populist leaders exist in both a vertical relation (as a leader) as well as a horizontal relation (as one of the people) with their followers. In order to prove that the leader is one of the people, he or she must establish and maintain a deep personal and emotional connection with them. This is symbolically well expressed by physical contact between the leader and the people. Even if most followers only watch such scenes on TV, pictures of the leader touching common citizens, eating their food, or appreciating their music are important for establishing this direct connection (Diehl 2011, 286; 2017). From the point of view of democratic representation, this kind of immediacy is deeply ambivalent. Although it is a sign of the leader's contact with the people, it performs representation without actually representing (Arditi 2005, 82–83).

The second level of identification with the leader is personal and more closely connected with what Sigmund Freud termed *Identifizierung*. For Freud (1922), identifying with something primarily means desiring to become like the object of identification. It happens when the "ego has enriched itself with the properties of the object" (76).[19] In that sense, the populist leader serves as an idealized object for the followers. Personal identification with the leader supplies his or her relationship to the people with sympathy and enables the followers to recognize themselves in the leader. When Chávez died in March 2013, a huge demonstration took place in Caracas. A reporter asked one of Chávez's followers why he supported his leader. The answer was quite clear: "Puede que no resuelva los problemas del país, puede que su gente se esté robando unos reales . . . pero él es como yo" (It could be that Chávez doesn't solve the country's problems, it could be that his people are stealing some of the money, but he is like me).[20] Here, identification provides the ground for political legitimation of the leader. The leader is presumed to be like the people.

There is a further populist twist here: the tension between "being one of the people" (horizontality) and "leading the people" (verticality) is eclipsed by identification with the leader; the distance between leader and followers is ignored, and, in its place, populist rhetoric suggests unity between the leader and the led. This represents a danger to democracy, since identification with the leader reduces the space for critique and accountability.

## Legitimation of Leadership through Similarity

Because identification is a necessary mechanism for populists to legitimize their leadership, it also renders acceptable the notion that their power is legitimate by virtue of their popular roots. Similarity operates on two levels of identification: political and personal. Politically, it legitimizes mirror representation and plays an important role in descriptive representation (Pitkin 1972) of minorities. Yet, when similarity is used to link the representative to the people as a whole and to convey the idea of popular power, the leader must at least appear to be "one of the people" in order to interpret and shape the people's will. "Populist leaders do not represent the people, rather they consider themselves—and succeed in being considered—an integral part of the people" (Pasquino 2008, 27).

In order to appear similar to the imagined people, populist leaders mimic the people: they dress down and show their preference for popular taste. Their choice of words is simple, and they often use colloquial language (Diehl 2011, 287; Diehl 2017). In the context of European right-wing populism, mimetic behavior is interpreted as folkish—both the former FPÖ chief Jörg Haider and the current chief Heinz-Christian Strache often wear traditional costumes to exhibit their closeness to the people (Diehl

2017). In the context of Latin American leftist populism, this closeness is illustrated by emphasizing the leader's proletarian origin with body language, mimicry, and clothes associated with the working class. Nonetheless, populists like Ollanta Humala (Gana—Peru) or Evo Morales (Movement for Socialism—Political Instrument for the Sovereignty of the Peoples, Bolivia) are known to mix class codes with ethnic elements of the native people of their respective countries.

Here, since an important element of accountability is missing, we shed light on another movement of the populist twist: justification. The leader doesn't have to justify his or her actions. His or her supposed similarity to the people suggests that they naturally share the same point of view and would thus make the same decisions.

### Emotional Bonds and Unquestioned Trust

Similarity and identification establish an emotional bond between the leader and the people and can promote unquestioned trust. Endowed with this trust, populist leaders are able to circumvent the tension between verticality and horizontality and suppress demands for accountability.

Chávez's speeches were always highly emotional and became more intense after his cancer diagnosis. At the peak of his last presidential campaign, in September 2012, Chávez invoked the possibility of his death. Thousands of supporters filled the streets of Caracas. Chávez described things he would do if he only could: travel his country, walk through the streets, feel the wind in his face, but he "couldn't at the moment," he said. At the end of his speech, he appealed to God to fulfill his dreams and to aide Venezuela on the path toward liberation. As often happened, the event ended with a popular song that Chávez joined in. The emotionality of this event peaked with the refrain of the song, "no voy a llorar" (I will not cry), which Chávez ended up doing.[21] Populist leaders transform the emotional tie between them and the people into trust.

Citizens' trust in institutions and official procedures is an important democratic resource. It enables the maintenance of the political order, fosters future cooperation, and provides political institutions with a long-term perspective. Office holders benefit from the public's trust in the democratic institutions they represent. If they squander this trust, they may damage the bond between the individual representative and the citizen without necessarily eroding the general loss of trust in the institution. On the other hand, trust in institutions bears on the qualities of the office holders (Petit

1998). Trust in representatives is important: it reduces the complexity of political life and makes politics possible (Luhmann 1979), but, if trust becomes something unquestioned, it destroys accountability. Paired with direct identification and the legitimation of power through similarity to the people, populist trust bears the risk that the representational tie turns into a "blank check" for the leader. "The followers of populist leaders put an exaggerated amount of faith in them and will often continue to believe that any and all improvements of their plight may only come from the action of a leader endowed with extraordinary qualities" (Pasquino 2008, 28). Here there is another populist twist. By transferring their cognitive power to the leader and not exercising their capacity to question his or her conduct, populist followers simply forget the initial reason they endorsed the populist leader: the demand for more popular power. In this case, verticality eclipses the horizontal dimension of the relationship between leader and people, even if it occurs only implicitly.

## The Totalitarian Risk

The populist twist happens through small but significant movements that shift the relationship between representative and constituents. It emerges when (1) the leader's shaping of the popular will is presented as a simple practice of popular expression, (2) deliberation and participation are circumvented while the followers are mobilized, (3) the power disparity and distance between the leader and the people are ignored while the leader's personal power is reinforced, 4) the people transfer their cognitive power to the leader and relinquish their capacity to question his or her acts. For the populist twist to occur, identification and the leader's legitimation through likeness and unquestioned trust are crucial. They make it possible for the leader to eclipse the will of the followers with his or her own will. The populist twist negates the tension between the verticality of leadership and the horizontality of equality while suppressing but not eliminating accountability.

The populist twist thus bears an important risk for democracy: by the steps described above, populist leaders lay the groundwork for an almost organic connection between the leader and the people. When political and personal identification are pushed to the extreme, the will of the leader replaces the will of the followers. This is the case in totalitarianism, where the tension between verticality and horizontality is extinguished, and it represents one of the most significant risks to democracy (Lefort 1986, ch. 9). If the leader becomes not only the object of identification but the subject of popular identity and of the popular will, populism can be the first step toward totalitarianism. In this case, the leader appears to be more than just one of the people; moreover, the people themselves want to become their leader. As Chávez supporters came together to mourn their leader after his death they carried posters with the slogan "Let's be like Chávez" (Seamos como Chávez). Descriptive representation was inverted: the people became the mirror of Chávez.

This corresponds to what Freud (1922) has called being in love. Being in love is different from simple identification and describes a situation in which the object of love (the leader) substitutes for the ego ideal. In this case, "the ego becomes more and more unassuming and modest, and the object more and more sublime and precious, until at last it gets possession of the entire self-love of the ego. . . . The object, has, so to speak, consumed the ego" (74–75). The wishes and desires of the subject transform into the desires of the object of love. Politically, this makes it possible for the leader to replace the will of the followers with his or her own. If being in love becomes the predominant emotional bond to the leader, the risk of totalitarianism emerges. Should identification turn completely into being in love, the line between the leader and the people is blurred, and representation is converted into embodiment.[22] In other words, representation becomes a state of pure authorization with no accountability. The basic tension between verticality and horizontality is extinguished, and populism had paved the way for totalitarianism.

## Conclusion

Even though the risk of totalitarianism remains, populism is distinctive. If totalitarianism opposes democracy, populism is much more ambivalent. Contrary to totalitarianism, populism functions within fundamental democratic values, namely the principles of popular sovereignty, equality, and the idea that the people should participate in decision-making processes and have the right to question and monitor their representatives. In totalitarianism, democratic horizontality between the leader and the people is eliminated. Accountability is effaced to empower the leader, and so no tension remains between verticality and horizontality, authorization and accountability, leadership and equality.

The problem populism poses for democracy is that leaders usually fall back on rhetoric that simultaneously radicalizes and negates the democratic tension, creating a twist in their representational relationship with their followers. The tension between verticality and horizontality apparently disappears since the leader's will is presented as the people's will, which remains suppressed but is not eliminated, as it is in totalitarianism. Another central distinction between populist and totalitarian leaders remains salient: populist leaders still insist on the idea that the people—and not the leader—are the actual sovereign.

The twisting mechanisms described here show the potential for populism to damage democratic representation. However, as mentioned before, populism is a gradual phenomenon and does not necessarily affect all dimensions of political practice equally. In addition, its relationship to democracy is ambivalent. For these reasons, populism can indeed be a revitalizing force for democracy. This is the case as long as the demand for popular participation in political organization and decision-making is put forward and the emotional bond to the leader helps to articulate social demands and reinforce popular sovereignty. But, if identification with the leader flowers into the state that Freud describes as being in love, the possibility for totalitarian power opens. Democracy is endangered if personal identification, legitimacy by likeness, and unquestioned trust entirely displace accountability. In this case, the representational tie degenerates into mere authorization, accountability disappears, and the road is paved for totalitarian leadership.

## Notes

1. Some examples of different approaches include populism as ideology (Mudde 2004), as political style (Taguieff 2007), as discourse (Laclau 2005b), and as a form of political contestation (Mény and Surel 2000; Canovan 1999).

2. My thanks to the anonymous reviewer who emphasized this aspect.

3. In his early works Ernesto Laclau (1997, 178–80) seems to approach this position and distinguishes two types of populism: the populism of the dominant classes and the populism of the dominated class.

4. It is important to underline the double meaning of the word *twist*. It indicates a turning movement occasioning an unexpected change. But the word also signifies distortion or perversion. In this sense, the populist twist expresses the complex relationship between populism and democracy.

5. In his latest article on the topic, Michael Freeden (2017, 3) expresses his doubts in applying the notion of thin-centered ideology to populism.

6. Torcuato Di Tella (1997) stated more precisely that the existence of anti-elite resentment does not necessarily imply popular leadership. Different forms of populism can emerge "mostly as a result of the type of anti-status quo elites involved" (196).

7. In this sense, I agree with Ernesto Laclau (2005a, 117) when he defines populism as "a political logic" and rejects the use of the concept as a category.

8. For a critical overview of different approaches to the concept of leadership, see Helms (2012).

9. Extreme right-wing parties use the populist structure to become politically acceptable within a context of democratic regimes. Today, the French Front National, for example, differs from its earlier right-wing extremist position "in its self-proclaimed acceptance of democracy" and its defense of the "free will of the French People in leading its destiny" (libre volonté du peuple français de mener son destin) as the Front National's homepage declares (http://www.frontnational .com/le-projet-de-marine-le-pen/refondation-republicaine/democratie/, accessed October 20, 2014). See also Marcus (1995, 102), which is quoted by Rydgren (2008, 176); Betz (2002).

10. The term *representatives* is employed here in a broad sense, which includes elected members of the executive and legislative branches.

11. According to Pasquale Pasquino, Sieyes considers the division of labor as a "véritable principe des progrès de la société," a principle of civilization able to be applied as a horizontal principle of political representation. Pasquino (1987) argues that for Sieyes "civilization, division of labor and representation correspond" (221).

12. Perón television interview from 1973, accessed October 20, 2014, http://www .youtube.com/watch?v=3lGXgiWYexk.

13. Ronsavallon later multiplies his concepts for the people. He identifies four forms of the people's manifestations: (1) as voters (the electorate), (2) as the manifestation of the social (social people), (3) as the people as-a-principle, and (4) as random people, described as the ones who are selected by a lottery system. For the purpose of this article, the earlier differentiation is important because it opposes the idea of the people to the social presence and voters' manifestation, which populism tries to blur. See Pierre Rosanvallon, "A Reflection on Populism," *La vie des idées*, September 27, 2011, http://www.booksandideas.net/A-Reflection -on-Populism.html

14. Grillo expelled parliamentarian Adele Gambaro in June 2013. See "Sì all'espulsione della Gambaro e I gruppi grillini si spaccano 'Sulla sua sorte decider la Rete," *La repubblica*, June 18, 2013.

15. The case of Grillo is even more complex, since he refuses to run for any particular office. Nonetheless, he remains the leader of the movement.

16. Strache's May 1, 2012, speech, "Dem Volk sein Recht," http://www.youtube .com/watch?v=KDFmb-264U4 (first published on May 2, 2012). As Margaret

Canovan (2002) points out, it is important to remember that, opposed to left-wing populists, right-wing populist leaders "also attack those they identify as clients of the elite and beneficiaries of taxes paid by ordinary, hardworking people, typically, asylum-seekers, immigrants, minorities who have been granted special treatment, welfare recipients and so on" (32).

17. For Laclau the dichotomous division of society is a necessary aspect of politics. Without the constitution of "popular camps" opposed to power structures, there is no possibility for the articulation of social demands. I partially agree with this position, because I recognize the need for naming the people facing the power structure. I disagree, however, that this naming process must by definition be antagonistic, as Laclau argues. Laclau's vision cannot embrace the possibility of a consensus that is not only an accommodation of popular demands to power structures but also a modification of power (Laclau 2005a, 83–86).

18. Panizza borrows the concept of naming from Stavrakakis, but the idea also plays a crucial role in Laclau's book. See Laclau (2005a, chs. 4 and 5) and Stavrakakis (2005).

19. Freud (1922) was convinced that identification is responsible for the "mutual tie between members of the group" (66) but that the relationship between the crowd and the leader is driven by the mechanism of "being in love," since the leader has been put in the place of the followers' ego ideal. His view of the crowd is not a democratic one, since the crowd is portrayed as a feminine and weak mass that needs strong leadership. However, this chapter uses Freud's categories to describe the complexity of the people-leader relationship better and does not rely on this assumption.

20. Quoted by the newspaper *El universal*, March 5, 2013, http://www.eluniversal .com/nacional-y-politica/chavez-entro-en-la-historia/130305/chavez-es-como-tu.

21. Chávez's March 5, 2013, speech "El Universal," accessed June 15, 2017 at http://www.youtube.com/watch?v=WBcg7e_efFY.

22. Carlos de la Torre (2013) uses Isidoro Cheresky's (2012) concept of semi-embodiment to describe the situation in populism. There is an interesting point here that shows how closely populism can approach totalitarianism without being confounded with it. However, facing the relationship between the leader and the people described above, populism seems to indicate embodiment without producing it. That is one of the elements of the populist twist.

## References

Akkerman, Agnes, Cas Mudde, and Andrej Zaslove. 2014. "How Populist Are the People? Measuring Populist Attitudes in Voters." *Comparative Political Studies* 47 (9): 1324–353.

Arditi, Benjamin. 2005. "Populism as an Internal Periphery of Democratic Politics." In *Populism and the Mirror of Democracy*, edited by Francisco Panizza, 72–89. London: Verso.

Barr, Robert R. 2009. "Populists, Outsiders and Anti-Establishment Politics." *Party Politics* 15 (1): 29–48.

Betz, Hans-Georg. 2002. "Rechtspopulismus in Westeuropa: Aktuelle Entwicklungen und politische Bedeutung." *Österreichische Zeitschrift für Politikwissenschaft* 31 (3): 251–64.

Borowiak, Craig T. 2011 *Accountability and Democracy: The Pitfalls and Promise of Popular Control*. Oxford: Oxford University Press.

Canovan, Margaret. 1999 "'Trust the People!' Populism and the Two Faces of Democracy." *Political Studies* 47:2–16.

———. 2002. "Taking Politics to the People. Populism as the Ideology of Democracy." In *Democracy and Populist Challenge*, edited by Yves Mény and Yves Surel, 25–43. New York: Palgrave.

———. 2005. *The People*. Cambridge: Polity Press.

Cheresky, Isidoro. 2012. "Mutación democrática, otra ciudadanía, otras representaciones." In *¿Qué Democracia en América Latina?* edited by Isidoro Cheresky. Buenos Aires: CLACSO Prometeo.

de la Torre, Carlos. 2013. "The People, Populism, and the Leader's Semi-Embodied Power." *Rubrica contemporanea* 2 (3): 5–20.

Di Tella, Torcuato. 1997. "Populism into the Twenty-first Century." *Government and Opposition* 32 (I.2): 187–200.

Diehl, Paula. 2011. "Die Komplexität des Populismus—Ein Plädoyer für ein mehrdimensionales und graduelles Konzept." *Populismus: Konzepte und Theorien.* Special issue, *Totalitarismus und Demokratie* 2:273–91.

———. 2017. "Populism and the Body." In *Handbook of Political Populism*, edited by Reinhard C. Heinisch, Christina Holtz-Bacha, and Oscar Mazzoleni, 361–72. Baden-Baden: Nomos/Bloomsbury.

Ellner, Steven. 2012. "The Heyday of Radical Populism in Venezuela and Its Reappearance." In *Populism in Latin America*, edited by Michael L. Conniff, 132–58. Tuscaloosa: University of Alabama Press.

Freeden, Michael. 2017. "After the Brexit Referendum: Revisiting Populism as an Ideology." *Journal of Political Ideologies* 22 (1): 1–11.

Freud, Sigmund. 1922. *Group Psychology and the Analysis of the Ego*. Vienna: The International Psycho-Analytical Press.

Helms, Ludger. 2012. "Introduction: The Importance of Studying Political Leadership Comparatively." In *Comparative Political Leadership: Challenges and Prospects*, edited by Ludger Helms, 1–24. London: Palgrave Macmillan.

Jansen, Robert S. 2011. "Populist Mobilization: A New Theoretical Approach to Populism." *Sociological Theory* 29 (2): 75–96.

Kazin, Michael. 1995. *The Populist Persuasion: An American History*. New York: HarperCollins.

Laclau, Ernesto. 1997. *Politics and Ideology in Marxist Theory: Capitalism, Fascism, Populism*. London: NLB.

————. 2005a. *On Populist Reason*. London: Verso.

————. 2005b. "Populism: What's in a Name?" In *Populism as the Mirror of Democracy*, edited by Francisco Panizza, 32–49. London: Verso.

Lefort, Claude. 1986. *The Political Forms of Modern Society: Bureaucracy, Democracy, Totalitarianism*. Edited by John B. Thompson. Cambridge: Polity Press.

Lits, Marc. 2009. "Présentation générale. Populaire et populisme: entre dénigrement et exaltation." In *Populaire et Populisme*, edited by Marc Lits, 9–27. Paris: CNRS Éditions.

Luhmann, Niklas. 1979. *Trust and Power*. New York: John Wiley and Sons.

Mair, Peter. 2002. "Democracy vs. Party Democracy." In *Democracies and the Populist Challenge*, edited by Yves Mény and Yves Surel, 81–98. Basingstoke: Palgrave.

Manin, Bernard 1997. *The Principles of Representative Government*. Cambridge: Cambridge University Press.

Marcus, J. 1995. *The National Front and French Politics: The Resistible Rise of Jean-Marie Le Pen*. London: MacMillan.

Mény, Yves, and Yves Surel. 2000. *Par le peuple, pour le peuple: Le populisme et les démocraties*. Paris: Fayard.

Mudde, Cas. 2004. "The Populist Zeitgeist." *Government and Opposition* 39:541–63.

Mudde, Cas, and Cristóbal Rovira Kaltwasser. 2012. "Populism and (Liberal) Democracies: A Framework for Analysis." In *Populism in Europe and the Americas: Threat or Corrective for Democracy?* edited by Cas Mudde and Cristóbal Rovira Kaltwasser, 1–26. Cambridge: Cambridge University Press.

Müller, Jan-Werner. 2014. "The People Must Be Extracted from Within the People: Reflections on Populism." *Constellations* 21, no. I.4 (December): 483–93.

O'Donnell, Guillermo. 1994. "Delegative Democracy." *Journal of Democracy* 5 (1): 55–69.

Panizza, Francisco. 2005. "Introduction. Populism and the Mirror of Democracy," *Populism and the Mirror of Democracy*, edited by Francisco Panizza, 1–31. London: Verso.

Pasquino, Gianfranco. 2008. "Populism and Democracy." In *Twenty-First Century Populism: The Spectre of Western European Democracy*, edited by Daniele Albertazzi and Duncan McDonnell, 15–29. New York: Palgrave Macmillan.

Pasquino, Pasquale. 1987. "Emmanuel Sieyes, Benjamin Constant et le 'gouvernement des modernes.' Contribution à l'histoire du concept de représentation politique." *Revue française de science politique* 37 (2): 214–29.

Petracca, Orazio. 1983. "Leadership." In *Dizionario di Politica*, edited by Norberto Bobbio, Nicola Matteucci, and Gianfranco Pasquino, 577–80. Torino: UTET.

Pettit, Philip. 1998. "Republican Theory and Political Trust." In *Trust and Governance*, edited by M. Levi and Braithwaite Russel, 296–99. New York: Sage.

Pitkin, Hanna F. 1972. *The Concept of Representation*. Berkeley: University of California Press.

Reisigl, Martin. 2002. "Dem Volk aufs Maul schauen, nach dem Mund reden und Angst und Bange machen. Von populistischen Anrufungen, Anbiederungen und Agitationsweisen in der Sprache österreichischer PolitikerInnen." In *Rechtspopulismus. Österreichische Krankheit oder europäische Normalität*, edited by Wolfgang Eismann, 149–98. Vienna: Czernic Verlag.

Rosanvallon, Pierre. 2000. *La démocratie inachevée*. Paris: Gallimard.

———. 2006. *La contre-démocratie: La politique à l'âge de la défiance*. Paris: Éditions du Seuil.

Rydgren, Jens. 2008. "France: The Front National, Ethnonationalism and Populism." In *Twenty-First Century Populism: The Spectre of Western European Democracy*, edited by Daniele Albertazzi and Duncan McDonnell, 166–80. Hampshire: Palgrave Macmillan.

Saward, Michael. 2006. "The Representative Claim." *Contemporary Political Theory* 5:297–318.

Schedler, Andreas. 1999. "Conceptualizing Accountability." In *The Self-Restraining State: Power and Accountability in New Democracies*, edited by Andreas Schedler, Larry Diamon, and Marc F. Plattner, 13–27. Boulder, CO: Lynne Rienner.

Stanley, Ben. 2008. "The Thin Ideology of Populism." *Journal of Political Ideologies* 13 (1): 95–110.

Stavrakakis, Yannis. 2005. "Religion and Populism in Contemporary Greece." In *Populism as the Mirror of Democracy*, edited by Francisco Panizza, 224–49. London: Verso.

Taggart, Paul. 2000. *Populism*. Buckingham: Open University Press.

Taguieff, Pierre-André. 2007. *L'illusion populiste: Essai sur les démagogies de l'âge démocratique*. Paris: Flammarion.

Urbinati, Nadia. 1998. "Democracy and Populism." *Constellations* 5 (1): 110–24.

Urbinati, Nadia, and Mark Warren. 2008. "The Concept of Representation in Contemporary Democratic Theory." *Annual Review of Political Science* 11:387–412.

Vignati, Rinaldo. 2013. "Beppe Grillo: dalla Tv ai palasport, dal blog al Movimento." In *Il partito di Grillo*, edited by Piergiorgio Corbetta and Elisabetta Gualmini, 29–36. Bologna: Il Mulino.

PART II

# Representation as Democratic Inclusion

# CHAPTER SIX

# Varieties of Inclusive Representation

Samuel Hayat

Insofar as political representation entails "making present . . . something which is nevertheless not present," (Pitkin 1972, 8–9) it is always suspected of excluding the represented from the political scene.[1] By speaking on behalf of the people or a group, a political representative (elected or self-appointed) renders their direct participation in decisions concerning them unnecessary. Such suspicion is reinforced by the importance given to representation by the minimalist (or realist) theories of democracy that dominated postwar politics (Bachrach 1980; Hindess 2000). In *Capitalism, Socialism and Democracy*, a reference work for these theories (despite the low importance it assigned to the issue of democracy), Joseph Schumpeter (2013) radically criticized direct participation—by asserting, for example, that "the typical citizen drops down to a lower level of mental performance as soon as he enters the political field" (262)—at the same time that he defended a view of democracy that understands the people as a mere arbiter between representatives competing for state power. According to realist theory, political exclusion of the people goes hand in hand with representing them. Therefore, constructing a more substantial or "strong" democratic theory based on the inclusion of citizens and aimed at creating political equality among them generally involves denouncing representation altogether (Pateman 1970; Barber 1984). At the very most, representative democracy might be accepted as a "second best" (Brennan and Hamlin 1999) or "defective substitute" (Mansbridge 2003) for direct democracy. From this perspective, the political inclusion of citizens—via participatory devices, social movements, public debates, and so on—matters above all else, whether outside of or even in opposition to representation.

To challenge the dichotomy between representation of citizens and direct participation by citizens, I would like to show that, as an act of speaking, standing, or acting for others, representation can function in two ways. On the one hand, it can be *exclusionary*, that is, tending toward the monopolization of power by representatives (especially the institutions of representative government) and the exclusion of the represented from the political scene. It can then be used to justify the division of political labor, the absence of citizen control over governance, and the complete suppression of any form of representation outside state institutions. On the other hand, representation can be used *inclusively* by involving the represented in political decision-making more than they were prior to or without representation. The reason representation can in fact facilitate direct political participation of the represented is linked to its constructivist aspects (Saward 2010; Disch 2015). When representatives—whether rulers and political professionals or spokespeople for social groups and the public—claim to speak and act on behalf of others, the represented become present in the political scene and are enabled to act directly in this scene. In this use of representation, it is precisely because the representatives speak and act on behalf of the represented that the latter are invited to judge them directly, control them, and create alternate forms of representation if they are not satisfied with how they are represented. Seen this way, only exclusionary representation obstructs direct participation by the represented and with it the prospects for the creation of substantial political equality. Conversely, inclusive representation offers a way to broaden direct political participation, making it possible for the voices of the dominated to be heard and, perhaps, for democratic institutions to give more room to citizens' direct participation in achieving collective outcomes.

But there is an imbalance between these two forms of representation. With the historical triumph of representative government, exclusionary representation effectively became a given, embedded in state institutions where the elected are rulers independent of their electors (Manin 1997). Exclusionary representation does not appear as just one form of representation; it has become the only politically valid form of representation and nearly synonymous with electoral delegation. Consequently, the vast majority of research on political representation examines only exclusionary applications, following the direction inspired by Pitkin's classic work and employing the inherently exclusionary principal/agent model (Przeworski, Stokes, and Manin 1999). Citizens may influence collective results directly through social movements and participatory devices or indirectly through their elected representatives, but the idea that representation itself could enhance the direct participation of citizens in the production of collective outcomes is rarely, if ever, explored.

Therefore, thinking about representation in its inclusive sense requires the additional explication that this chapter will introduce. To accomplish this, I will combine an analytical approach—one that uses theories of political representation and Pierre Bourdieu's political sociology to distinguish forms of inclusive representation—with predominantly historical material. Representation has been a central concept in European political vocabulary since the thirteenth century, long before the triumph of representative government (Hofmann 1973; Faggioli and Melloni 2007). If one desires to rethink representation beyond the exclusionary forms that representative governments adopted, unearthing the forgotten meanings and uses of the concept may be the best route. I will focus on the debates that accompanied the imposition and consolidation of the institutions of representative government in France during the century of controversies, revolutions, and institutional innovations begun by the 1789 Revolution (Rosanvallon 1998). Representation was discussed extensively during this period, which allows us to explore the concept of representation developed by those who opposed representative government for the sake of democracy. Through these historical examples, I hope to elucidate what inclusive representation could mean both theoretically and institutionally.

## Inclusion through Partisan Politicization

The reason it is possible to characterize the way representative government uses representation as exclusionary is that between one election and the next nearly all citizens—the represented—are excluded from political decision-making (Manin 1997). This division of political labor, a core feature of Benjamin Constant's "Liberty of the Moderns," is one of the elements of representative government in greatest conflict with the democratic ideal (Finley 1973). For this reason, radical criticism of this political form denounces the oligarchic tendency of representative government on the assumption that division of political labor inevitably establishes groups of professional politicians whose very existence excludes the majority of citizens (Michels 1962). Thus, the professionalization of politics goes hand in hand with exclusionary representation and with the construction of politics as a domain isolated from the citizenry. The sociologist Daniel Gaxie (1978) notes that "the exercise of the political profession is associated with the manipulation of a specific language, which therefore becomes a language of professionals. The mastery of this language by agents in the political field is at the source of the relative incompetence of other social agents, and tends to dispossess them of their potential to be involved in political activities" (95). According to the very mechanisms of representative government, the exercise of politics by elected representatives results in the dispossession of the constituents, since political competence is defined by the ability to speak the language of professional politicians.

However, electoral competition between professionals has historically taken forms that were not unequivocally exclusionary. In France, during the French Revolution, the Society of the Friends of the Constitution, better known as the Jacobins, which was at first a mere parliamentary club, soon opened itself to citizens, becoming the first mass party in French history. Then, during the whole nineteenth century, the professionalization of French politics went hand in hand with the development of parties that served both as electoral machines for professional politicians and as tools for mass political socialization (Huard 1996; Scarrow 2006). If we define inclusive representation as instances of representation where the represented gain access to decision-making they did not have previously, then participation in mass political parties may well constitute a form of inclusive representation. Through parties, citizens may fight against exclusion from professional politics by learning professional political language and using it to intervene in decision-making processes. This form of inclusive representation can be designated as the inclusion of citizens through their *partisan politicization*. Here, representation is inclusive in the sense that the represented may start a new direct political activity by entering a party and/or adopting a language they had not mastered before being represented. This may allow them to make their views heard in political arenas from which they were previously excluded; when mass political parties exist, representation may induce direct citizen participation through partisanship (Urbinati 2006, 30–33).

Understood this way, inclusion through partisan politicization occurs within the institutions of representative government when electoral competition is based on mass political parties. In these parties, the represented are included by direct interaction with the world of professional politicians and by using their language, which thus becomes a shared partisan language, that is, an ideology (Freeden 1996). Consequently, when representative government is a "party democracy" (Manin 1997, 206–18), representation is both exclusionary (due to the monopolization of political power by the representatives) and inclusive (as the excluded represented enter mass political parties and thus participate directly in politics). Seen this way, political representation in party democracies has a unique, intrinsically mixed meaning. Just as, for Bernard Manin (1997, 191), representative government is essentially mixed—in that it is based on a procedure that is both democratic and aristocratic, the election—it can be said that, according to this notion of inclusion through partisan politicization, representation is intrinsically both exclusionary and inclusive.

Should we then say that this inclusive power is a product of representation itself, irrespective of its institutional context? This is the underlying discourse of many authors who attempt to demonstrate the a priori compatibility between representation and democracy, advocating a "representative turn" in democratic theory (Brito Vieira 2017, 4–5). According to one of the founding texts of this approach, "the opposite of representation is not participation. The opposite of representation is exclusion" (Plotke 1997, 19). This perspective precludes the possibility of representation being exclusionary, despite the opposition to democratic participation of the founders of representative governments (Morgan 1974; Baker 1987; Dupuis-Déri 1999; Rancière 2014). According to most theorists of the representative turn, representation is intrinsically democratic and inclusive: to represent is to include, and therefore to be represented is to be included. Thus the idea of representative democracy constitutes a true tautology (Näsström 2006).

So why then have institutions of representative government faced constant criticism for being insufficiently democratic since they were established? Far from proving the tension between representation and democracy, according to authors of the representative turn, this criticism proves the inherently democratic aspect of representation. For example, for Georges Kateb (1981), the suspicion surrounding the discourse of representatives establishes the "moral distinctiveness" of representative democracy by creating a desirable distance between the represented and their government. According to Didier Mineur (2010) the crisis of representation is intrinsic to the concept itself, and for Bruno Latour (2003) it is a consequence of the specificity of political speech. All these arguments rest on the idea that representation is democratic because it opens the possibility of *judgment* of the actions of representatives by the represented. Far from preventing citizens from participating in politics, representation would be the only way citizens could acquire the ability to make political judgments. Applying his theories on aesthetic representation to political representation, Frank Ankersmit (2007) states that "the faculty of representation makes us into the inhabitants of two worlds, the private one (that we possessed already) and the public one (to which we can get access thanks to this faculty of representation)" (27). Mirroring the action of their representatives, the represented have their subjectivity split in two, thereby enabling them to move from the sphere of personal interest to that of political judgment. Not only would representation be inherently inclusive, it would be the only possible form of political inclusion.

However, this appealing theory is in contradiction with some prominent historical and sociological features of citizen politicization. Since the instauration of representative governments in Europe, political judgment was never exercised solely in reference to the political field. Democratic modernity entailed the development of mass political parties but also forms of mobilization and association that took place outside of the state, sometimes against it. For example, trade unions were not a byproduct of representative government; they developed from preexisting forms of trade organizations (Sewell 1980). This does not mean that these movements did not make use of representation. But they were not necessarily linked with the institutions of representative government. As political representation existed before representative government, representation continued to exist and develop outside of the electoral relation between the represented and their professional representatives. Inclusion through partisan politicization is but one aspect of inclusive representation. Other relations of representation take place outside the state; they may contribute to the inclusion of citizens—or extend their exclusion. To assess the inclusiveness of these, we need to take into account the processes of politicization that take place outside of the institutions of representative government.

## Inclusion through Autonomous Politicization

Recent years have seen the rise of both self-appointed representatives such as nongovernmental organizations (Montanaro 2012) and social movements like the *indignados* or occupiers that develop radical critiques of representative democracy (Ogien and Laugier 2014). It can always be argued, in a deliberative framework, that these new representative claim-makers participate in the representative system (Kuyper 2016). However, it is analytically useful to distinguish between two kinds of situation. On the one hand, popular sovereignty being "a diarchy of will and judgment" (Urbinati 2011, 26), passing judgments on representatives is part of representative democracy and can take place inside the institutions of representative government such as political parties. The inclusiveness of the representative system would then depend on the extent of partisan politicization. But, on the other hand, in certain situations citizen politicization may lead to a rupture between representatives and their constituents and to the subsequent invention of alternate forms of representation. As Urbinati (2005) puts it, "when the *continuity* between the representatives and the citizens is *interrupted*, the latter are likely to generate extra-parliamentary forms of (self-)representation" (198). The difficulty then is assessing to what extent these relations of representation that take place outside of the institutions of representative government are inclusive or exclusionary.

Such forms of representation become particularly visible during events in which the institutions of representative government simply no longer function. History shows that the break with institutions of representative government is not incompatible with representative claim-making. On the contrary, during the 1848 revolution—an example of a critical moment of questioning representative government—the brutal delegitimization of the July Monarchy was accompanied by the proliferation of rhetoric using the vocabulary of representation, along with the rapid establishment of alternative institutions of representation different from those of the representative government (Hayat 2014, 2015). The first of these institutions was the provisional government that seized state power after the success of the insurrection on February 24, 1848. It acted "in the name of the French people" (the sentence was used in every official act of the provisional government) and managed to have its representative claim recognized. In a way, it was using a form of exclusionary representation: its very existence implied a decrease of direct popular participation since the insurrection stopped, barricades were wiped out, and order was restored. Still, for several days, the provisional government faced demands from armed Parisian workers and during its ten weeks of existence received many petitions and delegates from demonstrations, associations, and intermediary bodies. Compared with previous representative bodies, the kind of representation implemented by the provisional government in 1848 was much more inclusive.

Nevertheless, in 1848 the real innovation in the representation system was not the provisional government but the other representative institutions born from the insurrection. First, the national guard, a previously bourgeois militia, became open to all male citizens, including workers, who received weapons and uniforms. National guards elected officers, who thus became important local representatives especially in popular neighborhoods (Hincker 2007). Then, due to popular pressure, the provisional government implemented a workers' parliament in the Luxembourg Palace—the former House of Lords—which was directly elected by the trades. Finally, in the weeks following the revolution, hundreds of clubs were created and were massively attended: an estimated one hundred thousand attended in Paris alone (Amann 1975). While these clubs were at first isolated, they soon federalized in order to create a unified club movement able to represent citizens, to organize demonstrations, and to control the actions of state authorities. These institutions were representative but born from an insurrection that destroyed previous elected assemblies. They triggered mass citizen participation and relied on it to work properly, especially the national guard and the club movement, but they were neither institutions of representative government nor invested with legislative power. They developed a relation of inclusive representation and contributed to politicize citizens but in a different way than partisanship. Here politicization and inclusion did not primarily mean acquiring the language of professional politicians or passing judgment on their actions. For citizens, it implied participating directly in the defense of their own neighborhood, in the definition of their own labor conditions, and in the expression of popular opinion. They were represented not as mere constituents but as active members of more partial and localized communities, increasing their *autonomy* through representation.

Therefore, we can describe this form of inclusion, which happens when relations of representation emerge outside the state legislature or government, as *autonomous* politicization. Autonomy here does not mean that citizens are not represented but that representation takes place outside of the institutions of representative government, sometimes in opposition to them. Autonomous politicization requires the creation of representative devices or bodies that should be at least partially autonomous from government, be it from their origin, their localization, or their goals. Contrary to parties, they do not primarily seek to participate in electoral competitions, and, while they may pass judgment on elected representatives, they may also have aims of their own. Some of these devices may be agonistic, aiming at exercising power over the institutions of representative government, in which case they would relate to what Pierre Rosanvallon (2008) calls "counter-democracy." Or they may develop with no reference to elected rulers, seeking to influence collective outcomes by expressing a will, as participative devices may enable participants to do, or through collective action.

The institutional consequences of these two forms of inclusion through politicization are therefore completely different. In partisan politicization, the inclusionary power of representation is located inside the institutions of representative government—exclusion and inclusion cannot be separated one from the other. Conversely, in autonomous politicization, inclusion takes place through processes of representation located outside of the institutions of representative government. This is, therefore, much more than a theoretical distinction. In the history of representative government, supporters of the inclusive effects of electoral representation long debated those who advocated supplementing electoral representation with other representative devices. In this regard, the 1848 revolution was an excellent testing ground because of its large-scale implementation of universal suffrage (despite continued exclusion of women). For some, universal suffrage was sufficient to guarantee the inclusion of all (male) citizens in the republic. This was Lamartine's position when speaking on behalf of the provisional government following the popular demonstration of March 17, 1848: "The election belongs to all without exception. As of the date of this [electoral] law, there are no longer any proletarians in France. Every adult Frenchman is a political citizen. Every citizen is a voter. Every voter is sovereign. The right is equal and absolute for all" (*Actes du gouvernement provisoire* 1848, 148–49). For Lamartine, universal suffrage was enough to guarantee the equal inclusion of all citizens, to the point of eliminating any class barrier and any inequality between rulers and the governed.

Conversely, other voices claimed that elections alone could not guarantee the inclusion of all citizens and that it was therefore necessary to add external devices of popular participation to the institutions of representative government. These would achieve inclusion by allowing citizens to organize themselves and express their will directly and potentially to monitor the elected assemblies. In 1848, clubs played such a role. Some club leaders even felt that this experience should last beyond the election of the National Assembly and proposed the establishment of a "Popular Convention" made up of club representatives. This unelected assembly, which would hold sessions on the premises of the former Chamber of Deputies, would not replace the National Assembly but would play a specifically inclusive role. It would "translate [the] acts [of the Assembly], relay [to it] a faithful expression of the feelings that they aroused in the People," but, even more importantly, it would become "a shelter for the great school of the people."[2] While the National Assembly would make laws, this Popular Convention would be aimed at developing citizens' political capacity, both through their direct participation in clubs and through their autonomous representation in the convention. This proposal, which was never put into practice because the counterrevolution soon submerged France, is a good example of the concept of inclusion through autonomous politicization. Electoral representation alone is not enough to guarantee the politicization of citizenry excluded through the division of political labor. It must be intensified by representative devices that are not focused on electoral competition but devoted to the politicization of the represented and the development of their direct participation.

Therefore, two forms of inclusion through politicization coexist. For the first, the partisan form, the institutions of representative government, especially in party democracies, have both inclusive and exclusionary aspects. For the second, the autonomous form, the exclusionary uses of representation must be offset by inclusionary devices outside of representative government. However, both conceptions of inclusion through politicization share an important feature. They imply that political representation excludes citizens as a collective whole. Therefore, whether they are based solely on election or on other devices, the proposed mechanisms of inclusion prove blind to the fact that exclusion is exercised differently depending on the social characteristics of the represented. Returning to the example of the 1848 revolution, inclusion through politicization can be accounted for by the extension of suffrage, the importance of electoral committees reviewing statements of principles by candidates (inclusion through partisan politicization), as well as the enormous increase in newspapers and clubs and the establishment of a democratized national guard and assembly of workers (inclusion through autonomous politicization). However, this fails to provide a framework of analysis sufficient to explain speeches made in the name of specific social groups, in particular workers and women. There was indeed some form of representation here in the sense that those who spoke on behalf of these groups considered themselves as their representatives and, particularly in the case of skilled workers, may sometimes actually have been elected by members of their social group. However, any analysis of this form of representation must consider the fact that it occurred within a social group and not within the overall framework of the relationship between citizens and their representatives.

## Inclusive Representation of Social Groups

All the represented are excluded from politics because of the exclusionary ways of using representation. However, we can add a second, more sociological meaning to the first definition of exclusionary representation, which stems from the social conditions under which the political field is organized. Representation as implemented by representative government is exclusionary for nearly all citizens in a general sense due simply to the division of political labor. But representation also excludes specific citizens who are "divested of the material and cultural instruments necessary for them to participate actively in politics" (Bourdieu 1991b, 172). Social actors less endowed with the cultural capital and free time required for political participation are left "no choice but delegation—a misrecognized dispossession of the less competent by the more competent" (Bourdieu 1984, 413–14). From this perspective, governments speak and act for the governed, but dominants also speak for the dominated, for whom representational exclusion is then doubled. Historically, suffrage based on the ownership of property accompanied representative government (Rosanvallon 1992). For its theoreticians and practitioners during the first half of the nineteenth century, this form of suffrage was the legal framework for the double exclusion noted above. However, the extension of suffrage did not eliminate this exclusion. That is, instead of being excluded from suffrage or eligibility by poll tax requirements, the dominated were excluded because of their lower "political competence" (defined as an "aptitude to speak the language of the professionals"), thereby leading to their "radical dispossession" (Gaxie 1978, 83, and 95). As dominated social groups suffer specific exclusion, it is necessary for a democratic representative system to implement specific ways of including them in the process of decision-making.

A primary way of carrying this out is to identify the groups that should receive specific representation and then grant within the institutions of representative government a certain number of positions or seats to representatives from these groups. This is the method adopted by those who support (particularly feminists) group representation (Williams 2000; Squires 2001), which is based on a descriptive concept of representation (Phillips 1995; Mansbridge 1999) that serves as a foundation of quota politics (Squires 1996; Achin 2001; Dutoya 2012). This form of representation assumes inclusion of dominated groups in the political field, based on the following principle: "a democratic public should establish mechanisms for actually recognizing and representing the individual voices and perspectives of those from these constitutive groups who are oppressed and disadvantaged" (Young 1990, 184). This demand for inclusion through group representation is not new. It was present in the strategies of the nineteenth-century workers' movement, from the seminal 1832 article by the republican and Saint-Simonian Jean Reynaud with respect to "the need for a special representation of the proletarians" to the 1864 *Manifesto of the Sixty*, which advocated separate candidacies for workers in the elections (Rosanvallon 1998, 87–129). This institutionalized collective inclusion is analogous to individual partisan politicization: excluded groups are included in politics through their presence in the institutions of representative government.

As with individual politicization, institutionalized inclusion is not the only possible option when thinking about the inclusion of dominated groups. It can also occur through the construction of autonomous forms of representation outside institutions of representative government. Correcting the exclusionary features of representation does not then occur by seeking greater inclusivity from established representative institutions but by constructing alternative autonomous means of representation specifically dedicated to representing an excluded social group. Because of the electoral exclusion of workers, the French labor movement of the 1830s was largely established around the right to association. This was understood to mean the right of workers not only to associate with one another but also to create a federative association on the national level, grouping together the various corporations and therefore ensuring the creation of an autonomous representative body. A similar demand was seen in the women's clubs of 1848, together with the demand for a broadening of suffrage. The exclusion practiced by institutionalized politics was thus challenged not only by demands for inclusion in the institutions of representative government but also by assertion of the right of autonomous association as women to defend the interests and rights of women. In his *Political Capacity of the Working-Classes* (1865), Proudhon responded to the *Manifesto of the Sixty* and theorized about the strategy of a split to ensure representation of the working class. According to him, by establishing autonomous federative institutions separate from the state, workers could collectively pursue their emancipation without waiting for an assembly of legislators to grant them the right to do so. This, for Proudhon, constituted the superiority of an autonomous representation strategy over the strategies of inclusion in the institutions of representative government. In the same way as it is possible to think about the inclusion of citizens by their politicization within or outside institutions of representative government, dominated social groups may pursue institutionalized or autonomous strategies of inclusion.

## The Exclusionary Risks of Group Representation

The parallel between individual and collective inclusion may be misleading. One could easily imagine that giving presence to social groups through inclusive group representation (institutionalized or autonomous) would induce the politicization of individuals belonging to these groups. According to Bourdieu (1984), however, the path to specific representation of the dominated always runs the risk of continuing their exclusion or even deepening it by giving the dominated the illusion that someone is speaking for them, since they would be "at the mercy of the discourses that are presented to them.... At best, they are at the mercy of their own spokesmen, whose role it is to provide them with the means of repossessing their own experience" (461–62). Therefore, to include the dominated by representing them is to make them dependent on a trustee who can always pass off her own interest as theirs. Since the dominated are excluded from representation, those who speak and act on their behalf can in fact claim to be authorized by them without the least assurance that these spokespeople are actually defending their interests. This is true for the working class studied by Bourdieu but also for any social group whose representation is based entirely on the goodwill of the representatives who advocate for them, whether from within the institutions of representative government or autonomous organizations. As far as dominated groups are concerned, representation as "advocacy" (Urbinati 2000) may well worsen their dispossession. Inclusive representation of dominated social groups does not entail inclusive representation of their members; the former gives presence to dominated social groups through representatives of these groups, while the latter requires direct participation from individuals belonging to these groups.

A significant historical example of this form of representation of the dominated by spokespeople acting as their advocates—with no guarantee that they are actually defending the interests of the represented or helping them to participate—can be found in France during the 1840s. In this period the combination of suffrage based on property ownership and the strict limitations for potential association or expression made workers largely dependent for their representation on the goodwill of deputies, who were not electorally accountable to them. The career path of Alexandre Ledru-Rollin exemplified this construct well. As a young, bourgeois, Parisian attorney, he was elected in 1841 in the course of making an uncommonly radical statement of principles. He began by invoking the "miseries with which the poor classes were plagued." He described the people as "a flock led by a few privileged beings," justified the people's uprising at the start of the 1830s, compared it to the work of Christ, and eventually advocated a break with representative government (Ledru-Rollin 1841, 52–53). In this statement of principles, which brought him immediate fame within radical circles, he presented himself as being authorized by the poor—considered by him as the only real people—and by worker insurrections to proclaim his primary political aim, namely, the struggle for the republic. Speaking of the workers and the poor as the excluded, he demanded their inclusion, and more generally spoke out in defense of their rights.

What gave force to Ledru-Rollin's discourse was not the substance of what he proposed (a regime change) but that he declared his objective to be the very goal of the workers, who he implied were on the verge of an uprising. Bourdieu (1991b) sees this as being at the heart of the representation process: "the speech of the spokesperson owes part of its 'illocutionary force' to the force (the number) of the group that he helps to produce as such by the act of symbolization or representation; it is based on the metaphorical *coup d'état* by which the speaker invests his utterance with all the power his utterance helps to produce by mobilizing the group to which it is addressed" (191).

The power in Ledru-Rollin's discourse stemmed from the power of the group that he claimed to represent (the workers, the poor, the people), despite the absence of proof of any specific relationship between him and this group, other than its exclusion and his speaking on its behalf. That Ledru-Rollin spoke in the name of workers did not in and of itself create workers' inclusion—it is well within the exclusionary forms of representation that workers are represented here. In a certain way, their double exclusion, as citizens and as dominated persons, earned them the right to a specific form of representation (by Ledru-Rollin in this case), but this representation is once again exclusionary: as doubly excluded, they are doubly represented, without this double representation necessarily being inclusive. Eventually, in June 1848, when workers appeared directly on the political scene, the spokesperson role established by Ledru-Rollin did not keep him from participating in repressing the same worker insurrections that he had justified just a few years earlier.

The risk of combining inclusive representation of a social group with exclusionary representation of its members is prominent when social groups are not recognized as such. Taking the French working class as an example: its recognition as a class was the result of a political process in which representative claims played a major role (Moss 1976; Sewell 1980). After the 1830 revolution some workers, who were admittedly a minority, began to rethink their traditional trade actions and organizations in terms that transcended the barriers between the trades. They established newspapers edited and written exclusively by workers, and it was only then that terms such as *working class* or *proletarians* started to refer to a class identity. Thus, worker identity was the result of an activity led by spokespeople to the extent that it can be said that the working class was created as a political subject by those claiming to represent workers. According to Bourdieu (1991c), such a process of *subjectivation* is at the core of the sociological mechanisms of representation. Spokespeople create the groups they claim to speak for through a "process of institution, ordinarily perceived and described as a process of delegation, in which the representative receives from the group the power of creating the group" (248). The process of instituting, masked by the idea of delegation, is based on the joint establishment of the representative and of the represented as an outcome of the emerging representative's activity: "*in appearance* the group creates the man who speaks in its place and in its name—to put it that way is to think in terms of delegation—whereas *in reality* it is more or less just as true to say that it is the spokesperson who creates the group. It is because the representative exists, because he *represents* (symbolic action), that the group that is represented and symbolized exists and that in return it gives existence to its representative as the representative of the group" (Bourdieu 1991a, 204). In this sense, unlike delegation, representation is not a transfer of power between two established social entities (the representatives and their constituents) but rather the establishment, by a signifying individual or group, of a signified group, which thereby acquires the status of a political subject.

This form of representation appears then to push its exclusionary features to the extreme; the spokesperson assumes the right, free of any control, to speak in the name of a social group that is not recognized yet, irrespective of the participation of the group's presumed members. But on the collective level it also involves an inclusive dimension, that of giving voice and presence to groups that have thus far been deprived of any recognized social identity. When new social groups are given presence by such a process of subjectivation, individuals that belong to these groups enter a relation of representation with them. These relations of representation may themselves be inclusive or exclusionary, depending on whether they stimulate or inhibit direct participation of group members in the collective decisions concerning it. Direct participation may then lead to new processes of subjectivation, questioning established identities as new divisions appear within the social groups represented. Anne Phillips (1995) explains this in regard to the representation of women: "In the subsequent development of feminist politics, the question of who can best speak for or on behalf of another became a major source of tension, for once men were dislodged from their role of speaking for women, it seemed obvious enough that white women ought also to be dislodged from their role of speaking for black women, heterosexual women for lesbians, and middle-class women for those in the working class" (9).

Representation involves a necessarily dynamic view of social identities. Since groups can be established through representational activity, the allocation of the ability to speak for the group cannot be set once and for all. Subjectivation processes constantly reveal new political subjects, who produce new dividing lines within the established social groups, thereby creating the need for new devices of inclusion.

## The Politics of Inclusive Representation

Far from being a simple way to justify the division of political labor, representation can be understood as a means of including the represented. Exclusionary representation assumes that the represented are absent, made present exclusively through the person of their representative. Inclusive representation, on the other hand, is measured by the fact that it gives presence to the represented. But presence does not mean the same thing for individuals and for groups. As far as individuals are concerned, representation may be called inclusive when being represented favors direct citizen participation in decision-making. This may entail either partisan or autonomous politicization, depending on whether citizens participate in the institutions of representative government such as political parties or in other organizations and movements. For social groups, inclusive representation rests on the inclusion of group representatives in decision-making, either inside the institutions of representative government or through the creation of autonomous representative bodies. These two forms of inclusive representation do not necessarily go hand in hand. On the contrary, the inclusion of dominated social groups may rest on processes of representation that exclude members of these groups, especially when their recognition requires the activity of self-appointed spokespersons.

Inclusive representation can assume various forms, but in every instance it is not the activity of representatives but the presence of the represented that constitutes the relevant criterion for defining the inclusiveness of representation. From this perspective, inclusive representation appears to stand in opposition to exclusionary representation and its norms. According to Pitkin, it is responsiveness on the part of the representative and the absence of conflict with those represented that signals good representation—while with inclusive representation it is the activity of the represented, going so far as to conflict with and break away from representatives, that determines effective representation. A representative system is inclusive to the extent that established representatives are subject to ongoing public judgment, competing with external forms of representation implemented by the represented themselves and by spokespeople for groups deemed poorly represented or not represented at all—spokespeople who may themselves be contested by those in whose name they speak. What makes representation inclusive is not that representatives have been elected, that they resemble the represented or defend their interests, but rather that the represented appear directly on the public stage, that they pass judgment, express their will, dispute what is said and done in their name, and construct alternative institutions. In this regard, inclusive representation policies would consist in multiplying the opportunities for dominated social groups to gain specific representation and for the represented to become directly involved in decision-making. It remains to be seen if such democratic reforms could fit in the malleable but deeply exclusionary institutions of representative government.

## Notes

1. A previous version of this article was published in French in *Raisons politiques* 50 (May 2013), and translated by Cairn International. I thank the Presses de Sciences Po for their permission to publish this modified version.

2. The petition was signed in May 1848 by *la Commission chargée du travail* (the commission responsible for labor) of the *Société des Droits de l'homme* (Human Rights Society).

## References

Achin, Catherine. 2001. "'Représentation miroir' vs parite: Les debats parlementaires Relatifs à la parite revus à la lumiere des theories politiques de la representation." *Droit et société* 47 (1): 237–56.

Amann, Peter H. 1975. *Revolution and Mass Democracy: The Paris Club Movement in 1848*. Princeton, NJ: Princeton University Press.

Ankersmit, Franklin Rudolf. 2007. "Political Representation and Political Experience: An Essay on Political Psychology." *Redescriptions: Yearbook of Political Thought and Conceptual History*, 11:21–42.

Bachrach, Peter. 1980. *The Theory of Democratic Elitism: A Critique*. Lanham, MD: University Press of America.

Baker, Keith Michel. 1987. "Representation." In *The French Revolution and the Creation of Modern Political Culture*, edited by Keith Michael Baker, Colin Lucas, François Furet, and Mona Ozouf, 1:469–92. Oxford: Pergamon.

Barber, Benjamin R. 1984. *Strong Democracy: Participatory Politics for a New Age*. Berkeley: University of California Press.

Bourdieu, Pierre. 1984. *Distinction: Social Critique of the Judgement of Taste*. Translated by R. Nice. London: Routledge and Kegan Paul.

———. 1991a. "Delegation and Political Fetishism." In *Language and Symbolic Power*, edited by John B. Thompson, 203–19. Cambridge, MA: Harvard University Press.

———. 1991b. "Political Representation: Elements for a Theory of the Political Field." In *Language and Symbolic Power*, edited by John B Thompson, 171–202. Cambridge, MA: Harvard University Press.

———. 1991c. "Social Space and the Genesis of 'Classes.'" In *Language and Symbolic Power*, edited by John B Thompson, 229–51. Cambridge, MA: Harvard University Press.

Brennan, Geoffrey, and Alan Hamlin. 1999. "On Political Representation." *British Journal of Political Science* 29 (01): 109–27.

Brito Vieira, Mónica. 2017. *Reclaiming Representation: Contemporary Advances in the Theory of Political Representation*. London: Taylor & Francis.

Disch, Lisa. 2015. "The 'Constructivist Turn' in Democratic Representation: A Normative Dead-End?" *Constellations* 22 (4): 487–99.

Dupuis-Déri, François. 1999. "L'esprit antidémocratique des fondateurs de la 'démocratie' moderne." *Agone*, 22:95–113.

Dutoya, Virginie. 2012. "La représentation de la nation à l'épreuve de la différence de genre : Quotas et représentation des femmes dans les Parlements de l'Inde et du Pakistan." PhD diss., Sciences Po, Paris.

Faggioli, Massimo, and Alberto Melloni. 2007. *Repraesentatio: Mapping a Keyword for Churches and Governance*. Berlin: Lit Verlag.

Finley, M. I. 1973. *Democracy Ancient and Modern*. New Brunswick, NJ: Rutgers University Press.

Freeden, Michael. 1996. *Ideologies and Political Theory: A Conceptual Approach*. Oxford: Clarendon.

Gaxie, Daniel. 1978. *Le Cens caché : Inégalités culturelles et ségrégation politique*. Paris: Seuil.

Hayat, Samuel. 2014. *Quand la République était révolutionnaire : Citoyenneté et représentation en 1848*. Paris: Seuil.

———. 2015. "The Revolution of 1848 in the History of French Republicanism." *History of Political Thought* 36 (2): 331–53.

Hincker, Louis. 2007. *Citoyens-combattants à Paris, 1848–1851*. Villeneuve-d'Ascq: Presses universitaires du Septentrion.

Hindess, Barry. 2000. "Representation Ingrafted upon Democracy ?" *Democratization* 7 (2): 1–18.

Hofmann, Hasso. 1973. *Repräsentation: Studien zur Wort- und Begriffsgeschichte von der Antike bis ins 19. Jahrhundert*. Schriften zur Verfassungsgeschichte. Berlin: Duncker & Humblot.

Huard, Raymond. 1996. *La naissance du parti politique en France*. Paris: Presses de la Fondation nationale des sciences politiques.

Kateb, George. 1981. "The Moral Distinctiveness of Representative Democracy." *Ethics* 91 (3): 357–74.

Kuyper, Jonathan W. 2016. "Systemic Representation: Democracy, Deliberation, and Nonelectoral Representatives." *American Political Science Review* 110 (2): 308–24.

Latour, Bruno. 2003. "What If We Talked Politics a Little?" *Contemporary Political Theory* 2 (2): 143–64.

Ledru-Rollin, Alexandre. 1841. "Profession de foi." *Revue du progrès politique, social et littéraire* 5:52–56.

Manin, Bernard. 1997. *The Principles of Representative Government*. Cambridge: Cambridge University Press.

Mansbridge, Jane. 1999. "Should Blacks Represent Blacks and Women Represent Women? A Contingent 'Yes.'" *The Journal of Politics*, 61:628–57.

———. 2003. "Rethinking Representation." *American Political Science Review* 97 (4): 515–28.

Michels, Roberto. 1962. *Political Parties: A Sociological Study of the Oligarchical Tendencies of Modern Democracy*. New York: Collier.

Mineur, Didier. 2010. *Archéologie de la représentation politique: Structure et fondement d'une crise*. Paris: Presses de la Fondation nationale des sciences politiques.

Montanaro, Laura. 2012. "The Democratic Legitimacy of Self-Appointed Representatives." *Journal of Politics* 74 (04): 1094–107.

Morgan, Robert J. 1974. "Madison's Theory of Representation in the Tenth Federalist." *Journal of Politics* 36 (04): 852–85.

Moss, Bernard H. 1976. *The Origins of the French Labor Movement, 1830–1914: The
Socialism of Skilled Workers*. Berkeley: University of California Press.

Näsström, Sofia. 2006. "Representative Democracy as Tautology Ankersmit and
Lefort on Representation." *European Journal of Political Theory* 5 (3): 321–42.

Ogien, Albert, and Sandra Laugier. 2014. *Le principe démocratie: enquête sur les
nouvelles formes du politique*. Paris: La Découverte.

Pateman, Carole. 1970. *Participation and Democratic Theory*. Cambridge: Cambridge University Press.

Phillips, Anne. 1995. *The Politics of Presence*. Oxford: Clarendon.

Pitkin, Hanna F. 1972. *The Concept of Representation*. Berkeley: University of California Press.

Plotke, David. 1997. "Representation Is Democracy." *Constellations* 4 (1): 19–34.

Przeworski, Adam, Susan Carol Stokes, and Bernard Manin, eds. 1999. *Democracy,
Accountability and Representation*. Cambridge: Cambridge University Press.

Rancière, Jacques. 2014. *Hatred of Democracy*. Translated by Steve Corcoran. London: Verso.

Rosanvallon, Pierre. 1992. *Le sacre du citoyen. Histoire du suffrage universel en
France*. Paris: Gallimard.

———. 1998. *Le peuple introuvable. Histoire de la représentation démocratique en
France*. Paris: Gallimard.

———. 2008. *Counter-democracy: Politics in an Age of Distrust*. Cambridge: Cambridge University Press.

Saward, Michael. 2010. *The Representative Claim*. Oxford: Oxford University Press.

Scarrow, Susan E. 2006. "The Nineteenth-Century Origins of Modern Political Parties: The Unwanted Emergence of Party-Based Politics." In *Handbook of Party
Politics*, edited by Richard S. Katz and William Crotty, 16–33. London: Sage.

Schumpeter, Joseph A. 2013. *Capitalism, Socialism and Democracy*. London:
Routledge.

Sewell, William Hamilton. 1980. *Work and Revolution in France: The Language of
Labor from the Old Regime to 1848*. Cambridge: Cambridge University Press.

Squires, Judith. 1996. "Quotas for Women: Fair Representation?" *Parliamentary
Affairs* 49 (1): 71–88.

———. 2001. "Representing Groups, Deconstructing Identities." *Feminist Theory*
2 (1): 7–27.

Urbinati, Nadia. 2000. "Representation as Advocacy: A Study of Democratic Deliberation." *Political Theory* 28 (6): 758–86.

———. 2005. "Continuity and Rupture: The Power of Judgment in Democratic
Representation." *Constellations* 12 (2): 194–222.

———. 2006. "Political Representation as a Democratic Process." *Redescriptions:
Yearbook of Political Thought and Conceptual History*, 10, 18–40.

————. 2011. "Representative Democracy and Its Critics." In *The Future of Representative Democracy*, edited by Sonia Alonso, John Keane, and Wolfgang Merkel, 23–49. Cambridge: Cambridge University Press.

Williams, Melissa S. 2000. *Voice, Trust, and Memory: Marginalized Groups and the Failings of Liberal Representations*. Princeton, NJ: Princeton University Press.

Young, Iris Marion. 1990. *Justice and the Politics of Difference*. Princeton, NJ: Princeton University Press.

# CHAPTER SEVEN

# Radical Democracy

## The Silent Partner in Political Representation's Constructivist Turn

Lisa Disch

The recent "democratic *rediscovery* of representation" has done a great deal more than dust off a concept and practice that fell out of favor in the participatory fervor that gripped academic political theory in the wake of the 1960s (Urbinati 2006, 5). It boldly reformulates the commonsense model of democratic representation as a mirror of or a "transmission belt" for constituency interests by orienting theory and empirical research alike toward the representative work of unelected agents such as nongovernmental organizations, advocacy groups, and even celebrities (Schwartz 1988, ch. 2).[1] At its most controversial, this new work emphasizes that political representation is constitutive: it "does not simply allow the social to be translated into the political, but also facilitates the formation of political groups and identities" (Urbinati 2006, 37). Urbinati's formulation makes it clear that the representative turn has entailed a constructivist turn to conceive political representation in mass democracies as functioning creatively, generatively, and dynamically—as theories of representation in culture, literature, and the arts would predict—rather than statically and unidirectionally as scholarly and popular common sense expects (Disch 2011). Saward (2006a, 186) writes, "there is an indispensable *aesthetic* moment in political representation because the maker [of a representation] has to be an artist, to operate aesthetically, to evoke the represented."

This chapter takes inspiration from scholars of deliberative democracy—many of whom have pioneered the representative turn—who balk at the constructivist turn. These critics worry that if political representation serves to shape social relations, to construct group identities, and to frame lines of conflict, it necessarily compromises a basic democratic intuition: that the "representative must be responsive to [the represented] rather than the other way around" (Pitkin 1967, 140). Some cast it as an "explicitly non-normative" account of political representation (Severs 2012). Others charge that, by giving up "on identifying criteria for distinguishing between persuasion and manipulation," constructivist accounts of representation reduce democratic theory to a normatively impoverished realism (Neblo 2015, 72, 114). Sofia Näsström (2015, 1) hones the question: "without recourse to election as a source of legitimacy, how do we know that such representation is democratic?"

I take inspiration from these critics, but I do not attempt to answer them. On the contrary, I argue that constructivist theorists of political representation *need not answer* the legitimacy brief. The preoccupation with legitimacy lands deliberative critics of constructivism in what I will term a manipulation impasse. This essay offers them a way out of that impasse through radical democratic pluralism, a rival tradition of democratic thought that makes it possible to think about both the dangers of mass democracy and the promise of constructivism in a different way.

## Deliberative Legitimacy and the Manipulation Impasse

Many critics who balk at the constructivist turn follow deliberative democrats in conceiving democratic theory as a normative project that assigns the theorist to the "first-order" role of specifying standards of democracy and then applying them—thereby acting as what Saward (2010, 146) has aptly termed an "adjudicator of occurrence." In this adjudicatory role, the theorist orients herself to a decision, act, or process as a judge and undertakes to evaluate whether it warrants recognition and acceptance as democratic. Deliberative democrats make legitimacy the measure of that judgment (Bohman 1996, 26; Cohen 1989; Habermas 1996). Applied to representative democracy, that measure requires the "entire representative system [to] contribut[e] to ongoing factually accurate and mutually educative communication" (Mansbridge 2003, 519). The distinction between education and manipulation—which even as she asserts it Mansbridge (2003, 519) acknowledges rests on irreducibly political claims about individual and common interest—holds the wheels on the adjudicatory project.

Setting aside the question of whether this distinction bears normative weight, deliberative legitimacy must strike anyone attuned to Rancière's (1991, 6) "myth of pedagogy" as an ideal that is riven from within.[2] It reflects a deep-seated commitment to political autonomy as Habermas (1996, 151) has defined it, the idea that democratic law and policies should command by the "generative force of communicative freedom" rather than by the threat of sanction. At the same time, because it defines democratically legitimate representation by its *educative* function, deliberative legitimacy puts the representative in a "pedagogical" relation to the constituency that Laclau and Mouffe (1985, 59) point out mirrors a specifically "authoritarian" representational mode.[3] At the extreme—which admittedly violates the deliberative injunction to mutuality—the association of representation with education authorizes vanguardism, where a party or group forges ahead on the authority of a public interest that its constituency does not (yet) recognize (59). Theorists of representation who feel obliged to take up the first-order problem of legitimacy meet an impasse if they engage democratic politics: they charge themselves to adjudicate a distinction between education and manipulation that they cannot formulate without presuming privileged insight into individual or common interests—a presumption that strains their commitment to autonomy.

I do not think it is wrong for democratic theory to take up the first-order concern with legitimacy, but I believe, with Saward, that this normative orientation does not exhaust its tasks. Saward (2010, 146–47) has suggested that democratic theory might also operate from the "citizen standpoint," using *citizen* in its broad political sense to mean democratic actors not passport-carrying nationals (see Disch 2015, 488, 493–96). The citizen standpoint confronts theorists not with the problem of legitimacy but with that of hegemony, where hegemony is understood as Laclau and Mouffe (1985) use the term to designate the conditions for and peculiar challenge of modern politics: to institute *politically* the division of the social into groups and to build alliances among some in opposition against others. True, there exists no ground from which to adjudicate the legitimacy of such alliances. The citizen's challenge is, rather, to judge the "equivalences" on which they are (or might be) based, to assess their potential to sustain a consequential power bloc that might extend relations of equality rather than scale them back (Laclau and Mouffe 1985, 128).

The argument unfolds over four sections. The first section sets the problem of legitimacy aside to elaborate the notion of hegemony as democratic practice. I read *Hegemony and Socialist Strategy* (1985) for its contributions

to democratic theorists' rediscovery of representation—contributions that
have been effaced by the tendency to narrate the representative turn as
a legacy of deliberative democratic theory.[4] The second section returns to
legitimacy from a critical vantage point, enlisting research on opinion formation to question whether scholars' concerns over elite manipulation of
citizens are empirically warranted. I take this research to demonstrate that
these concerns are both misplaced and overblown. Overblown because
manipulation is far more difficult to achieve than politicians and their pollsters fantasize it to be. And misplaced because "coordination," the systematic tendency in mass politics for group identifications to link up with
issue interpretations and "harden" lines of conflict, poses a much more
significant democratic threat than does manipulation (Chong 2000, 125).
Whereas manipulation attacks individual autonomy, coordination attacks
the "plurality" and "unfixity" of the social that radical democratic theory
establishes as a "precondition" for modern democratic politics (Laclau
and Mouffe 1985, 142).


## Constructivist Democratic Theory: From Topographical
## Categories to Hegemonic Practice

Published thirty years ago, Laclau and Mouffe's (1985) *Hegemony and
Socialist Strategy* remains the most significant statement to date of constructivist democratic theory. This work is constructivist for displacing the
normative orientation toward legitimacy to focus on hegemony, a term
they use to signal that social groups in their relations of antagonism and
cooperation are not the basis of politics but the first political task. This
constructivist position, while denying legitimacy its ground in the social,
does not reduce democracy to mere power politics. Laclau and Mouffe
understand it as struggle that plays on the "demonstration effect" of the
eighteenth-century revolutions to proliferate demand for equality across
"radically new and different political spaces" (181). Such struggle can serve
democracy, although there is no guarantee that it will.

Laclau and Mouffe link constructivism historically to the French Revolution, which, by stripping feudal social relations of the aura of sanctity
that sustained their necessity, gave rise to a distinctively "modern" politics
(138, 170). This politics, conditioned on the "plurality" or "radical unfixity"
of the social, takes the "problem of the political" in a different direction
from liberal social-contract theory (151, 170, 153). Whereas social-contract

theory poses the "problem of creating legitimate political power, establishing its origins, and setting *limits* on it" (Chambers 2004, 188), Laclau and Mouffe (1985) hold the revolution to pose the "problem of the *institution* of the social, that is, of the definition and articulation of social relations in a field criss-crossed with antagonisms" (153; emphasis added). In the liberal West, then, modern politics begins not with groups in either conflict or cooperation but with the task of soliciting group identities and defining the terms on which they might align with or oppose each other. This proposition, which is the starting place of radical democratic pluralism, identifies Western modernity with the "hegemonic form of politics" and as a break from politics based on "topographical categories" (138, 180).

A topographical politics represents both conflict and cooperation as the political expression of a sociological substrate. It is exemplified by but not limited to the symbolic order of the Ancien Régime, where terms such as *nobility*, *workers*, or *women* figure as demographic categories and static markers of "differences" understood as the substantive "contents" that "fix permanently" subjects' social roles and identities (180). This mapping of political conflict (and cooperation) onto social division represents "political struggle as a game in which the identity of the opposing forces is constituted from the start," rendering hegemonic practice inconceivable (170).

Laclau and Mouffe regard the French Revolution as the "last moment in which the antagonistic limits between two forms of society presented themselves . . . in the form of clear and empirically *given* lines of demarcation": the "opposition people/Ancien Régime" (151). By doing away with the Estates General and putting the National Assembly in its place, the French revolutionaries institutionalized a new imaginary of the social. Laclau and Mouffe, in their infamously "post-Marxist," poststructural appropriation of Saussure, characterize this nontopographical social as a "system of differences without positive terms" whose center or master term—that which Saussure holds to determine the relations among the terms—is "always finally absent" (112–13). In this new imaginary, there is no sovereign to rule decisively or master signifier to fix meaning. The absent center politicizes what might otherwise pass as fundamental building blocks of society, ushering in an order where there can be no "unity between agents" without "political construction and struggle," or "no politics without hegemony" (65, 151).[5]

This is what Laclau and Mouffe mean by hegemony: the creation of political unity by the articulation or linking together of heterogeneous struggles and demands that, absent any intrinsically shared quality or goal, can be joined only by rendering them equivalent in opposition to a system of domination. Although there is no ground from which to adjudicate among such linkages—to determine that one is more legitimate than another—still hegemony is not power politics *tout court*. It is not the imposition of order, either from above or in the name of a common essence, but the "*political construction* from dissimilar elements" of an "equivalential chain" (85, 127–34). Laclau and Mouffe give the example of the relation between the "trade union militancy of white workers and racism or anti-racism" (141). Trade unionists are not given to racism ontologically but solicited into it by "whiteness" (Roediger 1991), which symbolizes a chain of privileges that materialize race—which itself is not a fact but a quintessentially "empty signifier" (Laclau 2005, 96). Insofar as they are hegemonically solicited to racism, they might be counterhegemonically called to "anti-racist struggle" by the political consolidation of an equivalential relation "among such contents as anti-racism, anti-sexism, and anti-capitalism which, left to themselves, do not necessarily tend to converge" (Laclau and Mouffe 1985, 141). As Lasse Thomassen (2005, 106) emphasizes, hegemony is "essentially a relation of representation" understood in constructivist terms so that "the representation is not the representation of an original presence but what brings about the represented."[6]

Liberal and (many) Marxist accounts of politics will mute the force of this revolutionary break with topography by discovering in "interest" a new unifying force, one potentially more voluntary but no less prepolitical than the premodern belief that society rested on a natural and God-given order. Radical democracy is distinct for emphasizing the precariousness of the relationship between agents' political identity and their economic locations and interests, which do not come together spontaneously but only as the result of "an articulatory practice" that issues specific demands (Laclau and Mouffe 1985, 120–21). Again, these articulations are not subject to "an essential necessity" that requires one struggle be joined (or not be joined) to another (94, 120). Articulation effects a linkage that transforms: it is "not just a rationalist coincidence of 'interests' among preconstituted agents" but a grafting that specifies the direction and political import of what it links together (58). In linking, it also effects a "*division* of social space," joining various struggles by virtue of that to which they are antagonistically opposed (165).

"Antagonism," which Oliver Marchart (2007, 140) identifies as Laclau and Mouffe's "main contribution to contemporary political thought," is a confrontation between two forces in which the presence of each before the other prevents either from being what it either wants, feels obligated, or is confined to be. It "arises from the failure of the constitution of identity" (Thomassen 2005, 107).[7] Laclau and Mouffe (1985, 125) give the example of a landowner expelling a peasant from the land, which is an antagonism because land is simultaneously that *without which* the peasant cannot be a peasant and that which *when denuded of peasants* displaces the landowner from his position of mastery over persons. Expelling the peasant subjects both peasant and landowner to the order of commodity value, in which neither can continue to be what they were. For a more contemporary example, take Mulvey's (1975) classic analysis of narrative cinema and consider the disconcerting moment when the female subject returns the gaze: she fails as feminine "spectacle" and denies masculine "omnipotence" by collapsing the distance on which it depends.

Antagonism is not, as some readers have interpreted it, the opposite of engagement, generosity, or compromise (Coles 1996). Nor is it synonymous with disagreement, conflict, or "interminable hostility," as others have claimed (Barnett 2004, 505). The opposite of antagonism is what Laclau (1990, 92) terms the "ideological," which consists of "those discursive forms" that attempt to fix meaning and identity in place. In contemporary Western societies, such forms are manifest in discourses of race, sex, ethnic, and national identity that determine social identities, fix them to political claims, and thereby foreclose the practice of hegemony. Antagonism, as political struggle between existentially distinct possibilities, challenges habitual or essentialist parsings of the social. Laclau (1990, 18) credits it with "a revelatory function" to show identities to be contingent on institutions and make institutions perceptible *as* institutions rather than as expressions of natural differences or functional hierarchies. Antagonism makes it plain that institutions are hegemonic all the way down: they take the form that they do in the present not because they are legitimate but by the exclusion of "historically available and politically articulated alternatives" (Marchart 2014, 275).

Pamela Brandwein (2017) illustrates the "revelatory" aspect of antagonism and the "hegemonic" character of social order in a recent article that reexamines the debates over the Thirteenth Amendment. A crucial historical moment in the articulation of liberal individualism to market capitalism, these debates entertained a question that is nearly inconceivable today: whether contract labor is the quintessence of freedom or its opposite. Brandwein (2017, 32) narrates an existential conflict between two nineteenth-century discourses, "free-labor" republicanism and what she terms "labor-movement antislavery," which took mutually exclusive positions on this question. Today's scholarly consensus credits free labor with mounting at once a critique of slavery and a critique of class hierarchy, thereby making the Thirteenth Amendment available as a tool in the struggle for fair labor contracts today (e.g., VanderVelde 1989). Brandwein (2017, 16) establishes that despite its potent and historically consequential opposition to slavery, free labor did not extend that opposition to "wage laborers *qua* wage laborers." On the contrary, free labor's "promotion of self-ownership and the equal rights to contract" made it "an early language of modern capitalism," one that abetted the "assimilation of wage labor to 'freedom'" (32, 37). The triumph of free labor excluded labor-movement antislavery, an alternative ideology that likened the "equal right to contract" to slavery, as "a 'fraud,' [and] a function of forced dependency" (29, 32). This was a rival chain of equivalence; an attempted counterhegemonic articulation that failed. This excluded alternative offered a radical critique of capitalism by means of proposing an "equivalence" between the struggles of wage laborers and slaves.

Although she does not use the concept, Brandwein effectively narrates an antagonism. She demonstrates that free-labor republicanism and labor-movement antislavery were not allies pursuing a common abolitionist cause. They were opponents in an existential struggle whose competing and mutually exclusive constructions of the relationship between contract and freedom meant that each prevented the other from constituting itself as a force for emancipation. The triumph of free labor institutionalized wage labor in the United States as a condition of political independence not because "self-ownership and the equal rights to contract" are a *legitimate* basis for liberal freedom but because they emerged as *hegemonic* at a particularly consequential moment in the development of liberalism. Labor-movement antislavery, then, is significant as the excluded alternative that brings this hegemony to light.

It is also significant as an exemplary democratic struggle, one that aims to disclose "a relation of subordination [as] a relation of oppression" and, thereby, constitute it as the "site of an antagonism" (Laclau and Mouffe 1985, 153). The very fact that free-labor republicanism and labor-movement antislavery could contest whether "contract" should be regarded as the basis of freedom or its opposite confirms that democratic struggle does not emerge spontaneously from an empirical ground. Those subject to contract labor might or might not understand it as oppressive, depending on whether they subscribed to the free-labor position or to that of labor-movement antislavery. Hegemony comes in at the point of the struggle between them. As Laclau and Mouffe have put it, with a claim whose simplicity belies its radicalism, the "struggle against subordination cannot be the result of the situation of subordination itself" (152).

This claim devastates a basic democratic assumption common to liberalism, Marxism, the New Left, and what Judith Grant (1993) nicely terms "fundamental feminism": the idea that political struggle begins with the "experience" of oppression and has as its principal requisite a "raised" or otherwise enlightened "consciousness." Against this common sense, Laclau and Mouffe (1985) emphasize two important points. First, subordination is not "automatically" a political relation; it must be represented as "oppressive" to count as such (153). Second, oppression is not a sociological fact but a political accomplishment. What can be recognized as oppression depends on the languages available for making political demands, those languages being in their turn—as the antagonism between free-labor and labor republicanism exemplifies—objects of hegemonic contest. Together these two claims displace the individual subject, consciousness, and concerns about manipulation from the foreground to the background of democratic politics to focus on the logics of conflict that a political system makes available.

Subordination—being "subjected to the decisions of another"—is an everyday occurrence (153). It happens in the household, the workplace, at school, in interactions with the welfare state and the private insurer, and in consumer transactions with banks, automobile companies, the cable provider, and more. Such relations do not give rise to political struggle as a matter of course because they are, variously, imbued with authority (e.g., employer/employee), legitimized procedurally (e.g., majority rule), or passed off as natural (e.g., wife/husband "in certain forms of family organization"). Even such extreme examples of subordination, as "'serf,' 'slave,' and so on, do not designate *in themselves* antagonistic positions," however objectionable they may be to us, as inheritors of the revolutionary social imaginary (154; emphasis added). The mere experience of subordination, then, cannot give rise to antagonism. To become sites of political struggle, a new social logic must intervene to reconceive of "differential" relations, those that had been passed off either as following from nature or being authorized by divine will, as humanly imposed, arbitrary, and, hence, oppressive.

Oppression, then, is not an object of experience or perception but a hegemonic achievement that requires a "discursive 'exterior'" or repre-

sentation of society to redescribe as *political acts* power asymmetries that
are taken as mere *effects of differences* (154). Laclau and Mouffe regard
the French Revolution as not just a modern revolution but a distinctively
democratic one for introducing a powerful language of oppression with the
Declaration of the Rights of Man. The language of rights displaced a feudal
social system in which hierarchy was justified by logics of difference for a
democratic one in which the "logic of equivalence [became] the fundamental instrument of production of the social" (155). They trace this logic of
"equivalence" from the assertion of citizenship against monarchal rule to
the extension of citizenship from men of property to wage workers, to the
"displacement" of egalitarian demands from the field of politics to that of
economics, and to the proliferation, alongside the struggles of white men,
of struggles that displace the discourse of rights still further "from the field
of political equality between citizens to the field of equality between the
sexes" and the races (156, 154). This is the "profound subversive power"
of the democratic revolution to "allow the spread of equality and liberty
into increasingly wider domains and therefore act as a *fermenting agent*
upon the different forms of struggle against subordination" (155; emphasis added).

   This notion of rights as a "fermenting agent" of struggle is significant
precisely because it refuses to count rights as legal universals and markers
of democratic legitimacy. Laclau (1977, 107) has argued that rights function in what might be termed an interpellative sense as a way to hail a
"people" into being as subject in "confrontation with the power bloc."
Understood literally as legal universals, rights claims might serve to mark
struggles as democratically legitimate; understood in this interpellative
sense, they assuredly do not.[8] Laclau and Mouffe (1985, 168) insist "the discursive compass of the democratic revolution opens the way for political
logics as diverse as right-wing populism and totalitarianism on the one
hand and a radical democracy on the other." The direction of rights-based
struggle, like that of "*any other social struggle*, depends upon its forms
of articulation within a given hegemonic context" (86–87). Feminism, for
example, has been articulated to discourses and struggles ranging from
biological essentialism and "separate spheres" to Marxism and, so, has
given rise to various demands: "a radical feminism which attacks men as
such; a feminism of difference which seeks to revalorize 'femininity'; and a
Marxist feminism for which the fundamental enemy is capitalism, considered as linked indissolubly to patriarchy" (169). It is not topography but
hegemony—the *articulation*—that "gives [struggles] their character, not
the place from which they come" (169; emphasis added).

When Laclau and Mouffe call "hegemony . . . a political *type of relation, a form*, if one so wishes, of politics[,] but not a determinable location within a topography of the social," they put forward a democratic politics without guarantees (139). In their words, "radical and plural democracy" means that "there are no surfaces which are privileged *a priori* for the emergence of antagonisms" and no "discursive regions" that should be excluded "*a priori* as possible spheres of struggle" (191–92). This emphasis on antagonism offers a version of modern politics that is not *by definition* democratic. In contrast to social-contract theory, it centers not on legitimacy or consent but on the "openness and indeterminacy of the social" (144–45). Whereas in the feudal imaginary, every element has its group and every group has its place, this openness creates the conditions of possibility for "unsuspected articulations [that alter] the social and political identities that are permissible and even thinkable" (60). This is the radical democratic promise of hegemonic politics, for political actors to forge alliances such as that between economic liberalism and support for civil rights in late 1930s United States, which transformed the meaning of liberalism and set the Democratic and Republican parties on entirely new geographic bases (Schickler 2016). Whether or not such articulations serve democratic struggle—struggle that proliferates the demand for equality beyond the recognizably political targets of citizenship and voting rights—depends on the social divisions and alliances that articulation creates, not the experiences or social locations of the linked subjects (Laclau and Mouffe 1985, 167).

Laclau and Mouffe have no answer to Nässtrom's (2015, 1) question as she posed it: How do constructivists assure that representation is democratic absent "recourse to election as a source of legitimacy?" Their approach affords no principle with which to adjudicate among struggles and alliances in a first-order way. From the "citizen standpoint," the response to whatever one judges to be an undemocratic articulation of struggles is to attempt a rival articulation on the basis of an alternate equivalence. As Brandwein (2017) shows, it matters whether a critique of slavery proceeds by affirming an equivalence between wage labor and slavery or whether it juxtaposes the two by means of a rival equivalence between contract and freedom. As neither of these can be judged more manipulative than the other, legitimacy affords little critical traction here. But there is a politically consequential difference between them. As compared to free labor, labor-movement antislavery proposes a more far-reaching extension of equality, paired with a counterhegemonic interpretation of capitalism.

## The Manipulation Problem: Political or Metaphysical?

Deliberative democrats believe they have good reason to worry about manipulation and democratic legitimacy. This concern persists even among proponents of the "systemic approach" to democratic deliberation, who are willing to concede that even the most strategic forms of mass political communication may contribute to a deliberative process (Mansbridge et al. 2012, 1–2). Yet even as they recognize that both protest politics and "partisan campaigns and heuristics" can serve the deliberative process by providing information or promoting inclusiveness, proponents of the systemic approach maintain a normative orientation toward such activities. They continue to affirm the theorist's first-order responsibility to devise criteria by which to weigh the "pluses and minuses" of political protest and political campaigning in light of communicative norms (18). Their continued commitment to locate "where to draw the line between pressure and persuasion" (19) testifies that they remain in thrall to Pitkin's (1967, 233) basic injunction: that democratic representation necessarily falls on the right side of the "line between leadership and manipulation" however tenuous that line may be.

From this perspective, it may well make sense to worry about manipulation. But this perspective, like any perspective, is partial. So, what if deliberative democrats are worried about the wrong thing? Does the manipulation concern hold up to empirical evidence?

A significant body of empirical research suggests that the concern with manipulation is overblown. To begin with, scholars of public opinion and political preference formation have shown repeatedly that individuals are *not* easily induced to change the beliefs that underlie their attitudes. Elites can affect attitude formation only by "priming" to raise the salience of an issue and/or "framing" to influence the considerations an individual brings to bear in evaluating it (Chong and Druckman 2011). Experimental work on framing, especially in psychology, has tended to exaggerate elite control by studying political messaging out of the context of political debate (Chong and Druckman 2007). Sniderman and Theriault (2004, 158) indict the "whole body of studies on framing" for having "gone terribly wrong" by designing experiments that make "citizens look like puppets" because they fail to account for the "clash of political arguments" (see also Chong 2000, 130). In mass democratic politics, not only do elite messages play out in an uncertain context of people's "established views, sentiments, political orientations, or values" (Sniderman and Theriault 2004, 139). They must also contend against "competing messages ... sent by opposing parties" (Chong 2000, 130).

Put simply, in the competitive context of democratic politics, the capacity to frame does not confer the power to manipulate. In Chong's (2000, 131) words, "although the research literature is replete with examples of how public preferences are susceptible to framing effects and heresthetic, or agenda-setting, maneuvers, these discoveries tend to be made after the fact." And where discursive competition diminishes elite control over messaging, it can even give individuals a measure of control by stimulating them to "more careful evaluation of competing frames" (Chong and Druckman 2007, 652). This research yields two significant findings: that individuals tend to question the plausibility of various framings provided they are exposed to competing messages and that they are moved more by the relative *strength* of a frame than by its frequency of repetition (649, 645; emphasis added). Chong and Druckman are careful to note that the "strongest frames" are not necessarily the "most sound or meritorious arguments according to empirical, analytical, or normative standards" (652).

These two findings send a mixed message. Whereas individuals exhibit a kind of autonomy in the competitive political contexts where they typically encounter elite messages, they are moved by "strong" and "weak" frames rather than "true" and "false" ones. Is it really fair to say that research into "*competitive* political rhetoric" takes the deliberative democrat's concerns about manipulation off the table (Chong and Druckman 2013, 1; 2007)? Does it not validate those very concerns by showing that elites influence opinion formation by proposing issue framings that are false and misleading to have them taken up by the less-informed who perceive them to be "strong"? What is manipulation if not that?

Manipulation requires not simply *proposing* false framings but being able to assure that they will be taken up as "strong." Empirical studies of framing and opinion formation have repeatedly emphasized that elites *cannot* do this, however often they and their pollsters may overestimate their capacity to do so (Druckman and Jacobs 2015, chs. 5–6). Few framing scholars have undertaken to pose the crucial question of how any given frame comes to be perceived as strong or weak; they tend to test for framing effects in the controlled context of the experiment rather than analyze the chaos of discursive competition in a policy or electoral campaign. Chong (2000; 1996) is an exception in this regard. Through a combination of qualitative interviewing and case study, he has developed a metatheory of the framing process that governs how individuals come to view one frame as more pertinent than another in considering a particular issue. I contend that this metatheory brings to light a tendency of mass politics—a "coordination process" between issues and group identifications—that poses a more significant threat to democracy than does manipulation (Chong 2000, ch. 4). This threat, and its import to democracy, appears more readily to theorists of hegemony than it does to theorists of legitimacy because it targets not the autonomy of the individual but the plurality of the social, the condition of possibility for articulatory (or hegemonic) practice.

## Coordination: A Throwback to the Premodern Social

Chong (1996) argues that individuals differentiate between strong and weak frames by making use, more or less consciously, of "common frames of reference." A common frame of reference is an issue interpretation, "popularized by discussion," that teaches individuals to "base [their] opinion on certain pertinent aspects of the debate" and to dismiss "other features of the topic deemed to be irrelevant" (Chong 1996, 196; 2000, 118). A common frame of reference is a kind of heuristic or knowledge-building shortcut that enables individuals to orient themselves in a competitive rhetorical field. Common frames of reference affect opinion formation indirectly, constraining *how* an individual will approach an issue as opposed to dictating *what* they will think about it. There is nothing inherently troubling about them. Norms and principles, for example, are "one kind of common frame of reference" (Chong 1996, 196). But stereotypes, memes such as "death panels" or "weapons of mass destruction," and even "goals such as homeownership and open space" can serve equally well (Chong and Druckman 2007, 652; see also Druckman 2010).[9]

The theorist's first impulse when confronted with this phenomenon may be to propose a normative framework to differentiate between frames of reference that are more or less legitimate insofar as they are more or less normatively acceptable or epistemically valid. This is a perfectly reasonable first-order task, one that would enable a theorist and even a politician to offer commentary on a political competition. Yet, as 2016 Democratic presidential nominee Hillary Clinton's infamous "deplorables" comment and other similar gaffes illustrate, such an approach offers little critical or tactical advantage over common frames of reference in mass political discourse. It is rather more prone to backfire because individuals' common frames of reference are typically not open to argument: they tend to hold to them more out of group loyalty than intellectual conviction.

Chong (2000, 119) redirects attention from the content of these frames of reference to the dynamics that link frames of reference to group loyalties by introducing the concept *coordination process* to describe how frames of reference come to be held in common. The term *coordination* describes the systematic process whereby cue-giving elites and members of publics converge on particular issue interpretations as those interpretations prove successful in mobilizing collective action. This process (or tendency) links group identifications to issue interpretations, consolidating each of these as it secures the links between them. In what Chong (125–26) characterizes as a "self-reinforcing" relationship, "people's evaluations are systematically coordinated around group identifications and values, and those identifications and values are renewed and strengthened" by political victories. Once established, these frames of reference, the group identifications they consolidate, and the strategies of mobilization they engender are difficult to "displace" (125).

In short, coordination enables collective action successes by diminishing the heterogeneity and competitiveness of a discursive field. It reduces the plurality of arguments that individuals are willing to hear about an issue and "hardens" the links between issue interpretations and group identifications (125). This pays off in two distinct ways, by lowering the costs of opinion formation on the part of the individual and mitigating the uncertainty of political messaging on the part of opinion leaders. This is not manipulation; coordination happens without a coordinator. There is neither a decisive moment where a group chooses to define itself by a common frame nor a smoke-filled room in which politicians or other elites collectively scheme to rally their supporters around an interpretive frame. Chong emphasizes that the coordination process involves an "element of surprise" (130). A "politician [accidentally] discovers an issue that captivates" a numerically significant constituency and that success inspires others to follow suit, with the result that a line of conflict and its accompanying patterns of group identification and affiliation become more or less temporarily entrenched (132). In short, elites do not control this process, but they can exploit it by returning to and reinforcing "successful coordination around particular values and identifications" (132).[10]

The phenomenon of coordination suggests, along with constructivist theorists of representation, that mass political coalitions are built not primarily around preexisting values and interests but around conventions of argument that become politically charged. Moreover, it affirms that group identification is not rooted in an individual's social position or characteristics but, rather, produced and reinforced in speech and action. Individuals develop a sense of group membership as they learn, most forcefully through victories secured by such collective actions as voting, that others share their sense of what an "issue is and is not about" and that in acting on that sense they may expect "that others will follow suit" (Chong 1996, 200; Chong 2000, 129). Even as he charts the dynamics of a phenomenon that corroborates these central constructivist premises, Chong equivocates on a crucial question: whether group identifications enable common frames of reference to take hold or whether such frames of reference participate in consolidating group identifications. This is a critical point, not just for constructivist theories of political representation but for Chong's own argument; for if the coordination process tracks putatively prepolitical groupings, then there is little to "coordinate."

At his most foundationalist, Chong (2000, 123) affirms that an individual's "perspective" on issues follows from the "*reference groups* and values that have the greatest currency in their lives (e.g., race, ideology, partisanship, social class)." This terminology of *reference groups* is especially unfortunate because by all but reducing a group to a frame of reference it simply conflates the very phenomena—group identification and shared frameworks of interpretation—whose relationship is at issue. By contrast, at his most constructivist, Chong (2000, 129) emphasizes that "there is no self-explanatory, reflexive reaction to a new political issue." Individuals are "cross-pressured by several group memberships," and the social field is composed of a plurality of "norms, values, symbols, and group identifications" that could give rise to "many possible reactions" (126, 129). It requires "political organization" to raise the salience of particular group identifications, to define an issue as their signature, and to bring them to converge on a shared way of thinking about it (129).

This "coordination process" has significant consequences for democratic politics that are not well captured by a normative concern with manipulation (119). Coordination affects the social field's openness to articulatory practices. Alliances become predictable and opposition becomes difficult not because people dispute messages that might forge new lines of conflict but because they dismiss them altogether: the messages are regarded as neither wrong nor objectionable but as merely irrelevant. Under such conditions, a focus on the problem of manipulation will obscure what "coordination" puts at stake, which is the very possibility of democratic

politics understood as "distinctively the domain in which choices are contestable legitimately" (Sniderman and Theriault 2004, 140). Coordination
threatens choice not overtly, by repressing it as illegitimate, but by the
powerful compound of group loyalty and common sense.

This research suggests that the concerns about manipulation may not
just be overblown but altogether misplaced. Manipulation is an attack
on the autonomy of the political subject. Coordination, by contrast, is
an attack on the "plurality of the social" (Laclau and Mouffe 1985, 181).
Whereas both are forms of coercion, only the second affects what Laclau
and Mouffe take to be distinctive to modern democracy: its opening of
the "possibility of unsuspected articulations [which alter] the social and
political identities that are permissible and even thinkable" (60), and which
have the potential to transform hegemonic relations of power.

## Conclusion: Taking up the Citizen Standpoint

This chapter opened with a complaint. Critics charge that constructivist approaches to political representation lead normative theory into a dead end
because, being indifferent to the problem of legitimacy, such approaches
cannot account for the difference between democratic and undemocratic
acts of representation. These critics are not wrong. To hold that political
representation evokes the represented, shapes social conflict, and escapes
the discipline of election does indeed evacuate a pivotal distinction: that
between leadership and manipulation—a distinction by which deliberative
democrats distinguish acts of representation that are democratically legitimate from those that are not.

Even conceding this point, architects of the constructivist account might
well be puzzled to find their democratic credentials called into question.
They make the constructivist turn to disclose representation's capacity
to remap society—its group identities, national boundaries, and lines of
conflict. And they regard this as opening up various radically democratic
possibilities: to forge unprecedented political alliances (Laclau and Mouffe
1985, 60); to recognize representatives who do not count as such within
established party systems (Saward 2006b; 2010); and to create as subjects
of representation previously excluded groups or entities that can only be
imagined, such as future generations, microscopic species, and ecological
processes (Saward 2006a, 185; 2008). I have shown that select empirical
research, mostly on US politics, confirms the constructivist vision. Studies

document how consequential social programs have created and empowered their constituencies after the fact (Campbell 2003). They show that so-called target populations for policy are not socially given but politically contested (Soss 2005; Soss, Fording, and Schram 2011; Jensen 2005). And they demonstrate that episodes of partisan realignment do not simply redistribute groups but radically remake them (Schickler 2016).

The argument of this chapter may not satisfy the theorist who takes up the first-order question of when such group-making activities are legitimate and when they are not. I have argued that the theorist who takes up the citizen standpoint confronts a different question: that of hegemony, which, as Laclau and Mouffe (1985) use the term, poses a problem of alliances. It requires asking, What is this struggle to which I commit myself? Who or what is my opponent? Who might be an ally? And how might my struggle be transformed by choosing this alliance rather than that one? Legitimacy affords little traction over questions such as these because they are antagonistic: they involve "a choice between conflicting alternatives" that set different futures, different legitimacies, and different normativities in motion (Mouffe 2013, 3; Laclau 1990, 35). Resolving such conflicts involves appealing to ideologies and value commitments that are so deeply seated as to resist justification; this does not mean, however, that all outcomes are equal.

As citizens in the broad sense we are obligated to oppose futures that we cannot live with. Arguing their legitimacy is one way of mounting opposition. In well-regulated democratic regimes, legitimacy discourse has force in the juridical domain of courts and regulatory agencies (not just graduate seminars and the dinner parties of the so-called liberal elite). But it yields little leverage in the field of popular organizing where electoral and other mass majorities are built.

## Notes

This essay benefitted greatly from the spirited discussion at the Two Faces of Representation workshop (October 2015). I am grateful to all the participants but especially to Johannes Pollak and Dario Castiglione for inviting me to participate in it and to Jenny Mansbridge for hosting it. I am also grateful to the participants in the Political Theory workshop at Stanford, where an excellent discussion launched my revisions. Thanks go to Emilee Chapman for the invitation and to Bernardo Zacka for launching the discussion. In the final throes of revising, a careful and caring reading by Sam Chambers made all the difference.

1. Some key recent empirical and theoretical works include Bellamy and Kröger 2013; Celis, Childs, and Kantola 2014; Kröger and Friedrich 2013; Lord and Pollack 2013; Manin 1997; Mansbridge 2003; Monaghan 2013; Montanaro 2012; Plotke 1997; Rehfeld 2006; Runciman 2007; Sørenson 2002; Young 2000.

2. From Rancière's perspective, traditional education is fundamentally at odds with democratic politics. This is not to say that there can be no emancipatory pedagogy; on the contrary, that is exactly what Rancière's essays dramatize. But as Chambers's (2014) inspired reading of Rancière makes clear, even an emancipatory pedagogical relation would not translate easily into deliberative politics because it involves a degree of coercion and something other than a communicative exchange: it requires the teacher to impose "her will upon the student by requiring him to read [a] text, to write about the text, to say what he sees and observe what he hears."

3. Mansbridge (2003, 519) herself acknowledges the family resemblance, noting that the deliberative account of representation permits the influence of the representative over the represented to be "highly unequal," provided it serves educative ends "of nonmanipulation, illuminating interests, and facilitating retrospectively approvable transformation." She even concedes the difficulty of differentiating between democratic and authoritarian modes of representation given that "questions regarding voters' interests, in contrast to their preferences, are . . . 'essentially contested'" (519–20). But far from making her wary of casting democratic representation in an educative mode, this appears to deepen her commitment to it, as she suggests that "mutual communication" with the representative can be understood to illuminate interests insofar as it "deepens the base on which the voters' preferences rest" and does not frame issues and interests in ways that, "given adequate information and the time for adequate reflection, the voters would reject" (520).

4. In an influential and richly insightful review essay, Urbinati and Warren (2008, 393) credit Habermas (1996) and Manin (1997) for reawakening democratic theorists to the importance of political representation, Habermas by developing the notion of "public spheres of judgment" and Manin by proposing to regard elections "as a means of judging the characters of rulers."

5. Laclau and Mouffe's account of the French Revolution resembles that of Furet (1977) but without the conservatism. Furet holds that the Revolution made a lamentable break with an order that held political power appropriately in check by grounding it in the social. Laclau and Mouffe follow Lefort in conceiving the Revolution as a transformation of the symbolic practice of power. To be sure, the revolutionaries changed both society and politics. They did so, however, not by literally detaching politics from its social base but by disclosing something that every regime save modern democracy has dissimulated: that the unities (e.g., races, classes, interest groups) of which societies are supposedly composed do not "exist until they have been given a form" (Lefort 1988, 18).

6. Initially, Laclau and Mouffe (1985, 65) present their position as aiming to "replac[e] the principle of representation with that of *articulation*." Laclau's (1996, ch. 6; 2005) later work confirms that their account of hegemony can be read not as a replacement but as a reconceptualization of representation conceived simplistically "as transparency" (Laclau and Mouffe 1985, 58).

7. Thomassen (2005, 107–9) makes a brilliant critical reading of an ambiguity that arises from Laclau and Mouffe's (1985, 122) claim that antagonism is the "limit" of objectivity. He writes that whereas antagonism "is supposed to both *prevent* the fullness of identity and *arise from* the failure of fullness," it cannot do both (Thomassen 2005, 108–9). As the above example shows, it is necessary to presuppose the feudal ideal of an interdependent community to perceive that expelling the peasants will give rise to antagonism. Thus, Thomassen concludes, antagonism is "one possible discursive representation" of social relations, "but, as such, it is not the limit of objectivity or representation" (108–9).

8. Chambers (2004) argues convincingly that Laclau understands rights as "empty signifiers that mediate the gap between universal and particular," providing a language in which a specific demand can invoke an ideal that can provide a discursive framework for linking various demands in a broader struggle (197). Chambers insightfully concludes that the radical democratic understanding of rights not only dissociates rights-based struggle from liberal identity politics (the link that its critics have emphasized) but demonstrates that the "viability of hegemonic politics today depends on the discourse of rights" (198).

9. Some researchers have argued that in the United States, in debates over welfare provision to the poor, conservative framings that cast aid as being inconsistent with values of limited government and self-sufficiency have a competitive edge over liberal framings, because the latter must contend with the ambivalence that universalist, rights-based, state-centered framings inevitably generate in a cultural context of individualism (McCloskey and Zaller 1984).

10. The example of Fox News in the case of the Tea Party illustrates this point. In February 2009, a hodgepodge of groups mixing a variety of protest styles emerged to oppose President Obama's just-passed $750 billion economic stimulus. Over the next years, Fox News (and prominent conservative funders such as the Koch brothers and former congressperson Dick Armey's (R-TX) nonprofit advocacy group FreedomWorks) helped consolidate this geographically, demographically, and economically diverse assemblage into a forceful political agent. Williamson, Skocpol, and Coggin (2011, 34) demonstrate that "Fox News helped to construct a common ideological agenda for heterogeneous Tea Party supporters by priming issues such as deficits, government spending, immigration and border security." Its regular coverage "even in periods where actual political happenings [were] not occurring" made the group a fixture in the politics of the early Obama years whether it was active or not (29). It also participated in recruiting membership, "connecting the Tea Party to [Fox's] own brand identity," thereby carrying

into politics the relationship that a city's leading classical music station has with its symphony orchestra (29). See also Disch 2012.

## References

Barnett, Clive. 2004. "Deconstructing Radical Democracy: Articulation, Representation, and Being-with-Others." *Political Geography* 23 (5): 503–28.

Bellamy, Richard, and Sandra Kröger. 2013. "Representation Deficits and Surpluses in EU Policy-Making." *Journal of European Integration* 35 (5): 477–97.

Bohman, James. 1996. *Public Deliberation: Pluralism, Complexity, and Democracy*. Cambridge, MA: MIT Press.

Brandwein, Pamela. 2017. "The 'Labor Vision' of the Thirteenth Amendment, Revisited." *Georgetown Journal of Law and Public Policy* 15:13–57.

Campbell, Andrea. 2003. *How Policies Make Citizens: Senior Political Activism and the American Welfare State*. Princeton, NJ: Princeton University Press.

Celis, Karen, Sarah Childs, and Johanna Kantola. 2014. "Constituting Women's Interests through Representative Claims." *Politics & Gender* 10 (2): 149–74.

Chambers, Samuel A. 2004. "Giving Up (on) Rights? The Future of Rights and the Project of Radical Democracy." *American Journal of Political Science* 48 (2): 185–200.

———. 2014. "Walter White is a Bad Teacher: Pedagogy, Partage, and Politics in Season 4 of *Breaking Bad*." *Theory & Event* 17 (1). https://muse-jhu-edu.proxy .lib.umich.edu/article/539134.

Chong, Dennis. 1996. "Creating Common Frames of Reference on Political Issues." In *Political Persuasion and Attitude Change*, edited by Diana C. Mutz, Richard A. Brody, Paul M. Sniderman, 195–224. Ann Arbor: University of Michigan Press.

———. 2000. *Rational Lives: Norms and Values in Politics and Society*. Chicago: University of Chicago Press.

Chong, Dennis, and James N. Druckman. 2007. "Framing Public Opinion in Competitive Democracies." *American Political Science Review* 101 (4): 637–55.

———. 2011. "Public-Elite Interactions: Puzzles in Search of Researchers." In *Oxford Handbook of the American Public Opinion and the Media*, edited by Robert Y. Shapiro, Lawrence R. Jacobs, and George C. Edwards III, 170–88. Oxford: Oxford University Press.

———. 2013. "Counterframing Effects." *Journal of Politics* 75 (1): 1–16.

Cohen, Joshua. 1989. "Deliberation and Democratic Legitimacy." In *The Good Polity*, edited by Alan Hamlin and Philip Pettit, 17–34. Oxford: Basil Blackwell.

Coles, Romand. 1996. "Liberty, Equality, Receptive Generosity: Neo-Nietzschean Reflections on the Ethics and Politics of Coalition." *American Political Science Review* 90 (2): 375–88.

Disch, Lisa. 2011. "Toward a Mobilization Conception of Democratic Representation." *American Political Science Review* 105 (1): 100–114.

———. 2012. "The Tea Party: A 'White Citizenship' Movement?" In *Steep: The*

*Precipitous Rise of the Tea Party*, edited by Lawrence Rosenthal and Christine Trost, 133–51. Berkeley: University of California Press.

———. 2015. "The 'Constructivist Turn' in Democratic Representation: A Normative Dead-End?" *Constellations* 22 (4): 487–99.

Druckman, James N. 2010. "What's It All About? Framing in Political Science." In *Perspectives on Framing*, edited by Gideon Keren, 279–301. NY: Psychology Press/Taylor and Francis.

Druckman, James N., and Lawrence R. Jacobs. 2015. *Who Governs? Presidents, Public Opinion, and Manipulation.* Chicago: University of Chicago Press.

Furet, François. 1977. *Interpreting the French Revolution.* Translated by Elborg Forster. Cambridge: Cambridge University Press.

Grant, Judith. 1993. *Fundamental Feminism: Contesting the Core Concepts of Feminist Theory.* New York: Routledge.

Habermas, Jürgen. 1996. *Between Facts and Norms: Contributions to a Discourse Theory of Law and Democracy.* Translated by William Rehg. Cambridge, MA: MIT Press.

Jensen, Laura S. 2005. "Constructing and Entitling America's Original Veterans." In *Deserving and Entitled: Social Constructions and Public Policy*, edited by Anne L. Schneider and Helen M. Ingram, 35–62. Albany, NY: SUNY Press.

Kröger, Sandra, and Dawid Friedrich. 2013. "The Representative Turn in European Union Studies." *Journal of European Public Policy* 20 (2): 171–89.

Laclau, Ernesto. 1977. *Politics and Ideology in Marxist Theory: Capitalism, Fascism, Populism.* New York: New Left Books.

———. 1990. *New Reflections on the Revolution of Our Time.* New York: Verso.

———. 1996. *Emancipations.* New York: Verso.

———. 2005. *On Populist Reason.* New York: Verso.

Laclau, Ernesto, and Chantal Mouffe. 1985. *Hegemony and Socialist Strategy: Towards a Radical Democratic Politics.* New York: Verso.

Lefort, Claude. 1988. *Democracy and Political Theory.* Translated by David Macey. Minneapolis: University of Minnesota Press.

Lord, Christopher, and Johannes Pollack. 2013. "The Pitfalls of Representation as Claims-Making in the European Union." *Journal of European Integration* 35 (5): 517–30.

Manin, Bernard. 1997. *The Principles of Representative Government.* Cambridge: Cambridge University Press.

Mansbridge, Jane J. 2003. "Rethinking Representation." *American Political Science Review* 97 (4): 515–28.

Mansbridge, Jane J., James Bohman, Simone Chambers, Thomas Christiano, Archon Fung, John Parkinson, Dennis F. Thompson, and Mark E. Warren. 2012. "A Systemic Approach to Deliberative Democracy." In *Deliberative Systems: Deliberative Democracy at the Large Scale*, edited by John Parkinson and Jane J. Mansbridge, 1–26. New York: Cambridge University Press.

Marchart, Oliver. 2007. *Post-Foundational Political Thought: Political Difference in Nancy, Lefort, Badiou and Laclau*. Edinburgh: Edinburgh University Press.

———. 2014. "Institution and dislocation: Philosophical roots of Laclau's discourse theory of space and antagonism." *Distinktion: Journal of Social Theory* 15 (3): 271–82.

McCloskey, Herbert, and John Zaller. 1984. *The American Ethos: Public Attitudes toward Capitalism and Democracy*. Cambridge, MA: Harvard University Press.

Monaghan, Elizabeth. 2013. "Making the Environment Present: Political Representation, Democracy and Civil Society Organisations in EU Climate Change Politics." *Journal of European Integration* 35 (5): 601–18.

Montanaro, Laura. 2012. "The Democratic Legitimacy of Self-Appointed Representatives." *Journal of Politics* 74 (4): 1094–107.

Mouffe, Chantal. 2013. *Agonistics: Thinking the World Politically*. London: Verso.

Mulvey, Laura. 1975. "Visual Pleasure and Narrative Cinema." *Screen* 16 (3): 6–18.

Näsström, Sofia. 2015. "Democratic Representation Beyond Election." *Constellations* 22 (1): 1–12.

Neblo, Michael A. 2015. *Deliberative Democracy between Theory and Practice*. New York: Cambridge University Press.

Pitkin, Hanna F. 1967. *The Concept of Representation*. Berkeley: University of California Press.

Plotke, David. 1997. "Representation Is Democracy." *Constellations* 4 (1): 19–34.

Rancière, Jacques. 1991. *The Ignorant Schoolmaster: Five Lessons in Intellectual Emancipation*. Translated, with an introduction by Kristin Ross. Stanford, CA: Stanford University Press.

Rehfeld, Andrew. 2006. "Towards a General Theory of Representation." *Journal of Politics* 68 (1): 1–21.

Roediger, David R. 1991. *The Wages of Whiteness: Race and the Making of the American Working Class*. New York: Verso.

Runciman, David. 2007. "The Paradox of Political Representation." *The Journal of Political Philosophy* 15 (1): 93–114.

Saward, Michael. 2006a. "Representation." In *Political Theory and the Ecological Challenge*, edited by Andrew Dobson and Robyn E. Eckersley, 183–99. Cambridge: Cambridge University Press.

———. 2006b. "The Representative Claim." *Contemporary Political Theory* 5 (3): 297–318.

———. 2008. "Making Representations: Modes and Strategies of Political Parties." *European Review* 16 (3): 271–86.

———. 2010. *The Representative Claim*. Oxford: Oxford University Press.

Schickler, Eric. 2016. *Racial Realignment: The Transformation of American Liberalism, 1932–1965*. Princeton, NJ: Princeton University Press.

Schwartz, Nancy L. 1988. *The Blue Guitar: Political Representation and Community*. Chicago: University of Chicago Press.

Severs, Eline. 2012. "Substantive Representation through a Claims-Making Lens: A Strategy for the Identification and Analysis of Representative Claims." *Representation* 48 (2): 169–81.

Sniderman, Paul M., and Sean M. Theriault. 2004. "The Structure of Political Argument and the Logic of Issue Framing." In *Studies in Public Opinion*, edited by Willem E. Saris and Paul M. Sniderman, 133–65. Princeton, NJ: Princeton University Press.

Sørenson, Eva. 2002. "Democratic Theory and Network Governance." *Administrative Theory & Praxis* 24 (4): 693–720.

Soss, Joe. 2005. "Deserving and Entitled: Social Constructions and Public Policy." In *Deserving and Entitled: Social Constructions and Public Policy*, edited by Anne L. Schneider and Helen M. Ingram, 291–328. Albany, NY: SUNY Press.

Soss, Joe, Richard C. Fording, Sanford F. Schram. 2011. *Disciplining the Poor: Neoliberal Paternalism and the Persistent Power of Race*. Chicago: University of Chicago Press.

Thomassen, Lasse. 2005. "In/Exclusions: Towards a Radical Democratic Approach to Exclusion." In *Radical Democracy: Politics between Abundance and Lack*, edited by Lars Tønder and Lasse Thomassen, 103–22. Manchester: Manchester University Press.

Urbinati, Nadia. 2006. *Representative Democracy: Principles and Genealogy*. Chicago: University of Chicago Press.

Urbinati, Nadia, and Mark E. Warren. 2008. "The Concept of Representation in Contemporary Democratic Theory." *Annual Review of Political Science* 11: 387–412.

VanderVelde, Lea S. 1989. "The Labor Vision of the Thirteenth Amendment." *University of Pennsylvania Law Review* 437:138–206.

Williamson, Vanessa, Theda Skocpol, and John Coggin. 2001. "The Tea Party and the Remaking of Republican Conservatism." *Perspectives on Politics* 9 (1): 25–43.

Young, Iris M. 2000. *Inclusion and Democracy*. Oxford: Oxford University Press.

# CHAPTER EIGHT

# Who Counts as a Democratic Representative?

## On Claims of Self-Appointed Representation

Laura Montanaro

A history of suspicion clouds political representation. Participatory democrats have long emphasized the dangers of representation, arguing that it replaces direct participation in democratic processes. They are both right and wrong. Without political representation, the most vulnerable among us are excluded and marginalized. In addition to this structural benefit, the indirectness of representation is now lauded as a value, as a space between speech and decision that provides critical distance for thoughtful consideration (Urbaniti 2006). Its dangers nevertheless remain, as seen when "we are the 99 percent" is claimed by a small percentage, when white, middle-class, cisgender women claim to represent all women, and when organizations do better by their privileged members than by their less privileged members.

These are, I claim, examples of political representation. When an individual, group, or organization renders a group politically present to others, as people requiring consideration in decision-making, with the intent to influence a state or other body with the capacity to make binding decisions about them, that is representation. It is not necessarily an example of good representation, however. The Occupy movement was criticized for being mostly white, highly educated, and employed. That the women's movement was—and often is—racist, classist, and heterosexist is well known. And that the "unheavenly chorus" (Verba, Schlozman and Brady 2012) of interest groups sings with an upper-class accent remains as true now as it was when Schattschneider (1960) first famously said so.

This argument is inspired by Castiglione and Warren (2006), who more than ten years ago encouraged theorists of representation to broaden our understanding of who can legitimately claim to be a representative to include those who are unelected and informal and who exercise primarily public influence rather than coercive and administrative powers. Self-appointed representatives are a practical political reality, and yet our theories of representation have not been very good at conceptualizing such actors and are ill equipped to assess potential legitimacy, generally dismissing any unelected, informal actor as undemocratic.

Elsewhere, I argue that understanding the practice of representation as rendering others politically present to audiences—a practice not necessarily tied to a government and its institutions—helps us recognize nonelectoral actors *as* representatives (Montanaro, 2018). We are represented not only by our government officials, elected or otherwise, but also by the various actors who make claims for and about us in civil society and the public sphere. These representatives may be self-appointed—they are not elected and are without the power of state office, but, still, they render us politically present to audiences of decision makers, asking them to consider us in their deliberative processes. The political reality is that these actors function as representatives when their claims to represent others (Saward 2010) are recognized by powerful audiences (Rehfeld 2010). But the claim of a self-appointed representative calls on a relevant audience, in contexts that are not institutionalized and so where sources of authority, including the audience, are identified only once the claim is made.

If not an elected or legal constituency, then, who are these self-appointed representatives representing? The representative relationship is not limited to a formal representative and a given electoral district; it can exist between an organization and a group of people it claims to speak for. The represented may not fall within the boundaries drawn by electoral districting or nation-states, and they may not be limited to the accompanying interests and issues that are captured by residence. Instead, self-appointed representatives can speak for people outside of, or alongside, electoral institutions, creating a space for nonelectoral and nonterritorial constituencies to demand representation of interests unconnected to their location in a legal district.

This broader concept of representation, though it helps us to recognize a wide range of representative actors and practices including the claims of self-appointed representatives, also provides malicious or opportunistic political actors with an opportunity to claim legitimacy. Though necessary to understand and describe our political landscape, this broader concept leaves us without the normative goods and obligations that we usually associate with democratic representation, including free and fair elections, accountability, and responsiveness. Standard accounts of representation describe it as a constituency providing a mandate to its representative, delegating the representative's responsibilities and duties. We assume that the people involved already know their interests and come to the ballot box to register those preferences. When we assume that people know what is best for them, their representative is obliged to be responsive to them: to execute their directives and to provide justification when acting contrary to constituents' expectations. But a constituency does not always already know its interests and convictions, and representation can help a constituency learn and deliberate them. While we need a theory of representation that establishes that representatives may be unelected and informal, we must also be aware of the dangers. Nonelectoral representatives have mixed potential: they can provide representation for constituencies that need it and in the ways that they need it, or they can do otherwise.

In what follows, I discuss the mixed potential of informal representation, both its democratic potential and its potential dangers. The distinction turns, in part, on whether a representative empowers its claimed constituency to exercise authorization and demand accountability. The second part of the chapter discusses the representative-constituent relationship, particularly with respect to the nonelectoral mechanisms of authorization and accountability that might be exercised by claimed constituencies; we will add to this an assessment of whether and how representing the claimed constituency harms others. In the third part of the chapter, these concerns will help us distinguish between the democratic, skewed, surrogate, and failed outcomes of claims of self-appointed political representatives.

## The Mixed Potential of Self-Appointed Representation

Our representatives render us present in a political context where such presence may affect the decisions of a state or other body with the formal capacity to make binding decisions buttressed by a legitimate monopoly on violence. Where a group and its interests were unknown, neglected, or dismissed by an audience—and so absent in the sense of being invisible and inaudible in a given political sphere—a claim of representation makes them visible and audible within that realm (Ranciere 2004). Representation is one way that we gain a political identity in the eyes of decision makers, and so the danger of *mis*representation looms large. But going unrepresented can also be harmful. To be rendered politically present—to be represented—can mean that the interests of groups are properly considered in the decisions that affect them. When decision-making affects a group whose interests are not properly understood, the marginalization of that group can be exacerbated. An election, even with its clear authorization by constituents, does not fully mitigate the possibility of misrepresentation, but it can provide signals of approval or disapproval and establish a relationship of accountability. All the more suspect, then, to be the object of claims of self-appointed representation.

In informal and noninstitutionalized contexts, both grassroots and elite actors offer claims to represent others. We welcome the claims of grassroots actors because of the proximity of the claimant to the community; we are more suspicious of the claims of elite actors because the large distance between the socioeconomic circumstances of elite actors and their claimed constituencies provides more room for error. With celebrity activists, in particular, we suspect their motives to be calculating and self-interested, or we find them uninformed and naïve. Though we are right to be suspicious of power differentials, nothing follows necessarily from either grassroots or elite representation. Grassroots actors can get it wrong, and elite forms of representation do not necessarily compromise democracy, provided they engage the constituency they claim to represent. When democracy does not do what it should do—when citizens cannot influence decision makers or lack access to knowledge and audiences that would help them form claims of entitlement—then elite forms of representation may be essential in influencing decision makers to consider constituencies they otherwise would not. Furthermore, elite actors have a responsibility to acknowledge their own privilege and use it to bring attention to others—and to step aside when the circumstances are created for people to speak for themselves. Thus, I am interested in both types of actors and in their ability to render constituencies politically present to audiences.

The relationship between a self-appointed representative and a purported constituency should be subject to assessment. Is the self-appointed representative somehow authorized by and held accountable to the constituency he or she claims to represent? Or does the self-appointed representative claim to represent one constituency while receiving authorization from a different constituency? Do donors, for example, authorize a representative because they are sympathetic to the interests of the claimed constituency? In that case, the self-appointed representative may still achieve a good for the claimed constituency but not in a democratic manner. And, more than agreeing or disagreeing with the claims of a representative, is the claimed constituency somehow able to direct or influence the agenda? The answers to these questions help us determine whether, to what extent, and how power is managed in the representative relationship. When a self-appointed representative renders a constituency politically present to audiences of decision makers but does not empower the constituency to exercise authorization and demand accountability, to set or amend the agenda, then we need to be especially cautious in assessing effects or consequences of such representation.

Our assessment of self-appointed representation should further consider the effects of the representative relationship. There is the possibility, however doubtful, that a claimed constituency benefits from self-appointed representation even if it does not and perhaps cannot exercise authorization and demand accountability. When a representative speaks for constituencies that understand themselves (and that others understand) as affected by collective decisions, and who would otherwise be unable to influence those decisions, then representation contributes to democratic norms of inclusion, egalitarianism, and self-development. But it is just as likely—perhaps more likely—that self-appointed representation creates or aggravates inequality, undermining those same norms (Strolovitch 2007; Verba, Schlozman, and Brady 1995). This mixed potential and its impact on outcomes of representation highlights the importance of holding nonelectoral representatives accountable to those they claim to represent and certainly to those their claims affect, whether or not they claim to represent them.

## Nonelectoral Authorization and Accountability

Claims of self-appointed representation derive from an actor's influence and persuasion in the public sphere. The actor's capacity to represent others works primarily through discursive means of publicity, advocacy, and persuasion. Like Mansbridge (2003), who argues that democratic representation comes in many forms, each with its own norms, I argue that nonelectoral empowerments are appropriate to the discursive powers and functions of self-appointed representatives. For this reason, the thresholds and mechanisms of accountability for self-appointed representatives are and should be different from those for representatives who wield coercive power and particularly power that includes the state's monopoly on violence.

The discursive power of self-appointed representatives works through their ability to garner agreement or consent and, ideally, the agreement and consent of those for whom they claim to speak. Inherent in the concept of the representative claim, then, is a supposition of accountability in the sense of giving an account to others. The deliberative element of accountability requires that the representative explain and justify claims and activities to others. As Savage and Weale (2009, 69) argue, "accountability is a form of public reasoning, the presupposition of which is that when accountability is discharged there is an intelligible connection between the action for which an account is being rendered and the putative reasons that are offered to explain and justify that course of action."

In the case of self-appointed representatives, I refer to two categories of authorization and accountability: organizational (Grant and Keohane 2005) and discursive (Dryzek and Niemeyer 2008). *Organizational authorization* may take one or more of the following forms: (1) by joining organizations, members recognize self-appointed representatives and the representative claims made in an organization's formal or informal mission statement; (2) donors provide self-appointed representatives financial contributions to pursue their work; and (3) voting within organizations authorizes self-appointed representatives. Members can elect such representatives to formal positions of power in an organization, and boards of trustees can support or undermine such representatives through their votes on issues of policy such as grant-making, geographic focus, spending, investment, and management.

*Discursive authorization* (Dryzek and Niemeyer 2008) takes the form of public agreement. An authorizing constituency offers not only their money but also their allegiance and public approbation, expressed in both actions and words. When a self-appointed representative makes a public speech, the size and enthusiasm of an appreciative crowd signals a greater or lesser degree of authorization. Public agreement is also expressed through support of protests, boycotts, letter writing, and petitions, among others, all of which contributes to an actor's public reputation. Constituencies might employ social media, such as Facebook, Twitter, and YouTube to share ideas, report or announce events, and spread messages across borders.

The sources of sanction that a constituency can wield to hold the self-appointed representative to account are much the same as the resources that signal their authorization: organizational capacities, including money, and memberships as well as discourse-based accountability mechanisms. Just as the vote serves both as a method of authorization when one votes an actor into office and as a means of accountability when one sanctions an actor by voting him or her out of office, membership will serve both authorization and accountability: through joining (authorization) and through exit or anticipation of exit (accountability). And, if public agreement is a key authorizing mechanism, public *dis*agreement can serve as an accountability mechanism. Constituencies express public disapprobation of the self-appointed representation in actions and in words, effectively sanctioning the self-appointed representative by undermining his or her public reputation. One's public reputation is a way to solicit authorization from individuals, groups, and organizations, who donate time and money to those they trust (Grant and Keohane 2005). It can also be wielded by those same individuals, groups, and organizations to hold self-appointed representatives to account. The intent is that such accountability encourages a representative to do better; if they do not, the threat of reputational effects remains.

I warn that some of these mechanisms are more easily wielded by those with power and resources than by those without. Some constituencies have comparatively small resources of money and time with which to signal their authorization through organizational means, such as membership or followership, attendance at meetings, participation in protests, and so on. But they may still wield voice accountability within organizations when they articulate their opinions to leaders, explaining why they prefer change, and threaten or exercise exit by cancelling memberships and donations and ceasing participation in meetings, programs, and the like. "Exit" is less democratic than "voice," but the two are structurally related, with voice strengthened by the threat of exit (Hirschman 1970, 83). Discursively, members of affected constituencies may express public agreement with the self-appointed representative and even acclaim that individual or organization as a representative. Participation in and approbation of organizations signal their authorization. Social media can be a useful mechanism provided conditions of internet access—a challenge for the underprivileged and certainly for highly censored peoples in, say, North Korea—and, of course, freedom of association generally. Conversely, members of affected constituencies may publicly and vocally denounce any authorization. And, as those members take such actions of either authorization or deauthorization, they themselves act as self-appointed representatives.

Discursive and organizational empowerments are notable for their serial nature. If a constituency is persuaded by the representation claim, and continues to be persuaded, that constituency repeatedly authorizes the claims of the self-appointed representative by, for example, renewing their membership. In this way, consent is continually tested and reaffirmed. And through this continual testing, dissent is also found: the public agreement of the represented with their representatives can quickly and easily become public disagreement, and donations and memberships can be renewed—or not—yearly or even monthly. The representative voice of the self-appointed representative waxes and wanes with these serial and incremental authorizations. As Nadia Urbinati (2006, 53–54) argues, authorization is essential to a democratic view of representation, so long as it is understood as a process and not as an isolated act that occurs only at a moment of election.

The turn toward a process of authorization—what I have referred to as its serial nature—provides a reflexive benefit. The distance between the claim and its authorization implies a process of reflection. A self-appointed representative offers a claim of representation that must resonate with a people, so that it understands itself *as* a constituency, and then receive authorization. Because authorization happens serially, incrementally, its reflexive nature (i.e., its capacity to mobilize objections or approval) grows. This is a benefit of all types of authorization, including formal votes, but it is more visible in the context of self-appointed representation, which does not rely on an election as its primary moment of authorization. Accountability serves this constitutive understanding also. We know that accountability involves both deliberation (to give an account, to explain and justify one's behavior to others) and the possibility of control (to be held accountable, to be sanctioned in some way) (Savage and Weale 2009, 69). Mansbridge (2009) terms the former narrative or deliberative accountability for how it differs from accountability based on monitoring and sanctions: "In narrative and deliberative accountability, the representative explains the reasons for her actions and even (ideally) engages in two-way communication with constituents, particularly when deviating from the constituents' preferences" (370). But the simple idea of justifying one's actions in relation to a constituency that has registered its preferences neither fully captures the creative element of the discursive activity of the self-appointed representative nor gives us a full understanding of accountability. Indeed, accountability is not simply or even primarily a sanction. Instead, accountability provides understanding "of how we constitute the sense we have of ourselves (our identities) as well as shared ways of constructing the meanings that inform our social orders" (Shotter 1989, quoted in Ranson 2003, 461). A claim of representation offers a particular understanding of a constituency, which may be accepted or declined or refined through authorization and accountability. Viewed through the lens of representation, discursive accountability is constitutive, the medium through which latent constituencies come to be. Affected constituencies may be formed through public reasoning, justification, and explanation. "Accountability in this view, as discursive reason, is the very expression rather than denial of our reflective agency" (Ranson 2003, 461). Thus, when considered as a part of constituency formation, discursive accountability is in itself constitutive of interests.

## Outcomes of Self-Appointed Representation

Our assessment of self-appointed representation should include a determination based on, first, the relationship between the representative claim-maker and its claimed constituency—does the claim-maker empower the constituency for which it claims to provide political presence to audiences? A self-appointed representative provides political presence for a constituency with or without its empowerment. Empowerment—and at this level power means exercising authorization and demanding accountability as well as influencing the agenda—remains important in this sphere of representation. We want to know whether or not a representative is speaking for people in a manner that is acceptable to them and if he or she has enabled a constituency to exercise its judgment. Second, we should assess the democratic and nondemocratic effects of that relationship. Even if the claimed constituency authorizes its representative, the outcomes of this relationship may be detrimental to others in the broader democratic system. For this reason, in addition to empowerments of authorization and accountability, we should consider the effects of the representative-constituent relationship on democracy and democratization.

### Democratic Representative Outcomes

Claims of self-appointed representation begin with an unelected actor offering a claim of representation separate from formal elections and institutions. The claim includes self-identifying as one who makes others politically present to others and identifying the relevant audience (the group whose recognition is required for the self-appointed actor to function as a representative), the claimed constituency (the group the self-appointed representative claims to represent), and an authorizing constituency (the group empowered by the claim to exercise authorization and demand accountability), which may be distinct from the claimed constituency. When the audience recognizes the claim, in effect providing an actor with the standing to function as a representative (as when the EU includes a nongovernmental organization in its deliberation proceedings as a representative of civil society), we have an instance of representation that began with a claim of self-appointment. Though this is sufficient to achieve the standing of a representative, it is not necessarily democratic. An informal representative may empower the constituency he or she claims to represent to create (authorize) and regulate (hold accountable) obligations between them, or he or she may not. Instead, the informal representative might operate solely with the standing provided by an audience or empower an authorizing constituency distinct from the claimed constituency. The representative might benefit the claimed constituency, but it is dangerous to render others politically present without their authorization, because we might misrepresent people and their interests and undermine a people's autonomy and capacity to make decisions for themselves, including decisions about who best represents them. Even when authorized by its claimed constituency, a self-appointed representative might still misrepresent the interests of the constituency. Self-appointed representation produces democratic outcomes to the degree that the claimed constituency is empowered to authorize and demand accountability *and* when the effects of that representative-constituent relationship benefit the claimed constituency's affected interests.

The high standards for democratic outcomes leave several possibilities for outcomes that are undemocratic and that wrong others. The first is acting with authorization of the claimed constituency but still misrepresenting it or making a poor decision on its behalf, including unevenly representing subgroups within the constituency. I call these outcomes *skewed*. A second nondemocratic outcome involves acting only with the standing granted by the audience and authorizing constituency, and not empowering the claimed constituency. Even without the authorization of the claimed constituency, self-appointed representation might still produce a good for it, so the wrong here is one of disrespect rather than harm. If the self-appointed representative could mobilize objections from the constituency but does not (and we must leave open the possibility that such mobilization is not always possible), then he or she does not acknowledge the constituency's capacities to make its own choices. I refer to these outcomes as *surrogate*.

A third nondemocratic outcome is acting only with the standing granted by the audience and authorizing constituency and misrepresenting the claimed constituency. Here the self-appointed representative is responsible for a real harm—I refer to these as *failed* outcomes.

## Skewed Representative Outcomes

That a self-appointed representative might be deemed a success, even when it does not benefit or even undermines the interests of its constituency, is worrying. I refer to these as *skewed* outcomes because the representative may not wholly fail a constituency, but the outcomes asymmetrically benefit—indeed are skewed toward—its privileged subgroups. Even when a self-appointed representative provides an imbalanced representation among subgroups within its claimed constituency, audiences might still perceive the representation as legitimate, which is particularly worrying if a representative undermines that constituency's interests.

In the women's movement, for example, groups claimed to represent women of color but marginalized their concerns and did not sufficiently include them at an organizational level, producing a skewed representation.[1] There was—and remains—a tendency to subordinate race and class to gender and to treat women as a homogenous unit, represented via a commonality of gender. Emphasizing differences of class, race, disability, and sexual preference is seen to undermine the movement. Though claiming to broadly represent women, representation is skewed toward its white, middle-upper-class, cisgender members and away from those who are disadvantaged on multiple dimensions of identity (Crenshaw 1991). Policy outcomes are disproportionately weighted toward the advantaged rather than the disadvantaged; for example, policy affecting women in higher education is better served than policy affecting welfare reform (Strolovitch 2007).

Egregious examples of disparate political power occur also when policymaking is dominated by powerful business organizations and by a small number of economic elite rather than by average citizens, even when those average citizens have the resources to demand representation and organize. We have long known that socioeconomic factors contribute to a disparity of outcomes (Almond and Verba 1963). Business interests spend more time and money and so are more likely to be active and influential, which plays a role in ensuring policy that benefits business-oriented groups. They also boast a specificity of purpose that makes their demands clear, whereas broad-based groups that claim a universality that subsumes different interests under its umbrella tend to be less successful, particularly for the subgroups. Average citizens benefit only when their interests happen to coincide with, or at least do not run counter to, the interests of businesses.

However, when broad-based groups claim to speak for disadvantaged subgroups, self-appointed representatives will, ideally, be held to account for these claims, either by an authorizing constituency or by the claimed constituency itself. Such capacity building may occur because the claims made on behalf of disadvantaged subgroups enter common discourse, generating accountability. This may help to create the conditions under which the authorizing constituency might speak for those with affected interests, and/or eventually the constituency might speak for itself. Those who lobby on behalf of business interests do not invoke such relationships of accountability, comfortable as they are to bias policy toward the wishes of corporations and businesses, again emphasizing the importance not only of analyzing the representative-constituent relationship but also its effects on others. In this way, we can assess that representation—to which everyone has a right, including those who are privileged and empowered—is distributed in a manner that captures and prioritizes those whose interests in self-development and self-determination are most affected.

But not all representation is necessarily accountable to those for whom it speaks. The Occupy movement was roundly criticized for insisting on nonrepresentative leadership though arguably offering a claim of representation. "We are the 99 percent," claimed by a fraction of the same (both in numbers and in demographics of largely white, urban youth), was a space to air grievances and a commentary on a representative government of which they disapproved, sensitive as it is to business interests and not to the average citizen. But, if the campaign was to have any affect, it would have affected also the nonmembers for whom it spoke however disjointedly (Vieira 2015). There were few and ineffective ways for the 99 percent to exercise accountability over the movement. Its public reputation, a form of accountability as discussed, took a hit with its critics deriding it as the pastime of a group of privileged youth with little in common with those for whom they spoke. Actors might resist the status of a representative either to avoid associated obligations or even out of a genuine, if misguided, belief that one does not and should not speak for others, as did Occupy.

### Surrogate Representative Outcomes

When a representative renders a constituency politically present to an audience without the constituency's authorization, the outcomes might still serve the constituency and democracy more broadly. If the constituency's interests are affected by a policy, issue, or good without harming others but without empowering the constituency to exercise authorization and demand accountability, then the outcomes are surrogate. Of course, we must be careful when judging claims of representation that do not rely on the constituency's judgment of its own interests (Alcoff 1991), as misrepresentation of interests can cause serious harm. But such representation does not necessarily preclude the possibility of outcomes that serve democracy.

Umbrella organizations, for example, operate at a significant remove from those they claim to represent and so cannot be understood to generate relationships of authorization and accountability with their claimed constituencies. Often, they are necessary to consolidate influence and receive support from funding agencies, who may not have the staff to monitor local organizations and so prefer contributing to umbrella organizations instead. Their representation of others can serve their constituencies and democracy more broadly.

Constituencies will exercise organizational and discursive authorization and accountability over their local organizations, becoming members and withdrawing membership, participating in various events or boycotting in disagreement, and speaking favorably or unfavorably of its reputation. In turn, these organizations have an obligation to communicate relevant discontent among members to the umbrella organization and to partner organizations. Constituents only exercise influence indirectly, then, over the larger cooperative. They may exercise some discursive accountability in direct relationship with the umbrella organization, communicating with leaders in person, by letter, or the like. But the larger organization's fidelity to groups of local organizations will diffuse the influence of individuals.

There are other relationships of authorization and accountability that become more important in the absence of a constituency's own say-so. Member organizations are accountable not only to their claimed constituents but also to donors and supervisory boards who may act as proxies for the claimed constituency, who can request explanations for proposed plans or policy choices. Reputation can ensure that rigorous thought, research, and expertise are deployed to the benefit of the claimed constituencies; if not, the organization's reputation takes a hit, which could be detrimental to its success in securing funding.

Democracies operate under the assumption that the people are the best judge of their own interests. In extreme and unfortunate political circumstances, however, we may not have access to those we claim to represent—

when wars ensue, borders close, and so on—and will wish to continue the work of representation on their behalf. In other circumstances, representatives will find it easier and more efficient to conduct representation without empowerment. We might think that the choice to trade empowerment for efficiency is highly questionable. But given the soft powers of self-appointed representatives, of persuasion and influence without the backing power of coercion, the wrong here may be one of disrespect rather than harm. There is another, important circumstance to consider: when people do not yet have preferences or know their interests. Surrogate outcomes describe instances in which, even without empowerment, outcomes of representation serve the interests of constituencies and without harm to others. In such cases, it is worth classifying these actors, at least potentially, as engaging in disrespect rather than in harm.

## Failed Representative Outcomes

Representation *fails* when, in claiming to speak for others, the self-appointed representative does so not only without the authorization of the claimed constituency but also in a manner that undermines its interests in self-development and self-determination. Failed outcomes may be the most expected outcome of self-appointed representation. Indeed, many nongovernmental organizations are subject to just this criticism, as is so often seen when NGOs located in the global north make claims for constituencies in the global south. In attempting to "do good," such actors choose ends for others that undermine the interests of the very constituency they wish to help. Though these representatives do not necessarily intend to misrepresent a constituency, the danger of failed representation is located precisely in the agency of the claimant to render a constituency and its interests and convictions to others without that constituency's knowledge or approval. If we are not empowered by our representatives, then it will be left to others to decide who we are, what we need, and whether the demands made on our behalf produce outcomes that benefit our purported interests. The wrong here is not only one of disrespect, as with surrogate outcomes, but also of harm.

We might argue that, rather than defining ends for a constituency while showing little regard for its people as agents, representatives should instead pay attention to the goals people set for themselves and, where needed, focus on the conditions that enable them to achieve those goals. Simply put, empower the represented so that they may exercise authorization and demand accountability over claims about what they need. But if we take seriously the idea that constituencies are complex, change, and do not already have preferences formed on all issues as they arise (Ankersmit 2002; George 2004; Laclau 2007), then we can imagine that representatives are and should be responsible for eliciting that knowledge and rendering a constituency and its interests politically present to audiences until such time as they can represent themselves or select those whom they would wish to be their representative.

The emphasis on outcomes of representation should not lead us to the conclusion that social location is unimportant. Though I do not wish to argue that the privileged cannot or even should not speak for others— indeed, they may have a responsibility to do so precisely because of the asymmetry of their circumstances, which makes influence and access to decision makers more easily theirs—I also do not claim that social location is less important than outcomes that benefit a constituency. Representation cannot long benefit others and democracy without empowering the constituents affected. The time would inevitably come when the representative would begin to undermine the constituency by crowding out their voices and their choice about who best represents them. One of democracy's goods is to cultivate the capacities of those involved in it and, as I am arguing, political representation is essential to democracy. Through their claims, our representatives draw out thought and judgment from decision makers, the broader public and, ideally, from the people about whom the claim is offered. Even in surrogate and failed circumstances where the representative does not empower the claimed constituency, the discursive nature of the claim creates the space for that constituency to come to understand itself as affected by some good or policy and deserving of entitlements. And the relationship is mutually transformative: just as the representative elicits new understanding from the represented, so too can the represented change how the representative understands them. Surrogate and failed representation remain dangerous for the lack of links that make that transformation possible and communicable, but the potential of self-appointed representation remains: it might spark the organization of better alternatives that produce better outcomes for democracy.

Social location helps with both capacity building and mobilization. As Mansbridge (1999, 2015) and others have argued, where interests are not fully articulated or crystallized, descriptive representation, which captures something like social location, is essential. Descriptive representation improves the legitimacy of the process precisely because people recognize themselves in it (Guinier 1994; Phillips 1995; Mansbridge 1999; Kymlicka 1993). Failed representation might well increase in likelihood when distances in social location are too great. But, as Pitkin (1967) argues, descriptive similarity alone does not ensure good representation. Even in relationships where the representative descriptively represents others, we cannot take for granted that the relationship is empowered, and we must still question whether or not the effects serve democracy. These, I think, are criteria that matter for assessing representation.

## Conclusion

Who counts as our democratic representatives? If I am right about the democratic potential of self-appointed representation, the answers are more plural and varied than we thought and include those who, without legislative and coercive powers themselves, speak for others in contexts that intend to or would influence the decisions of those who do. Though without such powers, many of the outcomes of self-appointed representation are problematic. Our representatives—even of the self-appointed kind—shape how others understand our interests, which is precisely the source of representation's mixed potential. If they represent well, constituencies benefit and there are good effects on democracy. But misrepresentation can bias our discussions and decisions and produce policy that proves detrimental to people's interests. For this reason, empowerment is essential to democratic representation. Its dangers remain, of course, as people may choose to benefit themselves without concern for others. But authorization and accountability provide a means for channeling power through popular empowerment and through limits. If a constituency cannot exercise authorization and demand accountability, this opens the space for an abuse of power.

Political representation is fundamental to a well-functioning democracy. At its best, representation ensures the equal distribution of influence so that groups that are ignored, overlooked, or inadequately considered receive due consideration in discussion and decision-making. Furthermore, it elicits from a constituency an understanding of its interests and so does not take for granted a people that already exists with interests static and intact. Instead, at its best, it evokes the *demos* fundamental to democracy.[2]

## Notes

1. This is a highly stylized account. For more complexity, see Alice Echolls's *Daring to Be Bad* (1989) and Winifred Brienes's *The Trouble Between Us* (2007).

2. Thank you to Cambridge University Press for allowing me to draw on arguments I made in *Who Elected Oxfam? A Democratic Defence of Self-Appointed Representatives* (2018).

## References

Alcoff, Linda. 1991. "The Problem of Speaking for Others." *Politics & Society* 20:5–32.

Almond, Gabriel, and Sidney Verba. 1963. *The Civic Culture: Political Attitudes and Democracy in Five Countries*. Princeton, NJ: Princeton University Press.

Ankersmit, F. R. 2002. *Political Representation: Cultural Memory in the Present*. Stanford, CA: Stanford University Press.

Brienes, Winifred. 2007. *The Trouble Between Us: An Uneasy History of White and Black Women in the Feminist Movement*. Oxford: Oxford University Press.

Brito Vieira, Mónica. 2015. "Founders and Re-founders: Struggles of Self-authorized Representation." *Constellations* 22 (4): 500–513.

Castiglione, Dario, and Mark Warren. 2006. "Rethinking Democratic Representation: Eight Theoretical Issues." Paper presented at "Rethinking Democratic Representation," Centre for the Study of Democratic Institutions, University of British Columbia, May 18–19, 2006.

Crenshaw, Kimberle. 1991. "Mapping the Margins: Intersectionality, Identity Politics, and Violence against Women of Color." *Stanford Law Review* 43 (6): 1241–99.

Dryzek, J., and S. Niemeyer. 2008. "Discursive Representation." *American Political Science Review* 102 (4): 481–93.

Echolls, Alice. 1989. *Daring to Be Bad: Radical Feminism in America, 1967–1975*. Minneapolis: University of Minnesota Press.

George, Susan. 2004. *Another World Is Possible If . . .* London: Verso.

Grant, Ruth, and Robert O. Keohane. 2005. "Accountability and Abuses of Power in World Politics." *American Political Science Review* 99:29–44.

Guinier, Lani. 1994. *The Tyranny of the Majority: Fundamental Fairness in Representative Democracy*. New York: Free Press.

Hirschman, Albert O. 1970. *Exit, Voice, and Loyalty: Responses to Decline in Firms, Organizations, and States*. Cambridge, MA: Harvard University Press.

Kymlicka, Will. 1993. "Group Representation in Canadian Politics." In *Equity and Community: The Charter, Interest Advocacy, and Representation*, edited by F. L. Siedle, 61–90. Montreal: Institute for Research on Public Policy.

Laclau, Ernesto. 2007. *On Populist Reason*. London: Verso.

Mansbridge, Jane. 1999. "Should Blacks Represent Blacks and Women Represent Women? A Contingent 'Yes.'" *Journal of Politics* 61: 628–57.

———. 2003. "Rethinking Representation." *American Political Science Review* 97 (4): 515–28.

———. 2009. "A 'Selection Model' of Political Representation." *Journal of Political Philosophy* 17 (4): 369–98.

———. 2015. "Should Workers Represent Workers?" *Swiss Political Science Review* 21 (2): 261–70.

Montanaro, Laura. 2018. *Who Elected Oxfam?* Cambridge: Cambridge University Press.

Phillips, Anne. 1995. *The Politics of Presence: The Political Representation of Gender, Ethnicity, and Race.* Oxford: Oxford University Press.

Pitkin, Hanna F. 1967. *The Concept of Representation.* Berkeley: University of California Press.

Rancière, Jacques. 2004. *The Politics of Aesthetics: The Distribution of the Sensible.* Translated by Gabriel Rockhill. London: Bloomsbury.

Ranson, Stewart. 2003. "Public Accountability in the Age of Neo-Liberal Governance." *Journal of Education* 18:455–80.

Rehfeld, Andrew. 2010. "Offensive Political Theory." *Perspectives on Politics* 8 (2): 465–86.

Savage, Deborah, and Albert Weale. 2009. "Political Representation and the Normative Logic of Two-Level Games." *European Political Science Review* 1 (1) 63–81.

Saward, Michael. 2010. *The Representative Claim.* Oxford: Oxford University Press.

Schattschneider, E. E. 1960. *The Semisovereign People.* New York: Holt, Rinehart, and Winston.

Shotter, John. 1989. "Social Accountability and the Social Construction of 'You.'" In *Texts of Identity,* edited by John Shotter and Kenneth J Gergen, 133–51. London: Sage.

Strolovitch, Dara. 2007. *Affirmative Advocacy: Race, Class, and Gender in Interest Group Politics.* Chicago: University of Chicago Press.

Urbinati, Nadia. 2006. *Representative Democracy: Principles and Genealogy.* Chicago: University of Chicago Press.

Verba, Sidney, Kay Lehman Schlozman, and Henry E. Brady. 1995. *Voice and Equality: Civic Voluntarism in American Politics.* Cambridge, MA: Harvard University Press.

———. 2102. *The Unheavenly Chorus: Unequal Political Voice and the Broken Promise of American Democracy.* Princeton, NJ: Princeton University Press.

# CHAPTER NINE

# Future Generations and the Limits of Representation

Kerry H. Whiteside

O ver the last thirty years or so, the idea of "representing future generations" has become the preferred way of expressing democratic aspirations to take political responsibility for posterity. Among political theorists, environmental arguments for "representing" future generations appeared in the early 1980s and have been voiced with increasing frequency ever since (Kavka and Warren 1983; Dobson 1996; Eckersley 1999; Ekeli 2005, 2009; Agius 2006; Gardiner 2014; Wells 2014). By the turn of the new millennium, propositions for representing future generations found their way into the world of policy and parliaments. Hungary and Israel instituted special commissioners for future generations—reforms lauded in the language of representation (Göpel 2014a; von Uexkull 2008). The World Future Council (2010) cites these and other precedents in its review of "different existing models for the representation of future generations in national governments." The United Nations Future Generations Commission has been presented with ideas for the "institutional representation of future generations in the United Nations" (Horváth 2012). It is no exaggeration to say that, today, representing future generations has become the standard way of squaring democracy with obligations to posterity.

The moral logic underpinning this development is well illustrated by Dennis Thompson's (2010) essay "Representing Future Generations": "Democracy is partial toward the present," Thompson observes; it therefore has a tendency to "neglect long-term environmental risks" (17). Democracy's "presentism," he says, is overdetermined. People's "natural" preference for immediate gratification, the reliance of representative democracy on constituent preferences, and the short-term perspective induced by the electoral system all contribute to temporal myopia. Our democracies respond to citizens' desire for immediate benefits even if the quality of life of people in the future is damaged (by exhausting resources, failing to clean up dangerous waste, and so on). *Future* people cannot protect themselves, because they have no systematic representation in our political processes. Thompson concludes, "We need a revised conception of representation that enables democracies to represent future citizens who are not now present" (26).

Yes, it would be so good if we could have such "a revised conception of representation." Unfortunately, we cannot.

The nonexistence of future people makes them impossible subjects of the political practice we call representation. This is not just some philosopher's semantic quibble. Representation is the wrong way of thinking politically about concern for future generations. The idea of representing future generations has the unfortunate effect of channeling democratic thinking—futilely—in the direction of proposals for political reforms modeled on representative practices: with preferred spokespersons and popular mobilization, parties, elections, seats in the legislature. Yet the nonexistence of future people deprives those practices of elements that are essential to making representation effective, secure, ethically justified, and even meaningful.

Is there a democratic alternative? The claim here is that the goal of protecting future generations creates an especially strong case for drawing on features of institutional design that are commonly associated with deliberative democracy. This now-familiar turn of argument takes on new significance in relation to democratic concern for future generations. It is because posterity *cannot* be represented that designs emphasizing deliberation are called for. Democrats will further insist that deliberative venues reach out to embrace the community's full normative and epistemic assets. Future-regarding minipublics, supporting an Office for Future Generations, could help achieve this aim.


## Representing Future Generations in Practice

In 1987, the United Nation's Brundtland Report issued its famous definition of sustainable development as "development that meets the needs of the present without compromising the ability of future generations to meet their own needs." Since then, the language of "future generations" has become so commonplace that we easily forget its uncomfortable implication: we of "the present" are called to accept obligations that are likely contrary to our interests. Other-regarding obligations are familiar in relation to public goods, but obligations to future generations are even more demanding: Current generations may feel only the sacrifices and none of the benefits of such efforts. The resulting incentive structure challenges democratic decision-making. Presentism means that democratic majorities commonly find issues like protecting jobs or national security more compelling than future-regarding obligations. How can representative institutions acquire more future-regarding sensitivity?

A number of models have been suggested. The World Futures Council (2014, 4) lists "Constitutional Protections for the rights of future generations" among new "national instruments to represent the rights of future generations." The constitutions of eight member states of the European Union explicitly refer to future generations, and five others do so indirectly.

But the difficulty of representing future generations becomes apparent when we distinguish between declaring constitutional rights and the activity of representing. Respecting a constitutional principle does not in itself make a person into one who "stands for" or "speaks for" another, to use Pitkin's terms (1967, 80). Just because Henry rightfully gets benefits when Mary repays her debt to him does not make Mary into Henry's representative. Henry does not choose Mary to "stand for" him and Mary is probably unaware of Henry's unique identity. Likely, Mary is not envisaging a situation in which she receives Henry's criticism or support. As Michael Saward (2010) rightly insists, "representation claims" work when political actors make claims on behalf of a (potential) constituency and touch a chord in its members. Just abiding by a moral or constitutional principle does not do this.

More accurately, we might say that a constitutional principle *enables* better representation. When nongovernmental organizations make claims by referring to a future generations' constitutional rights, aren't such groups effectively their representatives? The World Futures Council's (2014) own words give reason for caution here: "to enshrine such rights in constitutional law is not effective unless a country also has institutions and systems in place to ensure that the environment . . . and the rights of future generations are respected in national policy-making processes" (4). Future-oriented claims too often fall flat without special institutional support. This is because future-oriented NGOs cannot do what most representatives try to do. They cannot assemble and animate a new group of affected constituents, constituents who—because they come to recognize themselves in their representative's voice—eventually lend their energy to the representative's campaign. In fact, future-regarding NGOs represent not future people but a select minority of present people—usually too few to change the presentist orientation of the representative system as a whole.

Not just political philosophers and NGOs but also many governments have come to recognize this as a problem. That is why some parliamentary regimes have set up new political spaces in which future-oriented claims get special attention. One favored model is to charge a distinct parliamentary commission with discussing potential future challenges. In 1999, Finland's parliament created a Committee for the Future whose "task is to conduct an active and initiative-generating dialogue with the government on major future problems and means of solving them" (Tihonen 2006, 74). Since 2004, Germany has had a special council, the Parlamentarischer Beirat für nachhaltige Entwicklung, responsible for checking legislation's conformity to established sustainability criteria. These are examples of representation of an easily recognizable sort. Regularly elected members of parliament do all the talking. These targeted efforts to construct a future-deliberative venue give some support to theorists who praise representative democracy for its ability to open constructive debate to new questions.

Still, we should take a deep breath before deciding that such committees resolve the conundrums of representing future generations. There is, first, the fact that the parliamentarians involved are in no way shielded from the territorial and temporal incentives created by their countries' electoral systems or their government's quotidian priorities. This already calls into question the polity's determination to create a genuine counterweight to the forces of presentism. Second, there is no serious attempt to proportion the committees' power to the numbers of people allegedly represented by their activity or the gravity of the risks imposed upon them. These committees have only advisory and cross-checking functions (Jávor 2006, 286). They do not originate, amend, or scuttle legislative proposals. One might imagine that if future citizens are our equals and current activities endanger their rights, then those who represent them must have power to protect them, just as we expect other representatives to use their prerogatives to stand up for their constituencies. In fact, the power discrepancy between the two cases is vast. In a representative system, the numbers of people represented and the intensity of their preferences are made to *count* in the polity's legislative machinery. Parliamentary spokespersons for future generations never count in that way and for good reason: we cannot tally numbers of future citizens, and we cannot know the intensity of their preferences. But this also casts doubt on whether the committees' deliberations are rightly thought of as a form of representation.

What if a country went beyond the parliamentary committee model and created an independent and empowered agency for future generations issues? Couldn't we then talk about this agency's commissioner as a representative of future generations? One example of this more daring model comes from Israel: the Commission for Future Generations of the Israeli Knesset (established 2001), appointed with parliamentary approval, was authorized to collect information on forthcoming bills with relevance to future generations and to provide recommendations to the whole chamber. The Israeli commissioner could initiate bills. He also had the authority to demand information from government agencies, an authority that could be used to delay the legislative process.

The second is Hungary's parliamentary commissioner for future generations, established in 2007. Scholars cite it as "the most notable precedent" for "an effective mechanism of temporal checks and balances" (Göpel and Arhelger 2010, 7). In the Hungarian model, the future generations commissioner is an ombudsperson who receives petitions and champions sustainability issues. The official has investigative authority with respect to suspected violations of environmental law (Jávor 2006, 290–93). The commissioner can push regulatory authorities to enforce the law and can initiate legal proceedings against those who violate the rights of future generations.

One hint that such models might fall short of hopes for a new and better type of representation is this: both commissions have since fallen by the wayside, Israel's in 2006, Hungary's effectively in 2012.[1] A report to United Nations written by a former lawyer for the Hungarian commission pinpointed the problem. "Strong and consequential institutional representation of future generations" easily leads to "structural conflict" with "national level economic and social policies." Citing the Israeli and Hungarian examples, the report mentions their fate: the "typical solution" to the conflict is the "elimination of the 'disturbing' structural element" (Horváth 2012). Eliminated they were. The Hungarian prime minister sensed there would be little price to pay for ending the existence of the self-standing Commission for Future Generations. NGO protests would be limited and politically manageable. There would be no disgruntled crowds of future people occupying the public square to protest their sudden disenfranchisement.

A second wave of disappointment comes with the realization that these commissioners barely dared to exercise their most substantial powers. In the Israeli case, the commissioner in theory had the power to delay legislation but avoided using it, because the risk of antagonizing the parties in parliament was too great (Shoham and Lamay 2006, 248). The commissioners knew that they did not have organized constituencies to back them up—and this created a de facto difference from other representatives. This relative weakness was not accidental. European deputy Benedek Jávor (2006, 287) recounts: "The creators of these institutions ... [had] difficulty in solving questions of competence and legal contradictions. ... Because of their unsure relation to state administration and the democratic institutional system, [it was necessary] to strictly limit their competence. They play rather a consultative role and cannot participate in effective decision-making processes." When so-called future representatives are created, their creators are careful to treat them *unlike* other representatives. Preserving the authority of *real* representatives requires circumscribing the powers of the new office. Presentism carries the day.

## Future Representation: Theoretical Proposals and Problems

Perhaps representing future generations requires even bolder reforms. Several political theorists have advanced proposals to reserve seats in the legislature for specially elected future generations deputies. I have analyzed some of these ideas elsewhere (Whiteside 2013). Each proposal foundered, I argued, because it violated one or another premise that makes the practice of democratic representation distinctive and legitimate. Electing "ecological proxies," for example, entails giving a priori preference to certain political values. Andrew Dobson (1996) talked of representatives whose mandate would come essentially from the "sustainability lobby." Kristian Ekeli (2005) at first thought of relying on courts to allow only authentic future-oriented parties to run for seats reserved for future generations representatives. Both theorists supposed that proxies could do their future-protecting work only if electoral arrangements somehow protected them from presentist pressures. But neutrally discriminating between genuinely future-oriented parties and mere pretenders will not work. If parliamentary seats (and, hence, possible swing votes for a parliamentary majority) were at stake, every party would figure out how to rebrand its policy orientations as expressions of a future-regarding ethic. All the forces of presentism could then continue to operate in the elections. Competing values exacerbate the problem. Some people see a future world better served by economic development than by resource conservation. Others favor technological audacity, not precaution, and so forth. Those are eminently ideological differences. Reserving legislative seats only for "green" defenders violates the supposed value neutrality of a liberal system of representation.

One other example illustrates how far the quest for future-oriented representatives might go: they might be children. The Stiftung für die Rechte zukünftiger Generationen (The Foundation for the Rights of Future Generations; FRFG) proposes abolishing the age qualification for voting (Stiftung für die Rechte zukünftiger Generationen 2008). After all, today's children are closer to "future generations" than older voters are. They will probably still be living seventy years from now, and therefore—unlike the majority of today's voters—have a direct interest in how today's policies play out in that longer term. At any rate, one can say that their inclusion at least helps "develop a culture of more forward-looking representation" (Matravers and Meyer 2015, 33).

Many people (myself included) are unpersuaded by the suggestion that equal electoral participation by children would improve democracy. Dispiriting questions come to mind: Wouldn't candidates fish for that last margin of votes with campaign pitches resembling advertisements for kid's breakfast cereals? How could adolescents bring independent judgment to tax proposals when they have barely handled money or encountered the complexities of rival ideologies? Children's future-regarding perspectives have yet to be tested under the pressures of competitive politics. But if we worry that children are too manipulable or too subject to others' opinions to be trusted with an independent voice in the electoral process, the FRFG has an answer: These same objections apply to many adult voters, too. Yet no representative democracy disqualifies them on those grounds.

That response, though, comes dangerously close to saying that democracy has no commitment to intellectual capability or independent judgment. The future-generations baby gets thrown out with our (dirty) presentist bathwater. Complex, long-term issues like managing energy transitions and protecting biodiversity challenge democracy to come up with more intelligence and maturity than it commonly musters, not less. Abandoning *all* notions that participation belongs to those who have attained "the age of reason" is self-defeating. (This does not rule out lowering the voting age, if "reason" can be shown at a lower age.) What drives the argument in this direction is the assumption that making democracy more future-oriented requires finding untapped future-regarding principals with whom representative agents can interact. If we are not convinced that such principals exist, it seems we have no choice but to go back to more standard representative models.

## The Future Gap in Representation Theory

"Representation," in David Plotke's (1997) winning phrase, "is democracy." Plotke put paid to romantic conceptions of direct democracy by showing that, in complex societies, assuring the rule of the people in a meaningful way actually requires the ongoing mediating activities of representatives who interpret people's preferences and negotiate among them. The conviction that "representation is democracy" probably explains why so many future generations advocates hasten to formulate their propositions in representational terms. Notwithstanding their doubts about the ability of existing institutions to address future generations questions adequately, future-regarding champions fall back on representation—more, better, or different—to supply surrogate forms of inclusive, pluralistic debate.

The problem is, future generations fit neither standard nor modified accounts of political representation. Standardly, representation implies a process in which "constituencies formed on a territorial basis elect agents to stand for and act on their interests and opinions" (Urbinati and Warren 2008, 389). Yet future people cannot form a constituency. They do not exist. They have no clear territorial location (who knows what the population distribution will look like one hundred years hence?). They have had no opportunity to develop anything like the detailed schedule of interests that existing individuals have. Moreover, as Andrew Rehfeld (2005, 187) reminds us, democratic representation usually includes the prima facie claim that "the group who authorized the representative . . . [should be] the same as the group to whom the representative is accountable." This arrangement puts citizens with affected interests in the position to judge whether representatives have been responsive to their concerns. In regard to future generations, though, representation's prima facie form of accountability is impossible—not exceptionally but *absolutely*.

True, standard accounts often take note of electoral representation's contingent defects and propose ways to reach out to absent or marginalized groups. As long as the concern refers to existing people, such extended representative measures make sense. Thus, we may be persuaded that, in cases where a group has historically been the victim of legal discrimination, some measures of "descriptive representation" may be justified to ensure that the group gets suitable numbers and types of spokespersons in legislative assemblies. A supplement of descriptive representation can help overcome "conditions of impaired communication" or "distrust" (Mansbridge 1999, 641). Yet shortcomings in our attention to future problems are unlike communications breakdowns with fellow citizens. In the latter case, representatives from once-excluded groups, now present in the assembly, can bring their life experience to confront directly the bearers of prejudice and misconceptions who previously disregarded them. Inattention to the concerns of future generations, however, does not stem from distrustful social relations. The problem is the utter absence of an interlocutor. There is no descriptively bounded group whose lived *future* experience allows them to contradict the claims of presentism and to make their claims resonate with an otherwise neglected constituency. No "politics of presence" (Phillips 1995) can fill in this absence representatively.

Perhaps the difficulty lies only with the standard account, though. After all, at a general level, representation is a matter of "making something present that is not present literally" (Pitkin 1967, 8–9). This formula seems to describe speaking for future generations quite well. Moreover, the trend in representation theory in recent decades has been toward emphasizing the complex *process* of democratic inclusion. "The spaces for representative claims ... are now relatively wide open," affirm Nadia Urbinati and Mark Warren (2008, 391). Contemporary democratic theorists have made room for new realities like proliferating nongovernmental organizations and transnational movements. Such groups play representative-like roles in assembling people into groups and animating them with a sense of common identity. Representation now appears less as responsiveness to preexisting constituent preferences by authorized legislative agents than as a *constructive* process through which political intermediaries at many levels of society mobilize people and shape matters of public concern (Urbinati 2006).

If we use this broader view, the idea of representing future generations seems more plausible. More constructivist accounts can relativize standard assumptions about the territoriality of representation. Some representatives, at least, attempt to assemble broad constituencies, far beyond district boundaries. In addition, since constructivist theory does not presume that constituencies are "there," it has a forward-looking perspective that seems fitted to the project of building groups that do not yet exist. Representation is productive; it can "call forth" new constituencies (Disch 2011, 107). Even if future generations do not have established interests and identities, constructivists can point out that the same thing is truer of existing people than we often think. Representative agents do much of the work of forming people's dispositions and stimulating their concern for emergent issues. So, it seems like a small step to imagine agents who make "representative claims" on behalf of "nonhumans" and "future generations" (Saward 2003, 175; Urbinati and Warren 2008, 404).

Yet the nonexistence of future people blocks this theoretical extension. For nonexistence makes it impossible to capture the interactivity that is the epistemic and ethical core of constructivist representation.

Constructivist theory, no less than the more standard model, rests on a supposition so obvious that it is seldom mentioned: Representatives interact with *currently existing* people. To *represent* another (and not just to lay out an independent argument about what is right) is to engage with the other person and subject oneself to the other's judgments. Representatives try to move people, they get feedback from them, and they risk rejection for their efforts. It is indeed helpful to think of "constituents" not statically, as a legally defined electorate, but more fluidly, as an "audience" constituted by political claimants' appeals (Saward 2003). Still, that audience consists of actually existing individuals who are, at least in principle, capable of reacting to claims ostensibly made on *their* behalf. Interactivity is essential to representation, precisely in order to take account of the otherness of the represented. That person is complex, with an evolving identity, with variable interests, with ideals and vulnerabilities. Aspiring representatives attend to how the other's interests vary situationally and temporally as circumstances change. They listen to the other's stories and concerns. They try out propositions that the potential constituent may never have considered. Representatives also anticipate how the other's interests can be traded off against one another. Protecting wetlands may be diminish the profits of real estate developers, but they might be persuaded to accept such policy if compensated with other benefits. Only flesh-and-blood others can make these judgments about *their* identities and interests. Real presence, here and now, is the epistemic precondition of political representation.

Representative interactivity is also normative. Representatives use the margin of maneuver created by people's fluid sensibilities to join disparate groups together into a functioning community. Representative democracy can claim to serve the *common good*, because it encourages representatives to engage in a sort of entrepreneurial prospecting for support, constantly widening the range of issues addressed. It demonstrates *adaptivity* to evolving social problems by forming agents who are attentive to emergent political sensitivities. It generates a feeling of *fairness* among the governed, who appreciate multiple opportunities to make their voices heard. It *avoids tyranny* by stimulating groups to demand accountability from those who claim to speak in their name. It promotes *reflexivity* by legitimating agents who stir people to challenge the status quo. These ethical advantages explain why, when representation is defective, reformers seek more and better representation. They combat corruption, change electoral systems, revise electoral rules, redraw boundaries, set quotas, make party finances more transparent, oppose policies that repress dissent. All these aim to revitalize the dynamic links between representation claimants and their potential constituents.

Yet a contingent lack of dynamism is not what is going wrong with respect to future generations. Representative interactivity *with them* is not defective. It is impossible. No representatives risk rejection of their claims *by them*. None of today's "performative" gestures (Saward 2014, 725) can be assumed to appeal to an audience that is decades distant. Even if political mobilizers "bring new participants into conflict" (Disch 2011, 112), this near-future orientation often does not reach the more distantly future people held at risk by policies like the long-term storage of dangerous nuclear waste. Future generations are absent in a more radical way than any marginalized or repressed or as-yet-unmobilized set of existing constituents. Future generations have no identity to assert and no power to interject into a political process. Absence without identity incapacitates representation as a practice. In the case of future generations, representation simply cannot do the work that democrats would like it to do.

## Future-Regarding Deliberation

Is there a democratic alternative in relation to future generations? I contend that in circumstances where protecting future generations is an explicit goal, institutional designs should aim to enhance their deliberative qualities—not their representative ones. This means giving up the search for specially situated agents who might claim to speak for future generations. Instead, we devote our efforts to designing alternative types of inclusive decision-making forums—ones particularly apt to redress the future-regarding deficiencies of ordinary representation. What does a deliberatively designed institution look like? For heuristic purposes, consider one model: the consensus conference.[2]

A consensus conference consists of an event in which something like a jury of citizens is assembled to hear information about a public policy issue, debate and reflect among themselves about how best to address the issue, and finally write up a report with recommendations. The first step in constituting such a forum is to select the participants more or less randomly. This task is usually delegated to an opinion-polling firm, which acts under certain inclusionary guidelines. The selected group is kept small— fewer than twenty—to preserve the possibility of discussion for all. Next, organizers set up the conditions for *informed* debate. A diverse panel of experts and activists in the relevant policy area is charged with compiling and presenting an instructional background dossier for the participants.

During the event, the entire dialogical process is overseen by a neutral moderator. The moderator—ideally, someone trained in facilitating debate and exchange of views—keeps the debate flowing, monitors the interventions by the experts and activists, and verifies that questioners feel that their questions have been answered (Steiner 2012). The internal procedures of these forums help assure democratic equality among participants, while encouraging a search for solutions that takes the perspectives of all parts of the community into account.

Finally, participants seek a collective judgment. They ponder, weigh, evaluate all the reasons they have heard. In identifying their areas of agreement, they may have to use voting and majority rule. Crucial from a deliberative point of view is that aggregating procedures come only *after* all the preceding steps, in which participants have sought to reason their way toward the best answer possible (Pierce, Neeley, and Budziak 2008). Using some aggregative methods is probably an essential condition of legitimating citizen forums in contemporary democracies. A single minipublic event is clearly too small to include a cross section of the community's diversity. Results would have to be confirmed across many such events for the public to be convinced that reasoned, general interests have attracted agreement.

This example clarifies how deliberation concerns much less the representative question of how to stimulate interactivity between one group and another, and much more the question of how to improve the quality of *reasoning* that goes into decisions. A "deliberative" process, explains Fishkin, "provides informative and mutually-respectful discussion in which people consider the issue on its merits" (2009, 11). Participants in a deliberative decision-making process try to persuade each other with the best reasons for their judgments (Baber and Bartlett 2005, 6). Here, reasoning refers not to imaginative philosophical ratiocination but instead to reflective exchange of views among differently situated citizens about matters of common concern.

Participants in a deliberative forum are not representatives in either the standard or the constructivist sense. They are selected, not elected, and they are not seeking reelection. In their exchanges of views, they are not asked to think of themselves as "standing for" anyone else. They are asked only to articulate reasons and to evaluate evidence to the best of their ability. They are not even claimants seeking to mobilize other people. It is not intrinsic to their function that they go back to outside groups and justify their positions.

A deliberative design is particularly appropriate to democratizing decision-making processes with respect to future generations. It answers to four challenges of making those processes more future-regarding.

## Insulation against Presentist Pressures

The greatest challenge facing any future-regarding decision-making process is attenuating our bias toward the present. Electoral representation has the most trouble doing this because its very mission is to attend to citizens' constantly evolving interests. To ensure that it does so, representatives are held accountable in regular elections that incentivize short-term thinking. Random selection works against these presentist forces. In Peter Stone's words, it "sanitizes" decision-making procedures of coercive pressures (2009, 376). The objective of random selection is to prevent the choice of participants for a deliberative body because of their party affiliation or their connections to outside interests. A deliberative design establishes conditions for an assembly that is relatively insulated from the powerful political and economic forces of presentism and therefore is freer to concentrate on future-regarding issues.

## Surmounting the Aggregation of Sectoral Interests

In a deliberative space, the future-regarding characteristics of issues can be consciously brought to the fore. This is much harder in a representative space. There, all issues tend to be put on the same plane. If representatives take up a future-regarding question, they look for coalitions of present interests to support one side or the other and often they use commensuration techniques (e.g., discounted present value calculations or opinion polls) to determine the appropriate "weight" of future concerns vis-à-vis contemporary ones. Both strategies turn ethical reasoning into a matter of summing up interests.

Deliberation resists such reductionist strategies. A deliberative forum is a discursive setting in which citizens confront plural values and still try to move toward reasoned conclusions about the general interest. Future-regarding discourse extends the "general" interest to include future people. Concern for the future can take the form, for example, of extrapolating information about possible resource exhaustion and demographic evolution (Rosanvallon 2013, 234). To make such information intelligible to a deliberative group, it can be worked up in several different scenarios. It must be shown how changes in variables are likely to produce different consequences (Andersen and Jäger 1999). Participants examine not only extrapolations of current trends but also multiple paths of future development, with varying degrees of probability (Johnson 2008, 87).

Discursively anticipating the long term (say, fifty years or more hence) brings new, irreducible values to the fore. In addition to the substantive questions at stake (e.g., Is it worth protecting biodiversity on territory $x$?) future-regarding deliberation implies discussing and making judgments about the ethics of dealing with uncertainty; the wisdom of strategies incorporating standards like reversibility, resilience, or precaution; the relative merits of artificial substitutes on the one hand and ecosystemically reproduced goods on the other. Debates may concern who human beings are or what they may become. Some of these issues, argue MacKenzie and Warren, "have no meaningful public opinion attached to them," because they "combine technical complexity with *temporal complexity*" (2012, 104). Minipublic deliberations can help loosen the grip of vested interests in determining the path of technological and territorial development, while still linking decisions to a form of public review.

## Compensating for Informational Deficiencies

Deliberative forums entail intentional efforts to raise the level of empirical awareness among participants. Electoral representation, in contrast, creates incentives for "rational ignorance" among voters (Fishkin 2009, 2). Each voter's effect on final decisions is so small that it makes little sense to invest the time and effort to become well-informed on a topic. In large democracies, representation is efficient, but it has a significant downside: Rationally ignorant voters are easily swayed by campaigns of misinformation and symbolic manipulation (Delli Carpini and Keeter 1996). Part of the promise of citizen forums is that they are designed explicitly to counter these phenomena. They do so by interjecting warranted factual information—and controversies surrounding it—into a discursive process of collective judgment.

Composing the briefing materials that are put before a citizen forum is a meticulous affair, one that emphasizes breadth of information and neutrality on the part of the event organizers (Boy, Donnet Kamel, and Roqueplo 2000, 783–84). The organizers get input from a wide range of stakeholders. They consult persons with a reputation for knowledgeable involvement in the relevant fields—credentialed scientists, yes, but also specialized activists and NGOs. The dossiers are carefully balanced to present arguments for and against various potential solutions; they acknowledge controversies and areas of uncertainty (Fishkin 2009, 115–16). Then experts and activists appear before the citizens and respond to their questions. So, this briefing process is anything but a matter of experts imposing Truth on the befuddled masses. Before a citizen panel, expertise meets counterexpertise. Participants then have to grapple with multiple descriptions of environmental phenomena, projections of trends, and alternative scenarios of their broader consequences.

### Going beyond Partial Mobilization

Representative processes depend on constituents to speak up for themselves or to open themselves to mobilization by political entrepreneurs. Either way, some groups in the population are always left out: the discouraged or disadvantaged or dispersed, the preoccupied or the intimidated. In sociological profile, representative institutions usually reflect the unequal power distribution current in society as whole. Now, one might rationalize the disproportionate numbers of certain groups in the assembly. The wealthy or the highly educated, for example, might be said to have special intellectual gifts or social skills that good governance requires. Or one might admit that, while the current sociological profile is problematic, representative systems nonetheless leave opportunities open for new political actors. In the long run, undermobilized groups do tend to find their representative champions.

In relation to future generations, such defenses ring hollow. Those who have mastered the art of wealth creation in today's high-consumption economies may be among the *least* likely to contemplate the challenges of sustainability. Many of the highly educated tenaciously cling to intellectual frameworks developed decades ago, perpetuating the embedded assumptions of an earlier era.[3] Anyway, even if representative democracies have a record of gradually reaching out to formerly excluded groups, future generations are another matter entirely. Future generations cannot respond to any "opportunities" to mobilize themselves. We have to speak for them.

## All of Us Are Future Generations' Decision Makers

But who are *we*? Seen from a future perspective, we-of-the-present are inevitably but a small fraction of the populations subject to our decisions. What would validate the claims of this partial collection of people to impose life-changing decisions on a vast and voiceless group? The impossibility of representative dynamics in relation to future generations makes these questions more urgent than ever. In the case of future-regarding decisions, I believe, *we* has to be *all of us*—or, more likely, a randomly selected cross section of all of us—consulted deliberatively. There are two reasons for thinking about the democratic consultative basis of a future-regarding decision-making process in these terms.

First, every partial group has moral or epistemological insufficiencies in relation to future generations questions. Consider today's elected representatives. Yes, they do have title to speak authoritatively about the concerns of their constituents, because those constituents authorized them or at least helped judge their representation claims. But today's representatives have no such legitimating relationship to future people. And it is precisely the presentism induced by electoral calculations that makes legislators suspect as future-regarding spokespersons. What about non-elected representation claimants like environmental NGOs—the "sustainability lobby," in Dobson's terms? These groups may well make the right sort of claims, but they lack the moral authority to make decisions that bind *the whole* of today's people. They are not political parties who attempt to reach a broad electorate. Many citizens are likely to feel little ideological sympathy with them. As a result, any decision-making process giving them special, *de jure* legislative influence would be experienced as oppressive by part of the electorate. Damage to democratic legitimacy would be worsened when nonsympathizers read studies showing that the sociological profile of environmental activists is often skewed in favor of certain class origins, educational attainment, and ethnicity (Wahlström, Wennerhag, and Rootes 2013). What about experts? Scientific work itself can reflect economic, gender, and ethnic biases (Haraway 1991). Moreover, expertise does not translate directly into a superior ability to make decisions about what constitutes a good life in the polity, where judgments involve aesthetic, distributive, and ethical controversies, not just technical or factual ones. A future-regarding assembly needs a broader social base to get at these values.

A process of elimination leads to this conclusion: In cases where the affected lives cannot *in principle* constitute a representatively responsive group, no partial group in the polity deserves special weight in a democratic decision-making process. Decisions must be made by present people, either all or some of them. But *some of them* always creates a morally compromising bias. *All of them* is our only current option that does not *add to* the partialities that discriminate against future generations, provided that consultations take place in a deliberative mode. No Rousseauean illusions about the uncorrupted people's superior insight into the public good backs up this conclusion. It claims only that, for future-regarding decisions, every alternative is worse. Thus, some parts of an institutional design for protecting future generations should draw indifferently on all adult citizens to deliberate about these issues.

The second reason for including *all of us* in future-regarding decisions is epistemic. Hélène Landemore presents this general argument in its most persuasive form. She maintains that a democratic system collects and filters information in a way that favors consequentially good decision-making—provided that the democracy is deliberative and widely inclusive. Democracy's "reason" is a form of collective intelligence. It is a systemic, emergent property that forms as a result of dispersed deliberative processes utilizing the polity's full range of cognitive diversity. Democratic decision-making systems have greater knowledge-producing potential than elitist ones, claims Landemore, because (a) they allow citizens to develop their moral and intellectual capacities; and (b) their political structures tap into the whole range of perspectives, interpretations, and heuristics available in society (Landemore 2013b, 89–90, 102–3). By implication, democratic intelligence decreases if this consultative process engages only a fraction of the community. This, unfortunately, is what our current representative processes do. Right-sized, sortition-based assemblies could better capture the community's cognitive diversity than elected assemblies with their well-known biases toward the wealthy and educated (Landemore 2013a).

Landemore does not orient her argument especially toward future-regarding issues, but her argument for trying to help democracies "immunize themselves against the worst forms of cognitive failure" may find its best application in that area (Landemore 2013b, 22). When it comes to protecting future generations or making decisions affecting the biological destiny of humanity—where no individual and no small group can possibly muster the intelligence to look at the questions from all angles—there is probably no more epistemically robust solution than, at some point(s) in the decision-making process, to draw on *all* of our cognitive differences in a deliberative framework.

## Institutional Applications

In sum, when searching for ways to make democracy more future-regarding, the challenge is not to extend representation in new ways. It is to focus on ways of integrating deliberative forums into a democracy's institutional architecture *alongside* representation, specifically to counter its presentist bias.

At what points might such forums be useful? Occasionally one hears a proposal for a full-fledged, future-oriented chamber of randomly selected citizens that would check the power of the other, representative houses (Read 2012). That, I fear, seriously underestimates the levels of political skill and cognitive sophistication needed to champion future-regarding issues in national and international politics. Protecting future generations probably requires a summit institution, with politically experienced, highly educated staff, competent in the skills of parsing modern legislation—that is, an Office for Future Generations (OFG). Precedents suggest that its functions should include sponsoring cross-disciplinary future-regarding research, evaluating legislative proposals according to future-regarding criteria, monitoring policy implementation, and formulating coherent future-oriented policy proposals in areas where the normal representative processes have yet to produce them (Göpel 2014b, 98–101). The critique of OFGs developed earlier in this chapter was not meant to suggest that OFGs are unnecessary. It was intended to show why, until now, OFGs have not been allowed to be strong enough to carry out their alleged function. Their powers have been strictly circumscribed because they have been held to the legitimating standards of democratic representation. Those standards subordinate the office to electorally constituted institutions and make its democratic status questionable. They virtually ensure that presentism keeps the upper hand.

Making OFGs both powerful and democratic would require three deviations from representative expectations. (1) An OFG would need a direct connection to the public as a whole, not just to self-selected participants. (2) It would need not just advisory authority but distinct forms of leverage in the legislative process. (3) To keep such power under democratic control, an OFG would need an alternative form of accountability, one that involved the broader public in selecting its officers and in checking its functioning without subjecting it to the short-term temporality of ordinary electoral politics. These public connections would help people to come to own the OFG's decisions and to support its continued existence (Smith 2015).

In line with these new expectations, deliberatively constituted minipublics might fulfill a number of functions designed to create an insistent future-regarding vector in the dynamics of democratic decision-making. First, citizen forums might act as an initial assessment board for future-regarding propositions coming out of civil society. One function of an appropriately structured deliberative forum could be to receive propositions from other groups and to select those worthiest of consideration by higher level bodies, whether an OFG or the legislature. James Fishkin has argued for a similar decision path in relation to the unwieldy proliferation of referendum propositions in California.[4] He would convoke an assembly of four hundred or so citizens to serve as a filter for initiatives that could actually make it to the ballot.

A similar model might be devised to serve as a legitimating gateway for proposals that would allegedly protect future generations. The deliberators' first responsibility would be to evaluate the authenticity of the proposal-making groups' future-regarding orientation. A citizen forum could include instructions that participants pay attention to the groups' sources of funding, commitment to public mobilization, and lobbying record. In this way, screening out present interests dressed up as future guardians becomes citizen work, not the task of courts or elected officials. After that, the minipublic assembly could deliberate over the comparative worth of various future-regarding proposals and rank them accordingly. This idea leaves the work of detecting issues, formatting them, and raising concern about them to the most concerned and informed actors—NGOs, professional organizations, even political parties and interest groups, acting independently. But it does not just leave those groups to their own devices to put their concerns on the public agenda. Establishing a roster of issues for higher level consideration becomes a citizen function.

A second task might be compliance monitoring. Deliberative forums could constitute an oversight mechanism for verifying the implementation of measures decided at higher levels. Citizen juries might monitor compliance with environmental laws (Carson and Martin 1999, 44). It is a common dysfunction of representative systems that, after laws are passed and policies put into place, their efficacy is undermined by the subsequent play of interests that representation invites. Systematized forms of deliberative citizen monitoring could be used to create an alternative source of effective resistance to presentist pressures. A procedural avenue could be opened for convoking something like environmental grand juries to evaluate the state of implementation of legislated future-regarding objectives. The jury's findings could be used by citizens, NGOs, and courts to press representative authorities to improve the implementation of law.

Most importantly, citizen juries might take on a new accountability function. They could oversee (check, regulate, question, improve) the future-regarding performance of other actors in the democratic system. The Jefferson Center in the United States has experimented with juries that review political candidates through a deliberative process (Crosby 1995, 159; Fung 2003, 350). Citizen juries have been tried in which citizens rated competing mayoral or senatorial candidates for their positions on employment or education policy, and so on. (Stewart, Kendall, and Coote 1994, 16). Some variant of this model is conceivable with respect to the performance evaluation of the OFG. One defect of the ombudsperson model is that it leaves the office suspended in political midair, as it were, without popular grounding. The ombudsperson's odd position is reconciled with representative democracy by having the elected government or parliament ultimately determine this guardian's fate. Counterproductively, this arrangement makes the ombudsperson vulnerable to the vicissitudes of partisan politics. But what if citizen juries—with their special inclusiveness and insulation from presentist pressures—were involved, in a binding way, in the nominating process and in performance evaluation? The deliberative schema would thus include a nonelectoral version of democratic accountability. The guardian might acquire something like a constituency— citizens willing to defend this institution when the forces of presentism attack it. Moreover, it finally becomes imaginable that the OFG could take on more substantial powers vis-à-vis elected representative institutions.[5]

## Conclusion

All of these functions make deliberative bodies into "second-order groups" (Carson and Martin 1999, 71–72). These groups do not make law or policy themselves, but they pass judgments to decision makers and monitor the execution of their directives. They are more than advisory councils. Their functions allow citizens, assembled in specially designed deliberative bodies, to influence the legislative and policy process.

Such ideas for empowering deliberative bodies are surprisingly rare even in the literature on deliberative democracy. Most advocates of minipublics see them as a means of injecting better-informed public opinion into the representative process. They are reluctant to empower them. Meanwhile, representation theorists tend to criticize minipublics as highly artificial venues based on an idealized portrait of a political process, one involving only rational discussion. The analysis of future generations presented here begins to answer, I hope, some of those concerns. Minipublics might have a unique and consequential role to play where the legitimating credentials of representative democracy are at their weakest. These could be forums where citizen participants extend reciprocal consideration both territorially and temporally, at the same time giving democratic backing to other institutions charged with protecting future generations. This ensemble would not replace representative processes, but it could help build a distinct pillar of effective future-regarding concern in the overall architecture of contemporary democracy. It is a matter of democratically supporting future-regarding commitments in ways that representation cannot steadfastly supply.

## Notes

I wish to thank Franklin and Marshall College, the Centre d'études européennes of the Fondation Nationale des Sciences Politiques in Paris; and the European Pademia network for material support in writing this chapter.

　　1. The Hungarian commissioner for future generations was not entirely eliminated. It was made subordinate to another commissioner—whose responsibilities are largely present-oriented—and the size of its staff was drastically reduced. See Göpel (2014b, 97).

　　2. Possible variants are many, including Peter Dienel's Plannungzelle (Dienel and Renn 1995), the Jefferson Center's citizens juries (Carson and Martin 1999, 44–46) and James Fishkin's deliberative opinion polls. See (Fung 2003).

3. For the inertia of political scientists in relation to some future-regarding issues, see Javeline (2014).

4. See "The Deliberative Initiative: Returning Direct Democracy to the People," *SFGate*, February 1, 2012, http://blog.sfgate.com/jfishkin/2012/02/01/the -deliberative-initiative-returning-direct-democracy-to-the-people/.

5. What powers? Suspensive vetoes over some legislation (Read 2012), a circumscribed right of legislative proposition (Bourg et al. 2011, 168), and the authority to call a referendum (Ekeli 2009) are sometimes mentioned in the literature. Each idea raises far-reaching constitutional questions about the authority of future guardians in relation to other democratic institutions. But necessary debates over powers appropriate to a future-regarding institution will barely begin so long as we assume that democratic legitimacy can arise only out of representative practices. That assumption overlooks the presentist orientation of existing institutions. The moral seriousness of democratic claims to protect future generations begins by challenging that orientation.

## References

Agius, E. 2006. "Intergenerational Justice." In *Handbook of Intergenerational Justice*, edited by J. C. Tremmel, 317–32. Cheltenham: Edward Elgar.

Andersen, I.-E., and B. Jäger. 1999. "Scenario Workshops and Consensus Conferences: Towards More Democratic Decision-Making." *Science and Public Policy* 26:331–30.

Baber, W. F., and R. V. Bartlett. 2005. *Deliberative Environmental Politics: Democracy and Ecological Rationality*. Cambridge, MA: MIT Press.

Bourg, D., J. Bétaille, L. Blondiaux, M.-A. Cohendet, J.-M. Fourniau, B. François, P. Marzolf, Y. Sintomer. 2011. *Pour une 6ᵉ République écologique*. Paris: Odile Jacob.

Boy, D., D. Donnet Kamel, and P. Roqueplo. 2000. "Un exemple de démocratie participative: la "conférence de citoyens" sur les organismes génétiquement modifiés." *Revue française de science politique* 50:779–810.

Carson, L., and B. Martin. 1999. *Random Selection in Politics*. Westport, CT: Praeger.

Crosby, N. 1995. "Citizens Juries: One Solution for Difficult Environmental Questions." In *Fairness and Competence in Citizen Participation*, edited by O. Renn, T. Webler, and P. Wiedemann, 157–74. Netherlands: Springer.

Dienel C., and O. Renn. 1995. "Planning Cells: A Gate to 'Fractal' Mediation." In *Fairness and Competence in Citizen Participation: Evaluating Models for Environmental Discourse*, edited by O. Renn, T. Webler, and P. Wiedemann, 117–40. Netherlands: Springer.

Delli Carpini, M. X., and S. Keeter. 1996. *What Americans Know about Politics and Why It Matters*. New Haven, CT: Yale University Press.

Disch, L. 2011. "Toward a Mobilization Conception of Democratic Representation." *American Political Science Review* 105:100–114.

Dobson, A. 1996. "Representative Democracy and the Environment." *Democracy and the Environment: Problems and Prospects*, edited by W. Lafferty and J. Meadowcroft, 123–39. Cheltenham: Edward Elgar.

Eckersley, R. 1999. "The Discourse Ethic and the Problem of Representing Nature." *Environmental Politics* 8:24–49.

Ekeli, K. S. 2005. "Giving a Voice to Posterity—Deliberative Democracy and Representation of Future People." *Journal of Agricultural and Environmental Ethics* 18:429–50.

———. 2009. "Constitutional Experiments: Representing Future Generations through Submajority Rules." *Journal of Political Philosophy* 17:440–61.

Fishkin, J. S. 2009. *When the People Speak: Deliberative Democracy and Public Consultation*. Oxford: Oxford University Press.

Fung, A. 2003. "Survey Article: Recipes for Public Spheres: Eight Institutional Design Choices and Their Consequences." *Journal of Political Philosophy* 11:338–67.

Gardiner, S. 2014. "A Call for a Global Constitutional Convention Focused on Future Generations." *Ethics and International Affairs* 28:299–315.

Göpel, M. 2014a. "Eine Stimme für die Nachkommen: Ombudspersonen für die Rechte zukünftiger Generationen." *Politische Ökologie* 136:91–95.

———. 2014b. "Ombudspersonen für zukünftige Generationen: Diktatoren oder Bürgervertreter?" In *Kann Demokratie Nachhaltigkeit?* edited by B. Gesang, 89–110. Wiesbaden: Springer VS.

Göpel, M., and M. Arhelger. 2010. "How to Protect Future Generations' Rights in European Governance." *Intergenerational Justice Review* 10:3–9.

Haraway, D. 1991. *Simians, Cyborgs, and Women: The Reinvention of Nature*. London: Free Association Books.

Horváth, L. K. 2012. "A Preliminary Examination of the Possibilities for the Institutional Representation of the Interest of Future Generations and Environmental Protection within the System of the United Nations." Available at www.stakeholderforum.org/fileadmin/files/Luca%20Final.pdf.

Javeline, D. 2014. "The Most Important Topic Political Scientists Are Not Studying: Adapting to Climate Change." *Perspectives on Politics* 12:420–34.

Jávor, B. 2006. "Institutional Protection of Succeeding Generations—Ombudsman for Future Generations in Hungary." In *Handbook of Intergenerational Justice*, edited by J. C. Tremmel, 282–98. Cheltenham: Edward Elgar.

Johnson, G. F. 2008. *Deliberative Democracy for the Future: The Case of Nuclear Waste Management in Canada*. Toronto: University of Toronto Press.

Kavka, G., and V. Warren. 1983. *Political Representation for Future Generations*. In *Environmental Philosophy*, edited by R. Elliott, 21–39. State College: Pennsylvania State University Press.

Landemore, H. 2013a. "Deliberation, Cognitive Diversity, and Democratic Inclusiveness: An Epistemic Argument for the Random Selection of Representatives." *Synthèse* 190:1209–231.

———. 2013b. *Democratic Reason: Politics, Collective Intelligence, and the Rule of the Many*. Princeton, NJ: Princeton University Press.

MacKenzie, M. K., and M. E. Warren. 2012. "Two Trust-based Uses of Minipublics in Democratic Systems." In *Deliberative Systems: Deliberative Democracy at the Large Scale*, edited by J. Parkinson and J. Mansbridge, 95–124. Cambridge: Cambridge University Press.

Mansbridge, J. 1999. "Should Blacks Represent Blacks and Women Represent Women? A Contingent 'Yes.'" *Journal of Politics* 61:628–57.

Matravers, M., and L. H. Meyer. 2015. *Democracy, Equality, and Justice*. New York: Routledge.

Phillips, A. 1995. *The Politics of Presence: The Political Representation of Gender, Ethnicity, and Race*. New York: Oxford University Press.

Pierce, J. L., G. Neeley, and J. Budziak. 2008. "Can Deliberative Democracy Work in Hierarchical Organizations?" *Journal of Public Deliberation* 4:1–37.

Pitkin, H. F. 1967. *The Concept of Representation*. Berkeley: University of California Press.

Plotke, D. 1997. "Representation is Democracy." *Constellations* 4:19–34.

Read, R. 2012. *Guardians of the Future: A Constitutional Case for Representing and Protecting Future People*. Dorset: Green House. Available at http://www.greenhousethinktank.org.

Rehfeld, A. 2005. *The Concept of Constituency: Political Representation, Democratic Legitimacy, and Institutional Design*. Cambridge: Cambridge University Press.

Rosanvallon, P. 2013. *La légitimité démocratique: impartialité, réflexivité, proximité*. Paris: Seuil.

Saward, M. 2003. "Enacting Democracy." *Political Studies* 51:161–79.

———. 2010. *The Representative Claim*. Oxford: Oxford University Press.

———. 2014. "Shape-Shifting Representation." *American Political Science Review* 108:723–36.

Shoham, S., and Lamay, N. 2006. "Commission for Future Generations in the Knesset: Lessons Learnt." In *Handbook of Intergenerational Justice*, edited by J. C. Tremmel, 89–113. Cheltenham: Edward Elgar.

Smith, G. 2015. "Report: The Democratic Case for an Office for Future Generations." Foundation for Democracy and Sustainable Development. Available at fdsd.org

Steiner, J. 2012. *The Foundations of Deliberative Democracy: Empirical Research and Normative Implications*. Cambridge: Cambridge University Press.

Stewart, J., E. Kendall, and A. Coote. 1994. *Citizens' Juries*. London: Institute for Public Policy Research.

Stiftung für die Rechte zukünftiger Generationen (FRFG). 2008. *Wahlrecht ohne Altersgrenze?* München: Oekom Verlag.

Stone, P. 2009. "The Logic of Random Selection." *Political Theory* 37:375–97.

Thompson, D. F. 2010. "Representing Future Generations: Political Presentism and

Democratic Trusteeship." *Critical Review of International Social and Political Philosophy* 13:17–37.

Tihonen, P. 2006. "Committee for the Future—A New Institution to Discuss the Future in Finland." In *Do We Owe Them a Future? The Opportunities of a Representation for Future Generations in Europe*, edited by B. Jávor and J. Rácz, 72–88. Budapest: Védegylet.

Urbinati, N. 2006. *Representative Democracy: Principles and Genealogy*. Chicago: University of Chicago Press.

Urbinati, N., and M. E. Warren. 2008. "The Concept of Representation in Contemporary Democratic Theory." *Annual Review of Political Science* 11:387–412.

von Uexkull, J. 2008. "Representing Future Generations." In *Ethical Prospects 2008*, edited by Z. Boda, L. Fekete, and L. Zsolnai, 231–32. Netherlands: Springer.

Wahlström, M., M. Wennerhag, and C. Rootes. 2013. "Framing 'The Climate Issue': Patterns of Participation and Prognostic Frames among Climate Summit Protesters." *Global Environmental Politics* 13:101–22.

Wells, T. 2014. "Votes for the Future." *Aeon*. Available at aeon.co/essays/we-need -to-listen-to-our-future-citizens-here-s-how-to-tune-in.

Whiteside, K. H. 2013. "The Impasses of Ecological Representation." *Environmental Values* 22:339–58.

World Future Council. 2010. *National Policies and International Instruments to Protect the Rights of Future Generations*. Hamburg: World Future Council.

PART III

# Changing Contexts

# CHAPTER TEN

# Synecdochical and Metaphorical Political Representation

*Then and Now*

Frank Ankersmit

This essay investigates the interaction between two of the most significant notions in the political history of the West: sovereignty and political representation. One needs only to think of democracy to immediately recognize their importance. Democracy differs from both absolute monarchy and aristocracy by granting sovereignty to the people. Political representation means that the people's will guides political decision-making. Hence, sovereignty and political representation are the two indispensable pillars of representative democracy—and without either, let alone *both* of them, real democracy is impossible.

Though both notions seem to blend together harmoniously in democracy, a mere cursory glance at their past indicates that their relationship is more complicated. The Middle Ages had political representation but no sovereignty. And when the latter came into being in the early modern period political representation lost all practical meaning, because the absolute monarchs had no use for it. So, if we look at hard historical facts from the late Middle Ages until 1800, it seems as though the two notions excluded each other. As we shall see, there is a zero-sum relationship between the two concepts. Everything depends on which of the two is the strongest—and this is undoubtedly sovereignty. We have no good reason to trust that this interplay of forces changed with the advent of democracy. As Rousseau argued in *Du Contrat Social* of 1762, "sovereignty cannot be represented for the same reason that it cannot be alienated; it consists basically of the general will and the general will cannot be represented; it is what it is, or something else, there is no other possibility." And was Rousseau not the herald of democracy—if ever there was one?

This provides me with the plot for this essay. I argue that we must discern between two basically different, even incompatible notions of political representation. These should be called, for reasons that will become clear in the course of my argument, *synecdochical political representation* and *metaphorical political representation*. We will find the more robust variant of the two—that is, synecdochical political representation—in the Middle Ages. This variant disappeared from the political scene with the advent of absolutism—or could subsist only insofar as absolutism allowed medieval political traditions to continue. The later, weaker variant—metaphorical political representation—is what we find in representative democracy. It is the weaker variant because it had to negotiate a deal with sovereignty in which it would inevitably be—echoing Rousseau's so very clairvoyant analysis—the losing party.

So much will be clear if we admit that what we like to call our representative democracies are, in fact, elective aristocracies. Hence, in political systems where sovereignty (being in the hands of an aristocracy) succeeded in taming political representation, the latter was reduced to the humble status of free elections. Surely, from a democratic perspective one is better off with free elections than without them. Nevertheless, free elections are not enough to achieve representation. They are neither a necessary nor a sufficient condition for representation. In the happy years between 1801 and 1804 Napoleon undoubtedly represented the French people, even though he had come into power with the *coup d'état* of 18 Brumaire 1799. Next, the peoples of the member states of the European Union elect the European Parliament, but it would be the *ne plus ultra* of naivety to infer from this that this Parliament represents the European people. European authorities have arranged free elections for the European Parliament in such a way that they could never be more than a caricature of political representation. Undoubtedly, they have done so without being aware of this, but that does not alter the fact. And in a modern plutocracy such as the United States, free elections are more theory than they are practice (Fukuyama 2014). As soon as sovereignty appears on the political scene, it is sovereignty that decides what will be left of representation. At the same time, a representative democracy cannot do without sovereignty: the will of the people and political representation are both helpless in the absence of an institution transforming their input into universally valid legislation. Sovereignty is both the greatest threat to democracy and the decisive condition of its possibility. In representative democracy political representation will be cut down to a size agreeable to sovereignty. Keeping a representative democracy in a relatively good shape is, therefore, much like walking a tightrope.

The consensus in the West is that we are presently less skilled at walking the tightrope than we were some thirty to fifty years ago. In this essay I shall argue that this has resulted in a return on the political scene of synecdochical political representation at the expense of its metaphorical rival. Populism is what we should think of in this context. Most people are not happy with populism—and if populism is what Mr. Trump does (or did, I am writing this in May 2017), they are undoubtedly right not to be. But as will become clear at the end of this essay, populism can only be condemned if one is prepared to exchange a democratic for an aristocratic pattern of argument. To believe otherwise is to acquiesce to hypocrisy.

## Sovereignty in the Middle Ages

As Bernard de Jouvenel insisted, in the Middle Ages there certainly existed a hierarchy in public or political authority,[1] which enabled people in many cases to establish who was higher or lower in that hierarchy. But there was no lowest or highest position in the hierarchy; just as in the world of numbers there is a hierarchy of numbers but no highest or lowest number. Sure, it was generally recognized that there should exist such a thing as the *plenitudo potestatis* (the fullness of power). And here we might, indeed, be tempted to see the medieval equivalent of the modern notion of sovereignty. But the conjecture is wrong. "For the king has no other power in his lands, since he is the minister and vicar of God, save that alone which he has of right (*de iure*). Nor is that to the contrary where it is said *quod principi placuit legis habet vigorem*, for there follows at the end of the law *cum lege regia quae de imperio eius lata est* (together with the lex regia which has been laid down concerning his authority)" (quoted in McIlwain 1947, 70).

In his commentary on this passage McIlwain points out that Bracton subtly manipulated the meaning of the Latin word *cum*. In the original Justinian code it says that the prince's will has the force of law *because* (*cum*) the people has delegated to him the authority to act in this way, whereas Bracton's *cum* expresses that the king has this authority *together* with, or *insofar* as it agrees with what the *lex regia* states about *imperio*

*eius*. McIlwain goes on to say, "Justinian's is a doctrine of practical absolutism; Bracton's seems to be a clear assertion of constitutionalism. In the
one the prince's will actually is the law, in the other it is only an authoritative promulgation by the king of what the magnates declare to be ancient
custom" (71).

But this is only part of the whole story. For on other occasions Bracton
says things such as "the king is under no man" or "no one can pass judgment on a charter or an act of the king." This gives rise to the question
of how to reconcile this with his pronouncements that the king is always
bound by the *lex regia* (or *lex digna* as this notion was often named on
the European continent), requiring the king to rule according to the laws
that the people (allegedly) have chosen (*quas vulgus elegerit*). McIlwain's
ingenious solution is to discern between *gubernaculum* and *jurisdiction*.
The former term stands for all the competencies and powers required to
control those who might rise in revolt and disturb the peace of the realm.
Briefly, all people having acted in open violation of the laws of the realm.
These competencies were exclusive to the medieval king. *Jurisdiction*, on
the other hand, concerns the "definition of right."[2] And "defining what is
right" is not merely a matter of *quod placet regi*, but can be decided only
against the background of the immemorial customs the king had promised
to respect in the oath he swore when being anointed. Hence, "defining
what is right" is primarily a matter of *interpretation* of existing law, and
here the king has no better testimonial than those of the realm's magnates,
the members of the *curia regis* and lawyers possessing the expertise to
establish the traditions of common law. Here the king can never be more
than a *primus inter pares*; and any intervention by the king in the definition
of what is right will need the approval of Parliament. The political regime
of the Middle Ages thus left very little room for despotism; an autocratic
prince would immediately be accused of tearing up the legal web of the
political order and of having no right to do so: "quod non est in textu iuris,
non est in mundo."

Observe that McIlwain used the term *jurisdiction* where we might have
expected him to speak of *legislation*. And this is most appropriate. As will
be clear from the foregoing, for Bracton *legislation* is restricted to what
falls within the scope of what is reducible to custom and the realm's constitution. Put differently, Bracton leaves no room for a government, or a
king, to be confronted by wholly new juridical challenges or a situation
where an appeal to custom and existing law would be of no use. In sum,
the medieval king was, at most, the supreme judge (*iurisdictio*) but not a
sovereign legislator (*legislation*); and neither was anyone else.

Now, when the Western world moved from the Middle Ages to the political realities of early modern Europe, it precisely needed answers to new juridical challenges. The printing press, the discovery of the Americas and other parts of the world, the birth of the nation-state, the rise of the bourgeoisie and of modern science, and above all the wars of religion were political realities that had no antecedents in the Middle Ages. There was need for legislation for human activities dealing with all these new realities, and an appeal to medieval law and the social and political world it presupposed and expressed was of no avail. After the invention of the automobile, it was necessary to legislate on whether to drive on the right or the left side of the road to reduce the number of traffic casualties. In a similar way, to enable society to function properly, it was necessary to create an institution with the right or the power to repeal old laws and customs and replace them with new and more timely ones. This most urgent need was satisfied by the notion of sovereignty, as defined by Bodin and Hobbes. This, then, is why the notion of sovereignty is, basically, a *modern* one with no antecedent in the Middle Ages.

## Synecdochical and Metaphorical Representation

Representation is a two-place operator in the sense that it requires both a representation and a represented,[3] as becomes clear from the locution "*a* represents *b*." In this sense representation is symbolic since symbols stand for or symbolize something else. This, then, is where symbols differ from signs. For example, letters are signs. Take the letter *s*—you cannot say that it stands for something else, as is the case with symbols and representations.[4] No, the letter *s* stands for itself, for the letter *s*. It follows, by the way, that things cannot represent or symbolize themselves. For, if they do, they are not representations or symbols but signs, in the sense that all the different letters *s* on all the different pages of a book or a newspaper stand for one and the same thing, namely the letter *s*.[5] Next, in the phrases "*a* represents *b*" and "*a* symbolizes *b*," the words *represents* and *symbolizes* set no limits as to what *a* and *b* themselves stand for, represent, or symbolize. *Anything* can represent or symbolize literally *anything else* if we wish or decide to make it do so. With the sole exception, as we saw a moment ago, that what *a* and *b* stand for may not be one and the same thing—for then we are dealing with a sign and not with a representation.

So, the relationship between *a* and *b* in the phrases "*a* represents *b*" or "*a* symbolizes *b*" is wholly open, and nothing is a priori excluded here (again, with the exception of the relationship of identity). We are therefore perfectly free to state what part of the world will contain the $a$'s and what *other* part will contain the $b$'s. I will now consider two ways, $W_1$ and $W_2$, of dividing the world up with the $a$'s in one part and with the $b$'s in another, such that if added together both parts would represent the whole world. Clearly, in this case (1) both $W_1$ and $W_2$ mutually exclude each other, and (2) they leave no room for an alternative way of dividing the world ($W_3$ being neither $W_1$ nor $W_2$ nor part of either of them). This trick (less complicated than the foregoing may suggest) is effortlessly achieved by the notions of synecdoche and metaphor.[6] Let me explain.

In the case of synecdoche, if $a$ represents or symbolizes $b$, $a$ is part of $b$, as in a *pars pro toto*. Moreover, it is an *essential* part: synecdoche always aims at the reduction of something to what is considered to be its essence, in a specific context. For example, the capital city of a country may synecdochically represent or symbolize that country, as one says "Washington decided to occupy Iraq." Washington is part of the United States (*pars pro toto*), and in this context clearly an essential part, since capitals are places where governments ordinarily make their political decisions. Now, at the risk of stating the obvious, it must be emphasized that what synecdoche achieves in this statement is performed exclusively by the phrase *Washington* and *not* by the rest of the sentence. There is no synecdochical semantic interaction going on between *Washington* and the phrase *decided to invade Iraq*. So much becomes clear if we think of someone finding him or herself unable to comprehend the sentence as a whole. And then we say, "Well, you know, *Washington* stands for, represents, or symbolizes the United States here." The meaning of the sentence will be clear to anyone hearing or reading it; and clarification has been achieved by what was said about *Washington* and not about *decided to invade Iraq*. Hence, *Washington* is the (synecdochical) symbol, and the phrase *decided to invade Iraq* is not part of it.

Now metaphor. Take the sentence "the Enlightenment contributed to the secularization of the European mind." Just as in the case of synecdoche, the metaphorical dimension is not to be associated with the sentence as a whole but only with the term *Enlightenment*. That term stands for, represents, or symbolizes a specific part of European history. But in this case the symbol is *not* a *pars pro toto*. The literal meaning of the word *enlightenment* cannot meaningfully be applied in any way to the historical period in question; its correct literal use is restricted to contexts in which we speak of someone enlightening something by lighting a match, a lamp, a torch, and so on. Metaphor aims at giving us the essence of $x$ with the help of something outside of $x$. If you say, "Queen Isabella of England was a snake (or a she-wolf)," you wish to capture the essence of her personality in terms of something that is outside herself. Hence, to no lesser extent than synecdoche, metaphor aims at making us aware of the essence of what the (metaphorical) symbol symbolizes. But, unlike synecdoche, the origins of the semantic meaning of the symbol *Enlightenment* fall here *outside* and are *not* part of what the symbol intends to symbolize.

Summing it all up, we may[7] discern between synecdochical and metaphorical symbolization or representation, and then these two variants of symbolization or representation mutually exclude each other. A symbol is either one or the other for the simple reason that the symbol symbolizing what it symbolizes is either part or *not* part of what it symbolizes (represents)—*tertium non datur*.


## Medieval and Modern Political Representation

I shall now argue that, insofar as the Middle Ages knew political representation, it was synecdochical representation (or symbolization), whereas modern political representation is typically metaphorical. The former conflicts with sovereignty (resulting in the latter) and representation's willingness to comply with the necessity of sovereignty will ultimately result in its political impotence.

The significance of synecdochical symbolization or representation in medieval juridical and constitutional thought can hardly be overestimated. Think of the example Ryle (1949) used for illustrating his refutation of the Cartesian mind/body distinction: "A foreigner visiting Oxford or Cambridge for the first time is shown a number of colleges libraries, playing fields, museums, scientific departments, and administrative offices. He then asks 'But where is the University? I have seen where the members of the Colleges live, where the Registrar works, where the scientists experiment, and the rest. But I have not yet seen the University in which reside and work the members of your University'" (17–18).

Ryle's big idea here is that, just as we should not look for the University of Cambridge apart from all the things mentioned in the quotation, we should not ask for a mind that exists separately from its manifestation in a person's behavior. Now, Ryle's argument here is strikingly similar to the one in the following quotation. It is taken from Kantorowicz's (1957) discussion of a treatise entitled *De consecratione pontificum et regum* of around 1100, which he refers to as *The Norman Anonymous*:

> there was an old struggle between and competition between Canterbury and York about the supremacy of either or the other see. What is it, asks the Anony-mous, that may claim supremacy? Is it the bricks and stones of the Church of Canterbury? Or is it the cathedral building of Canterbury that claims suprem-acy over the cathedral building of York? Apparently it is neither the stones nor the material building of the Church of Canterbury, but it is the immate-rial Church of Canterbury, the Archbishopric, which claims superiority. And wherein should the superiority of one archbishop over another archbishop be found? *In eone quod homo est, an in eo quod archiepiscopus est?* (56–57)

So, *The Norman Anonymous* began with an argument much like Ryle's and then immediately went on to translate it into juridical and/or political terms. He does so by distinguishing between the person of the archbishop of Canterbury on the one hand and the function represented in or by his person on the other. And observe that this is not in the least a minor prob-lem, not a question of typical scholastic hair-splitting about how many angels fit on the point of a needle! No, this problem brings into focus the relationship between, on the one hand, the archbishop of Canterbury as a private person and, on the other hand, the archbishop as a public person. So, this problem addresses nothing less than the demarcation of the private domain from the public domain in all their juridical and political aspects. From there we may move on to the demarcation of public and private law and to what belongs and does not belong to the domain of politics. In sum, everything that politics is about only emerges after this absolutely crucial issue has been taken into consideration.[8] No wonder, then, that it was a problem that truly obsessed medieval political thinkers and that recurs over and over again in their writing. Above all, as one might have expected, in matters concerning kinghood:

> The King has two Capacities, for he has two Bodies, the one whereof is a Body natural, consisting of natural Members as every other Man has, and in this he is the subject to Passions and Death as other Men are; the other is a body Politic, and the Members thereof are his Subjects, and he and his Subjects together compose the Corporation, as Southcote said, and he in incorporated with them, and they with him, and he is the Head, and they are the Members, and he has the sole Government of them; and this Body is not subject to Passions as the

other is, nor to Death, for as to this Body the King never dies, and his natural
Death is not called in our Law (as Harper said), the Death of the King but the
Demise of the King. (Kantorowicz 1957, 13)

This summary of words spoken by the justices Southcote and Harper
in a lawsuit of 1559 aptly sums up the medieval doctrine of the king's two
bodies. Self-evidently, we are dealing here with synecdochical representation, the mortal person of the king can be said to symbolize both his
Kingdom as well as being the head (or "essence") of the "corporation" of
which all his subjects are members. Next, insofar as the mortal king's body
is one part of the union—the other being the immortal body of kingship—
the union of these two bodies symbolizes the "corporation" of the realm.
About this union Sir Francis Bacon most perceptively observed "aliud
est distinctio, aliud separatio"; and he then went on to emphasize that the
king's person and the Crown were "inseparable, though distinct" (Kantorowicz 1957, 365). Admittedly, all this may sound unduly mysterious, but
let's recall that Ryle might have said something similar about what goes
on in our minds and how this manifests itself in our behavior. In this way,
one might well say that the medieval doctrine of the king's two bodies is a
kind of constitutional anti-Cartesianism (allowing it to claim for itself the
unexpected and welcome support of a great deal of Wittgensteinian reflection on the mind/body problem). So, the medieval, synecdochical concept
of political representation—as exemplified by the doctrine of the king's
two bodies—is surely to be taken most seriously and not to be rejected
straightaway as just one more example of regrettable medieval mysticism.

There are two dimensions to this principle: first, the king as a person is
the embodiment of kingship, but this embodiment is most clear and unques-
tionable when he is physically present in Parliament. His physical being is
wholly fused with his position as king; the union of the king's two bodies
becomes a tangible reality. Second, the ceremony of "the King in Parliament" achieves this sublimation of the king by agreeing with, reinforcing,
and, above all, expressing the realm's political constitution: "there can be
no doubt about that in the later Middle Ages the idea was current that in
the Crown the whole body politic was present—from king to lords and
commons and down to the last liege-man" (Kantorowicz 1957, 363).

In agreement with the doctrine of "the King in Parliament," Kantorowicz explicitly includes the king in this notion of "the whole body politic,"
with the result that the king in his role as "the King in Parliament" represents himself *as part of the body politic.* The king here is not some entity

outside or above the body politic, somehow possessing the power to represent or to stand for it—for that would be metaphorical representation—he is the body politic in its synecdochical essence. As such it can be said that the king represents *all* of the body politic, and that the latter is represented by him. In this way we may claim that medieval political representation is *synecdochical* representation.

*Modern* political representation, however, is wholly different. It is metaphorical instead of synecdochical. Think of Burke's canonical definition of modern political representation in the well-known letter he wrote to his voters in Bristol in 1774:

> Certainly, Gentlemen, it ought to be the happiness and glory of a representative to live in the strictest union, the closest correspondence, and most unreserved communion with his constituents. . . . But his unbiased opinion, his mature judgment, his enlightened conscience, he ought not to sacrifice to you, to any man, or to any set of men living. . . . Your representative owes you, not his industry only, but his judgment; and he betrays, instead of serving you, if he sacrifices it to your opinion. . . . *Authoritative* instructions, *mandates* issued, which the member is bound blindly and implicitly to obey, to vote, and to argue for, though contrary to the clearest conviction of his judgment and conscience— these are things utterly unknown to the laws of this land, and which arise from a fundamental mistake of the whole order and tenor of our Constitution. (Burke 1866, 95–96)

In medieval synecdochical representation—whether the king as the representative of his country; whether the representatives of the three estates as the envoys sent to the king by the estates, cities, or provinces they represented; whether the representatives of the guilds in their often tumultuous negotiations with a city's council—the representative was always and invariably conceived to be a (synecdochical) part of what or whom he represented. Contrarily, Burke regards the representative's main duty and virtue to be choosing a position *above* and *outside* the people he represents. Clearly, this is metaphorical political representation. By being required to rely on his own political wisdom, the wishes and desires of his voters can only be an ingredient, and not even an indispensable one, for the representative's political decision-making. In modern political representation this is considered to be the condition of optimal representation, or of the very *possibility* of political representation. The center of gravity in representation was thus shifted from *within* to *outside* the represented;

undoubtedly a wise decision under the circumstances, but one that furthers aristocracy rather than democracy. In this way, then, sovereignty pulled synecdochical political representation out of its medieval orbit and fixed a new orbit for political representation closer to itself: that of metaphorical political representation. It follows that modern representative democracy is an uneasy mix of the Middle Ages (from which it inherited political representation) and absolute monarchy (from which it inherited sovereignty). It is not surprising that whatever merits representative democracy possesses, (political) logic does not score high among them.

## After Ideology

We found in the previous sections that synecdochical (medieval) political representation and metaphorical (modern) political representation are truly incompatible: the successes of the one are the defeats of the other and vice versa; political representation can be either one or the other—and yet they are mutually dependent. But for almost one and a half centuries Western politics functioned in an *Umwelt*, making it possible to forget this. Political ideology, which came in four variants, may explain why. Christianity, either in a Catholic or a Protestant guise, could be the source of political ideology. Christian democracy, which still exists in many countries on the European continent, has always aimed at the realization of this variant of political ideology. Next, there was liberalism basing its political ideology on the idea of progress, on moral or secular ideals of what the political order should look like—and, though to a lesser extent—about a liberal civil society. Marxism, in its turn, took its inspiration from the Marxist conception of history and insisted on social reformation to agree with Marx's philosophy of history. Social democracy, finally, was a delicately balanced mixture of liberalism and Marxism: it accepted the liberal state but hoped to realize part of the Marxist program within that constitutional framework. And there have been many more political ideologies—as numerous as the stars in the sky—all of them being a mix of these four political world views, each believed to give the right answers to the political challenges of the present and the foreseeable future.

All of these ideologies were successful in hiding from view the either/ or relationship between synecdochical and metaphorical representation by marginalizing what kept these two types of political representation apart from each other. Thus, the tacit and never openly acknowledged belief came into being that modern democracy somehow bridged or transcended the gap between synecdochical and metaphorical representation. This belief announced itself most clearly in the claim—accepted in all Western democracies—that the people's representatives had the three tasks of (1) representing the people, (2) being part of the sovereign legislator, and (3) controlling the executive. Above all, the belief was revealed in the expectation that these three tasks could be reconciled with each other unproblematically. More specifically, that the people's representative could at all times shift easily, effortlessly, and without a change of heart or of political role, from being the people's representative to being its sovereign legislator and back again. Indeed, the miracle worked by political ideology has been to make both the people, or the voter, *and* the people's representative believe that the latter could both synecdochically represent when having their face turned to the people, while metaphorically representing when acting as legislator. In this way, synecdochical medieval political representation succeeded in surreptitiously making itself comfortable in the framework of metaphorical modern political representation, even though the latter is alien and even hostile to it.

It was so successful in this that metaphorical political representation was sometimes understood and analyzed in terms of synecdochical political representation. One may think here, for example, of what Gerhard Leibholz (1902–1982) understood by "identitäre Representation" where the representative and the represented are believed to be "identical" (Leibholz 1929, 44ff.; Hartmann 1979, 199–201.). It will need no elucidation that this is synecdochical representation, in which the representatives are considered to be themselves part of what they represent. Nor need we be surprised that Leibholz is regarded as one of the founders of contemporary German thought about political parties. In terms of the ideology of a political party, the voters and their representatives tend to fuse together: the political ideology of a political party, in the mind of the people's representatives, will be basically the same as that in the mind of those who voted for them.

Christian-democratic, liberal, Marxist and sociodemocratic political ideologies all identified a point on the political horizon toward which both the representatives and their voters were moving. On this route, the representatives were guides, leaders, and comrades rather than unpredictable arbiters between the desires of their electorate and those of others. This created an indestructible bond of trust and confidence between the people's representatives and their voters; the voters were convinced that their representatives were the best defenders of their interests and blindly accepted compromises with their ideological antipodes if their own representative told them that there was, alas, no other realistic way to achieve the (partial) realization of their shared ideological goals. Not only were they unconcerned about their representatives being their sovereign legislator, they welcomed it! The voters saw in the sovereign powers of their representatives the strongest weapon in their common political struggle. Without it, they would both have been powerless.

The voters thus remained oblivious of the realities of the actual power relationship between themselves and their representatives; they could relegate to the margins of their political awareness the fact that a representative democracy *sensu stricto* is an elective aristocracy based on metaphorical representation, and that their representatives have the curious double role of representing them *and* of being their sovereign lord and master. While, at the same time, the representatives never needed to worry about the allegiance of their rank and file, whose interests they served in Parliament. They knew that a more or less fixed part of the electorate would vote for them because they were considered to be "one of us." In sum, Rousseau's incompatibility between representation and sovereignty was given no chance to announce itself until quite recently in our Western democracies. Ideology did not actually meld together representation and sovereignty—for this is a constitutional impossibility—but nevertheless created a situation in which such a melding together *seemed* to have been achieved. What was, in fact, metaphorical political representation was experienced by both the voters and their representatives as if it were synecdochical representation. They lived in the postabsolutist democratic state but experienced it as if they relived the Middle Ages.

But now that political ideology is gradually fading away and political decision-making is more and more guided by the Baroness Thatcher's TINA principle (There Is No Alternative), requiring the politician to do what is seen as bitter economic necessity, it becomes ever more difficult to remain blind to the fact that representative democracy is structured by metaphorical representation and, therefore, is guided by an essentially aristocratic compass. For more than a century it was considered a blindingly obvious platitude, a banal and trivial truth that our Western political systems are democracies; but it is now dawning on us that underneath the comforting veil of political ideology was hidden a political system that is far from being democratic—at least if one wishes to understand *democracy* as not too remote from what its etymology suggests.

This, then, is the *démasqué* taking place in all Western representative democracies in the wake of the mortification of political ideology, compelling both the citizen and the politician to recognize that these political systems are, in fact, elective aristocracies.[9] Needless to say, the recognition of this disheartening fact about our democracies was like a cold shower on both the voters and their representatives. Until recently, the people's representatives were cherished by their voters as "one of us," whereas the basic fact is that they are *not* one of us but the members of an elected aristocracy. The representative is no longer part of the people but of the government. The representative no longer represents the people to the government, but the government to the people (Pot 2006, 639). The vector of representation has been turned around 180 degrees.

## Populism

We must answer the question of what this must have meant for both the voters and the people's representatives. Let's begin with the voters. Now that the ideological bond between the voters and their representatives was lost, the voters were confronted with the nasty dilemma of whether they should see their representatives as people's tribunes ready to fight to the bitter end for their interests or rather as dispassionate arbiters weighing their interests against those of others. The voters discovered that, when being addressed by their representatives, they could never be sure whether the latter did so as sympathetic solicitors or as severe judges. They now felt like the defendants in a lawsuit in which their solicitors were also their judges. How could they avoid getting the eerie impression of having somehow ended up in the world of Kafka? Everything their representatives told them placed the voters in the impossible dilemma of interpreting it either as the best synthesis of their interests and desires or as an attempt to marshal their support for goals they did not care about or, worse still, for which they had no sympathy at all. The dilemma came as a terrible surprise for the voters because they had not been prepared for it by the official account of democracy, once so eloquently summarized by Lincoln in his Gettysburg Address as "a government of the people, for the people and by the people" (quoted in Pasquino 2008, 15).

So how could one possibly blame the voters, or the people, for preferring to see their representatives in the role of a people's tribune defending their interests against those of others when confronted with the two faces of the people's representatives? And without being haughtily told by their representatives that they, their representatives, know what is best for them, the voters, and that they will decide accordingly in Parliament? Is that for them, the voters, not the best or even the most honorable option? Must compromise not already be a bad thing in the eyes of the voters? Should they not regard compromises devised and enforced by others upon them, as an unsupportable encroachment of their sincerest convictions and of *democracy* and what its etymology seems to promise? Will this not invite the voters to embrace populism, defined by Mudde and Rovira Kaltwasser as follows: "populism is defined here as a thin-centred ideology that considers society to be ultimately separated into two homogeneous and antagonistic groups, 'the pure people' and 'the corrupt elite,' and which argues that politics should be an expression of the *volonté générale* of the people" (Mudde and Kaltwasser 2012, 20).

Who can blame the voters, having been convinced by Lincoln's eloquent rhetoric, for seeing in the checks and balances built into our political systems by a "corrupt elite" frustrating obstacles to the realization of the people's will? Which, again, amounts to a de facto embrace of populism. As Pelinka put it, "populism is a general protest against the checks and balances introduced to prevent 'the people's' direct rule. The beginning of modern populism was a radical understanding of democracy as a government by the people, beyond the distinction between majority and minority, beyond limitations 'the people' are told to respect" (Pelinka 2013, 3).[10]

And are "populist forces" sometimes not just simply dead right when demanding, "for instance, . . . the re-politicization of certain topics which either intentionally or unintentionally are not being addressed by the establishment" (Mudde and Kaltwasser 2012, 20; see also Pelinka 2013, 3)? They follow Ernesto Laclau's observation that populist parties have the capacity to destabilize and question the establishment's political discourse (Mudde and Kaltwasser 2012, 65). And, as one might wish to add, the self-censure and intolerance of political correctness. Moreover, as Dick Pels (2011, 31) argues, populism may feel a natural affinity with a certain type of political question, such as, "What is the meaning of national identity, patriotism of a feeling at home in an individualist culture open to all of the world? What protection can the nation-state offer against unwanted social, cultural, and economic influences from abroad? What kind of community are we; who do and do not belong to it? Which cultural differences are valuable, and which are not? What are the limits of toleration, of freedom of speech and freedom of religion?"[11]

No trifles, to be sure. A case could be made for the claim that rather than the defender of representative democracy, the populist is the "true democrat" (if we understand by the terms *representative democracy* and *democracy* what they really mean). By embracing populism, the voters are not irresponsibly exploiting democracy for purposes alien to it; on the contrary, their choice reveals an inconsistency that has always been part and parcel of representative democracy.

This inconsistency was obscured in numerous definitions of democracy, such as Schumpeter's (1994) both unassuming and misleading description of democracy as "an institutional arrangement for arriving at political decisions which realize the common good by making the people itself decide issues through the election of individuals who are to assemble in order to carry out its will" (250). This definition eludes the real problem of democracy: namely, the problem of who makes decisions when the people are divided on some political issue; likewise it avoids the question of how the right to decide in such cases could possibly be squared with what we commonly associate with democracy. All attempts to address this problem have sooner or later manipulated the notion of "the people" and transformed it into something in which "the people" could no longer recognize itself. Indeed, "the people" is "never a primary datum but a construct," as emphasized by Laclau (2005, 48). The question then arises, who are the "constructors" of the people, and what gives them the right to "construct" the people? Surely, a question not easy to answer in strictly democratic terms!

Hence, why would the voters, if confronted with what we identified above as the main flaw in representative democracy, *not* vote for populism? Again, by choosing populism they do not sin against the nature and intent of representative democracy. For the voters' embrace of populism is the result of a realistic and rational appraisal of the nature of representative democracy and of what it can and, above all, can*not* give them. It is not a move against or beyond representative democracy but remains firmly within the logic of that political system. In sum, one may well regret populism and have excellent reasons for doing so—reasons with which I warmly agree—but the populist voters could not possibly be accused of antidemocratic sympathies in the sense of questioning either implicitly or explicitly the mechanisms of representative democracy.[12] Whoever deplores populism should begin by acknowledging that the defenders of representative democracy left ample room for populism by being so consistently unclear about democracy's nature and by having furthered illusions about it, which could never be transformed into political reality. Thus, Margaret Canovan

(2011) was right in her observation "that populism follows democracy like a shadow" (2–16).

In the foregoing I focused on the people and the voters. Let us turn, next, to the people's representatives. As we saw in one of the previous sections, since representative democracy came into being, it has generally been assumed as a matter of course that the people's representatives should have three tasks: (1) representation, (2) legislation, and (3) controlling the executive. And these tasks were believed not to conflict with each other but to be merely different aspects of one and the same political function. In the same way, a university professor is expected to perform certain managerial and administrative tasks apart from teaching and writing. Sometimes one does something, then at other times one does something else; but it is all part of one and the same job. These three tasks were perceived to *complement* each other: what better background for legislation could one possibly have than that of being the people's representatives? Are the people's representatives—having been elected to represent the people—not best informed about the wishes and desires of the people and, therefore, ideally suited for translating these into actual legislation? So, the very idea that there should be a tension, let alone a conflict, between representation and legislation seemed to be, if not absurd, at odds with both the theory and practice of representative democracy. And, as was argued above, as long as political ideology permeated representative democracy, this view of the relationship between the three tasks of the people's representatives had an immense plausibility. But, again, this changed with the death of political ideology. Since then, the people's representative finds himself in a position not unlike that of Goethe's Faust:

> Thy heart by one sole impulse is possess'd;
> Unconscious of the other still remain!
> Two souls, alas! are lodg'd within my breast,
> Which struggle there for undivided reign:
> One to the world, with obstinate desire,
> And closely-cleaving organs, still adheres;
> Above the mist, the other doth aspire,
> With sacred vehemence, to purer spheres.[13]

That is the people's representatives' current predicament: on the one hand, with "obstinate desire" (in derber Liebeslust) they are the representatives of their voters, while on the other, as sovereign legislator, they are the cultivator of "purer spheres" (Gefilden hoher Ahnen). On the one hand, they will identify with the private interests of their voters, whereas on the other, they must take the public interest as their political compass. Representatives increasingly experiencing the responsibilities of just and careful legislation as an obstacle to do justice to "the will of the people" will see in the dissolution of the link between representation and legislation an occasion for choosing in favor of the populist option. On the one hand, if consistently and candidly pursued, an honorable option, but, on the other, an option that cannot fruitfully contribute to a solution of existing political problems and that will render us helpless when facing the political challenges of the present and the future. The populist politicians typically run away from political responsibility, whereas their nonpopulist opponents will be painfully aware that Machiavellian "raison d'état" will often compel them to sacrifice the interests of their own voters to the public interest.[14] It is, therefore, the option requiring more self-confidence and political courage than the populist representatives need to have, since the nonpopulist's voters may make them pay dearly for their "unpopular" political choices.

Now that the constitutional twilight of the age of ideology is over, and the inconsistency between representation and sovereignty is exposed to broad daylight, the people's representatives will have to show their cards and reveal their choice in the Rousseauist dilemma between representation and sovereignty—between the Middle Ages and absolute monarchy. Will they primarily be tribunes of the people or their sovereign legislator? Will they be the successors of those sent to the medieval prince to represent a city or a province? Or, rather, will they be the successors of the absolute monarch? The former option compels them to identify with the needs, the pains, and the private interests of their voters, the other to regard these with the chilly objectivism of the general interest. Machiavelli's tragic conflict between public and private morals thus invades the heart of the people's representatives. Political ideology can no longer be relied upon to mediate between the two; there is no longer a point on the political horizon presenting an ideologically defined reconciliation of both morals. Hence, the people's representatives can no longer effortlessly switch roles here, let alone naively believe that their several political tasks nicely and harmoniously complement each other. Clarity is required now; this is what they owe to their voters.

Finally, after the end of political ideology the voters are likely to move in the direction of populism since they will now have a stronger grip on their representatives than they did under the regime of political ideology.

On the other hand, now that the people's representatives no longer have the political guidance of ideology, they will be compelled to weigh the desires of their voters continuously against the demands of the public interest. Their most eligible option in this dilemma will be to decide where these two coincide in their view. But they will have no guarantees that their voters will agree with them on how to achieve a fusion of the voters' wishes and the public interest. The contrary is more likely to be the case. Thus, the electorate can be expected to become increasingly populist, whereas the people's representatives (opting for political responsibility) will become ever less so. The result will be a growing alienation between the people and its representatives.[15]

## Conclusion

This essay was an attempt at political archaeology. Representative democracy is still the reassuringly solid surface of the political reality we inhabit. But some archaeological or geological digging yields less comforting insights. We discover, first, that below the surface political ideology protected representative democracy from the tensions, shocks, and clashes of deeper layers. Second, that the irreconcilable conflicts between sovereignty and synecdochical and metaphorical representation are responsible for these tensions and for the shocks and clashes resulting from them. To put it simply, representative democracy is the uneasy synthesis of two basically different political systems, of synecdochical political representation (the medieval legacy) and of sovereignty (the absolutist legacy). Under the thick cover of political ideology, the inconsistencies of representative democracy lost their contours.

But now that political ideology is as good as dead, these inconsistencies have revealed themselves. Both politicians and voters have become painfully aware of them. We need only recall their origin to predict along what lines the conflict between these inconsistencies will crystalize. Representative democracy will be pulled in two opposite directions: synecdochical political representation (the medieval legacy) and sovereignty (the absolutist legacy). It seems likely, therefore, that the future will give us either a revival of medieval political representation (at the price of political chaos) or of absolutism (at the price of the end of political, or positive, freedom). Or these inconsistencies will move us toward a new synthesis avoiding both chaos and the loss of liberty. Alas, which is the most preferable of these three possible futures is easier to say than how to realize it.

## Notes

Parts of this essay were previously published in Ankersmit (2016, 107–133). I would like to thank Springer VS most warmly for generously allowing me to use this material here again.

1. Jouvenel (1955, 218, 219) speaks of "une échelle des commandements" and of "des droits étagères."

2. Confusing is that McIlwain quotes a passage from Bracton in which Bracton explicitly equates *jurisdiction* with *gubernaculum* (McIlwain 1947, 76).

3. Admittedly, this is a simplification. I have argued elsewhere that representation is a three-place operator in the sense that representation not only represents the represented but also requires us to focus on a certain aspect of it (see Ankersmit 2012, ch. 4). But we can safely leave out the notion of the aspect in the present context.

4. It might be objected now that the letter *s* stands for a specific sound. But think of the pronunciation of the letter *a* in the English words *bad*, *bald*, or *bandage*, of the French *mal* or of compositions such as the French *beau* or the German *aussen*. Clearly, the proposal to conceive of letters as signs standing for certain sounds is a nonstarter.

5. Perhaps one might say that each occurrence of *s* in the text is a self-symbolization of *s*. We would then wipe out the difference between signs and symbols. But since it is hard to see what purpose doing so might possibly serve, we had better steer clear from the self-contradictory neologism of *self-symbolization*. The best solution is to distinguish between symbols and signs strictly as follows: symbols symbolize something different from themselves, whereas the sign is a symbol that stands for itself.

6. I shall accept here the way the two tropes "synecdoche" and "metaphor" were defined in White (1973). Some literary theorists have protested that what White ascribed to synecdoche is, in fact, how metaphor is ordinarily understood, and *vice versa*. But this labelling discussion is of no relevance in the present context.

7. I deliberately say here "may" instead of "should," since we saw a moment ago that there are no limits to what we may wish to propose as a symbol or a representation for something else. The distinction between synecdochical and metaphorical symbolization or representation is just one option—and I am only interested in this specific distinction since both mutually exclude each other and do so for the reason specified here.

8. Surprisingly, Kantorowicz never seems to have been aware of this, even though he wrote a book of over five hundred pages on this theme. More surprisingly, the same seems to be true of no less an authority on medieval English law than Frederick Maitland (see Kantorowicz 1957, 3, 4).

9. An observation that is, in fact, neither new nor surprising. The French revolutionary Pierre Louis Roederer (1754–1835) wrote in 1800, "aristocratie élective,

dont Rousseau a parlé il y a cinquante ans, est ce que nous appelons aujourd'hui démocratie représentative.... Que signifie le mot élective joint au mot aristocratie? Il signifie que ce petit nombre de sages qui sont appelés à gouverner ne tiennent leur droit que du choix, de la confiance de leurs concitoyens; en un mot, d'une élection entièrement libre et dégagée de conditions de naissance. Eh bien! N'est-ce pas justement ce que signifie le mot démocratie joint à celui de représentative? Aristocratie élective, démocratie représentative sont donc une seule et même chose" (quoted in Rosanvallon 2000, 114, 115).

10. The Rousseauist undertone of this definition of populism is striking, suggesting that populism and democracy are branches of one and the same tree.

11. It should be added that populism avidly exploits the potential of an "us" against "them." The result is a sense of injury if not of rancor: "populism vegetates on rancorous feelings of unease. Rancour typically here is the conviction of not to be taken seriously by politics and the ruling elites" (see Zijderveld 2009, 33). One may agree with Zijderveld here, but this cannot explain why populism could suddenly become so "popular" in our contemporary democracies.

12. It has even been claimed that populism should be placed in the republican tradition (Haan 2003, 26–39). Indeed, if one emphasizes (1) the link between populism and radical Rousseauist democracy and (2) Rousseau's own obvious affinities with the republican tradition, the suggestion makes sense. On the other hand, if populism can be regarded as a return to medieval, synecdochical representation, it cannot be doubted that populism belongs to a political world very different from classical republicanism.

13. "Du bist dir nur des einen Triebs bewusst, / O lerne nie den andern kennen! / Zwei Seelen wohnen, ach! in meiner Brust, / Die eine will sich von den andern trennen: / Die eine hält, in derber Liebeslust, / Sich an der Welt mit klammernden Organen: / Die andre hebt gewaltsam sich vom Dust / Zu den Gefilden hoher Ahnen" (Goethe n.d.).

14. Observe that "the public interest" is generally regarded as a *hurray* term and "raison d'état" as a *boo* term. Yet one cannot applaud the former and, at the same time, reject the latter.

15. As argued by Peter Mair (2013), "there exists in the practice of organized democracy a clear tendency to match citizen withdrawal with elite withdrawal. That is, just as citizens retreat to their own private and particularized spheres of interest, so too the political and party leaders retreat into their own version of this private and particularist sphere, which is constituted by the closed world of the governing institutions. Disengagement is mutual, and for all the rhetoric that echoes on all sides, it is general" (76, 7). Elsewhere Mair put it as follows: "I am concerned to emphasize the evidence of indifference on the part of both the citizenry *and* the political class; they are withdrawing and disengaging from one another, and it is in this sense that there is an emptying of the space in which citizens and their representatives interact" (18).

# References

Ankersmit, Frank R. 2012. *Meaning, Truth, and Reference in Historical Representation*. Ithaca, NY: Cornell University Press.

———. 2016. "Vom Mittelalter zur Demokratie und wieder zurück.'" In *Politische Repräsentation und das Symbolische. Historische, politische und soziologische Perspektive*, edited by Paula Diehl and Felix Steilen, 107–33. Wiesbaden: Springer VS.

Burke, Edmund. 1866. "Speech at the Conclusion of the Polls." In *The Works of Edmund Burke*. Vol. 2, 95–96. Boston: Little, Brown.

Canovan, Margaret. 2011. "Trust the People: Populism and the two Faces of Democracy." *Political Studies* 4 (1): 2–16.

Fukuyama, Francis. 2014. *Political Order and Decay*. London: Profile Books.

Goethe, Johann Wolfgang von. n.d. "Faust." In *Goethes Sämtliche Werke. Jubiläum-Ausgabe. Dreizehnter Band*. Stuttgart und Berlin: J. G. Cottasche Buchhhandlung.

Haan, Ido de. 2003. "Volkswijsheid in de politiek. Het populisme en de republikeinse traditie." *Nieuwste Tijd*, August 8, 2003, 26–39.

Hartmann, V. 1979. *Repräsentation in der politischen Theorie und Staatslehre Deutschlands*. Berlin: de Gruyter.

Jouvenel, Bertrand de. 1955. *De la souveraineté: À la recherche du bien publique*. Paris: Guénin.

Mair, Peter. 2013. *Ruling the Void: The Hollowing out of Western Democracy*. New York: Verso.

McIlwain, Charles Howard. 1947. *Constitutionalism: Ancient and Modern*. Ithaca, NY: Cornell University Press.

Kantorowicz, Ernst. 1957. *The King's Two Bodies: A Study in Mediaeval Political Theology*. Princeton, NJ: Princeton University Press.

Laclau, Ernesto. 2005. "Populism: What's in a Name?" In *Populism and the Mirror of Democracy*, edited by Francisco Panizza, 32–49. London: Verso.

Leibholz, Gerhard. 1929. *Das Wesen der Repräsentation*. Berlin: de Gruyter.

Mudde, Cas, and C. Rovira Kaltwasser. 2012. "Populism and (Liberal) Democracy." In *Populism in Europe and the Americas: Threat or Corrective for Democracy?* edited by Cas Mudde and C. Rovira Kaltwasser, 1–26. Cambridge: Cambridge University Press.

Pasquino. G. 2008. "Populism and Democracy." In *Twenty-First Century Populism*, edited by D. Albertazzi and D. McDonnell, 15–29. London: Palgrave Macmillan.

Pelinka, A. 2013. "Right-Wing Populism: Concept and Typology." In *Right-Wing Populism in Europe*, edited by E. Wodak, M. Khosravinik, and Birgitte Mral, 3–22. London: Bloomsbury.

Pels, Dick 2011. *Het volk bestaat niet. Leiderschap en populisme in de mediocratie*. Amsterdam: de Bezige Bij.

Pot, Combertus Willem van. 2006. *Handboek van het Nederlandse Staatsrecht*.

*Bewerkt door Prof. Mr. D.J. Elzinga, Prof Mr. R. de Lange met medewerking van Mr H.G. Hoogers. Vijftiende Druk*. Deventer: Kluwer.

Rosanvallon, Pierre. 2000. *La démocratie inachevée*. Paris: Gallimard.

Ryle, Giulbert. 1949. *The Concept of the Mind*. London. Penguin Books.

Schumpeter, Joseph A. 1994. *Capitalism, Socialism and Democracy*. London: Routledge.

White, Hayden. 1973. *Metahistory: The Historical Imagination in Nineteenth Century Europe*. Baltimore: Johns Hopkins University Press.

Zijderveld, Anton. 2009. *Populisme als politiek drijfzand*. Amsterdam: Cossee.

# CHAPTER ELEVEN

# Externalities and Representation beyond the State

## Lessons from the European Union

Christopher Lord

When Elizabeth II visited the London School of Economics during the banking crisis she asked why, in a world in which there are so many economists, so few of them predicted the collapse of the financial system. Is the populist crisis in representative democracy the Queen Elizabeth moment in the study of representation? Has, in other words, the study of representation turned out to be largely irrelevant to the problems that have in fact developed in the process of representation?

Take, for example, the huge literature that has emerged on political representation beyond the state. Much law and public policy originates not in single representative democracies but in coordination between states or within international bodies with varying powers of their own. How well individuals are represented in the making of laws and policies that affect their lives has become a two-level problem. It requires an evaluation of both how well citizens are represented within democratic states and how they are represented in rule- and policy-making beyond the state.

By representation beyond the state, I mean speaking or acting on behalf of others in the making of policy or law for several states. Thus understood, the most common form of representation beyond the state probably remains the role of elected national governments in agreeing to international commitments that are often then adopted into their own laws. So ubiquitous and complex has that practice become that it bears little resemblance to classic forms of diplomatic representation. Rather, it occurs across the range of modern government. Each government relies on its own experts and specialists to frame international commitments that frequently become a part of the domestic governance of that policy area. Publics are represented by their national governments, and national governments are typically represented by their own experts in rulemaking beyond the state.

But that is not all. Democracies can also associate together in original ways for the purposes of making law and public policy beyond the state. Just as they need not limit themselves to classic forms of diplomatic representation, they need not limit themselves to classic forms of organization in which international bodies are mere arenas for the representation of the different views of each participating democracy. Rather international bodies can develop claims of their own to represent publics in law- and policy-making beyond the state. European Union (EU) institutions, such as the European Commission (EC) or European Parliament (EP), often claim to represent a European interest or a European public in ways governments cannot do. Then, of course, nongovernmental actors often seek access to law- and policy-making beyond the state precisely on the grounds that representation of their views should not be entirely up to their own governments.

While, however, democratic theorists have debated at length what would be desirable forms of representation beyond the state, that question would probably be dismissed as hardly worth asking by many who subscribe to the populist critique at the center of the present crisis in representative democracy. Since they doubt elite "representatives" are ever likely to be any good at "representing" the people (Urbinati 2014), populists often see representation beyond the state as only compounding the sins of representation. In their view, representation beyond the state is unlikely to align representation to globalization (Castiglione and Warren 2006, 1) or provide publics with means of solving problems through representatives they can themselves influence and control. Rather, representation beyond the state is only likely to complete the domination of the representative process by representatives themselves. For representation beyond the state makes it still easier for representatives to exercise power in ways the represented find hard to control.

However, any analogy soon breaks down between the failure of the economics literature to anticipate the failure of markets and any failure of the literature on representation to anticipate present crises in processes of mass representation made more massive by representation beyond the state. To the contrary, political philosophers have had plenty to say about shortcomings in present forms of representation and the risks they pose of arbitrary domination beyond, within, and between democratic states. One criticism identifies a new rule by the few. Decisions *beyond* the state are dominated by a handful of actors who get to "represent" their democracies in forms of rulemaking and policy coordination beyond the state—forms that are neither public, nor inclusive, nor contested, nor debated, nor controlled, and which are, therefore, outside politics and outside the public sphere. Present arrangements for international policy coordination can neither respond nor be adequately responsible to public opinion if they are unconnected to forms of public debate needed for public opinion to form in the first place. Without public debate of many decisions taken beyond the state, technocracy is substituted for democracy (Habermas 2015, 11). Representation collapses into nonrepresentation in the absence of the constant interaction between representatives and the represented that is defining of representation itself (Ankersmit 2002, 191).

Unaccountable and unrepresentative decisions beyond the state can then spill back into arbitrary domination *within* national democracies. Rather than control international decisions on behalf of their publics, national governments can use intergovernmental bargaining to take decisions in ways their publics find hard to control (Bohman 2007, 7). Instead of representing their publics in decisions made beyond the state, governments can use intergovernmental forms of representation to collude to comanage and constrain their own national democracies. Thus, Habermas (2012) decries the commanding heights of intergovernmental representation in the EU as a "self-authorising European Council ... confined to heads of governments," who, in the Euro crisis, even undertook to "organise majorities in their own national parliaments under threat of sanctions" (viii). Moreover, the often intergovernmental nature of decision-making beyond the state risks arbitrary domination *between* democracies. Decisions reflect the unequal bargaining power of states, not the equal representation of democracies (Pettit 2010).

Yet there is, of course, one fundamental difference between populist and other critiques. Populists criticize representation beyond the state because they question the legitimacy of representation. In contrast, it is, of course, justifiable to criticize shortcomings in representation beyond the state precisely because there can be no legitimacy without representation, and present forms of representation beyond the state are insufficient to secure that legitimacy. Bad representation may be a source of alienation or disguised domination. Yet good representation remains a condition for freedom and democracy (Plotke 1997). Representation scales up democracy to mass polities and societies (Dahl 1970, 67–8). Hence, as Richard Bellamy (2013, 504) puts it, it is "equal and public representation" in decisions on rights and on collective action problems that secures "civic freedom."

If, then, there is to be decision-making beyond the state, we cannot avoid the question of what would be sufficient representation in decision-making to secure its legitimacy. I argue here that one standard by which representation beyond the state should be evaluated is how well it helps democracies manage externalities between themselves in ways that, in turn, help them uphold obligations to their own publics. The following sections argue, first, that the obligations of democracies provide a better standard than the consent of states for the legitimacy of representation beyond the state; second, that democracies are nonetheless structurally unable to meet core obligations to their publics where they are unable to manage externalities between themselves; third, that there are different ways in which representation beyond the state can overcome that difficulty; the final section concludes with some tentative suggestions for how democracies should choose between forms of representation beyond the state.

Three points need to be noted straightaway. First, I am interested in the obligations democracies owe their own publics, rather than obligations they might owe to all democracies, all states, or all persons. This is not because I believe that universal and cosmopolitan obligations are unimportant. Rather my point is that representation beyond the state should also be the concern of noncosmopolitans. Obligations democracies owe their own publics may also require representation beyond the state.

Second, I focus on the representation of democracies in the making of law and public policy beyond the state and not, for example, in mere opinion formation beyond the state. Decisions relevant to the making of shared laws and public policies are those that most require legitimacy. On the one hand, for instance, a decision may demand legitimacy because it requires coercive enforcement by law. Even if laws are not coercively enforced on whole democracies, it is common for cooperation beyond the state to influence laws that individual democracies subsequently enforce on their own citizens. On the other hand, a policy may need legitimacy because it allocates political values. Choices allocate values even where they are choices between multiple ways of leaving everyone better off. In any case, choices that leave all democracies better off will not necessarily have that happy effect for all individuals or groups in society. Cooperation beyond the state may even have ideological biases that do not just allocate values but make those allocations of value procedurally difficult to change (for a discussion of this in the case of the EU see, of course, Scharpf 2009).

Third, I illustrate the arguments of the chapter through the example of the EU. The Union is not just a critical case in the sheer extent to which it makes law and public policy beyond the state (Rodrik 2011, 214). It also contains, as will be seen, much internal variation. The Union alone practices various kinds of representation beyond the state.

## From Consent to Obligation

Do current arrangements for the exercise of political power from beyond the state really require any special justification? Even in the case of EU member states, only around 20 percent of law derives from the Union (Töller 2010), and, even in the making of Union law, publics continue to be represented by their own elected governments. Although those governments no longer have a monopoly of either agenda-setting or veto powers, it remains unusual for any EU law to be made without the participation of member governments and without high levels of agreement between them (Mattila and Lane 2001).

Indeed, in many ways, representation beyond the democratic state continues to be mediated through the democratic state. The key elements and infrastructures of representation—parties, organized interests, social movements, parliaments, and elections—have only developed patchily beyond the state. Nowhere are those elements so fully and evenly developed beyond the state that they fit together to form a complete system of representation in the same way as their equivalents within states do. Everywhere they remain constrained by their microfoundations in national democracies. Thus, in the case of the EU, European elections are largely dominated by the domestic politics of each member state (Reif and Schmitt 1980). Parties in the European Parliament are largely conglomerations of national parties. Interest representation mostly coordinates interests that are already organized in national arenas.

Certainly, the EU has developed forms of representation with some unusual elements of autonomy of national governments. Publics can choose for themselves who represents them in the European Parliament, which, in turn, has significant powers of its own over EU laws, budgets, and even over the appointment and dismissal of the Union's political leadership. But even representation through the EP is less autonomous of national politics than it is of national governments. Indeed, in a sense, the Union only achieves representation beyond the state by compounding together different forms of representation within the state (Fabbrini 2015). The EP—itself elected in contests between national parties in member states—can only use its admittedly significant powers by proposing amendments that are, in turn, acceptable to a council of the elected governments of member states.

Moreover, there are, arguably, important reasons of democratic legitimacy why representation beyond the state continues to be largely mediated through representation within the state. Consider the long and demanding set of conditions that may be needed for representative democracy to work. These might include: (a) freedoms of speech and association; (b) free and fair elections; (c) appointment of leading legislature and executive positions by popular vote; (d) a form of political competition that allows voters to control the political system; (e) a civil society in which all groups have equal opportunity to organize to influence the polity; (f) a public sphere in which all opinions have equal access to public debate, and (g) a defined *demos* with agreement on who should have votes and a voice in the making of decisions binding on all. Yet, achieving all these conditions simultaneously may be hard for a body that operates from beyond the state and is not, therefore, itself a state. The capacity of the state to concentrate power, resources, and legal enforcement has been useful in all kinds of ways to democracy: in ensuring that the decisions of democratic majorities are carried out; in guaranteeing rights needed for democracy; in drawing the boundaries of defined political communities; in motivating voters to participate in forms of democratic competition that manifestly affects their needs and values.

Given, then, the great difficulty of constructing representative democracy beyond the state, it is perhaps understandable that the consent of states has often been seen as sufficient to legitimate cooperation between democratic states. As Allen Buchanan (2011, 6) puts it, "the traditional ... answer to the question 'Are International Institutions legitimate?' is that they are rendered legitimate by state consent." Yet, there are two serious difficulties with that solution. First, the democratic state may itself be changed and even delegitimated by extensive cooperation beyond the state. Policy- and lawmaking beyond the state do not just build on democratic representation within the state; they also change it. Elected governments now have a dual representative function. They represent their publics in exercising powers of their own political systems through the institutions of their own political system. Yet they also represent their publics a second time in a huge amount of shared rulemaking and policy coordination through multiple international bodies, each with its own norms and procedures for shared decision-making. That model, as we have seen, is open to the complaint that governments do not straightforwardly control decisions beyond the state on behalf of their publics. Rather forms of policy coordination beyond the state allow governments to take decisions in ways that their publics find harder to control.

Second, there is, in any case, a fundamental conceptual error in building a theory of legitimacy beyond the state on the consent of democratic states. Consent is neither necessary nor sufficient for legitimacy. Even powers to which actors have consented can be wrongly used (Beetham 2013). Conversely, it may be wrong to withhold consent from forms of authority needed to meet obligations (Estlund 2009). Hence, a more satisfactory understanding sees power as legitimate where it helps actors meet their own moral and political obligations (Buchanan 2002). Core, then, to legitimate representation beyond the state is not the consent of states. Rather it is an understanding of how representation beyond the state can help democracies meet their obligations, including to their own publics. There is no reason why universal and cosmopolitan obligations owed to all humankind should have a monopoly on the justification of any form of politics beyond the state. Obligations democracies owe their own publics may be sufficient on their own to justify ambitious forms of representation beyond the state.

## Externalities

I have argued that a standard for its legitimacy is that representation beyond the state should help democracies meet their own obligations to their own publics. I now argue that democracies are structurally unable to meet their own obligations to their own publics where they cannot manage externalities between themselves. The problem of externalities is familiar. Externalities are uncompensated harms or benefits that are not reflected in rewards to those who produce them. Externalities are negative where actors do not pay the full cost of harms they impose on others. They are positive where actors do not receive the full benefits of their own actions. Negative externalities will be overproduced. Public goods—which function as "very strong" positive "externalities" (Begg, Fischer, and Dornbusch 1984, 352)—will be underproduced. So, for example, too little will be done to clean up climate change (a positive externality) and too much will be done to create climate change (a negative externality). Too little will be done to provide stable systems of human security and economic exchange (positive externalities) and too much will be done to create financial risks that put entire economic systems in peril (negative externalities).

The need to manage externalities has long been understood as a core justification for political authority. David Hume ([1739] 1978, 538–39) famously remarked that "political society easily remedies" the "difficulty" created by individuals who seek to "free" themselves of the "trouble and expense" of providing goods by laying "the whole burden on others." Thus, political authority can solve the free-rider problem that otherwise constrains the elimination of negative externalities and the provision of positive externalities. The result is that "bridges are built, ramparts raised, canals formed, fleets equipped, and armies disciplined everywhere under the care of government."

Still, useful though building bridges may be, it might be objected that only a moral need for political power—and not something as instrumental as managing externalities—can justify anything as morally problematic (Beetham 2013, 3) as the exercise of political power by some people over others. What then justifies political power is that it may be needed to help individuals meet their moral obligations to others: to respect their rights and to treat them justly. However, it seems to me a great mistake to believe that there are two distinct justifications for political power: one instrumental and to do with managing externalities; the other normative and to do with securing rights and core values.

Rather, managing externalities is something that needs to be done in securing rights and delivering values (Lord 2015). Take democracy itself. As Jim Bohman (2007, 2) puts it, democracy ideally "empowers . . . free and equal citizens to form and change the terms of their common life together." Yet democratic institutions will fail to do that if they are unable to manage externalities in matters as fundamental to "living together with others" as providing security, a functioning system of economic exchange, or a sustainable ecosystem. Next, take justice and in particular Rawls's (2003) argument that justice is a matter of how "political and social" institutions, laws, norms and practices all "hang together as one" more or less "fair system of co-operation" (8–10). So difficult is it to exclude any one individual from the external costs and benefits of the overall political, legal, social, and economic systems under which they live that, Rawls continues, those "basic structures" must be sufficiently just for individuals to live "entire lives" under them. Finally, if freedom is the absence of arbitrary domination, it will be incomplete without freedom from polluters, monopolists, or free riders; or, in short, freedom from externalities (Pettit 1997).

Yet, politics, democracy, institutions, and law are often misaligned with the externalities they are supposed to manage. One much discussed difficulty is that the political authority to provide public goods and eliminate other externalities has historically accrued to states. However, under conditions of interdependence, states may themselves become a part of the problem (Warren 2010). Interdependence increases the ability of states to impose negative externalities on other states and decreases their ability to provide their own citizens with the positive externalities of public goods (Collignon 2003, 88). Far from being immune to that difficulty, democratic states may even be especially prone to it. Democracy may itself be an incentive to create negative externalities and to free ride on the efforts of other states to provide positive externalities. If voters are purely self-regarding, electoral competition within any one democracy may only be in "equilibrium (where those competing for power have done everything possible to win votes) at precisely the point that maximizes negative externalities and free riding between democracies" (Grant and Keohane 2005). If, then, an ability to manage externalities is a justification for political authority within states, it may be a justification for political authority beyond them too.

## Varieties of Representation beyond the State

However, it is one thing to argue that one standard by which democracies should be evaluated is how well they are represented in any management of externalities beyond the state needed to meet their obligations to their own publics. It is quite another to demonstrate that this constitutes an operationalizable standard by which democracies can be evaluated and compared. Do democracies even have real-world choices of how they are represented in the management of externalities from beyond the state? In this section I distinguish three possibilities: namely, representation in bargaining; in the formation of shared norms; or in shared lawmaking. Each can contribute in different ways to managing externalities between democracies. Moreover, the third possibility can be subdivided into further institutional choices.

## Representation in Bargaining beyond the State

Robert Coase (1960) famously demonstrated that—where transaction costs are low, and everyone benefits from the removal of externalities—those externalities can be managed by actors merely bargaining together to their mutual advantage, with little need for shared institutions or even shared norms. Moreover, contrary to the objection that bargaining is purely strategic and without normative value, bargaining can have the special normative quality of allowing all participants to cooperate for their own individual reasons of value (Buchanan and Tullock 1962). Hence, the possibility that it might sometimes be enough that democracies are represented by their own elected governments in bargaining to their mutual advantage over the management of externalities may be especially appealing in the case of cooperation between democracies. For, as has been seen, core preconditions for deciding questions of value democratically—such as political competition, high levels of voter participation, a well-formed public sphere, and political community—may be easier to secure within democracies than between them.

## Representation in Norm Formation beyond the State

However, not all externalities can be managed by merely bargaining together to mutual advantage. In the absence of shared norms or institutions, the transaction costs of managing externalities may be prohibitively high. Above all, there is one kind of externality where it makes little sense to leave solutions to bargaining. Where externalities affect what people believe are their core rights, they expect negative externalities to be avoided and positive externalities to be provided as a matter of right, and not of negotiation (Nozick 1974). They do not expect to have to bargain for compensation, to split differences, to divide remedies between victim and perpetrator, or even to negotiate over who should be understood as the victim and perpetrator. Rather they just expect a clearly defined right—and a right to be able to live with the certainty of having clearly defined rights—not to have certain negative externalities imposed upon them and not to have others frustrate their own efforts to provide positive externalities that they deem essential to their own well-being.

Democracies may, therefore, want to accord one another rights over the management of some externalities and not merely bargain solutions to them. However, agreement on rights and values also requires a great deal of agreement on just how those rights and values should be specified and applied in particular cases (Miller 2007). Just what should count as externalities may also require interpretation. One ambiguity is that externalities (as Coase also observed) are often "two-way." If a democratic choice by country $x$ subverts a democratic choice by county $y$, should we understand that as a negative externality on $y$, or should we regard any restriction on $x$'s choice as a negative externality on $x$? If a balance between those democracies is not to be defined by bargaining, it can presumably only be established by norms. However, democracies may not need any shared authority to enforce norms aimed at managing externalities between themselves. They may be able to enforce those norms on themselves in the expectation that, if they do not comply, they will lose the benefits of reciprocation. Representation in making shared norms can, therefore, amount to something more than representation in bargaining and something less than representation in making shared laws aimed at managing externalities beyond the state (see some versions of "regime theory" in international relations [Keohane 1984]).

The Common Foreign and Security Policy (CFSP) of the EU might be one example of how democracies can be represented in a cooperation that uses shared norms—rather than enforceable shared laws—to manage externalities. Security is a public good and, therefore, a positive externality. Like other matters covered by the Union method (Bickerton, Hodson, and Pütter 2015), the CFSP mostly coordinates the powers of the EU's member states. The Union, therefore, has few powers of enforcement. Member states largely enforce commitments on themselves in the knowledge that failure to cooperate may weaken their own prospects of benefiting from any reciprocation. Yet, the CFSP is a normative order even if it is only minimally a legal order. The CFSP has a general (treaty-based) norm of loyal cooperation and specific norms that regulate its security missions. How well member-state democracies are represented in the specification and application of those norms then depends on how well they are represented in the various intergovernmental conferences and European and other councils that define the CFSP.

## Representation in Co-legislation beyond the State

If, however, democracies do agree to shared laws aimed at managing externalities between themselves, they will need to meet normative requirements different from those involved in agreeing to shared norms. Consider the debate on what is needed if units and forms of representation are not to be arbitrarily defined (Näsström 2011, 17). One view holds that all those affected by decisions should be represented in their making. Yet, representation in the making of shared laws seems to require something more than mutual affectedness: namely, shared acceptance of any responsibilities that go with coauthorship of laws through representatives, such as shared obligations to commit to the collective bindingness of laws; shared obligations to give all subjected to the laws equal opportunity to determine what the laws should be; shared obligations to consider what others feel about living under those laws, and so on. Hence, the so-called all-subjected principle holds that, in addition to affectedness, a right to representation in shared lawmaking requires a willingness to undertake the obligations of shared lawmaking (Bauböck 2009; Owen 2012, 143–48).

Perhaps the most ambitious example within the contemporary international order of a group of democracies agreeing to a procedure for how they should be represented in the making of laws aimed at managing externalities between themselves is the EU's so-called community method. Except where it has exclusive competence, the Union can make law only if an outcome can be better achieved at the European level than at a national level (Treaty on European Union, Article 5.3). Externalities are the obvious example of where member states will be systematically more likely to achieve an outcome by legislating together rather than alone. Under the community method, the Union can legislate on a proposal from the commission that is agreed by majorities of the council and Parliament. Hence, no one member state with an interest in imposing a negative externality or free riding on the provision of positive externalities by others can be sure of blocking a law aimed at curbing those externalities. Yet member states retain high levels of joint control even where they cede individual control (Lindseth 2010, 26). Large majorities of governments are still needed, even though no one government has a veto. Member-state democracies that conduct lawmaking through the community method are also represented in at least the following ways; each a form of representation that goes beyond classic forms of intergovernmental representation.

TRANSGOVERNMENTAL REPRESENTATION.    Article 10 (A10) of the Lisbon Treaty is endlessly quoted as evidence of the singularity with which EU member states have used a treaty to commit themselves to a "Union founded on representative democracy" in which governments do not even pretend to exercise a monopoly on the representation of their national publics. Rather, governments share that representation with an EP elected by citizens themselves. However, the rest of A10 is also significant for how it characterizes the share that governments retain in the Union's system of representation: "member states are represented in the European Council by their Heads of Government and in the Council by their governments, themselves democratically accountable either to their national parliaments or to their citizens." In other words—even if accountable to their parliaments and voters—it is national governments that A10 depicts as representing their member-state democracies in Union lawmaking.

Representation by elected national governments is hugely important to how the EU's national democracies are represented in its shared lawmaking beyond the state. Each corresponding agency of each national government engages intimately in the making of Union policy or law through a process that has been described by Helen Wallace and Christine Reh (2015) as "*trans*governmentalism," by Joe Weiler as "infranationalism" (1997), and by Wolfgang Wessels as "fusion" (1997). Undoubtedly, transgovernmentalism—itself the product of the Union's executive federalism—poses problems of "executive domination" and, therefore, of democratic control. Yet transgovernmernalism is not without originality in its representation of national democracies in shared lawmaking beyond the state. First it demonstrates that—even in a multistate body as ambitious and complex as the Union—it is still possible for each national government to be represented in great depth at multiple points in the making of shared laws. Second, intense transgovernmentalism seems to be able to support norms of justification, communication, and shared learning that are more typical of representation than bargaining. It was through the example of how governments are represented through the experts they appoint to comitology committees that Christian Joerges and Jürgen Neyer (1997, 294) advanced their argument that the Union has developed a framework of "law" and "deliberation" that aims to overcome a "constitutional defect in the state itself" by requiring governments to justify the "extra-territorial" implications of their own preferences and behaviors to their "neighbours" (Joerges 2006, 789).

SUPRANATIONAL PARLIAMENTARY REPRESENTATION. Not only is the Union the only international body with a Parliament that is directly elected by citizens. But member states have shared their power to the point that the EP codecides (a) legislation, (b) budgets, and even (c) the executive leadership of the Union. Yet, even though the EP is elected independently of national governments and exercises its powers autonomously of them, it is also important to understand the EP as one more way in which the EU has pioneered new means of representing *national* democracies in shared lawmaking beyond the state (Lord 2017a).

Of course, that suggestion risks upsetting everyone. For those who argue that the EP has already demonstrated that parliamentary legitimation of the EU is feasible (Hix, Noury, and Roland 2007, 220), a directly elected EP has succeeded by representing what is common to the Union's polity and not by representing what is separate from its national democracies. In contrast, others argue (Reif and Schmitt 1980) that even the original sin whereby EP elections are contested on national rather than European issues—specifically on the performance of national governments rather than that of anyone in the EP—lacks even the redeeming feature of connecting the EP to national democracies. To the contrary, second-order elections arguably license the irresponsibility of the EP by detaching its election from any kind of competition—European or national—for the people's vote. Members of the EP exercise their powers safe in the knowledge that whatever electoral sanction awaits them will be little affected by their own behavior as representatives.

However, it is a mistake to assume that competition and sanction are the only bases for representation. As Jane Mansbridge (2009) argues, there is the further possibility that representatives can be selected in ways that make it likely that they will already be internally motivated to represent voters in predictable ways. Now, there is at least one way in which members of the European Parliament (MEPs) are chosen that makes it likely that they will, as Mansbridge puts it, "already have policy goals much like the constituents" (369–70). The very fact that national parties continue to structure voter choice in European elections enables voters to choose MEPs on the basis of the known views of national parties. Thus, Hermann Schmitt and Jacques Thomassen (2000) found a high correlation between the left/right views of candidates in the 1994 European elections and those who voted for them. Even with limited competition, debate, knowledge, or attention to EU matters, citizens' own choices between the normal range of national parties may do something to provide them with representatives who are likely to use the EP's powers to make broadly similar left/right choices as they would themselves.

As I discuss elsewhere (Lord 2004), there are many reasons why this is likely to be an imperfect form of representation. Yet, it is hard to argue that it has *no* value. It uploads to the European level (Eriksen and Fossum

2012) a left/right form of representation that is both common to most member states and relevant to the exercise of the EP's powers. Since the degree of integration is mainly decided by treaty change, the Parliament's primary task is to make left/right choices regarding the existing powers of the Union. And when the left/right opinions of national voters change, they (to reiterate) can make left/right choices between the national parties that contest European elections to change the left/right composition of the representatives who exercise the powers of the EP on their behalf.

Moreover, precisely and paradoxically because the EP is elected in member states, and in contests in which national parties structure voter choice, the composition of each five-year Parliament is very much one of national party delegations. Behind the European party groups, which have indeed succeeded in representing a left/right cleavage common to member states, lies a second party system of two hundred or so national party delegations (Ringe 2010). The groups depend for their own cohesion on the discipline of the national party delegations. They attempt to decide voting instructions by a consensus of the national party delegations. Conflicts between national party delegations and party groups are rare, but, where they do occur, MEPs are four times more likely to vote with their national parties than with their European party groups (Hix, Noury, and Roland 2007, 193).

INTERPARLIAMENTARY REPRESENTATION.    As has been extensively documented (Hefftler et al. 2015), national parliaments are now often involved in Union decisions. Two unusual features mean this is yet another way in which the EU has innovated in the representation of democracies in shared lawmaking beyond the state. First, national parliaments do indeed have rights over EU lawmaking: equal rights with the council and Parliament to receive all legislative texts at key moments in their preparation and rights to act together under the early warning mechanism (EWM) to challenge legislative proposals on grounds of subsidiarity. Some argue that the latter innovation could be developed even further to allow national parliaments to combine to make proposals for Union laws (green cards) or to exercise joint veto rights over them (red cards) (Chalmers 2013). Second, national parliaments already act together as well as separately on Union matters. The Conference of Parliamentary Committees for Union Affairs of Parliaments of the European Union (COSAC) helps them share information during scrutiny of Union decisions. Ian Cooper (2015) has documented how the EWM has encouraged national parliaments to function as a collective actor or, as he puts it, a "virtual third chamber." Ben

Crum and John Erik Fossum (2009) have noted the development of a "parliamentary field" in which parliamentary representatives at all levels develop common role conceptions, resources, and networks aimed at the scrutiny of Union decisions.

Indeed, interparliamentary cooperation in the EU can function as both a public good and a network good. Certainly, asymmetries of information usually favor the very executive bodies parliaments aim to scrutinize (Krehbiel 1991), a problem made acute in the EU's case by the complexity of its decisions. Yet, any information that any one parliament can extract in its own scrutiny of Union decisions can be a public good from which other parliaments cannot easily be excluded (Lord 2017a). Moreover, communication between parliaments can also be a network good, which has the unusual quality that its value increases rather than depletes the more the network is used. Perhaps more speculatively, that in turn may open new normative opportunities—for example, to use interparliamentary networks to operationalize Jim Bohman's (2007) proposal that representative bodies should be able to put their concerns on one another's political agendas and have them considered seriously.

## Concluding Choices

I have argued that democracies may need to manage externalities between themselves if they are to meet their own obligations to their own publics to secure rights and deliver core values of democracy, justice, and freedom from arbitrary domination. Representation beyond the state should not therefore be the concern of cosmopolitans only. Noncosmopolitans are, arguably, also committed to any representation beyond the state needed to deliver the obligations that democracies owe their own publics and the obligations citizens of single democracies owe one another.

I have also argued that democracies have choices in how they are represented in the management of externalities beyond the state. Interstate bargaining, shared norms, or shared laws can all be used to manage externalities between democracies. Yet each entails different forms of representation. Indeed, the example of the EU shows how representation in shared lawmaking aimed at managing externalities can be further subdivided into different practices, including transgovernmental representation, representation through a shared supranational parliament, and interparliamentary representation between parliaments at all levels.

So, how should democracies choose between these possibilities? Let me sketch some tentative answers that might benefit from further discussion and investigation. First, if managing externalities between democracies affects how well those democracies are likely to meet their own obligations to their own publics, it is presumably a matter of normative and not just technical importance if some forms of representation beyond the state turn out to be better than others at discovering externalities. Now, even where preferences are so complete and consistent that they require little further communication or deliberation, actors may still be ineffective at discovering externalities. It is hard to discover what people are prepared to pay to eliminate externalities where any of them have incentives to overstate the costs and understate the benefits of cooperation (Cornes and Sandler 1986, 114). In the case of cooperation between democracies, that difficulty most obviously arises where governments have an incentive to misrepresent risks that proposals to manage externalities will be politically unsustainable in their own democracies (Collignon 2003). One answer may be to represent domestic opponents of governments in some procedure that requires them to take positions *of their own* regarding whether they will accept, reject, or amend laws aimed at managing externalities between democracies. That could be achieved either by representing national parties of opposition in a supranational parliament or by passing shared laws aimed at managing externalities through national parliaments.

However, far from having complete and consistent preferences regarding ways of managing externalities—albeit with incentives to conceal those preferences—actors may struggle even to discover externalities without public debate and politicization and, therefore, representative institutions. As John Dewey put it ([1927] 1954, 35), people need to be made aware of themselves as a mutually affected public and made "effective" by representatives with powers to legislate solutions to externalities.[1] Here representation by political parties may be important. Conservatives, greens, liberals, and social democrats are constituted precisely by their different understandings of how markets, security policies, and ecological problems create externalities and with what implications for values of fairness, non-domination, or democracy (White and Ypi 2011). That again might argue for forms of representation beyond the state that are not monopolized by national governments but that represent the party politics of each participating democracy in its full pluralism.

Second, once democracies engage in any shared lawmaking aimed at managing externalities, they may no longer be able to rely exclusively on a governmental (intergovernmental or transgovernmental) as opposed to a parliamentary (supranational parliamentary or interparliamentary) form of representation beyond the state. The norming of laws—that is, the specification of the exact obligations, values, and rights that laws aimed at managing externalities should secure and respect—may require some role for a specifically parliamentary form of representation. As Habermas has put it (1996, 170), only the "parliamentary principle" can ensure that (a) representatives elected on a basis of "one person, one vote" can (b) test justifications for laws in public (c) during the course of lawmaking itself, and that (d) this happens within institutions that have some encompassing control over the making, amendment, and subsequent administration of laws (see also Mill [1861] 1972).

Third, as the last point already suggests, representation beyond the state may be important to ensuring that any management of externalities between democracies is nonarbitrary. Rather than run the risk of decisions on externalities just following the distribution of bargaining power between themselves, democracies might prefer to precommit to what they can agree are fair norms and procedures of managing externalities between themselves. Norms of mutual consideration (Owen 2012) would surely include opportunities to represent concerns about externalities to representatives of other democracies (Joerges and Neyer 1997). Moreover, limiting negative externalities and providing positive externalities may require joint decisions that profoundly affect the life chances of citizens of each participating democracy—decisions that allocate values in their different societies and from which there are no easy exit options (Lord 2017b). Democracies that cooperate over the management of externalities may therefore acquire historic responsibilities (Miller 2007) that only make it cumulatively more important that they should develop the means of representing their concerns over externalities to one another.

However, externalities are not just sources of democracy-on-democracy domination. Managing them can create risks of "intra-democracy" domination. As has been seen repeatedly, international coordination allows governments to exercise powers with less control by their own publics. Recall John Locke's ([1690] 1924) famous objection that Hobbes' Leviathan presupposes that "men are so foolish that they take care to avoid what mischiefs can be done by polecats and foxes, but are content, nay, think it safety, to be devoured by lions" (163). It makes no sense to respond to mischiefs, such as externalities, by establishing forms of political authority beyond the state that can dominate the very democracies that need to manage externalities between themselves. The management of externalities between democracies may itself need to be embedded in horizontal and vertical checks and balances or, in other words, in a *system* of representation.

## Notes

1. I am grateful to Lisa Disch for pointing out this quotation from Dewey.

## References

Ankersmit, Frank. 2002. *Political Representation*. Stanford, CA: Stanford University Press.

Bauböck, Rainer. 2009. "Global Justice, Freedom of Movement and Democratic Citizenship." *European Journal of Sociology* 50 (1): 131.

Begg, David, Stanley Fischer, and Rüdiger Dornbusch. 1984. *Economics*. Maidenhead: McGraw Hill.

Beetham, David. 2013. *The Legitimation of Power*. Basingstoke: Palgrave Macmillan.

Bellamy, Richard. 2013. "An Ever Closer Union among the Peoples of Europe: Republican Intergovernmentalism and *Demoi*cratic Representation within the EU." *Journal of European Integration* 35 (5): 499–516.

Bickerton, Christopher, Dermot Hodson, and Uwe Pütter, eds. 2015. *The New Intergovernmentalism: States and Supranational Actors in the Post-Maastricht Era*. Oxford: Oxford University Press.

Bohman, James. 2007. *Democracy across Borders from Demos to Demoi*. Cambridge, MA: MIT Press.

Buchanan, Allen. 2002. "Political Legitimacy and Democracy." *Ethics* 112 (4): 689–719.

———. 2011. "Reciprocal Legitimation: Reframing the Problem of International Legitimacy." *Politics, Philosophy and Economics* 10 (1): 5–19.

Buchanan, James, and Gordon Tullock. 1962. *The Calculus of Consent: Logical Foundations of Constitutional Democracy*. Ann Arbor: University of Michigan Press.

Castiglione, Dario, and Mark Warren. 2006. "Rethinking Democratic Representation: Eight Theoretical Issues." Paper presented to Centre for the Study of Democratic Institutions. University of British Columbia, May 18–19 2006.

Chalmers, Damian. 2013. *Democratic Self-Government in Europe: Domestic Solutions to the EU Legitimacy Crisis*. London: Policy Network Paper.

Coase, Robert. 1960. "The Problem of Social Cost." *Journal of Law and Economics* 3 (1): 1–44.

Collignon, Stefan. 2003. *The European Republic: Reflection on the Political Economy of a Future Constitution*. London: The Federal Trust.

Cooper, Ian. 2015. "A Yellow Card for the Striker: National Parliaments and the

Defeat of EU Legislation on the Right to Strike." *Journal of European Public Policy* 22 (10): 1406–25.

Cornes, Richard, and Todd Sandler. 1986. *The Theory of Externalities: Public Goods and Club Goods*. Cambridge: Cambridge University Press.

Crum, Ben, and John Erik Fossum. 2009. "The Multilevel Parliamentary Field: A Framework for Theorising Representative Democracy in the EU." *European Political Science Review* 1 (2): 249–71.

Dahl, Robert. 1970. *After the Revolution?* New Haven, CT: Yale University Press.

Dewey, John. (1927) 1954. *The Public and Its Problems*. Athens: Ohio University Press.

Eriksen, Erik-Oddvar, and John Erik Fossum, eds. 2012. *Europe's Challenge: Reconstituting Europe or Reconfiguring Democracy?* London: Routledge.

Estlund, David. 2009. *Democratic Authority: A Philosophical Framework*. Princeton, NJ: Princeton University Press

Fabbrini, Sergio. 2015. *Which European Union? Europe after the Euro Crisis*. Cambridge: Cambridge University Press.

Grant, Ruth, and Robert Keohane. 2005. "Accountability and Abuses of Power in World Politics." *American Political Science Review* 99 (1): 29–43.

Habermas, Jürgen. 1996. *Between Facts and Norms*. Cambridge: Polity.

———. 2012. *The Crisis of the European Union: A Response*. Cambridge: Polity.

———. 2015. *The Lure of Technocracy*. Cambridge: Polity.

Hefftler, Claudia, Christine Neuhold, Olivier Rozenberg, and Julie Smith, eds. 2015. *Palgrave Handbook of National Parliaments and the European Union*. London: Palgrave Macmillan.

Hix, Simon, Abdel Noury, and Gérard Roland. 2007. *Democratic Politics in the European Parliament*. Cambridge: Cambridge University Press.

Hume, David. (1739) 1978. *A Treatise on Human Nature*. Oxford: Clarendon.

Joerges, Christian. 2006. "Deliberative Political Processes Revisited: What Have We Learnt about the Legitimacy of Supranational Decision-Making?" *Journal of Common Market Studies* 44 (4): 779–802.

Joerges, Christian, and Jürgen Neyer. 1997. "From Intergovernmental Bargaining to Deliberative Political Processes: The Constitutionalisation of Comitology." *European Law Journal* 3 (3): 273–99.

Keohane, Robert. 1984. *After Hegemony: Cooperation and Discord in the World Political Economy*. Princeton, NJ: Princeton University Press.

Krehbiel, Keith. 1991. *Information and Legislative Organisation*. Ann Arbor: University of Michigan Press.

Lindseth, Peter. 2010. *Power and Legitimacy: Reconciling Europe and the Nation State*. Oxford: Oxford University Press.

Locke, John. (1690) 1924. *Two Treatises of Government*. London. Everyman.

Lord, Christopher. 2015. "Utopia or Dystopia? Towards a Normative Analysis of Differentiated Integration." *Journal of European Public Policy* 22 (6): 783–98.

———. 2017a. "An Indirect Legitimacy Argument for a Directly Elected European Parliament." *European Journal of Political Research* 56 (3): 512–28. https://doi.org/10.1111/1475-6765.12204.

———. 2017b. "The Legitimacy of Exits from the European Union." *Journal of European Integration* 39 (5): 499–513. https://doi.org/10.1080/07036337.2017.1333117.

Mansbridge, Jane. 2009. "A 'Selection Model' of Political Representation." *The Journal of Political Philosophy* 17 (4): 369–98.

Mattila, Mikko, and Jan-Erik Lane. 2001. "Why Unanimity in the Council? A Roll-Call Analysis of Council Voting." *European Union Politics* 2 (1): 73–97.

Mill, John Stuart. (1861) 1972. *Utilitarianism: On Liberty and Considerations on Representative Government.* London: Dent.

Miller, David. 2007. *National Responsibility.* Oxford: Oxford University Press.

Näsström, Sofia. 2011. "The Challenge of the All Affected Principle." *Political Studies* 59 (1): 116–34.

Nozick, Robert. 1974. *Anarchy, State and Utopia.* Oxford: Blackwell.

Owen, David. 2012. "Constituting the Polity, Constituting the Demos: On the Place of the All Affected Interests Principle in Democratic Theory and in Resolving the Democratic Boundary Problem." *Ethics and Global Politics* 5 (3): 129–52.

Pettit, Philip. 1997. *Republicanism: A Theory of Freedom and Government.* Oxford: Oxford University Press.

———. 2010. "Legitimate International Institutions: A Neo-Republican Perspective." In *The Philosophy of International Law*, edited by Samantha Besson and John Tasioulis, 139–60. Oxford: Oxford University Press.

Plotke, David. 1997. "Representation Is Democracy." *Constellations* 4 (1): 19–34.

Rawls, John. 2003. *Justice as Fairness: A Restatement.* Cambridge, MA: Belknap of Harvard University Press.

Reif, Karl-Heinz, and Hermann Schmitt. 1980. "Nine Second-Order National Elections: A Conceptual Framework for the Analysis of European Election Results." *European Journal of Political Research* 8 (1): 3–45.

Ringe, Nils. 2010. *Who Decides and How? Preferences, Uncertainty and Policy Choice in the European Parliament.* Oxford: Oxford University Press.

Rodrik, Dani. 2011. *The Globalization Paradox: Democracy and the Future of the World Economy.* New York: W. W. Norton.

Scharpf, Fritz. 2009. "Legitimacy in the Multilevel European Polity." *European Political Science Review* 1 (2): 173–204.

Schmitt, Hermann, and Jacques Thomassen. 2000. "Dynamic Representation: The Case of European Integration." *European Union Politics* 1 (3): 318–39.

Töller, Annette Elisabeth. 2010. "Measuring and Comparing the Europeanisation of National Legislation. A Research Note." *Journal of Common Market Studies* 48 (2): 417–44.

Urbinati, Nadia. 2014. *Democracy Disfigured. Opinion, Truth and the People.* Cambridge, MA: Harvard University Press.

Wallace, Helen, and Christine Reh. 2015. "An Institutional Anatomy of Five Policy Modes." In *Policy Making and the European Union*, edited by Helen Wallace, Mark Pollack, and Alasdair Young, 72–111. Oxford: Oxford University Press.

Warren, Mark. 2010. "Beyond the Self-Legislation Model of Democracy." *Global Ethics and Politics* 3 (1): 47–54.

Weiler, Joseph. 1997. "Legitimacy and Democracy of EU Governance." In *The Politics of European Union Treaty Reform*, edited by Geoffrey Edwards and Alfred Pijpers. London: Pinter.

Wessels, Wolfgang. 1997. "A Dynamic Macropolitical View on Integration Processes." *Journal of Common Market Studies* 35 (2): 267–99.

White, Jonathan, and Lea Ypi. 2011. "On Partisan Political Justification." *American Political Science Review* 105 (2): 381–96.

# CHAPTER TWELVE

# Liminal Representation

Michael Saward

In politics, representation is as representation does. Or—it is the contingent product of what is done with it or in its name. Against this background, efforts by theorists to extract representation's essence from its contexts and functions do not necessarily advance our understanding (Derrida 1982, 301). Likewise, neat distinctions between, for example, two or more types, forms, or qualities of representation are common in democratic theory, but the practices that produce representation often traverse and disrupt static and neat distinctions. Consider the example of "self-appointed representation" (SAR) (Montanaro 2012) and its implied opposite "other-appointed representation" (OAR). SAR, to *be* representation, depends in some form on recognition by others. OAR, to be representation, depends on a presentation of a self adequate to representation. This is one instance of representation's diverse and common *liminal* qualities, which see it traversing and complicating neat categorizations.

Bearing consequences for how representation is understood, analyzed, and evaluated, liminal qualities are evident in the instability of several key distinctions in the study of representation. Liminality renders as fragile some efforts to fix and limit the concept's meanings and range of reference. The diversity and changeability of practices and experiences of representation pose a basic challenge to would-be boundaries (be they empirical or conceptual) between, for example, the formal and the informal and the normative and the descriptive. I argue that we can productively *embrace* representation's liminality, developing fruitful analyses that *track* its changeable character.

After elaborating the idea of liminality and briefly defending an understanding of representation as practice, the chapter will focus on four distinctions often deployed to divide and map conceptually the field of political representation. Representation's liminal character presses us to question the neatness and the realism of many such distinctions. For each of the four distinctions, I focus on the transitional or intermediate nature of representation and the consequences that follow for theoretical analysis. Finally, I show how these four contribute to a larger and more encompassing distinction between *representative democracy* and *democratic representation*, arguing that the former—often the sole focus of debates on representation—is one (crucial) part of the latter.

## Characterizing the Liminal

According to the *Oxford English Dictionary* (2nd ed.), the *liminal* is "characterized by being on a boundary or threshold, especially by being *transitional or intermediate* between two states [or] situations" (italics added). The notion of the liminal gained prominence with the anthropological work of Victor Turner, who (drawing on the ideas of van Gennep) discussed "social dramas" such as initiation rituals in which participants undergo a *transformation* from one cultural state or role to another. We may understand a liminal time, phase, or space as one that (variously) features uncertain or indeterminate identities and outcomes (a realm of *possibility* rather than certainty, established fact, or known outcome); a moment where the normal undergoes a degree of *suspension* (Turner 1981, 159–61). The idea has since been deployed in a variety of styles and contexts, capturing "*in-between* situations and conditions characterized by the *dislocation* of established structures, the reversal of hierarchies, and *uncertainty* about the continuity of tradition and future outcomes" (Horvath, Thomason, and Wydra 2015, 2; emphases added). Liminal states may feature *hybrid* identities and an *ambivalence* in subjects and observers (Giesen 2015). Accounts of liminality and liminal states carry an emphasis on the close reading of contexts and events and on the experiential dimension. Liminality can be understood and applied to contexts and events in a great variety of ways. It can also have maximal and minimal interpretations—on the one hand, liminality may be used to characterize normality; on the other hand, it may describe a particular, shorter, special moment—in between more stable or regular states. I do not enter these wider debates, as my discussion of liminality follows close readings of specific places or events.

## What Is Representation?

My argument is premised on the account of political representation as the contingent product of "representative claims."[1] According to this perspective, representation's political presence arises primarily by virtue of its being *done*—practiced, performed, claimed. Representative roles and relations gain a presence in our politics because myriad actors make claims to speak for others (and for themselves). Representation is a performative product in two linked senses: it is performed in the theatrical sense (i.e., it is both done and shown to be done [Schechner 2002]) and in the speech-act sense (it is a speech or other act that establishes or contributes to establishing a state of affairs) (Austin 1975; Butler 1997). Representation's meaning, in a given time and space, is a contingent sedimentation of meanings within an ecology of more or less public claims, acts, and events about representation and cognate terms. The ecology of claims (and responses to claims) consists in who stands for, speaks for, or symbolizes whom or what—more or less familiar, more or less institutionalized, and so on. The contingent meaning of representation in such a context reflects predominant senses of its instantiation and purposes.

The claim-based approach avoids (a) privileging historically contingent modes of representation as the heart of the phenomenon and (b) the settled dictates of academic disciplinary and subdisciplinary conventions. A number of attempts to fix and to limit representation's meaning and reference—historically, institutionally, or according to the received wisdom of academic disciplines—are strongly challenged by its basis in practice and its liminal qualities. Hence the importance of generating definitions and norms of representation that track its liminality. There is no loss in precision or rigor in such an approach to definition and evaluation, and, if the arguments work, the gain is in versatility, purchase, and indeed the realism of our concepts.

## Liminal Representation

To show that liminal spaces and phases are evident and consequential in a range of features of political and democratic representation, in this section I select four key areas where a strong black-and-white conceptual distinction has generally been maintained by political theorists and others:

between the elective and the nonelective, the formal and the informal, the institutional and the noninstitutional, and the normative and the descriptive. My critique focuses on an indicative demonstration that paying due attention to liminality in such cases and areas undermines the fixity of common distinctions and categories. In so doing, it also demonstrates that representation is a practice and process that has critical liminal qualities, and that this fact has important lessons for the analysis of representation.

## Elective and Nonelective

For representative democracy, citizen political choices conventionally are seen as expressed through the mechanism of voting in elections, while in the wider societal domain they are seen as operating in more informal settings primarily through voice. Maintaining a sharp and clear distinction between elective representation on the one hand and nonelective representation on the other hand is a familiar step in political science and political theory (and also in the wider world of politics). Doing so serves different purposes, not least establishing a major and ongoing source of legitimacy for democracy. If democratic legitimacy is founded on the clear and open practice of political equality entrenched within voting procedures that provide one person, one vote, one value, then free and fair elections are at the core of such legitimacy. Major historical struggles for democratization have, of course, been over access to this franchise, as the latter represents practical and symbolic acceptance as a social and political equal in the polity. In this normative context, politics that is not (in some reasonably direct sense) electoral is pushed to the outer margins of arguments for democracy's legitimacy. So, for example, civil society activity and organizations—depending on how they are configured—may make a positive contribution to the maintenance of quality of democracy, but their presence and features are not formally electoral and therefore not at the core of what legitimizes democracy.[2] In this line of argument, to be democratic and legitimate representation must be electoral representation; nonelectoral representation, by virtue of *being* nonelectoral, may be either undemocratic or at best a marginal contributor to the broader democratic character of a system.

Consider how this standard position fares, however, if we set aside the presumption that representation is defined by its formal institutionalization in representative democracy. If we take *practices* of representation as the primary analytical focus, unpacking the politics of representative claims and their reception, this normatively driven, narrowing, and sharp electoral/nonelectoral distinction loses purchase on political reality. Framed in this way, representation has distinctive liminal qualities. First, the nonelectoral realm of civil society contains many and varied types of electoral practice. Depending on the society concerned, a great many clubs, corporations, unions, education establishments, policing and health bodies, interest groups, and so on have an elective component to their practice. An elected official to, say, a local education or police advisory board occupies a liminal position—elected but in a realm of practice where elections are not typically understood as contributing to democracy at the national or systemic level. Further, there are across civil society many forms of accountability in small and large nonstate organizations that to a degree may act as functional substitutes for (and indeed supplements to) formal election—Montanaro (2012) for example discusses voice, exit, hierarchical, financial, supervisory, and legal accountability. A range of unelected actors will find themselves by such means and to varied degrees answerable to constituencies (used in a broader sense), even if there is no electoral component to their position.

Second, elected actors may or may not act in accordance with the specific constituency-representative electoral relationship that put them in their legislative post. Mansbridge (2003) has elaborated influentially on the notion of "surrogate representation," where an elected official chooses to act for a "constituency" which may overlap little with his or her specific electoral constituency. For example, an Aboriginal member of the Australian Federal Parliament may take it upon himself or herself to speak for Aboriginal communities and interests more widely (Sawer 2001). Note, in this context, that Hanna Pitkin's (1967) preferred definition of representation—as a "substantive acting for others"—does *not* in principle require election (as distinct from others she discusses that do, notably the "authorization" and "accountability" definitions). Pitkin does not pursue this point, but arguably a substantive acting for others is different from the means of achieving it, and in certain contexts electoral means may be inferior ones.

There are likewise many respects in which elective representation contains, or is perhaps haunted by, a nonelective or supraelective component. All electoral systems have some noncompetitive component; the normative account criticized above tends to skate over this fact and to sideline widespread debates about how different electoral systems and arrangements may or may not enhance equality through free and fair competition for votes and offices. Incumbency effects, nonmajoritarian practices, undue hurdles to voter, candidate, or party registration, gerrymandering, and vote-buying are factors variously at play across democratic systems. It still matters greatly to democracy that an elected official may have the formal and constitutional status of a parliamentarian, but bases other than equal votes of equal value will commonly contribute to the achievement of the status. In reality, a semielective status, in between electoral and non-electoral, built on a significant but also thin or fragmentary manifestation of political equality, will influence representative status and practice (e.g., "nondemocratic" postelectoral influence by big campaign donors). To return to a distinction noted earlier, in these and other respects there is probably no such thing as a purely "self-appointed" representative (Montanaro 2012) or indeed a pure form of "other-appointed representative"; even if there are strong examples of the latter, the "others" who do the effective "appointing" often exceed the voting members of an electoral constituency.

Third, there are liminal statuses and actors in a range of electoral contexts. A candidate is already one—in between ordinary citizen and elected representative, in a state of active suspension or uncertain transformation. This status may demand shifting among different and hybrid personas for different voter audiences. A president-elect or a presumptive party nominee occupies a liminal position of transformation and possibility; a defeated candidate, too, prior to concession, may be similarly regarded. Former elected officials also carry with them something of the status that they no longer hold formally; for example, ex-US president Jimmy Carter carried out high-profile international humanitarian work for decades after he left elective office, leading to his Nobel Peace Prize in 2002. Distinctive features of democratic transitions may throw up unusual liminal roles— consider the Burma/Myanmar leader Aung San Suu Kyi, undisputed leader of the winning party in the national elections of 2015 but barred from assuming formal office. Figures who gain their political credibility and impetus in part from resisting the blandishments of electoral politics may run in elections in insurgent mode, gaining office as "outsiders" occupying the citadels—such as Spanish antiausterity activist turned Barcelona mayor Ada Colau. One might likewise note the campaigns of 2016 US presidential candidates Donald Trump and Bernie Sanders as "outsiders," in a way insurgents, or rhetorically in the case of Sanders "revolutionary." These examples raise a range of issues about liminal representation's challenges and opportunities and exhibit the commonality of not only being representative but also claiming, becoming, ceasing to be, and acting "as if" representative.

To be clear, the formality, regularity, publicity, and transparency of free and fair elections remain a profound source of strength for representative claims for the duly elected. Nothing in the claim-based perspective on representation runs counter to this fact. But a range of statuses and practices of representation are—in different ways—located between the strictly electoral and the strictly nonelectoral. Political figures that seek and hold these statuses or enact these practices are best seen as liminal figures, negotiating transitional or ambiguous zones of practice.

## Formal Authority/Informal Authority

Representation consists of variable claims that one person or group can or does stand or speak for another—across different spaces, times, and scales, and importantly *across and between degrees of formality*. The making and reception of such claims in myriad ways *unsettles* fixed ideas of representation. The unsettling can be understood in three interlinked senses.

First, both the so-called formal and the so-called informal rest upon common and contestable grounds. Even widely accepted, institutionalized, and familiar instances of representation depend for their acceptance or legitimacy on a claim or set of claims, and no claim is beyond reasonable contestation.[3] Even an elected parliament representing the people or demos of a nation-state is dependent upon more or less incessant and minimally effective claim-making to underscore its representative status. Explicit representative claims for parliaments are often made by officials working for them or, for example, by architects of the buildings housing legislatures rather than by the elected members themselves, whose claims tend to the more specific and partisan. From a different angle, a venerable and well-established parliament without active members whose practices symbolize their and the institution's implicit claims to represent would in short time be little more than a relic and perhaps a physical symbol of its own impotence. As recent events in Egypt and Tunisia attest, such representative status can be disputed and shattered in short time.

The formal/informal distinction may not overlap at all neatly with the institutionalized/noninstitutionalized distinction with which it is equated or upon which it is sometimes built. Informal and nonelectoral politicking can characterize statal as well as nonstatal governance and politics. Formality, including electoral formalities, can characterize nonstatal governance and politics, as suggested above. (Many more electoral events and relations than the most prominent national and local ones in contemporary societies fly under the radar of studies of democracy.) In line with its liminal quality, claims and practices of representation operate in and across all of these modes and domains.

Second, efforts to pinpoint the boundaries of the formal are likely to founder; so-called informal claims can invade or cut across the realm of the formal. Conventional senses of who can represent and how they do it (or how it is claimed they do it) are shaken up. Disparate informal claimants, for example Indian Ana Hazare and Pakistani education advocate Malala Yousafzai,[4] may be highly unconventional representatives. But their informal claims can become part of local, national, and international formal politics, posing questions about the mix of constraints and opportunities attending (degrees and manifestations of) formality and informality. They show how highly resonant claims can cut across standard representative accounts of institutions, nations, and cultures. Claims for such actors as Hazare and Yousafzai push the envelope further than political theory and political science work on political representation is prepared to go. However, we face the unsettling fact that there is no clear way to decide that one type of acknowledged claim is an instance of representation and another is not, regardless of their location in a nominally formal or informal space, phase, or manner.

Third, both so-called formal and so-called informal representation rest on critically unstable and unsettled "subject effects" and "object effects."[5] Subject and object are effects of the act of claim-making, whether understood as formal or informal. Ana Hazare may be many things, but the subject effect in his claim to speak for India highlights his grand ideals and courage. What matters in political representation is this subject effect, Hazare's capacity to create and sustain it, and the extent to which it resonates with audiences. Yousafzai likewise is many things—no doubt courageous as well as poised and confident beyond her years—yet representative claims will (necessarily) select or construct a subject effect, a picture of her attributes to support the claim to stand for a certain group, aspiration, or cause.

All representations are claims, however sedimented and institutionalized—formal or informal—they may be. The reliance of representation on practice, the presence of the informal in the formal and vice versa, and representation's trade in effects rather than identities underlines its liminality—its "in-betweenness," between protean or shifting boundaries.

Further, note that the implicit assumption of this distinction is that the formal + informal exhausts the manifestations of representation in or across the political community. But we might equally argue that the formal + informal constitutes a continuous political sphere (including varied modes of semiformality, for example) of the included. The excluded may not (be able to) participate in the formal + informal, being outside the community of representative politics, or effective or recognized representative claims. Consider also the latency of the formal in the informal. The civil sphere gives rise to movements or bodies that enter the state (political parties, green or social democratic, for example). It may germinate and grow representative practices and functions that, in time, become statal. As Rosenau (2000) has made clear in the context of transnational politics, we do not know which of the emergent institutional configurations may crystallize into widely accepted and lasting forms of democratic practice. By the same token, institutionalized formal representation may be present by proxy in the informal sphere, for example through what Americans sometimes call "AstroTurf" campaigns. Such actors, movements, organizations, or campaigns may possess liminal qualities (whether to their political benefit or disadvantage) and operate across liminal political spaces.

Our sense of what the subject (that which represents) and object (that which is represented) of representation are or could be is, in this light, not reasonably confined to a given set of institutions or relationships, as important as democratic elections and representative parliaments are.

The elective/nonelective and formal/informal distinctions are at the heart of Urbinati's effort to sustain a narrower conception of representation in her contribution to this volume. It is worth attending to that argument briefly to see the work that conventional normative approaches to representative democracy must undertake to cleave to tenuous and narrow definitions. Urbinati argues that a claims-based approach is only relevant to "expressive" politics that seeks "attention" outside formal elective and state structures. As such it is not genuine representation; only formal electoral, decisional, and judicial procedures and institutions can house genuine representation and indeed democracy. In this argument, however, "representation" and "democracy" are stipulated as statal properties to sustain a specific normative stance, an ideal image of strictly party-based and national democracy that, despite the nostalgic tone, has probably never been realized. The claim-based approach makes it clear that statal and nonstatal processes (e.g., electoral and nonelectoral) involve representative claims, counterclaims, and support. This is the complex dynamic of representative politics. Do not electoral candidates most fundamentally make claims to represent? Are claims not made for and about the representativeness of legislatures? Is not voting in elections and referenda a central mechanism of citizens pronouncing on these claims?

Urbinati also argues that claim-making is only about audiences, but it is constituencies (closely defined and including but not limited to formal electoral constituencies) and not audiences that in a democracy may reasonably judge claims to represent (Saward 2010; 2014). Likewise, for Urbinati, claim-making is merely about rhetoric and performance. Aside from its apparent alignment to the "anti-theatrical prejudice" (Barish 1981), these remarks suggest that electoral candidates and other public officials do not use rhetoric, do not perform, do not pose claims, and so on. This line of thinking has also not caught up with well-established political science critiques, such as that political parties are often today "cartel" rather than "mass" responsive or representative entities (Bartolini and Mair 2001) and that the substantive representation of women more significantly depends on "critical actors" rather than "critical mass" in legislatures: "Who these 'critical actors' are remains an open question. Taking their role seriously, however, requires careful attention to a wide range of possible players, including male and female legislators, ministers, party members, bureaucrats, and members of civil society groups" (Celis et al. 2008, 104). Urbinati's sweeping appraisal of the internet does not acknowledge, for example, the highly significant uses of interactive media in the Obama and Sanders US presidential campaigns. Specifically, from the angle of the present chapter, Urbinati's contribution shows how much realism, how much politics, how many instances of representative (and potentially democratic) practice must be expunged from a selective normative-led picture to sustain an account where ambiguity, shifting roles, and indeed liminality play no part in representative democracy.

## Institutional and Noninstitutional

Representation displays liminal qualities also with respect to its practices between "institutional" and "noninstitutional" sites. An institution is not an institution without the constant practice that defines and sustains it. With the possible exception of the workings of memory and anticipation, a parliament building and a legislative procedure that are empty of legislators are no longer a functioning institution. Practices animate, but they do more; they reconstitute the institution on an everyday basis.

To what extent can institutional models—especially normatively in-flected models of democracy that are built on privileging a specific set of political practices, such as deliberative democracy—be selective or in certain ways held separate from a range of experiences, perspectives, and practices of representation? If the models contain or recommend rules, there is a danger analogous to the relationship between rule utilitarianism and act utilitarianism: it is difficult to defend holding the rule to be prior to acts where the directions of the two (if not the overarching normative goal) diverge for a given choice or strategy. The general norm is reducible—must be reduced—to the practices or acts on which it is founded. I take account of the phenomenological call to attend to the specific things and acts that appear to us and how they do so: "to the claims themselves!" one might say. There is no doubt that there are varied ways of going to the claims them-selves. The assumption I make here is that, if representation is made and disputed in real-world politics on larger and smaller scales, then it happens daily and in detail below the standard-issue radar of political theory and in a realm more akin to that of the political anthropologist. To build a model of democracy on a small subset of claims is to risk oversimplifying and re-ducing its relevance to real-world democratic and representative practice.

As John Parkinson (2015) suggests, it is a mistake to equate the institu-tions of government with a fixed set of roles and personnel. First, formal representative roles do not automatically map onto state organizations. Second, "it is important to separate democratic roles from the actors who perform them." And third, democratic roles—such as "deciding what to do," "defining collective problems," or "articulating interests"—are not areas for action confined to set or fixed institutions or institutionalized positions (21–24).

If practice is at the core of institutions, consider the dynamism of rep-resentative roles within the institutions of representative democracy, such as (classically) trustee and delegate roles performed by members of par-liament or cabinet members. Liminal representation works between and across such seemingly fixed binary options. Arguably, categories of repre-sentation are parasitic on a performative or role-oriented conception of, for example, acting as a trustee or a delegate. A representative claimant plays the role of delegate or trustee. In the practice of a would-be repre-sentative such roles can be mixed and matched by "shape-shifting" claim-ants and actors outside and across their original theoretical or political points of departure (Saward 2014). The would-be representative's shape-shifting and consequent movement through phases of transition and ambiguity contributes directly to the transitory, in-between, liminal character of representation.

What seems solid—the types, the roles—becomes more malleable (de- and reattachable) than binary or other familiar typologies suggest. For example, representative roles are often best conceived as flexible resources for use by would-be representatives in their claiming and jockeying for position. In this light, for example, election candidates, social movement figures, or "shock jock" political talk-radio hosts position themselves as subjects with respect to constituents, supporters, or listeners; in other words, they adopt not so much roles as subject positions. Subject positions are intersubjective, culturally and discursively constituted stances that are (differentially) available for adoption by actors. For example, subject positions of descriptive or sociological likeness, and of trusteeship, are available to potential Western representative claimants (at least) as a social resource. If Chabal and Daloz (2006) in their three-country comparative study of representation are right, for example, a claim such as "I can speak for you because I am like you an ordinary person, doing the things you do and concerned with the things that concern you" expresses a local cultural resource within which a Swedish politician may fruitfully position herself but which would be less likely to work in Nigeria.

Subject positioning introduces into work on representation an interactive dynamism: claims by representatives position themselves and their audience, and claims by the represented position both them and the representative. Representatives do not so much have or occupy roles as pause at or move through available subject-positional resources, which in turn they play a part in creating or reshaping. Consider, for example, Fenno's (2003) view of "trustee" and "delegate" not as representative roles but as resources for congressmen and congresswomen to use to justify their actions to constituents. In this way, the shape-shifting representer, in between and in transition, contributes through his or her liminality to the liminal character of representation.

## The Normative and the Descriptive

In a different vein, we can also trace the liminal quality of representation with respect to analytical approaches to the subject. The dominant styles of analysis are normatively driven (the present volume contains varied examples). Representation is framed in such work by a prior stipulation of why and where it ought to appear and be regarded as acceptable within a certain conception of democracy (or perhaps of justice or equality). But, unless such an account is descriptively at least plausible, it risks revealing (the extent of its) characteristic detachment from real-world representative politics. Representation's liminality rests in part on its occupying spaces in and between the normative and the descriptive. The descriptive blends in to the normative, and my claim here is that descriptive depth and breadth in analyzing representation is more important than normative approaches tend to embrace or provide. The normative blends into the descriptive, but (I argue) evaluative work can most appropriately *trace* representative practice in all its real-world multiplicity, embracing the important element of analytical colocation or overlap between the two.

Let me pick up the second point in particular. Democratic legitimation of representation, I argue, concerns ongoing *acceptance* of representative claims by specific appropriate constituencies under certain *conditions*.[6] Democracy, whatever else it may require, is based on popular power or control, so in principle evident acceptance of representative claims by the relevant constituency is the key, with no necessary or decisive place for independent criteria of, for example, what might make for a good representative. Democratic criteria will apply within the context in which actual acceptance is given or denied to a claimant. Evidence of an *accepted or authorized* claim to representation can be taken, contingently, as an example of democratic representation. Many claims fail to be heard, fail to resonate with relevant constituencies, die a political death (often deservedly!). Evidence that they are heard and accepted (or not) by a sufficient proportion of constituents can be hard to find at times; that in itself justifies no easy assumptions, but it may justify taking the time to locate evidence. The conditions within which that acceptance is given or denied will need to be conducive to reasonably open and uncoerced choices by members of the appropriate constituency if democrats are to recognize its legitimizing force. In practice we are dealing with a spectrum of possibilities here. A choice or acceptance may be uncoerced, but none are entirely unconstrained. Following Simmons's discussion of consent, acceptance must be given intentionally and voluntarily, and without threats of violence or undue burdens (Simmons 1976, 276–77). This will be the case for a specific or discrete representative claim. It will also apply more widely across society, with a concern for the extent to which conditions conducive to uncoerced and open acceptance acts are replicated across a diverse range of spaces, sectors, and groups.[7]

This approach to evaluation tracks representation's liminal character; that is, it follows the texture of specific claims in context across state and society. It does not require a restricted view of representation's political instantiation. Nor does it require a defense of democratic principles—a description of such principles and a description of practices that accord with them suffices. The reasonable conditions of judgment likewise describe the conditions that would enable such acceptance or authorization to operate in the real world, and the appropriate constituency is given a careful non-normative definition (see Saward 2010). These are descriptive evaluations (closely linked to Skinner's "evaluative descriptions"), not independently derived normative standards; the flexibility of description enables evaluations to track representation's liminality—that is, its traversing of the formal and the informal, the elective and the nonelective, and so on.[8] The sources of democratic normativity can be allowed to emerge from descriptions of the texture of representation's practices.

Normative political theory sometimes assumes a privilege that may be more tenuous than it thinks. The claims-based approach sets aside acontextual normative judgment, arguing that more detailed description of representative practice is needed. Evaluation in context matters. The claims-based approach is more phenomenological, bracketing received assumptions about normativity. A constructivist approach will precisely trace meanings of principles and concepts as they are invoked, altered, and so on in practice. In normative political philosophy, acontextual normative judgments are uncontroversial—but crucially, perhaps because they are so widely accepted, they tend not to be defended. The fact that clear and independent normative standards may be *desired* by scholars does not speak to their defensibility. As Anne Phillips (2000) writes, "We can hardly stake the universality of our principles on the fear of what would happen if we abandoned this claim. The case against foundationalism cannot be countered by arguments of an instrumental nature, for if ever the 'preference' for firm foundations is revealed as such (we 'need' universal principles, we 'need' a secure vantage point from outside), the case collapses on itself. We cannot appeal to the consequences as the basis for returning to foundationalist thinking; the only basis for this return would be the knowledge of sure foundations" (249).

## Representative Democracy and Democratic Representation

I turn finally to the wider distinction that is implicated in each of the four areas under discussion, that between representative democracy (the normal home of democratic or legitimate or proper representation for much

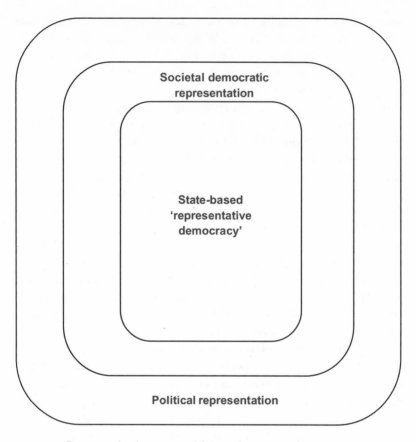

FIGURE 12.1 Representative democracy and democratic representation

of democratic theory) and the wider field of which it forms a part, which I
call democratic representation (see fig. 12.1). In other words, demonstrat-
ing representation's liminality with respect to the four areas discussed also
acts as a wider demonstration that representation's practices traverse the
seemingly separate realms of state-based representative democracy and
society-based political and democratic representation. Showing that much
representative practice is between—and often in transition between—the
polar elements in the four areas under scrutiny also shows that representative democracy is in fact one, critical part of a wider set of practices encompassing the statal *and* the societal dimensions of democratic representation
(within the field of political representation as a whole).

Representation is "done" (or, at least, "claimed") by a wide array of

TABLE 12.1 **Key distinctions in representation**

|  | Representative democracy—comprising statal representative institutions and processes | Democratic representation—comprising all features of representative democracy plus wider societal representation practices |
| --- | --- | --- |
| Modes of choice | Elective | Nonelective and elective |
| Types of authority | Formal authority | Informal and formal authority |
| Forms of practice | Institutional | Noninstitutional and institutional |
| Understanding and evaluation | Normative | Descriptive and normative |

local, national, and international groups and individuals, elected or chosen or not elected and rejected. Democratic representation concerns a *quality of practice* that may be more or less present in a wide and diffuse set of locations, including across transnational contexts. *Representative democracy* in formal national or other governance structures enacts but does not exhaust the enactment of democratic representation.[9] To choose to focus on representative democracy in the state more narrowly as the sole or only significant site of representation is to make a stipulative choice *from within* a wider set of significant representative practice.

Table 12.1 captures the ways in which characteristics of statal representative democracy become part of a broader spectrum in selected areas of concern for observers of representation and democracy. Representation's pervasive liminality means that no one mode of choice, type of authority, or form of practice may be regarded a priori as *the* democratic form of political representation.

It may be objected that this conclusion prevents the positive pursuit or advocacy of more democratic forms or practices of representation due to the fact that actors and practices may significantly blur the boundaries between, say, the formal and the informal. A key further factor is that nonelective representative claims involving informal modes of (potential) authority, which are not tied to or contained within a specific institution, *can* be instances of *democratic* representation. This factor may, for some observers, be a step too far in analysis of political representation; they may argue that democratic legitimacy is solely a matter of election and institutionalization, for example, and that if we are to assess how democratic representation is (and advocate its furtherance) we need to sharpen our focus despite representation's often liminal character. The arguments in this chapter militate against such a stipulation. However, democrats may of course look to enhance democratic representation *across* statal and societal domains. For example, given that citizen acceptance of representative claims on the basis of clear and fair electoral rules is a comparatively clear and strong form of acceptance, a reformer looking to strengthen democratic representation (and within that, representative democracy) could productively focus on improving the rules and conduct of elections. Reducing gerrymandering, facilitating voter registration, fair regulation of campaign funding, and perhaps compulsory voting might in this way be on the agenda. Similarly, our reformer may look to the uses of voting and elections in nonstatal contexts: could they be expanded and improved? He or she might seek to develop measures of citizen acceptance of a variety of representative claims in more informal or noninstitutional spheres, where it is normally more difficult to gauge degrees of support for an actor's representative claims. This could form part of an effort to more effectively trace representational political practice.

There are, in addition, analytical and evaluative payoffs stemming from the broadly constructivist approach set out in this chapter, adding rich strategies and questions to the representation research agenda, such as the following. First, if tracking representative claims is an important though neglected part of advancing our understanding, then we can learn more about local and specific interpretations of representation in varied contexts and cultures, "grounding" and "locating" the concept (Schaffer 2016); extended case studies by Fenno (2003) and Schaffer (1998) are highly illuminating exemplars of this approach. Second, in what *ways* and to what *extent* do elections legitimize political actors? To ask this question is to assume less and press ourselves to discover more what importance elections may have for democratic representation. Third, how can liminal statuses be *managed* by political actors or would-be representatives? How are they deployed or disguised, for instance? Can liminality be a *resource* for representative claim-makers?

## Conclusion

There are further areas where representation's liminal qualities are evident and may further inform the wider distinction and relation between representative democracy and democratic representation. Consider the *permanent* and the *ephemeral*: there is a common perception that representative democracy in the state involves permanent political presences (parliaments, departments of state, and so on), whereas the wider societal domain consists of representative relationships that are more temporary or ephemeral. But all claims to representation have a "becoming" quality; occupying liminal ground between being and not being representative, they are always not yet or not quite representation. Further, it is important to note that the statal can be ephemeral, and the nonstatal can be persistent. Or consider representation as *acting for* versus *standing for*, the subject of a sharp distinction by Pitkin (1967). It would be easy to assume that *acting for* is about performing claims to represent in civil society, and that *standing for* is solidly institutional and statal (as well as including symbols like national flags). But, as the broad thrust of this chapter suggests, nothing can stand for another thing without action (or performance) that alleges or claims or points out that it so stands. Though state structures may be deeply embedded, widely accepted, implicit, and institutionalized ("We the People"), they are rooted in allegations or claims of what they may represent and what is represented.

Representation, in these and the earlier examples, traverses familiar empirical and conceptual distinctions and boundaries. Or, by engaging in practices of representation, individual and collective actors "take representation with them" through liminal phases and contexts. It may not be an overstatement to claim that representation's liminality means that its primary characteristic is to be in dynamic transition across fields defined by more static perspectives.

Critics of constructivist approaches to representation look to limit and fix the concept's meaning and reference; they center on political or democratic representation meaning properly formal, permanent macro-level models and types within a conventional representative-democracy framework, often to underline strong and singular lines of normative legitimacy. However, the liminal nature of representation renders this project vulnerable, with its key positions somewhat artificial and at times difficult to sustain. It is political actors who often, across many contexts, invoke representation and position themselves to speak or to stand for others. Why redouble our efforts to underscore conventional stipulations of concepts when the effort may oversimplify the richness of the concept in practice? Similarly, it may be objected that embracing representation's liminality expands too much the scope of reference or application of the concept, encompassing most forms of political action and institutions. But tracking representative claims—for example, through the machinations of shape-shifting by would-be representatives—is a far cry from ascribing representation to political phenomena more generally; it is a difficult, disciplined, and focused research activity born of an aspiration to realism and relevance.

If my argument is right, then there are significant consequences for the analysis of representation; a need to embrace, rather than seeking to ignore or erase, representation's dynamic liminality, drawing on a phenomenological sensibility, and centered on the importance of context. And a need to go back to the actual practices and claims of representation, with all their changeability and variation, avoiding overhasty normative judgment. Whatness matters, and it should both delay and guide assessments of rightness and wrongness.[10]

## Notes

1. The representative claim is defined in Saward (2010, 38) as "a claim to represent or to know what represents the interests of someone or something."

2. Saward (2016) offers an account for distinctive types of political equality that are evident in nonelectoral contexts.

3. The actual words used in a representative claim may vary, but not just any discursive act can be a representative claim. Such a claim will always assert or imply a relationship between two or more entities whereby one stands, speaks, or otherwise acts for others.

4. Ana Hazare, an Indian activist and former soldier, went on an anticorruption hunger strike in India in 2011. Hazare, according to reports, "claims inspiration from Mahatma Gandhi" and "has described his protest against corruption as India's ... second freedom struggle." Pressing for anticorruption legislation in parliament, Hazare claimed that "I will live and die for India ... bigger than the parliament at Delhi is the parliament of the people" ("Indian Activist Ana Hazare on Hunger Strike as MPs Debate Anti-graft Bill," *The Guardian*, December 28, 2011). Hazare had support from at least one major Indian political party and from demonstrators across India during his hunger strike. Malala Yousafzai, a former Pakistani schoolgirl blogger and activist, was shot and gravely wounded by the Taliban on her way to school in Sind province. She is now resident in the UK while continuing high-profile advocacy of access to education for girls. One supporter, Paula Fletcher, notes that "Malala represents the countless young girls in Pakistan and around the world who are unwilling to accept the denial of their basic human rights" ("Malala Yousafzai for the Nobel Peace Prize," November 2, 2012, http://councillorpaulafletcher.ca/malala/). Former British prime minister Gordon Brown said that "Malala's dreams represent what is best about Pakistan" ("Pakistan 'to Pay Cash to Poor to Send Kids to School,'" BBC, November 10, 2012).

5. This idea is adapted from its use by Louis Marin (2001) who writes in *On Representation* that "to represent signifies to present oneself as representing some-

thing, and every representation, every sign or representation process, includes a dual dimension—a reflexive dimension, presenting oneself; a transitive dimension, representing something—and a dual effect—the subject effect, and the object effect" (256). An important contemporary pioneer of these ideas was Bourdieu (1991).

6. For detailed discussion of the "appropriate constituency" and other specific features of this account, see Saward (2010; 2014).

7. Within a democratic frame, this concern with the conditions within which acceptance is evident or denied can be broadened. The democrat should examine the extent to which there exist a plurality of sites, moments, or opportunities for representative claim-making and reception (the extent of openness to many claims and their contestation); uncoerced equal access to subject-positional resources for claim-making in the given context; variation in the nature and bases of representative claims in the given context (the extent of openness to different sorts of claims by different sorts of claimants); reflexivity, in the sense that claim-makers are responsive and contestation is encouraged (see Disch 2011); and evidence of extreme marginalization that effectively excludes some groups from both formal and informal modes of representative politics.

8. Lord and Pollak (2013, 521) ask, "How can we differentiate between legitimate and preposterous claims? Is it merely left to the constituency to decide about the legitimacy of claims?" My response is, in a democracy, yes!

9. A fuller account of this point is available in Saward (2011).

10. The term is borrowed from Ben Bradlee (1995), who wrote of the Vietnam War, "By instinct and habit, I was more interested in the whatness of the war rather than in the rightness or wrongness."

## References

Austin, J. L. 1975. *How to Do Things with Words*, 2nd ed., edited by J. O. Urmson and M. Sbisa. Cambridge, MA: Harvard University Press.

Barish, Jonas. 1981. *The Anti-Theatrical Prejudice*. Los Angeles: University of California Press.

Bartolini, Stefano, and Peter Mair. 2001. "Challenges to Contemporary Political Parties." In *Political Parties and Democracy*, edited by Larry Diamond and Richard Gunther, 327–44. Baltimore: Johns Hopkins University Press.

Bradlee, Ben. 1995. *A Good Life*. New York: Simon and Schuster.

Butler, Judith. 1997. *Excitable Speech: Politics of the Performative*. London: Routledge.

Bourdieu, Pierre. 1991. *Language and Symbolic Power*. Edited and Introduced by John B. Thompson. Translated by Gino Raymond and Matthew Adamson. Cambridge, MA: Harvard University Press.

Celis, Karen, Sarah Childs, Johanna Kantola, and Mona Lena Krook. 2008. "Rethinking Women's Substantive Representation." *Representation* 44:99–110.

Chabal, Patrick, and Jean-Pascal Daloz. 2006. *Culture Troubles: Politics and the Interpretation of Meaning*. London: Hurst & Co.

Derrida, Jacques. 1982. "Sending: On Representation." *Social Research* 49:294–326.

Disch, Lisa. 2011. "Toward a Mobilization Conception of Democratic Representation." *American Political Science Review* 105:100–114.

Fenno, Richard F., Jr. 2003. *Home Style: House Members in their Districts*. New York: Longman.

Giesen, Bernhard. 2015. "In-Betweenness and Ambivalence." In *Breaking Boundaries: Varieties of Liminality*, edited by Agnes Horvath, Bjorn Thomassen, and Harald Wydra. New York: Berghahn.

Horvath, Agnes, Bjorn Thomassen, and Harald Wydra. 2015. "Liminality and the Search for Boundaries." In *Breaking Boundaries: Varieties of Liminality*, edited by Agnes Horvath, Bjorn Thomassen, and Harald Wydra, 1–8. New York: Berghahn.

Lord, Christopher, and Johannes Pollak. 2013. "The Pitfalls of Representation as Claims-Making in the European Union." *Journal of European Integration* 35:517–30.

Mansbridge, Jane. 2003. "Rethinking Representation." *American Political Science Review* 97:515–28.

Marin, Louis. 2001. *On Representation*. Translated by Catherine Porter. Stanford, CA: Stanford University Press.

Montanaro, Laura. 2012. "The Democratic Legitimacy of Self-Appointed Representatives." *Journal of Politics* 74:1094–107.

Parkinson, John. 2015. "Performing Democracy: Roles, Stages, Scripts." In *The Grammar of Politics and Performance*, edited by Shirin M. Rai and Janelle Reinelt, 19–33. London: Routledge.

Phillips, Anne. 2000. "Equality, Pluralism, Universality: Current Concerns in Normative Theory." *British Journal of Politics and International Relations* 2:237–55.

Pitkin, Hanna F. 1967. *The Concept of Representation*. Berkeley: University of California Press.

Rosenau, James N. 2000. "Governance in a Globalizing World." In *The Global Transformations Reader*, edited by David Held and Anthony McGrew. Cambridge: Polity.

Saward, Michael. 2010. *The Representative Claim*. Oxford: Oxford University Press.

———. 2011. "The Wider Canvas: Representation and Democracy in State and Society." In *The Future of Representative Democracy*, edited by Sonia Alonso, John Keane, and Wolfgang Merkel, 74–95. Cambridge: Cambridge University Press.

———. 2014. "Shape-Shifting Representation." *American Political Science Review* 108:723–36.

———. 2016. "Fragments of Equality in Representative Politics." *Critical Review of Social and Political Philosophy* 19:245–62.

Sawer, Marian. 2001. "Representing Trees, Acres, Voters and Non-voters: Concepts of Parliamentary Representation in Australia." In *Speaking for the People*, edited by Marian Sawer and Gianni Zappala. Melbourne: Melbourne University Press.

Schaffer, Frederic C. 1998. *Democracy in Translation: Understanding Politics in an Unfamiliar Culture*. Ithaca, NY: Cornell University Press.

———. 2016. *Elucidating Social Science Concepts: An Interpretivist Guide*. New York: Routledge.

Schechner, Richard. 2002. *Performance Studies: An Introduction*. 2nd ed. New York: Routledge.

Simmons, A. John. 1976. "Tacit Consent and Political Obligation." *Philosophy and Public Affairs* 5:274–91.

Turner, Victor. 1981. "Social Dramas and Stories about Them." In *On Narrative*, edited by W. J. T. Mitchell, 137–64. Chicago: University of Chicago Press.

# CHAPTER THIRTEEN

# Recursive Representation

Jane Mansbridge

The representative system is coming under increasing strain in many democratic countries. To take only one example, the 2016 referendum vote in Britain to leave the EU ("Brexit") underscored the fragility of the representative system in both Britain and the EU. That the elected representatives in Britain decided to hold a referendum itself demonstrates the widespread belief that for many British citizens the existing system of electoral representation in Britain was not sufficiently legitimate to carry the weight of such a foundational decision. The referendum itself revealed that the opinion of the referendum majority in Britain differed dramatically from majority opinion among the democratically elected representatives. In the referendum process the elected representatives did not help cultivate a high standard of deliberation in the press and throughout the country. Many Brexit voters also considered their representation in the EU laughable. They believed that they and their country's interests were not adequately represented in the EU and that insensitive bureaucrats in Brussels were harassing them with unjustifiable regulations. None of these weaknesses were surprises.

Britain may leave the EU, but it cannot return to the past. Nor is it possible to return to the past in either the practice or the theory of representation. I argue here that the conceptions of representation forged in the eighteenth century are inadequate to the world of the twenty-first. Over the past century, human beings acting together have forged new practices that do not map easily onto the categories of earlier understandings of representation. New practices require new theories.

As the legitimacy of current systems of representation continues to decline, we need to pay more attention to the representative-constituent connection. The roles of "delegate" and "trustee," devised in the eighteenth century, may have made some sense for a world in which representatives left the constituency for faraway capitals and found it hard to return for regular visits. They make little sense in a world of fast transport, emails, and internet chat rooms. The representative can now visit her constituents weekly and respond to communications from them every day. As constituents become accustomed to greater contact, they want more. In the United States, representatives in Congress consequently are spending more and more time in their constituencies and less and less time mastering the details of policy. Representation has in practice taken a communicative turn.

One can respond to these changing dynamics by either resisting or embracing them. I recommend embrace. In response to the declines in the legitimacy of representation that we see almost everywhere, I suggest—as only one among many possible interventions—expanding the cluster of ideals that now apply to the representative role to include a new ideal, which I call *recursive representation*, based on an aspiration for iterative, ongoing communication between constituents and their representatives. Like most ideals, this one can never be fully achieved. In the full ideal the representative would hear what the constituent says, take it in, consider it, and respond accordingly, while in turn the constituent would hear what the representative says, take it in, consider it, and respond on the basis of that consideration. This is a deeply interactive and communicative ideal.

Within recursive representation, the ideal role for the representative is as *interlocutor*, a discursive intermediary between the representative's legal constituents and several other entities: the constituents in other districts, the legislative representatives from other districts, the "administrative representatives" who in practice make many of the laws, the organized groups that represent their own constituents' interests and sometimes help craft the laws, and the lobbyists those groups hire to represent their interests. The representative as interlocutor links the representative system together less by making policy herself than by helping those in all the other parts of the system understand one another.

Traditional normative understandings of representation rarely consider the question of constituent/representative communication. When they do consider it, they conceive the ideal as simply "two-way" communication. In this traditional ideal, constituents make demands or give information, while the representative, often at another point in time, explains her position or in other ways tries to persuade the constituents of her perspective.

By contrast, the recursive ideal stresses interactivity. In recursive representation, both constituents and representatives can learn from one another through interactions in which those on each side hold open the possibility of changing their positions, concepts, and conclusions on the basis of what they learn. Recursive representation should be an ideal throughout the full representative system, which includes not only legislative representatives but also administrative and societal representatives.

Traditional normative understandings of representation also rarely consider the representative functions of administrators and organized interest groups. When they do incorporate these entities, it is often to argue that they should not be "usurping" lawmaking functions or that for their actions to be legitimate they must be subject to careful direction and oversight from the legislative branch. Such direction and oversight might have been possible one hundred, or perhaps even just fifty, years ago. With the increasing complexity of collective decision-making, it is no longer possible. We should be assessing the legitimacy of administrative and societal rulemaking not only with the criteria of clean and uncorrupt delegation and of effective legislative direction and oversight, but also with the same cluster of criteria by which we assess the legitimacy of legislative lawmaking. These criteria include the equal or appropriately proportional power of those affected, the degree to which the process makes participants aware of their interests and gives them the capacity to promote those interests, the degree to which the process meets the standards of good deliberation, and now, the degree to which the process incorporates productive and egalitarian recursivity, in which both the represented and the representative have the capacity to learn from one another. Of course, recursive representation is meaningless without the capacity and desire to respond to the citizens' interests with action.

The reasons for articulating an ideal of recursive representation spring from a crisis in legitimacy. In other work, I have argued that as our global and intranational interdependence grows, we face a growing number of collective action/free-rider problems and therefore a growing need for state coercion. That coercion should be both normatively legitimate, so that citizens can live in a state that is morally grounded, and perceived to be legitimate, so that it may be effective. Yet while the need for legitimate state coercion is rising, the supply is declining. Every ounce of both normative and perceived legitimacy is becoming increasingly precious.[1]

Readers need not accept my strong claim regarding the increasing need for legitimate coercion and its decreasing supply to agree that recursive representation may in any context help increase democratic legitimacy. Yet my conviction of a crisis, stemming from my analysis of the reasons that we will henceforth require increasing amounts of state coercion, provides the reason for my own current intense attention to the problems of legitimacy in representation. I will therefore take the first few pages of this chapter to sketch out the logic by which I arrived at that conclusion.

To begin, why coercion at all, and why *state* coercion? I have argued that free-use goods—goods that, once produced, anyone can use[2]—trigger the logic of the free-rider problem (or collective action problem). This logic, uncovered between 1950 and 1965, shows us that in large societies, where reputational sanctions are insufficient to get most people to contribute to free-use goods, state coercion is often the only option. Without state coercion we cannot get clean air or water, enough fish in the sea, or a stable climate, let alone the narrower goods that eighteenth-century theorists identified (but did not understand as free-use goods) of law and order, defense, and harbors.[3]

Why a *growing* need for state coercion? First, our increasing national and global interdependence requires effective regulation, backed by state coercion, to facilitate the market and protect both consumers and workers. Not only does almost every new transaction and contract require state backing to guarantee mutual compliance, but many new transactions create externalities or free-rider problems that require state regulation to control (e.g., exports require stronger and more transparent food safety standards than local markets demand). Second, we must now through human action produce vital free-use goods—such as clean air, clean water, a reproducible number of fish and trees, and a stable climate—that "nature" provided in an earlier era.

Coercion (the threat of sanction or the use of force) is intrinsically a bad thing, its point being to make you do something you would not otherwise do against your (first-level) will. Thus, in generating enough coercion to produce the needed free-use goods, states should craft it to be minimal, not to drive out the intrinsic incentives to promote collective goods (e.g., incentives deriving from a core of other-regarding public spirit, duty, and solidarity, as well as the interest, excitement, and enjoyment of the work), and to the greatest degree practicable to emerge locally to respond to local needs. Such crafting defines good state coercion; it does not eliminate the need for state coercion. Even the participatory, bottom-up processes of voluntary supply and locally based coercion that Nobel laureate Elinor Ostrom made famous almost all need to be "nested," in her word, in a larger state coercive apparatus (Mansbridge 2010a, 2014b; see Ostrom 1990). On the scale of a nation-state, some "periphery" of coercion must usually surround the "core" of solidarity, duty, intrinsic interest, and enjoyment that otherwise induces people to contribute. That periphery of coercion, designed to be as narrow as possible, provides an ecological niche in which the motives of duty and solidarity in the core can survive and thrive (Mansbridge 1990).[4]

To be effective, the necessary state coercion should be perceived to be legitimate. To be rightful, that coercion should be justifiable to those affected. In both perceived and normative legitimacy, the legitimacy is a matter of *degree*, not a binary. No law, regulation, or state act can be fully legitimate, because the democratic norms that legitimate the law are all *aspirational* (or "regulative," in Kant's word); they are standards at which to aim but which cannot, or can only rarely, be reached fully. This aspirational quality applies, for example, both to the ideal of equal power that animates the practice of an equal vote and the ideal of no power that animates the practice of good deliberation (Mansbridge et al. 2010, 65n3).

Both perceived and normative legitimacy have *plural* sources. Legitimacy may derive from fair procedures, such as free and equal elections ("input" or "participative" legitimacy). It may derive from just and good outcomes ("output" or "performative" legitimacy). It may derive from fair and just administrative lawmaking and the application of the laws ("throughput" legitimacy). It may derive from appropriate justification.[5] Although occasionally input legitimacy derives directly from the people— through referenda in some countries, through direct face-to-face assemblies in small New England towns in the United States, the cantons of Glarus and Appenzell Innerrhoden in Switzerland, a handful of kibbutzim in Israel, and the "horizontalist" movement structures in Argentina and elsewhere in Latin America, and through direct internet democracy in some of the new social movements and political parties in Europe—almost all current democratic attempts to establish ongoing input legitimacy in large polities depend on some form of electoral representative democracy. This is the representative democracy now so severely under strain.

How to *relieve* this strain? I argue that we must look to all three realms of electoral representation, administrative representation, and societal representation, and in these realms restructure current practices to facilitate *recursive communication* between represented and representative. In this process, each realm can be supplemented with imports from the others. In normative theory we should recognize and value from the perspective of recursive representation many of the new representative practices in all three realms that have already evolved to meet our changing needs.

What has *changed*? Advancing education and familiarity with democracy has undermined old assumptions of hierarchy in representation along with the (always somewhat confusing and practically inapplicable) categories of trustee and delegate. A growing acceptance of pluralism has undermined the old denigration of descriptive representation while validating a cacophony of competing voices. The growing complexity and extent of the regulation required by the increasing number of free-use goods we must produce has undermined the assumption that representation and lawmaking legitimately take place only in the legislature. Over time, citizens in democratic societies have responded (although still inadequately) to the growing need for legitimate state coercion by moving from these old assumptions in practice without developing a theory that would legitimate these moves. Some new practices have formal legal legitimacy but little perceived legitimacy. Some have perceived legitimacy but little normative legitimacy. To guide the evolving practice and provide tools for evaluating it, political theory must elaborate both more nuanced ideals and more helpful standards for practice. This chapter, which adopts an *interactive* and *communicative* perspective on the three realms of legislative, administrative, and societal representation, and stresses the legitimating qualities of *recursive* representation, takes only one small step in this direction.

## Recursive Communication in the Representative System

Michael Saward (in this volume) has suggested a conceptual map of existing relations of representation that helps make sense of the larger representative system in which state electoral representation is embedded. He proposes "political representation" as the largest and most inclusive category, within which is nested "democratic representation" (including nonelectoral societal democratic representation), within which is nested "state-based 'representative democracy.'" He points out that each realm interpenetrates the other.[6] I adopt this general idea with a few modifications. I focus on the two categories of *electoral* representation and *administrative* representation within "state-based 'representative democracy.'" When I discuss *societal* representation, I include both internally democratic and nondemocratic forms. I address only the appropriate normative structures for democracies, leaving aside the monarchies, theocracies, rule by meritocracy, and other forms of state organization that would fit into Saward's most inclusive category of political representation. In each of the three interpenetrating realms of electoral, administrative, and societal representation, I argue that democratic norms apply both to what I will call the *internal* relationship between represented and representative and to the *external system* of representation within which that relationship is embedded. Leaving aside for this chapter the crucial points that *demo*cracy requires rough equality among the citizens and that demo*cracy* requires the capacity to act, and although I think that in the long run and more broadly the health of democracy depends on the communicative characteristics of the entire representative *system*, including recursive communication among the citizens and among the representatives, I focus here primarily on one relatively narrow ideal, mostly internal to the representative-represented relationship: the ideal of good recursive communication.[7] I do so partly because the topic has been neglected and partly because lack of recursive communication is one cause of the strain in democratic representative systems that may be open to some remediation.

Within the large category of "state-based 'representative democracy,'" the *standard* model of democratic electoral representation assumes that voters choose and influence representatives (either legislative or presidential), who then choose and influence those who administer the laws. The *recursive* model involves iterative communication (circular, not two-way, arrows) all along the standard categories, with the addition of societal representation.

The recursive ideal requires more and better iterative communication between elected representatives and their constituents, between administrators and those to whom they apply the law, between societal representatives and their constituents, between legislatures, administrators, and the societal realm, and between societal representatives and their constituents. The societal representatives may or may not in practice be democratically organized.[8] But in democracies, a set of ideals regarding recursive representation should apply throughout the entire representative system.

In this revised model, recursive communication is critical for maintaining a normatively justifiable and perceptually legitimate relationship between represented and representative, including the mutual constitution of each by the other.[9] The deliberative ideals that normatively should inform that communication include mutual respect, inclusion, and coming as close as is practical to the absence of power.[10] The newly introduced

**Standard model:** Voter → Elected representative → Administrator → Citizen

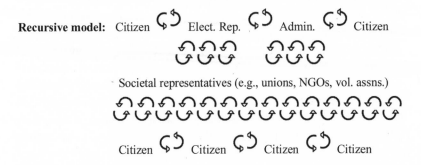

FIGURE 13.1 Recursive model

recursive element, in addition, responds both to the current widespread perception among citizens in many democracies that their voices are not heard and to the reality that in practice representatives very often do not hear those voices.

*Electoral Representation*

In the recursive communicative democratic ideal, both citizens and individual representatives or political parties should hear one another, communicate well with one another, and change one another for the better through their interaction. David Plotke (1997) and Melissa Williams (1998) first articulated this ideal, the first arguing for reforms "enhancing communications between representatives and constituents" (33) and the second writing of accountability that "the representative's accountability requires a movement back and forth between consultations with constituents and deliberations with other legislators. . . . [The representative should] engage in a project of persuading her constituents of the reasons for her judgments. At the same time . . . she should further revise her judgments in the light of her discussions with them" (231–32).[11] Recursive communication is thus more than "two-way" communication, although the two-way imagery more accurately describes current reality, even at its best. With electoral representation, for example, Michael Neblo and his colleagues (2010) describe their ideal of "republican consultation" as "communication between citizens and their representatives in which the representatives seek *input* from their constituents in forming agendas and in advance of their formal votes, as well as [making] efforts to *explain* their votes to constituents post hoc" (6; my emphasis). Both input and explanation are usually one-way. If each responds to the other, it is usually indirectly. The first cycle of hearing, understanding, and response is rarely repeated.[12]

Recursive communication between representatives and constituents is not easy, and there are tradeoffs with the other work that representatives are expected to do. In the Single Member Plurality (SMP) electoral system that characterizes the United States, and on the federal level in which each member of the House of Representatives has about 650,000 constituents, a representative's attempt to explain a vote in the face of a well-funded advertising blitz may simply make constituents angry. As one representative said about his vote in the legislature against his own perception of the public interest, "Very frankly, if I had a chance to sit down with all of my constituents for 15 minutes and talk to them, I'd have voted against the whole thing. But I didn't have that chance" (Kingdon 1981, 48, quoted in Mansbridge 2003, 520).[13] Normative and perceived legitimacy both suffer when constituents do not understand what the representative is doing and why, while the representative does not understand, except through a circle of political activists, the media, or occasionally a survey, what the constituents want and why.

To my knowledge, only one researcher has gone into the field and asked constituents, in an open-ended way, what they wanted from their elected representative. This group of only twenty-eight constituents at one point in time (1997–98) in one small region (upper New York State) in the United States said that the main thing they wanted from their representative was communication. They stressed again and again their desires that the representative listen to and be available to them (Grill 2007).[14] This small in-depth study reinforces Richard Fenno's (1978) conclusion, also based on the United States: "Responsiveness, and hence, representation, require two-way communication. Although the congressman can engage in this kind of communication with only some of his supportive constituents, he can give many more the assurance that two-way communication is possible." Fenno concludes, "Access and the assurance of access, communication and the assurance of communication—these are the *irreducible underpinnings of representation*" (239–40; emphasis in original).

In countries other than the United States and where electoral systems direct attention away from the internal represented-representative relationship and toward the external characteristics of the system, constituents' desires that representatives listen and be available to them as individuals may be less strong. If this is so, more recursive communication would not generate greater perceived legitimacy. Normatively, however, good democratic representation must rest in part on the capacity of representatives to hear, to respond, to explain legislative actions, and to act on citizens' responses to those explanations. As Iris Marion Young (2000) put it, "We should evaluate the process of representation according to the character of the relationship between the representative and the constituents. The representative will inevitably be separate from the constituents, but should also be *connected* to them in determinate ways. . . . Representation systems sometimes fail to be sufficiently democratic not because the representatives fail to stand for the will of the constituents but because they have lost connection with them. In modern mass democracies it is indeed easy to sever relations between representatives and constituents, and difficult to maintain them" (128, emphasis in original).[15]

In recursive communication, representatives can deepen their constituents' understandings of the issues and incite them to action, while constituents, ideally, can deepen the understanding of their representatives and incite them to action as well.[16] When the interests of representatives and constituents conflict, the inequalities of individual power between them are likely to move the interaction away from ideals of democratic legitimacy, even though the constituents may have greater collective power in their capacity to unseat the representative. In general, recursive communication should be judged by the criteria of good deliberation, particularly those of inclusion, mutual respect, and as close an approach as possible to the absence of power. Promoting such characteristics and facilitating recursive communication—in which both representatives and constituents take in what the other is saying, update, revise, and respond on the basis of their own experience, and then listen to the others' response—requires us to restructure and supplement electoral representation as well as recalibrate our democratic norms.

RESTRUCTURE. *Electoral systems* affect representative communication. With all their faults on the dimension of systemic political equality, SMP electoral systems produce more incentives for the representatives to listen to and speak with constituents than closed-list Proportional Representation (PR) systems and perhaps even open-list PR systems.[17] On the other hand, closed-list PR systems allow parties to balance their tickets to produce more descriptive representation, which in turn usually fosters communication. Normatively, the degree and quality of recursive communication in the representative relationship should affect how we judge one system in comparison to another. Empirically, we could use greater study of the degree and quality of recursive communication in different electoral systems. Practically, we can find ways to restructure all these systems, and particularly closed-list PR systems, to facilitate representative-constituent interaction.

Types of representation also affect communication, but again we have little empirical work on how. In earlier work I have noted the advantages, when feasible, of what I have called *gyroscopic* representation (Mansbridge 2003).[18] In the ideal pure case of gyroscopic representation (all real cases being mixed, none pure), voters select representatives on the basis of their judgment of the representatives' internal motivations and goals, place them in office, and deselect them when the representatives' goals or capacities are no longer congruent with the voters' needs. They do not try to change the representatives' behavior through monitoring that behavior and threatening sanctions in the next election. Gyroscopic representation is possible only when some representatives have internal motivations and goals roughly congruent with the voters' own and the voters have sufficient basis in the representative's past actions and reputation for making warranted judgments about the representative's internal motivation. This form of representation has some characteristics of traditional trustee representation, but without its hierarchical element: the voters may simply want a representative "like me" (Mansbridge 2011). The main contrast is to *anticipatory* representation, where the voters try to control the behavior of the representative through monitoring, threats, and promises, while the representatives adjust their behavior to forestall potential sanctions in the next election.[19]

Gyroscopic representation has the normatively attractive quality of generating and reflecting warranted trust between constituent and representative, a feature that allows the representative some flexibility,[20] facilitates effective negotiation,[21] and in some ways promotes recursive communication. When voters want to communicate, they may engage more deeply, informally, and continuously with a representative they think is "like them." On the other hand, in gyroscopic representation the voters have little prudential incentive to pressure the representative on policy because they have good reason to believe that the representative will be pursuing, with integrity, the policies the voter prefers. Nor has the gyroscopic representative much prudential incentive to contact the voters. By contrast, with anticipatory representatives, the voters have an incentive to organize in ongoing pressure groups to communicate with the representatives, while the representatives, trying to anticipate what the voters will want in the next election, have many incentives to initiate contact, thus opening up a potential field of recursive communication in which they can try to influence the voters to be more favorable to them in the next election, while the voters can convey to the representatives their possibly changing needs and demands. Any move from anticipatory to gyroscopic representation in the electoral realm should thus emphasize opening up and deepening channels for recursive communication.

All else equal, *descriptive* representation (often gyroscopic) seems to improve communication between elected representatives and constituents, particularly for the more marginal members of the polity and particularly in the context of a history of communicative distrust. In the United States, where black Americans have a justified historical mistrust of whites, black constituents are more likely to contact black than white representatives. The same may well be true of other marginalized groups (Gay 2001).[22] Even when the descriptive representation is "passive" (the representative simply having a background similar to the represented in relevant respects) rather than "active" (the representative acting consciously as an advocate for those with similar background features), restructuring electoral systems to make descriptive representation more likely would almost certainly increase the number and quality of communicative channels for marginalized groups.[23]

A more radical communicative restructuring, as suggested here, could reposition the representative as *interlocutor*. Even today in the British Parliament and the US Congress, the representatives themselves do not make much policy. In Britain, the cabinet does most of this work. In the United States, according to one report, the Congressional staff do 95 percent of the policy work.[24] If we stop thinking of the representative's main job as policy-making and reconceptualize it as communicating, we would provide the representatives with relatively expert staff, allocate more staff time to policy-making, and expect the representative, prepared by the staff on policy issues, to dedicate most of her time to communicating with other representatives and with constituents. Running for election and winning is a better test of capacity to communicate than it is a test of policy expertise. A restructured division of labor, in which the elected representative did more communicating with both constituents and other legislators while the staff did more policy-crafting, would make recursive communication more possible. Although a significant departure from current norms, the model of *representative as interlocutor* would give the representative more time for communication with constituents, producing better representation and perhaps even better policy.

SUPPLEMENT.   In SMP electoral systems, *surrogate* representation (in which representatives represent constituents outside of their districts) currently serves as an important nonelectoral supplement to district representation. Surrogate representation may not derive from an explicit claim by a representative to represent anyone outside her district. When in the late 1980s an administrator for Mickey Leland, a black member of the US Congress, exclaimed in frustration, "What people don't understand is that Mickey Leland must be the [black] Congressman for the entire Southwest" (Swain 1993, 218, quoted in Mansbridge 1999), she did not mean that Leland had ever made an explicit claim to represent the entire Southwest. She meant that throughout the southwest US, black citizens from other districts and even states turned to Leland to help represent their interests. In a 2013 study, black state legislators responded more often than white legislators to a request for help from a person outside their districts with a black name (Broockman 2013).[25] In both of these cases the representative claim originated with the represented.[26] Although representatives do not usually initiate communication with their surrogate constituents, they open up through their policy stances or similar backgrounds opportunities for communication to and from citizens who feel relatively unrepresented in their own districts. Because those represented are not constituents, the communication in surrogate representation is not likely to be deeply recursive unless the surrogate constituents are also represented by advocacy groups, which are better equipped to carry on a more continuous conversation with the representative.

In an inventive and practical recursive supplement to the current ways that representatives communicate with their constituents, Michael Neblo and his coauthors (2018) use computer-generated random selection to create discussion groups of constituents who discuss an important issue with their representative in the US Congress online for an hour. In their first experiment, 95 percent of the participating constituents said they considered such sessions "very valuable to our democracy" and wanted to repeat the experience with other issues (Neblo et al. 2010, 2, 9; Neblo et al. 2018). The participants generally felt more politically efficacious later and gained information on the policy discussed. Most participants in such a session also talked about the session later with family members or friends, including those who disagreed with them on the issue, thus spreading the communication (Minozzi et al. 2015; Neblo et al. 2018).[27] Using this process, the elected representatives at the federal level, even in a nation as large as the United States, could hold each week two meetings of one hour each and be in recursive communicative touch with about a quarter of their voting-eligible constituents every six years.[28]

Representatives in these sessions would also be in touch with constituents who usually are less active in political affairs, including the young, racial minorities, and people with lower incomes, because, so far, these groups are as likely as others to participate in these sessions. The only overparticipation in the sessions comes from the unemployed and people with children under twelve in the home, who probably have more time than most to spend in the house on their laptops.[29]

If such online recursive communication through discussion groups were to become a regular part of the way representatives did their work, citizens would learn about these experiences through friends, media, and the school system. Schools would probably run simulations to teach children how to participate when they reached voting age. Friends might ask one another what they would say if they were chosen for such a session. Interest groups and scholars would monitor the processes and outcomes to see if they mirrored, increased, or reduced existing inequalities in power. If these experiences became everyday parts of the representative system, the communicative quality of that system should increase, as should the quality of its outcomes and its normative and perceived legitimacy.

Randomly selected minipublics (groups of "citizen representatives" randomly selected to represent the population and brought together to deliberate over a weekend or a year) could provide another recursive communicative supplement to electoral representation.[30] Because of the expense involved in producing a sufficiently representative sample with trained facilitators and materials agreed upon by opposing parties and experts,[31] such minipublics are best used contingently, when elected legislators need public legitimation for a potentially damaging vote[32] or the elected legislators might have interests that diverge from those of the public.[33] Such minipublics must also be embedded, as Neblo puts it, in "a larger system of democratic contestation," including public review and criticism, to reduce the likelihood of intentional or unintentional elite cooptation (2015, 181, see 179–89). Although discussions are admirably recursive within such minipublics, the question of how such fully developed minipublics would link communicatively with representatives has not been fully explored.

Ironically the one current supplement to electoral representation that most enhances recursive communication between the representative and some constituents also greatly undermines both normative and perceived legitimacy. This is the supplement of money: the financial dependence of electoral campaigns on individual citizens with significant monetary resources. In the United States, which of all the advanced democracies is most vulnerable to this form of political inequality, representatives in Congress currently actively reach out in person, often four hours a day, to past and potential donors through phone calls and at fundraising parties to solicit the advice of those donors on the laws the donors think the country most needs and why. Communication between candidates for office and the donors outside their district (one segment of their "surrogate" constituents) is often far more frequent, personal, and recursive than communication between the candidates and their district constituents (see Barber and McCarthy 2015 for the rapidly increasing percentage of outside-district donors). Perhaps relatedly, the representatives in Congress vote more in the interests of the wealthy than in the interests of the majority (Gilens and Page 2014). Perhaps relatedly as well, in the United States 67 percent of the citizens in 2012 said they believed that "Rich people buy elections," compared with only 17 percent in Germany (ANES 2012; World Values Survey 2012; Norris 2015).

RECALIBRATE. The content and quality of communication between representatives and constituents in different systems of electoral representation has been both normatively undertheorized and empirically underinvestigated. A recalibration of our theory and empirical study to forefront communication would begin by distinguishing communicative persuasion from strategic manipulation. It would recognize that unequal power inevitably accompanies communication, identify the most significant power resources in communication on both sides, and suggest institutional changes to facilitate greater equality along with greater recursivity. Such a recalibration would resist the common temptation to define politics only as power and conflict or to see power- or conflict-oriented analyses as more realistic than analyses that also consider persuasion. It would consider the deliberative side of the representative-represented relationship valuable, and it would analyze the capacities of differently organized democracies to enhance or undermine the recursive and deliberative quality of that relationship.[34]

Although in everyday speech we often use the term *persuasion* to include power-based strategy and manipulation, I will stipulatively redefine the term here for analytic purposes to exclude power strategies and manipulation but include both what Habermas called the "force of the better argument" and emotionally based efforts to understand others and respond authentically to them.

On the broadest definition of *power* in general, as preferences and interests causing, or changing the probability of, outcomes,[35] all communication is intended to exercise power. In this chapter, however, I use the term *power* to mean coercive power, namely one's preferences and interests causing, or changing the probability of, another's outcomes through the threat of sanction (involving the other's will) and the use of force (changing the other's behavior without engaging their will). By contrast, I define persuasive power (henceforth persuasion) as the capacity to cause, or change the probability of, outcomes through good argument and emotional insight.

In human interaction, no persuasion exists without power, because the very words we must use to communicate draw from millennia of human practices that embed in those words assumptions, often hierarchical, of which we are not aware. Language thus encapsulates a form of force, working independently of the actor's will. The ease with which different members of society can draw upon these words also differs greatly from individual to individual in ways inflected heavily by the relations of domination and subordination in the society at large. Yet just as persuasion cannot exist without power, so, conversely, in human interaction power never exists outside a field shaped by persuasion. All human beings grow up in a universe that they navigate in large part by relying on forms of communication grounded to some degree in the common interest of the communicating parties in mutually accurate persuasive communication.[36]

Despite the inevitable presence of power in persuasion and vice versa, we can and do distinguish conceptually between manipulation (coercive power as force, often in the guise of persuasion) and persuasion.[37] And despite the well-known difficulties in distinguishing between these two in practice, the distinction in ordinary speech reflects a norm in favor of persuasion and against manipulation that, whether explicitly expressed or not, may be coexistent with human culture. In the represented-representative relationship, the normative standard for communication is nonmanipulative persuasion, not as a form of interaction that can exist without power but as an aspirational ideal, despite being always already embedded in and shaped by power. Thus, in the model of recursive communication, the aspirational ideal is to come as close to mutual deliberative persuasion as realistically possible.

The meaning of communication in the recursive model becomes more complicated when we realize that the arrows of mutual communication are not only arrows of reciprocal power and continuing mutual influence but also arrows of mutual constitution. Representatives help shape the represented; the represented help shape the representatives.[38] Both representatives and represented (although dwarfed in this process by many others outside the representative relationship) by themselves and in interaction also help shape the larger social and political system within which both act. Such mutual constitution is a feature of the larger human social condition, but it poses a conceptual problem for democratic representation as traditionally and linearly conceived. That standard model begins with a constituent's preexisting and static interests, which cause preferences, which ideally cause representative or legislative behavior (which then causes administrators' behavior, which then affects citizens). As Warren (citing Disch 2011, 2015, and Montanaro 2012) points out in this volume (p. 47), if the preferences of constituents are at least in part constituted by their representatives, it is hard to understand those constituents as purely "choosing and directing their representatives—authorizing them to stand, speak, or act on their behalf. Nor can they hold representatives accountable, since what people understand their interests to be are at least partially constructed within the representative relationship itself."

The mutual constitution of everyone by everything would seem simply to pose no more than the familiar question of the possibility of individual autonomy[39] but for an important wrinkle: in this relationship of mutual constitution, power is usually not equal. The external political and social system is structured in ways that give some individuals and groups more power to choose the words we use and set the frames of our thinking, including the interests we perceive as essential parts of our identities and those we perceive as humanly and politically salient. We cannot learn as human beings or as citizens except within these frameworks. Within them, elites by definition have more power than others. Electoral representatives figure among the many who, because of their privileged access to the means of communication or greater resources to craft those communications, will reach more people and have more impact.

Yet although in the cocreation of the process of representation elites in general have more cultural capital, organizational resources, access to the microphone, and attention from the media, those members of elites who

function as electoral, administrative, and societal representatives of seg-
ments of the public are in addition particularly vulnerable to the constituting efforts of others, in this case the represented. To arrive at the positions
in which they speak and act for others, representatives have often crafted
themselves in gross and subtle ways to respond to the anticipated needs of
the represented. Their publics have also, subtly or unsubtly, selected them
for such good self-crafting. Even in the very course of speaking to and for
others, in venues such as political rallies where the audience and the represented are much the same, representatives are likely to select their words,
sometimes spontaneously, to respond to what the people for and to whom
they are speaking want them to say. Such anticipatory, often preconscious,
processes are hard (often impossible) to track.

Coconstitution is thus the human condition, but the conditions in which
coconstitution occurs are to some degree under human control. Thus Fra-
ser, Disch, Warren, Neblo, and many others have rightly urged us to work
toward reducing the inequality and increasing the alternatives available in
the larger social and political system.

Recognizing that the reduction of political and social inequality is a
large and important goal, in this chapter I attempt something far smaller—
only a recalibration in the weights we give respectively to citizen control
and communication. Democracy requires voter control of the legislature,
at least indirectly. Yet more control is not always and automatically better.
If the available options make relatively gyroscopic representation possible,
then constituents occasionally can select and deselect their representatives,
not focus on actively steering them, and instead focus on recursive communication with those representatives, as a matter primarily of mutual
persuasion rather than power. As I wrote in an earlier work, "if the quality
of citizen deliberation at election-time is good and if the electoral system
makes it relatively easy both to maintain representatives in office and to
remove them, then it is normatively quite consistent with democracy to
leave them alone. Let us dislodge, normatively, the standard single-minded
focus on voter control of representatives, with its across-the-board opposition to incumbency and obsession with turnover in office. When an initial
selection has been a good one, neither voter control of the representative
nor turnover [is] necessary for good democratic representation" (Mansbridge 2005, 240–41).

Whenever we can make good gyroscopic representation possible, instead of resting our democratic expectations primarily on control, monitoring, transparency, and accountability (in the recently popular sense of

monitoring plus sanctions rather than giving an account),[40] we can shift our sights toward greater recursive communication. Indeed, whether representatives are primarily gyroscopic, responding to inner motivations and selected in part on that basis, or anticipatory, responding to anticipated sanctions from voters, we can still recalibrate our normative and practical theory to stress institutions through which citizens can enter the democratic process on an equal basis, educate their elected representatives about conditions on the ground (including the citizens' own changing thoughts and emotions), and educate themselves, through their representatives, about the effects of their interdependence with other citizens. To create such recursive communication on a genuinely equal basis would require eliminating the massive structural and political inequalities that now distort both the electoral and the communicative features of all representative systems, in some countries far more than in others. Eliminating such inequalities is the aspirational ideal. As we try to move toward that systemic ideal, it is still possible, as a congruent but somewhat separate goal, to try to improve the conditions for recursive communication in the representative relationship.

*Administrative Representation*

I cannot provide in this chapter anything like a full discussion of recursive communication in administrative representation.[41] The important point, however, is that we must take administrative lawmaking seriously as not only a pervasive but also a legitimate creator of state coercion. In the twenty-first century, we need administrative lawmaking. And we need a lot of it—much more than can be directed by the legislature, except in the most general way, and much more than can be subject to legislative oversight, except relatively superficial oversight supplemented by the "fire alarms" set off by interest groups and other observers (McCubbins and Schwartz 1994).

The electoral strand in the representative system, even when restructured and supplemented to create more recursive communication, is still too weak a reed to carry the weight of all the legitimacy required for our growing needs for state coercion. Thus, when we see a democratic deficit, rather than looking first or only for solutions in the field of electoral representation, we should recognize and willingly incorporate administrative lawmaking into the representative system, finding ways to make it more legitimate and more democratic.

At the higher policy-making level, both those who appoint administrators and the administrators themselves usually recognize the administrative policy-making role. The normative legitimacy of administrators in making policy derives primarily from the legislature's formal delegation of powers and continuing decision not to remove those powers. It derives from lack of corruption as the legislature delegates those powers and chooses the administrators. In addition, it derives in great part from the quality of the justifications, or reasons, the administrators can give those affected for their decisions and actions. Yet even in the cases in which the formal processes of delegation and selection meet the highest standards of legitimacy and the justifications meet high rational standards for accuracy and relevance, other factors—such as the current great volume and importance of administrative policy-making, the long lines of delegation required and consequent distance from the original legislative authorization, and the difficulty relevant publics may have in understanding the justifications—mean that the law administrators promulgate requires additional support in normative and perceived legitimacy. In modern democracies administrative representatives have thus often instituted formal procedures for communication with the public both to improve the result and to increase the perceived and normative legitimacy of the decision. They have also instituted informal practices, such as making the administration more descriptively representative (see, e.g., Selden 1997). In addition, they have developed ways of consulting with the organized societal entities that represent some affected interests (see, e.g., Sabel and Zeitlin 2010). These procedures deserve more empirical and normative attention.

In the standard democratic account, once the public has gone through a discursive period of opinion formation and the elected legislature its own discursive period of will formation, a public will emerges from the legislature that administrators then implement and reflect back to the public as the public's will. In this model, the barrier between legislature and administration is a vital protection against domination. As John Locke put it, "The Legislative cannot transfer the Power of Making Laws to any other hands" (Locke [1679–1689] 1963).[42] In the work of Jürgen Habermas and his progenitors, a barrier between state and society serves the same protective role.

Current conditions of interdependence and complexity make these traditional visions untenable and undesirable. The numbers and complexity of regulations required to solve free-rider problems today make it impossible in almost every case for a legislature to enact anything with sufficient detail to be applicable.[43] Administrators at both the higher policy-making levels and the street level must fill in the blanks. At either of these levels, if they do not consult with the public in their policy-making, the policy they make will be of lower quality and have less normative and perceived legitimacy. A normative approach more congruent with today's needs would make both the higher level administrative lawmaking function and the street-level function of reflecting the public back to itself more recursive. It would be improved by greater capacities to explain to citizens the reasons for the administrative legislation and to find out from citizens what legislation they think they need. Recalibrating our understanding of the roles of administrators at all levels makes it possible to criticize administrative representation and suggest reforms that would make that representation, the resulting policies, and the eventual coercion more relevant to the citizens' worlds, more effective, and more legitimate.

In circumstances when for exogenous reasons the civil service is already honest, competent, and acting in the overall directions that the public desires, what democracies need, in the realm of administrative representation as in the realm of electoral representation, is not necessarily more citizen control, or power, but more citizen capacity to initiate deliberation and *deliberative accountability*—defined not so much as the capacity to monitor and sanction but as a requirement that administrators explain the reasons for their actions, listen well to citizens' disagreements or suggestions, and recursively respond (Mansbridge 2014a). Administrators need to understand better how what they do affects the lives of the citizens on the ground, and they need to hear it from the citizens themselves. For their part, citizens need to hear the ideas of the administrators in contexts where the citizens can pursue their questions, pressing deeply and interactively into the responses. Citizen power may be required to make administrators listen well, but in this case that power is instrumental to the goal of communication, not a legitimating feature of the system itself.

At the street level, bureaucrats in all countries also make law. The police, teachers, social workers, even customs inspectors and clerks at the motor vehicles registry usually have some, sometimes considerable, discretion. When they use that discretion, they make law. For reasons much like those of administrators at the policy level, these street-level administrators sometimes engage the public in coproducing these laws. The police may institute community policing measures to bring the public into the decisions they make about how to put into effect their broader mandate (e.g., Fung 2004). The schools may rely for some decisions on parent-teacher associations or their equivalents. A broader normative mandate for greater recursive communication would encourage other street-level bureaucracies to devise institutions to consult citizens deliberatively and regularly. Such a mandate might mean restructuring administrative representation to be more descriptively representative of the relevant population, to give citizens more power to initiate communication from below, and to provide communicative incentives for administrators.

The democratic landscape is today dynamic and quickly changing, trying to adapt in practice to exponentially increasing interdependence and complexity. Recalibrating our understanding of administrative representation should allow us to accept, from a normative democratic perspective, some relative autonomy among administrators selected for their competence and public-interest motivation. We can then provide deliberative counterweights to that autonomy by adding to present systems institutions that promote a greater responsiveness to informed public desires, a greater respect for public knowledge and perceptions, a greater and more equal public voice in decisions, and a greater recursive capacity for mutual education, communication, and deliberation between administrative representatives and the public. In many such instances the arrows of control and communication may rightly bypass the electoral system to go directly from the citizens to those administratively responsible for a policy.

Ideally, the causality can become in many cases recursive, with power and persuasion traveling in both directions and affecting the next moves of all the communicative partners. This ideal of democracy is deliberative as well as aggregative. It is educative rather than static. It respects all three crucial sets of actors in the political world—the citizens, the elected representatives, and the administrative representatives—and asks what settings will encourage all of them to develop their capacities, including their institutional capacities, in ways that foster critical intelligence and concern for the public good, and the ability to listen and communicate across the lines of caste, class, and culture.

## Societal Representation

Many useful supplements to both electoral and administrative representation come from the social, private, or societal realm.[44] This realm is often far less democratic and more susceptible to entrenched inequalities than either the electoral or the administrative realms. Perceived legitimacy in this realm may be high, because many still-held eighteenth-century norms support a market perceived, in contrast to the realities, to be "free." Perceived legitimacy may also be high for other reasons—because formal processes of policy-making in the societal realm often involve willing key stakeholders, private organizations are not expected to be subject to democratic standards, and the expertise of the groups involved may be or seem to be merely technical. Normative democratic legitimacy, however, may be low—either because the societal representatives for different groups do not speak accurately for or are not authorized by or accountable to the groups for whom they speak, or because the larger system of societal representation is biased.

Because the societal sector is such a crucial piece of the larger representative system, it deserves significant normative attention. Yet at present normative democratic standards for societal representation are only beginning to be developed and are much in contest. Some developing standards apply to what I will call *internal* legitimacy problems. They are problems within the represented-representative *relationship*,[45] including problems of misrepresentation, authorization, and accountability. Other standards apply to *external* questions of bias within the *system* in which the representative relationship is embedded.

In both the internal-relational and external-systemic realms, democratic standards should become more demanding as the form of societal representation takes on a more formal relation to the state. Some societal organizations have powers *directly delegated* by the state. Some organizations *consult formally* with state agencies. Some organizations and individuals aim only at *informal influence* on the state. Many organizations play more than one of these roles. The content and level of the standards required for the democratic legitimacy of these organizations and individuals should vary contingently with the closeness of connection to the state.[46] Public perceptions of legitimacy sometimes, but not always, follow this pattern. Our current norms regarding external, or systemic, bias are stronger and clearer than our norms regarding the internal governance of organizations.

At the level of direct *delegation* of powers, the strongest connection with the state, both elected and administrative representatives often rely on societally organized representative institutions. Elected representatives rely, for example, on political parties. Although the parties are strictly speaking private entities, in most nations the state legally regulates the parties; in the EU parties receive state funding. Because the connection of societally organized parties with the state is strong, one would expect significant public concern with both the internal representative processes of the parties and their external systemic bias. Although in most nations the political parties have their own internal rules for selecting candidates, over time the public has become more concerned with these issues. In the United States the public has favored, but not legally mandated, primaries over more informal methods of candidate selection. In Europe the public has favored, and occasionally even legally mandated, party gender quotas. Regarding external, systemic legitimacy, the public has also over time taken more interest in the degree of democratic bias that different party systems produce. Electoral methods are usually a matter of state decision. When states decide to move from one electoral method to another, issues of systemic bias usually play a major role in the public debate.

Administrations also directly delegate many powers to the societal sector. The nexus of administrative and societal representation has received less public scrutiny than the nexus of electoral and societal representation, and the norms are correspondingly less well developed. Administrations can delegate powers to almost any societal organization, from a multinational for-profit corporation to a village nonprofit. Sometimes governments create private organizations in order to give them policy and enforcement responsibilities. Sometimes governments delegate their powers to existing private entities and simply enforce the rules those entities make. Sometimes administrations formally adopt as law the codes developed by private entities. Considering all three of these processes, Rudder, Fritschuler, and Choi (2016) estimate that "Taken together, agency rulemaking and the policy decisions of private groups account for most policy-making in advanced societies."[47] Accrediting organizations provide an example. In the United States, the federal government adopts the accounting standards of one private nonprofit group, the Financial Accounting Standards Board, and gives another private nonprofit group, the Financial Industry Regulating Authority, the legal power to discipline the firms and individuals who violate those standards (61–62 and ch. 4). These groups have their own internal mechanisms for selecting their officers, unregulated by the state and almost entirely ignored by the public. The question of whether these mechanisms may incorporate systemic bias has rarely been addressed. Scholars are only beginning to develop norms for internal governance, recursive and otherwise, to apply when state administrators delegate powers to societal organizations (see, e.g., Hirst 1994; Smith and Teasdale 2015).

When we move from delegation to state *formal consultation* with societal organizations, the normative issues get even more complex. Elected representatives consult with lobbyists for many societal organizations. Administrators often give specific societal organizations a privileged place, either formally or informally, in public hearings or in informal meetings. The EU consultative system works this way and so do many US agencies. There is probably much more formal mandated consultation with the public in both electoral and administrative representation than there is formal delegation of lawmaking or enforcement capacity to societal organizations. Yet normative theory about representative democratic legitimacy in these processes of formal consultation is in its infancy. As that theory develops, both equality and recursivity should serve as legitimating features.

Finally, at the level of *informal influence* on the state, the way that societal organizations represent the public almost always falls far short of existing normative democratic standards on both the internal and the external dimensions. Much recent work in democratic theory has focused on the *internal* dimension, the representative/represented relationships within the organizations. Nancy Rosenblum, for example, warns against "government intervention in the lives of associations" on the grounds of freedom of association and freedom to organize one's association as one wants. In her analysis, choice and exit, the processes of "shifting involvements," and pluralism *give us all the democracy and accountability we need*.[48] Yet the closer the formal relationship with the state, the greater the normative justification for states requiring internal associational democracy.[49]

Often the organizations, and even individuals, that influence the state in the name of those they claim to represent are what Montanaro calls "self-appointed representatives." Although much of their effectiveness derives from recognition by powerful audiences such as the state, much of their legitimacy derives from recognition by those they claim to represent.[50] When the represented publicly refuse to recognize the claim of an individual or organization to represent them, the audience to whom the representative claim is addressed (such as potential donors) also often wavers in recognizing that claim. "Organizational authorization" and "discursive authorization" both provide serial, or sequenced, legitimacy: "The representative voice of the self-appointed representative waxes and wanes with these serial and incremental authorizations."[51] In judging the legitimacy of such claims, we might also add the depth and quality of recursive communication that the representatives have with those they claim to represent.

Both internal and systemic biases in societal representation are hard to correct. Even the internet, theoretically open to all and in practice sometimes responsive to interventions by the marginalized, significantly favors the verbally advantaged and the already well-connected (Schloz-man, Verba, and Brady 2010). Occasionally deviations from this pattern emerge. After 1830 in France, workers established newspapers edited and written exclusively by workers, such as *L'Artisan*, *Le Journal des Ouvriers*, and *Le Peuple*.[52] In the United States, from the mid-1920s to 1986, the Communist Party USA newspaper *The Daily Worker* included columns and letters to the editor by workers, serving as an authentic, although censored, means of mutual communication. That paper was, however, subsidized by the Communist Party, in turn partially funded by the USSR during the Cold War. The more usual unequal descriptive representation by class on the internet and in the print media does not necessarily translate into unequal substantive representation, but it suggests at least a potential problem of systemic bias.

We may conclude that in societal representation our democratic norms regarding the representative relationships internal to organizations are in flux, but our norms regarding the external representative system seem relatively clear: individuals should be represented societally either proportionally to their numbers within an existing democratic polity or proportionally to the degree that they are affected. As in electoral and administrative representation, societal representation on all three levels—the organizations to which the state delegates lawmaking powers, those the state consults, and those that influence the state—is deeply biased (see Schlozman, Verba, and Brady 2012; Schlozman and Tierney 1986). Even in regard to internal governance, our norms are becoming clearer: the closer a societal organization comes to influencing the state definitively, the more the public has a legitimate normative claim that the organization act to counter, rather than perpetuate, the biases in the representative system and that it organize itself along recursively communicative, democratic lines.

## Conclusion

As the representative systems of many developed democracies come under strain, the growing citizen distrust of government poses both a practical and a normative challenge. Distrust undermines legitimate state coercion at a time when our increasing interdependence and need for more free-use goods require increasing state coercion to solve the resulting collective free-rider problems.

In this widening crisis, many progressive thinkers are suggesting not new ways of legitimating state power but new ways of resisting it. The reason is understandable. As the number of free-rider problems we must solve increases, state power has increased. As state power increases, it is of crucial importance to develop increased capacities to resist it.

Yet resistance cannot be our only answer. In response to growing state power, it would be a fatal mistake to identify the appropriate normative agenda solely as resistance, disruption, destabilization, and the multiplication of veto points against that state power. These steps prevent state action. In the absence of democratic state action (the *kratia* part of democracy), the world will become even more unequal and open to oppression than it is now.[53]

Given our great and growing needs for legitimate state coercion, the job of representing citizens democratically in all requisite decisions is both more important and more difficult. To approach this goal more closely, we need to stop anchoring all democratic legitimacy in elected office. Instead of deploring the "outsourcing of the law," we need to use our ingenuity to find ways of making electoral, administrative, and societal representation not only more democratic but also more communicatively thoughtful and recursive, so that as citizens and representatives together coproduce their own and the public's interests they do so in conditions close to those the citizens would approve, either hypothetically or in retrospect. Most developed democracies today have relatively good systems of electoral, administrative, and societal representation. But "relatively good" is far from good enough to meet our present needs. This chapter has indicated some ways of restructuring and supplementing representation in all three realms to bring that representation closer to democratic norms, particularly recursive communicative norms. In the societal realm, which is currently the least exhaustively theorized, both internal organizational relations of authorization and accountability and system-wide relations are important to democratic representation. We cannot analyze those system-wide ideals effectively if we conceive legitimacy as based only on consent—unless we work out, which I do not attempt here, the normative conditions that would authorize a subtle form of what I would call *diachronic consent*, a tacit Burkean consent, based on good justifications and developed in good conditions over the centuries.

Outside the currently developed democracies, the greatest challenge today to democratic representation is no longer fascism or communism but the Chinese ideal that combines meritocracy and what I will call *demo-*

*benia*: government guided by the good of the citizens (jarringly conjoining the Greek root *demos* and the Latin root *bene* or good).[54] This system ideally represents the citizens' interests through an arrangement that combines fair meritocratic selection to positions of power, peer accountability, some local democracy and other methods for gauging citizen needs, with responsiveness based on the representatives' internalized norms to "serve the people," their underlying apprehension of sanctions from above for poor performance, and, ultimately, some fear of collective citizen disaffection and sanctions from below. This representative ideal can be undermined in practice by favoritism, group power, fear, and groupthink. It can be undermined by manipulating the methods or ignoring the results. The check on the representatives' power based on an underlying fear of citizen sanctions can be undermined by increasing economic productivity, promoting nationalism, and suppressing dissent. Nevertheless, the current Chinese system has found ways to practice a version of meritocratic representation that seems in its country to be perceived as relatively legitimate.

It is just conceivable that such a system could be combined with the rule of law, not only in the civil code, as is currently more or less the case in China, but also in the criminal code, where in China it is currently largely absent (Hurst and Kinkel 2011). It could conceivably be combined with effective human rights. It could conceivably be combined with effective forms of communication, even recursive communication, between the represented and the representatives (see He and Warren 2011). It could relatively easily be combined with certain forms of individual dignity, such as the dignity of work, the dignity that derives from food security, and possibly even the dignity of being treated with respect by street-level bureaucrats.[55] It does not, however, seem compatible with the dignity that we associate with democratic citizenship: the particular dignity of standing tall or looking directly in the others' eyes that derives from equal political liberty, the equality of self-government.[56]

In both democracy and meritocratic demobenia, the electoral, administrative, and societal representative systems can all use recursive communication with constituents to generate better outcomes and greater legitimacy, both perceived and normative. Democracy is unique in giving power to the citizens behind that recursive communication and having a legitimating aspirational norm of political equality. As we try to make sense intellectually of the complicated implicit norms that have arisen slowly in existing democracies through the practice of electoral, administrative, and societal representation, we might look particularly for democratic features that reinforce the republican dignity of self-government, both through appropriate guarantees of power in the larger system and through the specific mechanisms of recursive communication in the representative relationship. Today governments are by necessity taking on more tasks that require state coercion, citizens are more educated and more demanding, and the capacities for constituent-representative communication have expanded dramatically. As a result of these growing demands and capacities, the dignity of the democratic citizen now rests not only on casting a vote but also, as an aspirational ideal, on being heard, and in the best case being responded to and having the capacity to respond to the response, recursively, throughout the representative process. By making this ideal of recursive communication among constituents and representatives explicit, we can formulate it as a newly important component of the cluster of ideals that make up what we mean by representative democracy.

## Notes

For insightful comments I thank the participants in the Stanford Political Theory Workshop (particularly James Fishkin and Juliana Bidadanure), the University College of London Political Theory Colloquium, and the Oxford Blavatnik School Workshop on the Performance of Democracies, as well as Ben Crum, Michael Neblo, Wendy Salkin, and the anonymous reviewers for this volume.

1. See Mansbridge 2014c. I thank Claus Offe (personal communication) for the language of supply and demand and for thoughts on the causes of the decline in supply.

2. Although free-use goods are often called "public goods" or "nonexcludable" goods, both of those terms are technically inaccurate (Mansbridge 2014c).

3. Lord's similar analysis (this volume) uses the language of externalities.

4. For solidarity, see recent work on innate altruism, e.g., Rand and Nowak 2013; Warneken et al. 2007; for duty, see the classic works of Sen 1977 and Hirschman 1985; for other intrinsic motives, see, e.g., Fourier (1808–1837) 1971 on "attractive labor" (*travail attrayant*); for the problem of extrinsic motivations driving out intrinsic, see Deci and Ryan 1985; for "nudges," using primarily preconscious psychological incentives rather than overt coercion, see Thaler and Sunstein 2008 and for criticism Waldron 2014. (One's stance toward nudges may differ depending on whether the alternative is explicit state coercion or no coercion, and on how valuable one considers the transparency of explicit state coercion).

5. See, e.g., Scharpf 2003 on input and output legitimacy; Beetham and Lord 1998 for performative legitimacy; Schmitt 2013 on throughput legitimacy, Cohen 1989 and Chambers 2003 on justification. Although I usually use the word *justice*

to apply to outcomes and *legitimacy* to apply to procedures, this terminology is not universal; I thus adopt Scharpf's much-used "output" terminology here.

6. Saward (this volume) emphasizes this liminal interpenetration. Saward's conceptual map could easily incorporate international representation, with his category of "state-based" representation referring to the state-like structures that provide legitimate coercion in the international realm. For simplicity, my analysis focuses on the national realm and ignores judicial representation within this realm. For an excellent discussion of international representation, see Lord (this volume).

7. These internal "intersubjective" (Disch 2011, 106) relationships are embedded in and partially constituted by the larger external representative system, a relation that places limits on the very concepts of "internal" and "external."

8. They may thus fall into either of Saward's two outer circles. See below for an argument that the more closely the state consults and adopts the advice of societal groups, the more these groups should be democratically organized internally.

9. See Disch 2011 (citing Pitkin 1967), 2012, 2015, and Saward 2010 on representatives' claims and other actions creating, mobilizing, and in other ways "constituting" their constituencies.

10. For a more extended summary of these ideals, their aspirational quality, their evolution from "first" to "second" generation, and the continuing contest over their meaning, see Mansbridge 2015 and Bächtiger, Dryzek, Mansbridge, and Warren 2018. Throughout that evolution, theorists have maintained consensus on the importance of the two aspirational ideals of mutual respect, which includes listening for difference as well as commonality, and absence of power, which includes rejecting threats and manipulation (see discussion below).

11. The normative goal is for citizens to "have a better chance to be heard, understood, and have an impact on the thinking of all of their elected and appointed representatives, while conversely, those representatives have a better chance to be heard, understood, and have a productive impact on the thinking of the constituents" (Mansbridge 2005, 13). See Castiglione and Pollak (this volume, 15) on political representation as an "interactive relationship" in which "citizens need to have an ongoing (deliberative and participatory) engagement with the representatives"; Warren (this volume, 55) on representatives' "deliberative interaction with constituents"; and Fossum (this volume, 98) on representation as dynamic "ongoing communication and interaction between representatives and represented."

12. In "response," I include the possibility of saying, "I have heard what you said (which is a, b, c), and am not persuaded, for these reasons."

13. Note the one-way locution "talk *to* them," which taken literally would almost preclude the possibility of his constituents convincing him that they were right, even in part.

14. So, too, a majority of African Americans in the United States have indicated that they prefer legislators who spend time on district-based service more than lawmaking (Tate 2004, ch. 6).

15. Young continues on pages 129–30: "A representative process is ... better to the extent that it establishes and renews connection between constituents and representative." Melissa Williams discusses how constituency and representative mutually constitute one another (1998, 203–5).

16. On representative institutions encouraging more inclusive citizen participation, see Hayat (this volume).

17. Open-list (preferential) PR systems, especially in interaction with vulnerability in the next election, also create incentives for time spent in the constituency and constituency service. (For an introduction to the literature on constituency work, see Heitshusen, Young, and Wood 2005; André, Depauw, and Martin 2015; and Arter 2011; thanks for these and other references to Claire McGing, currently studying constituency service in Ireland). To my knowledge, the representative work of constituency service has not been analyzed from a normative perspective, although such work probably provides an important source of communication, particularly between working-class constituents and their representatives. Vivian Schmitt notes that in Europe, unitary (as compared with federal) and SMP (as compared with PR) systems have more incentives for elected representatives to listen to and speak with their constituents. As for the EU, it has "elaborate ... coordinative discourses" but only "the thinnest of communicative discourses" between political leaders and the public (Schmitt 2006, 40). On the capacities of different electoral and party systems for accountability and conflict negotiation, see Warren and Fossum in this volume.

18. The name refers to a ship's internal gyroscope, which keeps it on course; for greater detail, see Mansbridge 2009 on the "selection model" of electoral representation.

19. In European PR list systems, the gyroscopic element among individual representatives is likely to be large, because the representatives are usually chosen by party officials with good information about the representatives' inner motivations, goals, and principles. In such systems the political party, more than the individual representative, anticipates the voters' sanctions in the next election and adjusts accordingly.

20. In some cases, however, constituents may desire inflexibility and accordingly select an inflexible gyroscopic representative to represent them.

21. Constituent trust facilitates negotiation at the legislative level, because, to be effective, negotiation must be conducted behind closed doors, preventing the monitoring necessary for anticipatory representation (Warren and Mansbridge et al. [2013] 2015).

22. For a contingency analysis of when descriptive representation most furthers democratic aims, see Mansbridge 1999; one relevant context is a history of communicative distrust.

23. See Selden 1997 for passive and active descriptive administrative representation and Mügge (n.d.) for passive and active descriptive electoral representation.

24. "Ninety-five percent of the nitty-gritty of work of drafting [bills] and nego-tiating [their final form] is now done by staff" in the federal legislature (Senator Edward Kennedy 2009, 486, quoted in Kaiser 2013, 28).

25. For "promissory," "anticipatory," and "surrogate" representation, see Mans-bridge 2003.

26. See Saward 2010 for examples and an analysis of the dynamics of a "repre-sentative claim" by nonelected representatives.

27. Participants discussed the session with approximately 1.5 others.

28. Michael Neblo, personal communication. The time cost to the member would be less than an hour per session (two hours a week), far less than mem-bers spend now soliciting donors, while the monetary costs of setting up the soft-ware, headphones, and outreach interface could be less than $100,000 a year for the entire Congress. The goal of reaching one-quarter of the constituents every six years would require members of both the House and the Senate to convene groups of 175 constituents (shown feasible and attractive to participants in Neblo et al. 2018) twice a week for all 52 weeks of the year. Lesser efforts would still cover considerable numbers of constituents.

29. For the way in which these groups use the hypothetical opportunity to par-ticipate in such a deliberation, see Neblo et al. 2010, 11, table 2, and Neblo et al. 2018. Future studies could test whether and what the member of Congress learned from the experience. Such studies could also investigate in depth the quality of the interactive experience with different group sizes and instructions.

30. Random selection in practice always includes an element of self-selection after the random draw. The best designs minimize self-selection by providing strong incentives to attend (Mansbridge 2010b). For citizen representatives, see Urbinati and Warren 2008. For a critique of such minipublics, see Lafont 2017.

31. Assemblies designed for accurate representation by lot are expensive. Fish-kin (personal communication) indicates that the cost of a well-structured Delib-erative Poll, with balanced materials, experts, facilitators to bring out minority opinion, a sample of two hundred or more to make meaningful descriptive repre-sentativeness possible, and sufficient incentives to bring out those least likely to at-tend spontaneously, exceeds US$1 million; Warren (personal communication) in-dicates that the British Columbia Citizens Assembly of 161 citizens, also relatively well-designed for representativeness and including six meetings on weekends over the course of a year as well as many public hearings, also exceeded US$1 million.

32. In Rome, the elected representatives knew that hospitals had been over-built and some needed to be closed, but no representative had dared advocating closures for fear of electoral sanction. A Deliberative Poll moved heavily in the direction of such closings, thus allowing representatives to use the citizen delibera-tion to legitimate their votes (Fishkin 2009, 151).

33. The rationale for asking a randomly selected British Columbia Citizen As-sembly (BCCA) to recommend a new electoral system after a year of deliberation

was that elected representatives often cannot be trusted to vote without undue self-interest on changing the electoral system that has brought them to power. (The BCCA recommendation garnered more than 50 percent of the votes in a subsequent referendum but failed because the mandated threshold was 60 percent; Warren and Pearse 2008.)

34. Other related recalibrations of normative theory, not stressed in this chapter, would derive legitimacy from plural sources, recognize the communicative values in descriptive representation, and explore the ways that anticipatory representation and the "like me" forms of gyroscopic representation undermine in different ways the hierarchy inherent in the representative relation.

35. More technically, this broad understanding of power ("power as capacity") is "the actual or potential causal relation between the preferences or interests of an actor or set of actors and an outcome or the changed probability of an outcome," a definition adapted from Nagel 1975 by adding "interests," "set of actors," and probability (see Mansbridge and Shames 2008, 624; Mansbridge et al. 2010, n. 44).

36. See Neblo 2015, 89–91, on "buying into the game" of giving nonstrategic reasons. More empirical and theoretical work is needed on the cognitive and emotional capacities required for listening to understand the meanings, the intents behind the meanings, and even the preferences and interests behind the intents in another's speech.

37. For the distinction between manipulation and persuasion, see, e.g., Neblo 2015, 71–76. For formulations that subsume manipulation under the "force" in being moved against one's will, see Bachrach and Baratz 1963, 636; Lukes 1974, 32 (Lukes later rightly considered it a "mistake" to identify persuasion with common interests as the sole criterion for distinguishing it from manipulation: 2005, 12, 109). In a book-length treatment of the manipulation/persuasion distinction, which notoriously is not "easy to operationalize" (Mansbridge 2003, 519; Disch 2011, 101; Neblo 2015, 72), Klemp (2012) parses the normative spectrum into the three categories of *deliberative persuasion*, which includes openness to revision, sincerity in intention, and a focus on the merits; *strategic persuasion*, which includes unwillingness to revise, selective use of facts and arguments, and an orientation to winning; and *manipulation*, which includes the intent to deceive, unwillingness to revise, insincerity, and the use of "hidden or irrational force," which overwhelms or bypasses "the listener's capacity to choose" (47–62). Although the descriptor *irrational* needs more unpacking (because all communication is to some degree irrational) and intent is not absolutely required (see Nagel's improvement on Dahl's definition of power), Klemp nevertheless makes a start on operationalizing these distinctions by mapping them onto concrete examples of political action. For critical discussions, including the role of intentional and unintentional psychological framing in communication, see Lisa Disch 2011 101, 2015, and this volume. At approximately the same time as Bachrach and Baratz, Habermas formulated

the idea of "the force of the better argument" ([1962] 1989). He later concluded that "reaching understanding" was the "inherent telos" of speech ([1981] 1987) and distinguished analytically between "communicative" and "strategic" action ([1983] 1990). One need never have read Habermas, however, to cede that the aspirational (inherently unreachable) ideal of communication through persuasion in the absence of (coercive) power is both meaningful and conceptually distinguishable from manipulation, even though there are no pure cases of either, the lines in any case are often unclear or contested (particularly when the distinction involves a determination of individual interests, intent, or rationality), and the broadest meaning of the term *manipulation*, shorn of intent (Mansbridge and Shames 2008), can cover many sources of power, including the many sources of systemic power in a political or social system.

38. See note 10 above. Although some theorists have conceived of representation as "a recursive process: a movement from represented to representative, and a *correlative* one from representative to represented" (Laclau 2005, 158, cited in Disch 2012, 604; my emphasis), most, including Pitkin herself (see Disch, 2012) stress only the capacities of the representative to constitute the represented (e.g., Bourdieu 1984, 11, quoted in Hayat, this volume). Saward 2010 (see Warren, this volume) and Disch 2012 have more recursive views, Disch stressing the greater power resources of representatives in relation to most constituents.

39. This problem may be our generation's equivalent of the medieval conundrum of free will. For two excellent treatments of autonomy, see Hirschmann 1992 and Nedelsky 2012.

40. See Mansbridge 2014a on the distinction between "deliberative accountability" as giving an account and the more recent meanings of accountability reduced to monitoring and sanctions, along with an argument for, in appropriate cases, *transparency in rationale* in contrast to *transparency in process*. See also Phillips 1995, 145 and Chambers 2003 on the core of legitimacy deriving from deliberative accountability, and Warren 2014 and this volume on "discursive accountability."

41. See appendix A in Mansbridge 2017 for further notes.

42. See also Habermas (1962) 1989; Lowi (1969) 1979. The language of opinion-formation and will-formation comes from Habermas (1992) 1996.

43. As the US Supreme Court decided in *Wayman v. Southard* (1825).

44. See appendix B in Mansbridge 2017 for further notes. The terminology for this sector is still unstable. The term *informal* representation is inaccurate because many of the organizations that provide societal representation have highly formal structures and are formally connected with electoral or administrative representation. The term *nonelectoral* is empty and too broad, confusingly including administration. The term *private* is too restrictive, as many of these organizations have a semipublic character. I have adopted *societal* (Saward this volume) because, although it has the connotation of nongovernmental, it does not explicitly exclude

mixed institutions. See Saward (this volume) on electoral and nonelectoral, formal and informal, and the liminality of the entities in this and other sectors.

45. I take the term *representative relationship* from Montanaro (this volume) and Warren (this volume).

46. For a two-by-three table of internal and external by direct delegation, see appendix B, Mansbridge 2017. For normative contingency see, e.g., Mansbridge 2014a.

47. Moving to the normative realm, the authors conclude, "To the degree that private groups are making public choices about values to pursue, they should be evaluated on the grounds of democratic legitimacy, including the organizations' inclusiveness, transparency, and accountability in their government roles, just as government should be" (Rudder, Fritschuler, and Choi 2016, 4). These suggested norms need more scrutiny.

48. Rosenblum 1998, 6, 17, 20, 25, 27, citing Hegel, *Philosophy of Right*, ¶235; emphasis in original.

49. See Schmitter 1992 for a voucher scheme allowing voters to select voluntary associations to represent them in state-sponsored consultations and negotiations, and requiring internal democracy from the associations that agree to state funding.

50. For the role of the audience in representative claims, see Saward 2010. For self-appointed representatives, see Montanaro 2012 and this volume; see also Urbinati and Warren 2008. Warren (this volume) points out that while representatives may self-appoint, the "represented need to judge." In some cases, however, recognition and judgment by the represented is difficult or impossible, as with unborn generations (Whiteside this volume).

51. Montanaro (this volume). This sequential and sometimes recursive process of authorization in societal representation contrasts with the singularity of the formal authorizing moment in electoral representation.

52. Hayat (this volume). Hayat's careful phrasing is that "some workers, who were admittedly a minority," established these papers. They were the informal representatives of those who did not edit or write for the papers. Many report on bias in the system of societal representation. See, e.g., Strolovitch 2007.

53. See, e.g., Scott 2009 for arguments to the contrary.

54. None of the Greek words for "the good"—*agathon, sumpheron*, and *lusiteloun* (Mansbridge 2013, 915)—has a recognizable English cognate; hence this mongrel coinage. It allows one to speak, for example, of "meritocratic demobenia" rather than "meritocratic autocracy" (Fishkin and Mansbridge 2017). A better term might be "*minben* legitimacy" (*minben* meaning "the people as root"), "which holds that the well-being of the people, and not the interests of the rulers, should guide the exercise of political power" (Williams, Chan, and Shin 2016, 6).

55. During the Cultural Revolution, Chinese street-level bureaucrats adopted the phrase "I'm sorry to have made you passive" to apologize for taking away the initiative from the persons served rather than soliciting their suggestions. A citizen

might correspondingly complain to a bureaucrat, "I feel very passive" (Fincher 1972, 334).

56. See Waldron 2012 on "moral orthopedics" and Pettit 2014 on the "eyeball test."

# References

ANES (American National Election Study). 2012. www.electionstudies.org/Core Utility/varfiles/Q2239_2012.txt.

André, Audrey, Sam Depauw, and Shane Martin. 2015. "Electoral Systems and Legislators' Constituency Effort: The Mediating Effect of Electoral Vulnerability." *Comparative Political Studies* 48 (4): 464–96.

Arter, David. 2011. "The Michael Marsh Question: How Do Finns Do Constituency Service?" *Parliamentary Affairs* 64 (1): 129–52.

Bachrach, Peter, and Morton Baratz. 1963. "Decisions and Non-Decisions: An Analytical Framework." *American Political Science Review* 57:632–42.

Bächtiger, André, John Dryzek, Jane Mansbridge, and Mark Warren. 2018. "Introduction." In *Oxford Handbook of Deliberative Democracy*. Oxford: Oxford University Press.

Barber, Michael, and Nolan McCarthy. 2015. In *Political Negotiation*, edited by Jane Mansbridge and Cathy Jo Martin. Washington, DC: Brookings.

Beetham, David, and Christopher Lord. 1998. *Legitimacy in the European Union*. London: Addison Wesley Longman.

Bourdieu, Pierre. 1984. "Espace social et genèse des 'classes.'" *Actes de la Recherche en Sciences Sociales* 52/53 (June): 3–14.

Broockman, David E. 2013. "Black Politicians Are More Intrinsically Motivated to Advance Blacks' Interests: A Field Experiment Manipulating Political Incentives." *American Journal of Political Science* 57 (3): 521–36.

Chambers, Simone. 2003. "Deliberative Democracy." *Annual Review of Political Science* 6:307–26.

Cohen, Joshua. l989. "Deliberation and Democratic Legitimacy." In *The Good Polity: Normative Analysis of the State*, edited by Alan Hamlin and Philip Pettit, 17–34. Oxford: Basil Blackwell.

Deci, Edward L., and Richard M. Ryan. l985. *Intrinsic Motivation and Self-Determination in Human Behavior*. New York: Plenum.

Disch, Lisa. 2011. "Toward a Mobilization Conception of Democratic Representation." *American Political Science Review* 105 (1): 100–114.

———. 2012. "Democratic Representation and the Constituency Paradox." *Perspectives on Politics* 10 (3): 599–616.

———. 2015. "The 'Constructivist Turn' in Democratic Representation: A Normative Dead-End?" *Constellations* 22 (4): 487–99.

Fenno, Richard E., Jr. 1978. *Home Style: House Members in Their Districts*. Boston: Little, Brown.

Fincher, Beverly Hong. 1972. "Impressions of Language in China." *China Quarterly* 50 (April–June): 333–40.

Fishkin, James S. 2009. *When the People Speak: Deliberative Democracy and Public Consultation.* New York: Oxford.

Fishkin, James S., and Jane Mansbridge. 2017. "Introduction: The Prospects & Limits of Deliberative Democracy." *Daedalus* 146 (3): 6–13.

Fourier, Charles. (1808–1837) 1971. *Harmonian Man: Selected Writings of Charles Fourier.* Edited by Mark Poster. Garden City, NY: Doubleday.

Fung, Archon. 2004. *Empowered Participation: Reinventing Urban Democracy.* Princeton, NJ: Princeton University Press.

Gay, Claudine. 2001. "The Effect of Black Congressional Representation on Political Participation." *American Political Science Review* 95 (3): 589–602.

Gilens, Martin, and Benjamin I. Page. 2014. "Testing Theories of American Politics: Elites, Interest Groups, and Average Citizens." *Perspectives on Politics* 12 (3): 564–81.

Grill, Christopher J. 2007. *The Public Side of Representation: A Study of Citizens' Views about Representation and the Representative Process.* Albany: State University of New York Press.

Habermas, Jürgen. (1962) 1989. *The Structural Transformation of the Public Sphere: An Inquiry into a Category of Bourgeois Society.* Translated by Thomas Burger with the assistance of Frederick Lawrence. Boston: MIT Press.

———. (1981) 1987. *The Theory of Communicative Action.* Vol. 2, *Lifeworld and System.* Translated by T. McCarthy. Boston: Beacon.

———. (1983) 1990. *Moral Consciousness and Communicative Action.* Translated by Christian Lenhardt and Shierry Weber Nicholsen. Cambridge, MA: MIT Press.

———. (1992) 1996. *Between Facts and Norms.* Translated by W. Rehg. Cambridge, MA: MIT Press.

He, Baogang, and Mark E. Warren. 2011. "Authoritarian Deliberation: The Deliberative Turn in Chinese Political Development." *Perspectives on Politics* 9 (2): 269–89

Heitshusen, Valerie, Garry Young, and David M. Wood. 2005. "Electoral Context and MP Constituency Focus in Australia, Canada, Ireland, New Zealand, and the United Kingdom." *American Journal of Political Science* 49 (1): 32–45.

Hirst, Paul. 1994. *Associative Democracy: New Forms of Economic and Social Governance.* Cambridge: Polity.

Hirschman, Albert O. 1985. "Against Parsimony." *Economics and Philosophy* 1:7–21.

Hirschmann, Nancy J. 1992. *Rethinking Obligation: A Feminist Method for Political Theory.* Ithaca, NY: Cornell University Press.

Hurst, William, and Jonathan Kinkel. 2011. "Access to Justice in Post-Mao China: Assessing the Politics of Criminal and Administrative Law." *Journal of East Asian Studies* 11 (3): 467–99.

Kaiser, Robert G. 2013. *Act of Congress: How America's Central Institution Works, and How It Doesn't*. New York: Knopf.

Kennedy, Edward M. 2009. *True Compass: A Memoir*. New York: Twelve.

Kingdon, John W. 1981. *Congressmen's Voting Decisions*. New York: HarperCollins.

Klemp, Nathaniel J. 2012. *The Morality of Spin: Virtue and Vice in Political Rhetoric and the Christian Right*. Lanham, MD: Rowman & Littlefield.

Laclau, Ernesto. 2005. *On Populist Reason*. New York: Verso.

Laclau, Ernesto, and Chantal Mouffe. 1985. *Hegemony and Socialist Strategy: Towards a Radical Democratic Politics*. New York: Verso.

Lafont, Cristina. 2017. "Can Democracy be Deliberative and Participatory? The Democratic Case for Political Uses of Mini-Publics." *Daedalus* 146 (3): 85–105.

Locke, John. (1679–1689) 1963. *Two Treatises of Government*. Edited by Peter Laslett. Cambridge: Cambridge University Press.

Lowi, Theodore J. (1969) 1979. *The End of Liberalism: The Second Republic of the United States*. New York: W. W. Norton.

Lukes, Steven. 1974. *Power: A Radical View*. London: Macmillan.

———. 2005. *Power: A Radical View*. 2nd ed. London: Palgrave Macmillan.

Mansbridge, Jane. 1980. *Beyond Adversary Democracy*. New York: Basic Books.

———. 1990. "On the Relation of Altruism and Self-Interest." In *Beyond Self-Interest*, edited by J. Mansbridge, 133–43. Chicago: University of Chicago Press.

———. 1999. "Should Blacks Represent Blacks and Women Represent Women? A Contingent 'Yes.'" *Journal of Politics* 61 (3): 627–57.

———. 2003. "Rethinking Representation." *American Political Science Review* 97 (4): 515–27.

———. 2005. "The Fallacy of Tightening the Reins." *Österreichische Zeitschrift für Politikwissenschaft* 34 (3): 233–47.

———. 2009. "A 'Selection Model' of Political Representation." *Journal of Political Philosophy* 17 (4): 369–98.

———. 2010a. "Beyond the Tragedy of the Commons." *Perspectives on Politics* 8:590–93.

———. 2010b. "Deliberative Polling as the Gold Standard." *The Good Society* 12 (1): 55–62.

———. 2011. "Clarifying the Concept of Representation." *American Political Science Review* 105 (3): 621–30.

———. 2013. "Common Good." In *The International Encyclopedia of Ethics*, vol. 2, edited by Hugh LaFollette, 913–26. Oxford: Wiley-Blackwell.

———. 2014a. "A Contingency Theory of Accountability." In *The Oxford Handbook of Public Accountability*, edited by Mark Bowens, Robert E. Goodin, and Thomas Schillemans, 55–68. Oxford: Oxford University Press.

———. 2014b. "The Role of the State in Governing the Commons." *Environmental Science and Policy* 36:8–10.

————. 2014c. "What Is Political Science For?" APSA Presidential Address. *Perspectives on Politics* 12 (1): 8–17.

————. 2015. "A Minimalist Definition of Deliberation." In *Deliberation and Development*, edited by Patrick Heller and Vijayendra Rao, 27–49. Washington, DC: World Bank.

————. 2017. "Recursive Communication in the Representative System." Paper presented at the annual meeting of the American Political Science Association, San Francisco. https://papers.ssrn.com/sol3/papers.cfm?abstract_id=3049294.

Mansbridge, Jane, and Shauna L. Shames. 2008. "Toward a Theory of Backlash: Dynamic Resistance and the Central Role of Power." *Politics and Gender* 4 (4): 1–11.

Mansbridge, Jane, with James Bohman, Simone Chambers, David Estlund, Andreas Follesdal, Archon Fung, Cristina Lafont, Bernard Manin, and José Luis Martí. 2010. "The Place of Self-Interest and the Role of Power in Deliberative Democracy." *Journal of Political Philosophy* 18 (1): 64–100.

Minozzi, W., M. A. Neblo, K. M. Esterling, and D. M. J. Lazer. 2015. "Field Experiment Evidence of Substantive, Attributional, and Behavioral Persuasion by Members of Congress in Online Town Halls." *PNAS* 112 (13): 3937–42.

Montanaro, Laura. 2012. "The Democratic Legitimacy of Self-Appointed Representatives." *Journal of Politics* 74 (4): 1094–107.

Mügge, Liza. n.d. "Passive and Active Descriptive Representation in the Dutch Parliament." Upublished paper.

Nagel, Jack H. 1975. *The Descriptive Analysis of Power*. New Haven: Yale University Press.

Neblo, Michael A. 2015. *Deliberative Democracy between Theory and Practice*. Cambridge: Cambridge University Press.

Neblo, Michael A., Kevin M. Esterling, and David M. J. Lazer. 2018. *Politics with the People: Building a Directly Representative Democracy*. Cambridge: Cambridge University Press.

Neblo, Michael A., Kevin M. Esterling, Ryan P. Kennedy, David M. J. Lazer, and Anand E. Sokhey. 2010. "Who Wants to Deliberate—And Why?" *American Political Science Review* 104 (3): 1–18.

Nedelsky, Jennifer. 2012. *Law's Relations: A Relational Theory of Self, Autonomy, and Law*. Oxford: Oxford University Press.

Norris, Pippa. 2015. *Why Elections Fail*. Cambridge: Cambridge University Press.

Ostrom, Elinor. 1990. *Governing the Commons: The Evolution of Institutions for Collective Action*. Cambridge: Cambridge University Press.

Pettit, Philip. 2014. *Just Freedom: A Moral Compass for a Complex World*. New York: W. W. Norton.

Phillips, Anne. 1995. *Politics of Presence*. Oxford: Oxford University Press.

Pitkin, Hanna F. 1967. *The Concept of Representation*. Berkeley: University of California Press.

Plotke, David. 1997. "Representation Is Democracy." *Constellations* 4 (1): 19–34.

Rand, David, and Martin Nowak. 2013. "Human Cooperation" *Trends in Cognitive Sciences* 17 (8): 413–25.

Rosenblum, Nancy. L. 1998. *Membership and Morals: The Personal Uses of Pluralism in America*. Princeton, NJ: Princeton University Press.

Rudder, Catherine E., A. Lee Fritschuler, and Yon Jung Choi. 2016. *Public Policy-Making by Private Organizations*. Washington, DC: Brookings.

Sabel, Charles F., and Jonathan Zeitlin. 2010. *Experimentalist Governance in the European Union: Towards a New Architecture*. Oxford: Oxford University Press.

Saward, Michael. 2010. *The Representative Claim*. New York: Oxford University Press.

Scharpf, Fritz W. 2003. "Problem-Solving Effectiveness and Democratic Accountability in the EU." *MPIfG Working Paper* 3, no. 1 (February).

Schlozman, Kay Lehman, and John T. Tierney. 1986. *Organized Interests and American Democracy*. New York: Harper and Row.

Schlozman, Kay Lehman, Sidney Verba, and Henry E. Brady. 2010. "Weapon of the Strong? Participatory Inequality and the Internet." *Perspectives on Politics* 8 (2): 487–509.

———. 2012. *The Unheavenly Chorus: Unequal Political Voice and the Broken Promise of American Democracy*. Princeton, NJ: Princeton University Press.

Schmitt, Vivian A. 2006. *Democracy in Europe: The EU and National Polities*. Oxford: Oxford University Press.

———. 2013. "Democracy and Legitimacy in the European Union Revisited: Input, Output *and* 'Throughput.'" *Political Studies* 61:2–22.

Schmitter, Phillipe C. 1992. "The Irony of Modern Democracy and Efforts to Improve Its Practice." *Politics and Society* 20 (4): 507–12.

Scott, James. 2009. *The Art of Not Being Governed: An Anarchist History of Upland Southeast Asia*. New Haven, CT: Yale University Press.

Selden, Sally Coleman. 1997. *The Promise of Representative Bureaucracy: Diversity and Responsiveness in a Government Agency*. New York: Taylor and Francis.

Sen, Amartya K. 1977. "Rational Fools." *Philosophy and Public Affairs* 6:317–44.

Smith, Graham, and Simon Teasdale. 2012. "Associative Democracy and the Social Economy: Exploring the Regulatory Challenge." *Economy and Society* 41 (2): 151–76,

Strolovitch, Dara Z. 2007. *Affirmative Advocacy: Race, Class, and Gender in Interest Group Politics*. Chicago: University of Chicago Press.

Swain, Carol M. 1993. *Black Faces, Black Interests: The Representation of African Americans in Congress*. Cambridge, MA: Harvard University Press.

Tate, Katherine. 2004. *Black Faces in the Mirror: African Americans and Their Representatives in the U.S. Congress*. Princeton, NJ: Princeton University Press.

Thaler, Richard H., and Cass R. Sunstein. 2008. *Nudge: Improving Decisions about Health, Wealth, and Happiness*. New Haven, CT: Yale University Press.

Urbinati, Nadia. 2000. "Representation as Advocacy: A Study of Democratic Deliberation." *Political Theory* 28 (6): 758–86.

————. 2006. *Representative Democracy: Principles and Genealogy*. Chicago: University of Chicago Press.

Urbinati, Nadia, and Mark E. Warren. 2008. "The Concept of Representation in Contemporary Democratic Theory." *Annual Review of Political Science* 11: 387–412.

Waldron, Jeremy. 2012. *Dignity, Rank, and Rights*. Oxford: Oxford University Press

————. 2014. "It's All for Your Own Good." *New York Review of Books*, October 9, 2014, 9.

Warren, Mark E. 2014. "Accountability and Democracy." In *Oxford Handbook of Public Accountability*, edited by Mark Bovens, Robert E. Goodin, and Thomas Schillemans, 39–53. Oxford: Oxford University Press.

Warren, Mark E., and Jane Mansbridge, with André Bächtiger, Max A. Cameron, Simone Chambers, John Ferejohn, Alan Jacobs et al. (2013) 2015. "Deliberative Negotiation." In *Political Negotiation*, edited by Jane Mansbridge and Cathy Jo Martin, 141–97. Washington, DC: Brookings.

Warren, Mark E., and H. Pearse. 2008. *Designing Deliberative Democracy: The British Columbia Citizens' Assembly*. Cambridge: Cambridge University Press.

Warneken, Felix, Brian Hare, Alicia P. Melis, Daniel Hanus and Michael Tomasello. 2007. "Spontaneous Altruism by Chimpanzees and Young Children." *PLoS Biology* 5 (7): e184.

Williams, Melissa S. 1998. *Voice, Trust, and Memory: Marginalized Groups and the Failings of Liberal Representation*. Princeton, NJ: Princeton University Press.

Williams, Melissa S., Joseph Chan, and Doh Chull Shin. 2016. "Political Legitimacy in East Asia: Bridging Normative and Empirical Analysis." In *East Asian Perspectives on Political Legitimacy: Bridging the Empirical-Normative Divide*, edited by Joseph Chan, Doh Chull Shin, and Melissa S. Williams, 1–24. Cambridge: Cambridge University Press.

World Values Survey. 2013. www.worldvaluessurvey.org/WVSOnline.jsp.

Young, Iris Marion. 2000. *Democracy and Inclusion*. Oxford: Oxford University Press.

# Contributors

FRANK ANKERSMIT is Eminent Professor in Intellectual History and the Philosophy of History at Groningen University. He has published some fifteen books and many articles on the philosophy of history, political philosophy, and aesthetics. The notion of representation is at the center of most of his writings.

DARIO CASTIGLIONE teaches political theory at the University of Exeter. His main research interests are democratic and constitutional theory, the nature of civil and social relationships, and the history of political thought. His recent publications as coeditor and contributor include *Les Défis de la Representation* (Garnier Classiques 2018) and *Institutional Diversity in Self-governing Societies* (Lexington Books 2017).

PAULA DIEHL is Senior Lecturer for Theory, History, and Culture of the Political at the University of Bielefeld. Author of *Das Symbolische, das Imaginäre und die Demokratie. Eine Theorie politischer Repräsentation* (Nomos Verlag 2015), she is currently working on a book on right-wing populism and mass media.

LISA DISCH is Professor of Political Science and Women's Studies and an affiliate of the Program in the Environment at the University of Michigan. Author of *The Tyranny of the Two-Party System* (Columbia University Press 2002) and coeditor (with Mary Hawkesworth) of *The Oxford Handbook of Feminist Theory* (Oxford University Press 2016), she is currently working on a book on the constructivist turn in political representation.

JOHN ERIK FOSSUM is Professor of Political Science at ARENA Centre for European Studies at the University of Oslo, Norway. He has published extensively on democracy, federalism, and constitutionalism in the European Union. His latest publication (coedited with Markus Jachtenfuchs) is *Federal Challenges and Challenges to Federalism. Insights from the EU and Federal States* (Routledge 2018).

**SAMUEL HAYAT** is a CNRS Researcher in Political Science at the Lille Centre d'Etudes et de Recherches Administratives, Politiques et Sociales (CERAPS). He works primarily on political representation and on nineteenth-century revolutions and worker movements. He recently published *Quand la République était révolutionnaire: Citoyenneté et représentation en 1848* (Le Seuil 2014) and coedited several journal issues on political representation (*Trivium, Raisons politiques, Revue française de Science politique*).

**CHRISTOPHER LORD** is Professor at ARENA Centre for European Studies, at the University of Oslo, Norway. He has published widely on democracy, legitimacy, and the European Union. His books include *A Democratic Audit of the European Union* (Palgrave 2004). His most recent journal articles include "Utopia or Dystopia: Towards a Normative Analysis of Differentiated Integration" (*Journal of European Public Policy* 2015) and "An Indirect Legitimacy Argument for a Directly Elected European Parliament" (*European Journal of Political Research* 2017).

**JANE MANSBRIDGE** is Charles F. Adams Professor of Political Leadership and Democratic Values at the Harvard Kennedy School. She is the author of *Beyond Adversary Democracy* and *Why We Lost the ERA [Equal Rights Amendment]*, and editor or coeditor of *Beyond Self-Interest, Feminism* (with Susan Moller Okin), *Oppositional Consciousness* (with Aldon Morris), *Deliberative Systems* (with John Parkinson), and *Political Negotiation* (with Cathie Jo Martin). She is currently working on problems in political representation, deliberation, negotiation, and everyday activism. She is a past president of the American Political Science Association (2012–2013).

**LAURA MONTANARO** is a Lecturer in Political Theory at the University of Essex. Before joining Essex, she was a Harper Schmidt Fellow at the University of Chicago. She earned her PhD (2010) from the University of British Columbia. She has recently published *Who Elected Oxfam?* (Cambridge University Press 2018).

**JOHANNES POLLAK** is Professor of Political Science at Webster Vienna Private University and Senior Researcher at the Institute for Advanced Studies, Vienna (currently on leave). He is the author of *Repräsentation ohne Demokratie* (Springer 2007) and coeditor of *Political Representation* (jointly with C. Lord). His recent publications concern the pitfalls of the representative claim, representation at the supranational level, and democratic theory.

**MICHAEL SAWARD** is Professor of Politics and International Studies at the University of Warwick. Author of *The Representative Claim* (Oxford University Press 2010) and coeditor (with Engin Isin) of *Enacting European Citizen-*

*ship* (Cambridge University Press 2013), he is currently working on issues of democratic design with the support of the Leverhulme Trust.

**NADIA URBINATI** is Kyriakos Tsakopoulos Professor of Political Theory in the Department of Political Science at Columbia University. She is the author of *Democracy Disfigured: Opinion, Truth and the People* (Harvard University Press 2014) and *The Tyranny of the Moderns* (Yale University Press, 2015).

**MARK E. WARREN** holds the Harold and Dorrie Merilees Chair for the Study of Democracy at the University of British Columbia. He is especially interested in democratic innovations, civil society and democratic governance, and political corruption. He is currently working with an international team on a project entitled *Participedia* (www.participedia.net), which uses a web-based platform to collect data about democratic innovation and participatory governance around the world.

**KERRY H. WHITESIDE** is the Clair R. McCollough Professor of Government at Franklin & Marshall College (United States). He specializes in modern political theory and environmental philosophy. His recent publications concern the precautionary principle, political ecology in France, and democratic theory from an environmental point of view.

# Index

Aboriginal communities, 280
absolutism, 232, 249
abstract universalization, 55
accountability, 55–58, 120, 126–32, 188–92
    authorization and, 20, 40, 111–12, 118,
        131, 188
    deliberative, 193, 318
    democratic, 11, 112, 120–21, 223
    direct, 119, 124
    discursive, 7, 47, 58, 194, 198
    lack of, 117, 121, 124
    mechanisms, 17, 192
    mediated, 119, 124–25
    nonelectoral, 18, 190–94, 198, 201, 320,
        324
actors
    democratic, 164
    elite, 189
    grassroots, 189
    informal, 187
    nonelectoral, unelected, 187, 190–94,
        280
    nongovernmental, 255
    political, 71, 110, 113, 115, 172
    social, 151
advocacy, 51, 106, 153
    and civil society, 9
    discursive, 71
    groups, 41, 73, 162, 310
    public, 42
agency, 5, 56, 194, 199, 208, 266, 321
    collective, 58
    political agent, 16, 28, 181
    principal-agent, 3, 21, 89; as relationship,
        89; structure of, 89
agendas, 104, 181, 190, 194, 292, 324

normative, 324
partisan, 103
political, 96, 101–3
public, 102–3, 223
setting of, 174, 258
alliances, 179
Anglo-American literature, 17, 32
Ankersmit, Frank, 12, 33, 49–50, 146
antagonism, 94, 115, 125, 165–72, 181
Arditi, Benjamin, 117
Arendt, Hannah, 53–55
arrangements, 91, 256, 258
    consociational, 102
    electoral, 209
    institutional, 32, 66, 246
    political, 57, 93
audiences, 5, 21, 44, 56, 214
    and democracy, 5
    and the internet 77–81
    political presence to, 187–200
    power of, 187, 322
    role of, 73–76
Aung San Suu Kyi, 281
authority, 26, 47, 119, 164, 170, 222, 250
    advisory, 222
    collective, 92
    delegated, 119, 233
    dimensions of, 116
    formal, 282
    forms of/types of, 260, 291
    informal, 282
    investigative, 208
    moral, 219
    political, 81, 233, 261, 271
    shared, 264
    sources of, 75, 187

authorization, 17, 118, 190
    discursive, 198, 322
    organizational, 322
    process of, 193, 331
autonomous association, 152
autonomous federative institution, 152
autonomy, 45, 164–65, 174–75, 178
    of acceptance acts, 45
    among administrators, 319
    of citizens, 47, 78
    development of, 48–49
    of the individual, 165, 175, 314
    of the people, 195
    political, 8, 78–79, 164
    of the political subject, 178
    relative, 319
    through representation, 148

Bellamy, Richard, 257
Bentham, Jeremy, 67
Berlusconi, Silvio, 113, 115–16
Blair, Tony, 115
Böckenförde, Ernst-Wolfgang, 26
Bohman, Jim, 261, 269
Bourdieu, Pierre, 143, 153–55
Brandom, Robert, 56–57
Brandwein, Pamela, 168–69, 172
Brundtland Report, 205
Bryce, James, 106
Buchanan, Allen, 259

Canovan, Margaret, 134, 246
capacity
    to act, 304
    building of, 197, 200
    of citizens, 5, 54–56, 130, 150, 195, 318
    for democratic action, 19
    of elite, 174
    formal, 188
    political, 28, 150
Carré de Malberg, Raymond, 82
Carter, Jimmy, 281
Casaleggio, Roberto, 77. See also Five Star
    Movement
Chambers, Simone, 102, 180
Chartier, Robert, 23–24, 30, 33
Chávez, Hugo, 117, 125–26, 128–29, 131, 134
Chong, Dennis, 174–77
citizen control, 315, 318
    absence of, 142

citizenship, 8, 63, 17
    democratic, 7, 40–49, 51–58, 64, 69, 325
    effective power of, 63
    modern, 79
citizen standpoint 164, 172, 179
civil peace, 65
civil rights, 63, 65, 67, 74, 81, 172
    "fermenting agent" upon, 171
    free speech, 68
    legal universals, 171
    right to vote, 73–74, 79
    See also freedom; liberty
civil society, 27, 122, 259, 280
    groups, 285
    organizations, 27, 279
    See also constituencies; people, the
Clinton, Hillary, 175
Coase, Robert , 263
coercion, 180, 199, 318
    forms of, 178
    state, 300–303, 316, 323–24, 326
collectivity, 43, 49, 51, 114
    of action, 49, 149, 176, 257, 300–301
    of decisions, 11, 31, 53, 54, 190
    of intelligence, 220
    of subjects, 72
common frame of reference, 175
common good, 93, 96, 214, 246
communication, 52
    between constituents and representa-
        tives, 299
    dynamics of, 31
    horizontal means of, 78
    and populism, 114–17
    political, 173
    recursive, 6, 302–22, 325
    two-way, 14, 193, 305–6
competence, 209
    exclusive, 265
    political, 144, 151
competition, 62, 66–67
    democratic, 259
    discursive, 174
    electoral, 66, 75, 144, 148, 150, 262
    political, 62, 175, 259, 263
compliance monitoring, 223
conflict, 8
    absence of, 157
    between national party delegations, 268
    civilizing, 8, 86, 100, 104

handling of, 8, 86–89, 109
   lines of, 163, 176–78
   management of, 70, 87
   structural, 208
consent, 193, 257, 259–60
   democratic, 34
   diachronic, 324
   electoral, 69
   informal, 75, 80
   of the many, 66, 68
   state, 257–60
constituencies
   authorizing, 191, 195–97
   claimed, 188, 190, 194–200
   informal, 75, 80
   interests of, 162
   *See also* civil society; people, the
constitutionalism, 234
contestation, 19, 31, 62, 75, 282, 295
   democratic, 311
   political, 94, 132
corruption, 124, 214, 294, 317
credibility, 281
Crum, Ben, 269, 326

Dahl, Robert, 69
decision-making, 13, 17, 42
   beyond the state, 257
   citizen participation in, 144, 156–57
   collective, 5, 30, 92, 300
   democratic, 40, 206, 220, 222
   diarchy of, 64
   group representatives in, 157
   political, 142–43, 231, 240, 243
   process of, 13, 61, 81, 91, 131, 151, 209,
      216, 219–21
   shared, 260
   transparency of, 120
delegates, 27, 147, 286–87, 299, 303
deliberation, 2, 93
   by citizens, 315, 329
   democratic, 10, 173
   discursive, 73
   forums for, 217, 223
   future-regarding, 217
   legislative, 3
   political, 55, 77
   process of, 68, 82, 173, 223
   quality of, 72
   secrecy in, 102

theory of 68; deliberativist, 68–70; and
   first-order role, 163, 173, 175; and
   second-order groups, 224
democracy
   deliberative, 55, 68–69, 71, 92, 162, 205,
      224, 286; and self-monitoring, 69
   democratic deficit, 76, 316
   democratic diarchy, 63, 76
   democratic ideal, 305
   democratic intelligence, 220
   democratic pluralism, 163, 166
   democratic principles, 68–69, 289
   democratic procedures, 69, 81
   democratic process, 2, 7, 64, 68, 316
   democratic quality, 102–3
   direct, 141, 211
   electoral, 69, 78–80
   modern, 2, 8, 12, 61, 118, 178, 180, 242
   normative theory of, 80
   procedural, 67
   radical, 167, 171
   representative, 1–7, 10–16, 111, 223–24,
      231–33, 277, 279; mechanisms of, 246;
      nature of, 65–67, 70; practices of, 32
      participation in, 43; populist crisis in,
      254–55; state-based, 13, 290, 303–4,
      326; tensions of, 26; theory of, 56, 247
   Western, 242–44
demos, 72, 74, 119–20, 201, 259, 282, 324
Dewey, John, 44, 270
diarchy of will, 7, 61, 147
dichotomy, 114, 142
dignity, 63, 325
Disch, Lisa, 10, 42, 46, 106, 315, 330
discourse
   political, 12, 24, 72, 79, 245
   populist, 9, 114, 125, 127
distrust, 52, 212, 309, 323, 328
Di Tella, Torcuato, 133
division of political labor, 142–43, 150–51,
   156
Dobson, Andrew, 209, 219
Druckman, James N., 174
Dworkin, Ronald, 75

Echolls, Alice, 202
education, 180, 303, 319
   distinction between manipulation and,
      163–64
Ekeli, Kristian, 209

elections
    and appointments, 72
    and electorates, 99, 133, 213, 242–43, 249
    financial dependence of campaigns in,
        312
    free, 62, 232
    mechanisms of, 89
    and party-in-the-electorate, 98
    systems of, 56, 205, 306, 315, 319, 329;
        proportional representation in,
        58, 307–8; short-term perspective
        induced by, 205; Single Member Plu-
        rality (SMP), 306–7, 310, 327; West-
        minster systems 57–58
    See also suffrage
elite, 97, 102, 124, 133–34
    control by, 173–74, 176
    corruption among, 114, 245
    political, 41, 116
Elizabeth II, 254
emancipation, 126, 152, 168–69
    antislavery, 169–170, 172
empowerment, 27, 194, 199, 201
    of authorization and accountability, 194
    democratic, 3–8, 31, 74, 76 (see also
        inclusion: democratic)
    discursive and organizational, 192
    nonelectoral, 190
Enlightenment, 236–37
entitlements, 200
environment, 49, 98, 206
equality
    arithmetical, 62
    between members of society, 118, 171
    between representatives and their con-
        stituencies, 111
    horizontal, 9 (see also horizontality)
    political, 73, 89, 141–42, 279–81, 294, 307
European Commission, 255
European Parliament, 232, 255, 258, 267
    members of, 267
European Union (EU), 206, 232, 254–55,
    265, 268
    and Brexit, 298
    Common Foreign and Security Policy
        (CFSP) of, 264
    community method of, 265
    Conference of Parliamentary Com-
        mittees for Union Affairs of Par-
        liaments of the European Union
        (COSAC) of, 268

and early warning mechanism (EWM),
    268
    lawmaking in (see under lawmaking)
    Norwegian membership in, 88
    and Norwegian Progress Party, 103
    transgovernmentalism in, 266
exclusion, 31, 75, 141–42
expression
    direct, 73
    of contestation, 75
    of the general interest, 70
    political, 8, 166
    of political judgment, 75
    popular, 124, 130
    of popular opinion, 148
externalities, 12–13, 255–60, 272–55, 301, 326
    management of, 261–71

feminism, 170–71
Fishkin, James, 215, 222, 224, 326, 332
Five Star Movement (M5S), 77, 124
formal consultation, 321–22
freedom
    of association, 68, 74, 78, 81, 192, 322
    indirect, 62
    liberal, 169
    of public opinion, 32
    of speech, 76
    See also civil rights; liberty
Freedom Party of Austria (FPÖ), 117, 125,
    128
free labor, 169, 172
French Revolution, 27, 144, 166, 171, 180
    1789 Revolution, 143
    1848 Revolution, 147, 149–50
Furetière, Antoine, 23, 33
future generations, representation of, 6, 11,
    178
    in citizen forums, 215, 218, 222
    in citizen juries, 223
    and consensus conference, 215
    constitutional protection of, 206
    expressions of a future-regarding ethic,
        210
    and future-regarding issues, 216, 221, 225
    organizations concerning: Office for
        Future Generations, 221; Commis-
        sion for Future Generations of the
        Israeli Knesset, 208; Hungary's par-
        liamentary commissioner for future
        generations, 208; Stiftung für die

Rechte zukünftiger Generationen (Foundation for the Rights of Future Generations), 210
and other-regarding obligations, 206
and sustainability, 207–9, 219

Gadamer, Hans-Georg, 30, 31
gag rules, 101–2
Gambaro, Adele, 133
Garsten, Bryan, 47
Gaxiem, Daniel, 144
governance, 1–2, 6–7, 11–12, 86, 142, 218, 255, 282, 291, 320–21, 323
domestic, 255
modern systems of, 86
nonstatal, 282
process of, 7
of self, 7
Grant, Judith, 170
Green Parties, 103
Grillo, Beppe, 77, 124, 133. *See also* Five Star Movement

Habermas, Jürgen, 69, 82, 164, 180, 256, 271, 313, 317, 330
Haider, Jörg, 128. *See also* Freedom Party of Austria (FPÖ)
Harper Canadian Conservatives, 104
Hazare, Ana, 283, 294
hegemony, 10, 164–69, 171–79, 181
Hirschman, Albert O., 95
Hobbes, Thomas, 24, 26, 33–34, 71, 235, 271
Hofmann, Hasso, 22–23, 25, 33–34
Humala, Ollanta, 129
Hume, David, 261
horizontality, 111–12, 118, 120–25, 128–32

identification
group, 176–77
partisan, 93
with populist leaders (*see under* populism)
identity, 24–30
class, 155
common, 212
formation of, 32
institutional, 72
national, 168, 245
non-identity, 30
political, 3, 62, 93–95, 98–99, 127, 167, 188
popular, 123, 131

principle of, 30
of self, 27–28
social, 156
symbolic, 76
ideologies, 66, 97, 113–14, 132, 144, 169, 177
bonds of, 244
differences among, 210
political, 66, 241–44, 247–49
immigration and asylum policy, 104
inclusion
autonomous strategies of, 153
collective, 153
democratic, 19, 31, 212; process of, 212
equal, 149
and the included, 74, 284
through autonomous politicization, 146, 150
through partisan politicization, 143–45, 150
indignados, los. *See* los indignados
inequality, 149, 190, 312, 315
influence
of constituents, 119, 142, 198
of elite, 174
exercise of, 62
informal, 320, 322
integration, 12, 268
interdependence, 6, 262, 300–301, 316–19, 323
international commitments, 254–55
international policy coordination, 256
internet, 61, 77
and e-citizens, 78
*See also* new media; social media

Jacobins, 144
Jefferson Center, 223–24
journalism, 79
Jouvenel, Bernard de, 233
judgment
autonomy of, 5, 7, 100, 106
of citizens, 46
ethical, 55
formation of, 8
moral, 7, 40, 54
political, 8, 41–42, 47, 62, 67, 75, 146
jurisdiction, 234, 250
Justinian code, 233

Kant, Immanuel, 52–53, 55, 302
law of reason, 53

Kantorowicz, Ernst 237
    "king" concept, 233–34, 239, 240; the
        body natural, 238; the body politic,
        239–40
    *The Norman Anonymous*, 238
Kateb, Georges, 145

Laclau, Ernesto, 164–72, 178–81, 245–46. *See
    also* Mouffe, Chantal
Landemore, Hélène, 220–21
language
    body, 129
    colloquial, 128
    of externalities, 12, 326
    of oppression, 171
    ordinary, 21, 24
    political, 21, 144
    of political representation (*see* represen-
        tation: political: language)
    verbal, 115
Latin America, 126, 302
Latour, Bruno, 145
lawmaking, 64, 300–303, 316–18, 322–23, 327
    administrative, 302, 316, 318
    in the European Union, 268
    process of, 78
    representative, 71
    shared, 262–70
Ledru-Rollin, Alexandre, 154–55
legislation, 32, 52–53, 234–35
    beyond the state, 264–66
    direction of, 32
legitimacy
    damage to, 219
    deliberative, 163–64
    demands of, 10
    democratic, 45–46, 73–75, 171–73, 225,
        279, 291, 332
    formal, 71
    manipulation and, 173
    normative, 320–24
    first-order problem of, 164
    formal, 73
    input, 302, 326
    internal, problems of, 320
    legal, 303
    normative, 293, 302–3, 316–18
    of nonelectoral, nonauthorized forms of
        representation, 4
    output, 326
    perceived, 303, 306–7, 311–12, 317

perceptions of, 75
problems of, 301
serial, 322
source of, 81, 122, 163, 172, 279
systemic, 321
theory of, 260
Leibholz, Gerhard, 22, 26–29, 34, 242. *See
    also* Schmitt, Carl
Lewis, C. S., 25
liberal individualism, 168
liberty, 63–5, 74, 78–79, 171, 249, 325
    equal political, 63, 74, 325
    individual, 74, 79
    loss of, 249; and disenfranchisement,
        209
    political liberty of the moderns, 78–79
    *See also* civil rights; freedom
Lisbon Treaty, 265
literature, Anglo-American, 17, 32
Locke, John, 271, 317
los indignados, 111, 146
loyalty, 93–100, 104, 176, 178
    group, 176, 178
    as a means of self-binding, 99
    preservation of, 99

Madison, James, 51–54
Mair, Peter, 1, 4, 78–79, 91, 101, 115, 251
Manin, Bernard, 19, 32, 42, 82, 118, 145, 180
    principle of distinction, 19
manipulation, 67, 122, 173–78, 312–13,
        330–31
    by elite, 165
    by false framings, 174
    impasse, 163
    partisan, 67
    strategic, 97, 102
    symbolic, 218
Mansbridge, Jane, 48, 55, 106, 163, 180, 190,
        200, 267, 280
Marchart, Oliver, 167
marginalized groups, 309
market capitalism, 168
Martin, Louis, 30
Marxism, 166–67, 171, 241–42
Mény, Yves, 110. *See also* Surel, Yves
Middle Ages, 12, 231–35, 237, 239, 241, 243,
        248
Mineur, Didier, 145
minimalism. *See* representation: theory of:
        minimalist

minipublic, 215, 222
misinformation, 218
Moffitt, Benjamin, 98, 107
Morales, Evo, 129
Mouffe, Chantal, 10, 71, 164–68, 170. *See also* Laclau, Ernesto
Muirhead, Russell, 93–95. *See also* Rosenblum, Nancy
Mulieri, Alessandro, 33

Napoleon, 232
Näsström, Sofia, 76, 163, 172
nation-states, 235, 245, 282, 302. *See also* states
Neblo, Michael, 305, 310–11, 315, 328
Nedelsky, Jennifer, 48, 330
network good, 269
new media, 77–78. *See also* internet; social media
normative approach, 73, 318
norms, 66–69, 100–106, 260–66, 302, 304, 307, 309, 331
    communicative, 173, 324
    cultural, 90
    democratic, 69, 190, 302, 304, 307, 323–24
    implicit, 325
    internalized, 325
    of mutual consideration, 271
    of representation, 278
    shared, 262–64, 269
    social, 106
    of system preservation, 94

objections, 18, 29, 45–47, 50, 263, 271
    explicit, 47
    mobilized, 195
    non-objection criterion, 18, 45–46
    relative, 29
Occupy movement, 186, 197
O'Donnell, Guillermo, 119
opinions
    costs of forming, 176
    elite influence on forming, 174
    formation of, 3, 8, 10, 32, 68, 165, 175, 317
    language of forming, 331
    minority, 329
    online media and forming, 8
    popular, 148
    power of, 75–76
    public, 32, 50–51, 97, 120, 173, 217, 256

order
    decision-making, 80
    first-order (*see* deliberation: deliberative theory)
    institutional, 95
    institutional and legal, 69
    international, 265
    legal and constitutional, 67
    normative, 264
    political, 234, 241
    social, 168
organizations
    member, 198
    nongovernmental (NGOs), 146, 162, 199, 206–8, 212, 218–19, 222–23
    partner, 198
    umbrella, 198
Ostrom, Elinor, 301

Panizza, Francisco, 127, 134
participation
    citizen, 57, 144, 148, 156
    democratic, 64, 80, 145
    direct, 141–43, 150, 153, 156, 186
    electoral, 78, 210
    equal, 68
    expressive, 80
    informal, 64, 79
    nonelectoral forms of, 79
    and overparticipation, 311
    partisan, 64
    political, 43, 57, 77, 142, 151
    popular, 125, 132, 147, 149
    and pseudoparticipation, 125
    quality of, 70
partisanship, 91–99
Pasquino, Pasquale, 133
Pels, Dick, 245
people, the
    construction of, 28, 123
    political unity of, 26, 27
    trust of, 114
    voice of, 114, 121–22, 124
    *volonté générale* (general will) of, 114, 123, 245
    will of, 70, 121–22, 124, 127–28, 132, 231–32, 245, 248
    *See also* representation: and the represented
Perón, Juan Domingo, 121–22, 124, 133
personification, 22–23, 34

persuasion, 75, 92, 163, 173, 190, 199, 319, 329
  communicative, 312
  deliberative, 314
  mutual, 315
  nonmanipulative, 313
  strategic, 330
Petracca, Orazio M., 116
Phillips, Anne, 18, 156, 289
Pitkin, Hanna, 18–19, 21–23, 25–26, 28–30,
      32–34, 39, 41–42, 45–47, 67, 90, 111–
      12, 118–19, 128, 141–42, 157, 163, 173,
      201, 206, 212, 280, 293, 326, 330
  *The Concept of Representation*, 2, 17,
      71, 106
  and different theories of representa-
      tion, 21
  and meaning of representation. *See
      under* representation
  and presence. *See* presence
  and standard theory of representa-
      tion, 19
  and substantive representation, 18
Plotke, David, 10, 30, 211
policy coordination, 256, 260
  process of, 175–77
  international, 256
political action, 5, 20, 29, 63, 91, 101, 293,
      330
political construction, 166–67
political leaders, 64, 93, 99, 113, 327. *See
      also* elite: political
political parties, 62, 77, 79, 81, 91, 93–94, 98–
      99, 242, 294, 328
  European party groups, 268
  second party system, 268
  representative role of, 104
political practice, 7, 72, 113, 115–16, 120, 123,
      132, 205, 292
political process, 11, 18, 75, 119, 155, 214, 224
political sphere, 188, 284
political subjectivity, 5–6, 9–10, 20, 32
political unity, 26–29, 166
politicization, 10, 144–56, 245, 270
  autonomous, 146, 148–50, 156
  individual, 152
  partisan, 143–52
politics
  and antipolitics, 1, 9
  feminist, 156
  international, 221

modern, 8, 99, 164, 166, 172
  transnational, 284
  Western, 241, 243
populism
  anti-institutional and anti-elite attitude
      of, 122, 124–25
  discourse of (*see under* discourse)
  dualism of, 77
  idealization of, 122
  Latin American leftist, 129
  leaders, 98, 111–16, 121–28; people's
      identification with, 126–28, 132
  movements, 8, 110–11, 122, 124
  parties, 8, 97, 100, 105, 245
  *See also* Five Star Movement; Freedom
      Party of Austria (FPÖ)
power
  asymmetries in, 171
  authoritarian structures of, 124
  coercive, 201, 313
  direct delegation of, 320
  formal delegation of, 316
  fullness of, 233
  governmental, 28
  political, 62, 114, 145, 166, 180, 196, 258,
      261; and equality, 62, 75
  totalitarian, 112, 132
preferences, 7, 90, 93, 128, 173, 196, 204, 209,
      289
  autonomous, 41
  formation of, 48
  manifested, 25
  of representatives, 40, 42
  of voters, 41, 87
  *See also* political parties
presence
  approach, 19–20
  of citizens, 61
  democratic, 5, 16–17, 19, 21, 23, 25, 27,
      29, 31–33, 35
  direct, 5
  political, 5, 7, 16, 194, 278
  as political agents, 16
presence/absence, 21–23, 25, 28–30, 34
  dialectic, 23, 28
  model of, 22
  paradox of, 21, 25, 30
presentism, 204, 207, 210, 212, 216, 219, 223
  pressures of, 209, 223
proceduralism, 65

procedures
    democratic, 69, 81
    voting, 81
proletarians, 149, 152, 155
Przeworski, Adam, 65
public agreement, 191–92
public opinion. *See* opinions: public
public policy beyond the state, 255, 257–58
public sphere, 69, 72–73, 187, 190, 256, 259,
    263

Rawls, John, 55
    theory of justice, 54, 261
realist theory, 141
reciprocation, 264
recursive communication, 6, 302, 304, 307–9,
    311–13, 316, 318, 322, 326
reference group, 177
Rehfeld, Andrew, 211
Reisigl, Martin, 114
representation
    administrative, 302, 316, 318–19, 328
    aesthetic, 146
    anticipatory, 309, 328
    ascriptive, 75 (*see also* Dworkin, Ronald)
    autonomous, 150, 152
    bad, 121
    balanced, 18
    beyond the state, 254–60, 269–71
    concept of, 21–22, 33, 112, 143, 151
    corporative and privatistic forms of, 28
    crisis of, 1–2
    democratic: modern, 26; standard model
        of, 8, 213, 304, 314
    descriptive, 19, 200, 212, 303, 307, 309,
        328–29
    diplomatic, 254
    direct, 29; and self-representation, 78
    of the dominated, 153
    educative function of, 164
    elective, 64, 279, 280
    electoral, 8, 48, 89, 149, 211, 279, 298,
        302–5, 307, 311–12, 318, 328, 331; and
        rational ignorance, 217
    ephemeral and permanent, 292–93 (*see
        also* representation: liminal)
    exclusionary, 142–47, 150–57
    external system of, 304
    failed, 199–200
    formal, 119, 284

good, 157, 186, 201, 256
grassroots, 189
gyroscopic, 66, 308–9, 315, 328–29
    and identity, 23
    inclusive, 9, 142–44, 146, 148; of social
        groups, 151–55; politics of, 156–57
    informal, 283, 331
    intergovernmental, 256, 265
    interparliamentary, 268–69
    left/right forms of, 268
    liminal, 281, 286 (*see also* representation:
        ephemeral and permanent)
    linguistic and visual, 30
    linguistic origins of: *Abbild*, 23, 34;
        *repraesentare*, 23–24, 42; *Repräsenta-
        tion*, 23, 26–27; *Urbild*, 23, 34
    meaning of, 19; *Darstellung*, 19; *Stellver-
        tretung*, 26; *Vertretung*, 26
    metaphorical, 235, 240–43, 249 (*see
        also* representation: synecdochical)
    and misrepresentation, 189
    nonelective, 80
    norms of, 278
    other-appointed, 276, 281
    outcome of: democratic, 195; failed, 188,
        196, 199; nondemocratic, 195–96;
        skewed, 196; surrogate, 197–200
    outside state institutions, 74, 142
    paradox of, 19, 21–22, 25
    partisan, 92
    phenomenology of, 61, 72, 81
    political: institutional system of, 32; lan-
        guage of, 11; modern, 20, 26, 237, 240,
        242; performativity of, 20
    practices of, 21, 24, 279, 282–83, 286,
        291, 293
    problem-based approach to, 22, 33
    problem of, 26
    process of, 19, 254, 307, 314
    recursive, 299–300, 303
    reflexivity of, 46–48, 70–71, 214, 295
    relations of, 146–48, 303
    and the representative (person), 34, 41,
        43, 50, 119, 128, 155, 164, 180, 195,
        200–201, 240–44, 305–10; aspiring,
        213; as interlocutor, 212, 299, 309–10;
        mediating activities of, 211; other-
        appointed, 281; as trustee, 42
    and representative bodies, 19, 86, 93,
        147, 157

representation (*continued*)
  and representative claims, 3, 5, 7, 44–52,
      99, 155, 191, 195, 213, 278, 288, 291–
      93, 331; claim-based approach, 278,
      284; claim-making, 8, 47, 51, 54–57,
      62–67, 71–81, 90, 95, 106–7, 147, 282–
      83, 285, 295; competition among,
      46–47, 56; future-oriented, 206; rhe-
      torical, 63
  and representative relationships, 7, 41,
      45, 89–90, 100–102, 104, 187, 190, 308,
      313–14, 316, 320, 332; two-way com-
      munication in, 14, 306
  and the represented: activities of, 7, 39–
      40; interests of, 18, 19, 41–42, 153;
      judgments of, 43, 47; presence of, 18,
      20, 157; self-determination of, 122,
      197, 199; self-development of, 197,
      199; self-understanding of, 21, 49;
      subjectivity of, 5, 9–10, 20, 32 (*see
      also* representation: subjects of)
  self-appointed, 187–203, 276
  societal, 6, 302–4, 320–25, 331
  sociological mechanisms of, 155 (*see also*
      representation: subjectivation)
  structure of, 90
  subjectivation of, 155–56
  subjects of, 26, 74 (*see also* representa-
      tion: the represented)
  substantive, 19, 285, 323
  supranational parliamentary, 12, 266,
      269–71
  surrogate, 280, 310
  synecdochical, 12, 237, 240, 242 (*see
      also* representation: metaphorical)
  system of, 12, 16, 19, 32, 210, 266, 272, 304
  theory of: constructivist, 3, 7, 10, 40, 87,
      89, 162–63, 178; deliberative, 68, 72,
      80; deliberativism 70, 73; minimal-
      ist, 63–64, 67, 69, 73, 80, 141; political
      representation, 2; representative, 20,
      145, 162, 165
  transgovernmental, 265
  trustee, 308
  of the working class, 152
reputation, 71, 76, 191–92, 197–98, 218, 308
responsiveness, 25, 42, 46, 86–95, 100–105,
      157, 188, 212, 319, 324
  norms of, 89, 101
  partisan, 93, 104
  social, 94

Reynaud, Jean, 152
rhetoric, 9, 68, 71, 114, 122, 124, 128, 132, 147,
      174, 245, 251, 285
  political, 174
  populist, 9, 124, 128
Rosanvallon, Pierre, 123, 133, 148
Rosenblum, Nancy, 86, 91, 93–95, 322. *See
      also* Muirhead, Russell
Rousseau, Jean-Jacques, 2, 53, 70, 220, 231–
      32, 243, 248, 251
Runciman, David, 18, 29, 46, 50–51
Ryle, Giulbert, 237–39

Sanders, Bernie, 281
Sartori, Giovanni, 91
Saward, Michael, 3, 19–21, 45–46, 71, 73, 90,
      95, 106, 206, 304
  *The Representative Claim*, 44, 72
Schattschneider, Elmer E., 86, 186
Schmitt, Carl, 22, 25–30, 34. *See also* Leib-
      holz, Gerhard
Schmitt, Hermann, 267. *See also* Thomas-
      sen, Jacques
Schmitt, Vivian, 327
Schumpeter, Joseph A., 65, 68, 141, 246
second-order groups, 224
second public, 50–51
Second World War, 88
self-rule, 48–49, 66
Sintomer, Yves 33, 81
social-contract theory, 165, 172
social location, 200–201
social media, 191
sovereignty
  democratic, 6, 73
  popular, 3, 47, 113, 117, 119, 121, 123,
      126, 131–32, 147
speech acts, 44–45, 56–57
Stanley, Ben, 113
states, 20–29, 64, 66–67, 310, 317, 320–23
  constitutional, 1, 74
  democratic, 27, 243, 258–59, 324
  institutions of, 61, 67, 74, 81, 142
  liminal, 277
  modern, 26
  *See also* nation-states
Stavrakakis, Yannis, 134
Strache, Heinz-Christian, 117, 125, 128, 133.
      *See also* Freedom Party of Austria
      (FPÖ)
subordination, 169–71, 313

suffrage, 66, 69, 71, 73–74, 79–80, 149–52, 154
    abolishing the age qualification for, 210
    universal, 66, 71, 149
    voting power and, 63
    *See also* civil rights: right to vote; elec-
        tions
Surel, Yves, 110. *See also* Mény, Yves
surveillance, 75, 80

Taggart, Paul, 110, 122
Thatcher, Baroness Margaret, 243
    *There Is No Alternative Principle*, 243
Thirteenth Amendment, 168–69. *See
    also* emancipation
Thomassen, Jacques, 267. *See also* Schmitt,
    Hermann
Thompson, Dennis, 204–5
totalitarianism 130–32, 134, 171
transaction costs, 263
transparency, 9, 68, 112, 181, 282, 315, 326,
    331
Trump, Donald, 233, 281
trust, 14, 61, 114, 118, 132, 308, 328
    between the representative and the
        represented, 242
    role of in populism, 121–30
trustees, 42, 50, 153, 287, 299, 303

United Socialist Party of Venezuela (PsUv),
    117. *See also* Chávez, Hugo

United States, 91, 111, 169, 172, 181, 223, 232,
    236, 299, 302, 306, 309, 311–12, 321,
    323, 327
universality, 196, 289
Urbinati, Nadia, 42, 51, 106, 147, 162, 193,
    212, 284–85

verticality, 111–12, 116, 118, 121–23, 126, 128,
    130–32
Voegelin, Eric, 34
voices
    competing, 303
    democratic, 8, 11
    partisan, 97
    plurality of, 6
    representative, 322

Weber, Max, 113, 116
Westminster systems, 57, 58
White, Jonathan, 92–93, 95. *See also* Ypi, Lea
Williams, Melissa, 305, 327
Wittgenstein, Ludwig, 21–22, 24, 239
women's movement, 196
World Future Council, 204
World War II, 88

Young, Iris Marion, 29, 30, 71, 307, 327. *See
    also* Plotke, David
Yousafzai, Malala, 283
Ypi, Lea, 92–93, 95. *See also* White, Jonathan